T0270947

A key theme in the West African trading system of the nineteenth century is the transition from the slave trade to 'legitimate' commerce, and its significance for the African societies of the region. In this period of transition, trade in palm oil was at the core of relations between Britain and West Africa, and of immense importance to the economies of large parts of West Africa. Filling an important gap in the literature, Martin Lynn's authoritative and comprehensive study of the palm oil trade covers the whole of this critical period for all of West Africa. Emphasising the continuities of West African history in the first half of the nineteenth century, it explains how the palm oil trade grew organically out of the organisation of the slave trade. The situation changed sharply with the development of steam communication between Britain and West Africa from the 1850s, leading to severe problems for commerce in the second half of the century, the erosion of African brokers' powers, and the restructuring of the trade thereafter. The result was a crisis within the trade towards the end of the century and, eventually, with the arrival of colonial rule, the ending of the long-established structures of the commerce.

Commerce and economic change in West Africa

African Studies Series 93

A list of books in this series will be found at the end of this volume

Commerce and economic change in West Africa

The palm oil trade in the nineteenth century

Martin Lynn
Queen's University, Belfast

CAMBRIDGE
UNIVERSITY PRESS

CAMBRIDGE
UNIVERSITY PRESS

University Printing House, Cambridge CB2 8BS, United Kingdom

Cambridge University Press is part of the University of Cambridge.

It furthers the University's mission by disseminating knowledge in the pursuit of education, learning and research at the highest international levels of excellence.

www.cambridge.org
Information on this title: www.cambridge.org/9780521590747

© Martin Lynn 1997

First published 1997
First paperback edition 2002

A catalogue record for this publication is available from the British Library

Library of Congress Cataloguing in Publication data
Lynn, Martin, 1951–
Commerce and economic change in West Africa: the palm oil trade in the nineteenth century / Martin Lynn.
    p.   cm. -(African studies series; 93)
Includes bibliographical references and index.
ISBN 0 521 59074 4
1. Palm oil industry – Africa, West – History – 19th century.
I. Title. II. Series.
HD9490.5.P343A3585 1997
380.1′413851′0967–dc21 97-7352 CIP

ISBN 978-0-521-59074-7 Hardback
ISBN 978-0-521-89326-8 Paperback

For Hannah and Megan

Contents

Maps

Tables

Preface

Historians of Africa owe an immense debt to K. O. Dike's *Trade and Politics in the Niger Delta, 1830–1885*, published in 1956. Not only did *Trade and Politics* present a new way of looking at West Africa's past from the point of view of West Africans themselves, it also played a major role in the emergence of the modern academic study of the history of the African continent. For me as for many of my generation, it was *Trade and Politics* that provided one of the earliest entries into the rewards of studying West African history and first stimulated my interest in the issues that are covered in this work. Although this book covers much of the same ground, namely the development of the palm oil trade, it is not an attempt to replace *Trade and Politics*. The present work eschews Dike's concentration on political conflict to present an entirely economic history of the palm oil trade. It thus does not engage with the debate on the origins of British imperial expansion in West Africa, except tangentially; its aim is to provide a contribution to West Africa's economic history, an aim which I consider valuable in itself.

This book's focus is on a commodity – palm oil – that for centuries has been of importance to millions of Africans and which in the nineteenth century became similarly important to Europeans, and it examines the relationship between West Africa and Britain that ensued from its trade. It attempts to go beyond the usual studies that look simply at the British side of this relationship or at the West African; it tries to look at all those involved in the production, trading, and consuming of palm oil in the nineteenth century – from West African producer to British consumer – and consider the consequences for them of the growth of West African exports after 1800.

Shipping, and more particularly the steamship, is the other theme of this work. It was shipping that first established the relationship between West Africa and Britain in the days of the slave trade; it was ships that brought palm oil from Africa to Britain; and, it is argued here, it was changes in shipping technology that generated the transformation in the oil trade of the later nineteenth century, with the effects for West Africa and its exports that followed. Excellent studies of shipping in the West African trade have been produced, but none, I feel, that fully addresses the impact of shipping technology on the history of West Africa itself.

The focus of the book is on exports to Britain; the French and German oil trades are mentioned only in passing. This is not simply because the British sources were more easily available to me, but also because Britain was the major market for West African palm oil throughout the nineteenth century. Material on the French and German markets has been utilised where appropriate.

Spellings of place-names, titles, etc., have relied on current practice. The main exception is 'Old Calabar', which has been used to distinguish the Efik from the Kalabari state. Equally, the 'Bight of Biafra' has been used in preference to the modern name of Bight of Bonny. A further piece of shorthand I have utilised is – in defiance of geographical fact – the inclusion of Old Calabar in the Niger Delta by using the term 'Delta area' to describe the region between the Slave Coast and the Cameroons. This follows Dike's practice and can be justified given that the trading system in Old Calabar was essentially the same as that in the Delta proper. One final policy adopted is the use of the term 'broker' to refer to those in West Africa who bulked palm oil and kernels on the coast for sale to those who transported them to Europe; the term 'trader' has been used to refer to those responsible for purchasing oil and kernels in West Africa and shipping them overseas. This practice has been followed for stylistic convenience.

Many debts have been built up in the writing of this book. Not least, major acknowledgement is due to the British Academy for the grant of funding to visit archives in Nigeria and Ghana. Gratitude is also due to the Queen's University, Belfast, for the study leave that was necessary to complete this work. In addition a number of individuals have helped in a variety of ways. I would like to thank Omoniyi Adewoye, Jim Bradley, Tony Cole, Alun Davies, Peter Davies, John Dransfield, D. Dyer, Christopher Fyfe, Janice Jardine, David Johnson, John Levi, Joseph Miller, Andrew Porter, Maura Pringle (for drawing the maps), Gloria Rickard, Yvonne Smyth, and Mike Stammers. I would also like to thank Karen Anderson Howes for her indefatigable copy-editing and Jessica Kuper for her patience over several years. Material in tables 1.8, 4.1, 5.1, 6.1, 6.2, 6.3, 7.1, and 7.2 first appeared in articles I published in the *Journal of African History*, vol. 22 (1981) and vol. 30 (1989). I am grateful to the editors of the *Journal* for permission to reproduce this material here. In addition thanks are due to Lever Bros. Ltd, Port Sunlight, for arranging a visit to their factory to see modern soap making in practice. My debt to Alice Clark, who has had to live with palm oil for longer than anyone has a right to expect, is unquantifiable.

Thanks are also due to the numerous librarians and archivists who assisted during the research for this book. The bibliography outlines the libraries and archives that helped me during the past few years; gratitude is expressed for permission to consult and quote from their papers. If it is a truth universally acknowledged that working conditions for university lecturers have sharply deteriorated in recent years while working loads have increased, then it is also true that conditions for librarians and archivists have declined equally significantly. As I made my way around the libraries and archives of Britain and West Africa, what became increasingly striking were the difficult circumstances, financial and otherwise, that the staff of these institutions were facing, coupled with the good humour and immense kindness with which they set about helping me. This applied to every institution without exception, but was particularly marked in the libraries and archives I visited in Nigeria and Ghana, where staff maintained service often in the most difficult of circumstances. A heartfelt 'thank you' is expressed to all the librarians, archivists, and depository staff who helped in the producing of this book.

Abbreviations

AEH	*African Economic History*
CMS	Church Missionary Society
CMSP	Church Missionary Society Papers, University of Birmingham Library
CO	Colonial Office
CUST	HM Customs and Excise
EDR	Elder Dempster Records, Merseyside Maritime Museum
FO	Foreign Office
IJAHS	*International Journal of African Historical Studies*
JAH	*Journal of African History*
JHPL	John Holt Papers, Liverpool Record Office
JHPO	John Holt Papers, Rhodes House, Oxford
JHSN	*Journal of the Historical Society of Nigeria*
JRGS	*Journal of the Royal Geographical Society*
NAGA	National Archives of Ghana, Accra
NNAE	Nigerian National Archives, Enugu
NNAI	Nigerian National Archives, Ibadan
PP	*Parliamentary Papers*
PRGS	*Proceedings of the Royal Geographical Society*
PRO	Public Record Office, Kew
THSG	*Transactions of the Historical Society of Ghana*
UACP	United Africa Co. Papers, Unilever Archives, Port Sunlight

Introduction

'This palm oil is of great use to the inhabitants [of Guinea] in several respects', wrote John Barbot in the seventeenth century, 'for besides its serving to season their meat, fish, etc., and to burn in their lamps to light them at night, it is an excellent ointment against rheumatick pains, winds and colds in the limbs, or other like diseases.' It is, he added, 'no despicable sauce, especially when new'.[1] The palm oil that Barbot eulogised is derived from the fruit of the oil palm, *elaeis guineensis*. The nuts produced by the oil palm contain a fleshy outer pericarp, from which palm oil is produced, and an inner kernel from which palm kernel oil is derived. The latter is a colourless, translucent oil, similar to coconut oil, while palm oil itself is a bright orange-yellow colour, with an odour often compared to violets; on exposure to air the oil turns white, thickens, and over time its odour becomes rancid.[2]

Elaeis guineensis was classified by Nicolaas Jacquin in 1763. While it can now be found in many parts of the world besides West Africa, most notably South-East Asia and South America, it is clearly of African origin. Fossil pollen similar to the pollen of the oil palm has been identified in Miocene layers in the Niger Delta, while archaeological evidence suggests palm oil was known to and traded by third-millennium Egyptians.[3] Conversely, the South American palm is clearly from the post-Columbian era. Linguistic evidence shows that the names used for the oil palm in South America are derived from West African origins. Further, pre-Columbian European travellers to West Africa found the oil palm common.[4] Cadamosto, writing in the 1460s, gives the first literary reference to palm oil in European sources; he found palm wine being drunk and palm oil being used in cooking in the Senegal region, while Pacheco Pereira, writing of visits to West Africa in the 1480s, referred to palm oil being offered for sale along the Forcados River and palm leaves being used to thatch houses in Benin.[5]

The oil palm in Africa flourishes between 12° N and 12° S, but most particularly within 7° north and south of the Equator. It is distributed widely between the Gambia and Angola and can be found in scattered spots in Central and East Africa and on Madagascar. Its greatest concentration, however, is in West Africa between Sierra Leone and Congo (former Zaire), with a particular concentration in southeastern Nigeria.[6] It grows some distance inland from the coast, thriving in a moist, equable climate with a rainfall of between 70 and 100 inches p.a.; it does not do well in the swamps or the dry sandy soils characteristic of much of the West African seaboard. Nor does the oil palm flourish in dense rain forest, needing more light than such forest allows; for this reason its origins as a plant are likely to be in the ecotone between forest and savanna.[7] Today it is found concentrated in a belt running some 20 to 150 miles from the coast. It is a plant of the lowlands; though it has been found at 3,000 ft or more, it does not grow above 4,000 ft. According to Hartley, it does best in conditions with a rainfall of 80 inches evenly spread over the year, a mean temperature between 22° and 33° C and sunshine of around five hours per day.[8] It reaches its full height after twelve years of growth, though it can begin fruiting from as early as its fourth year; most commonly it produces fruit after seven years of growth. The tree can live for up to two hundred years and bears fruit for at least sixty. In West African conditions it produces two crops a year: one in May–July and a second in December–January. Its yield is significantly determined by rainfall; rainfall variations produce a cycle of poor yields every four to six years in parts of West Africa.[9]

Palm oil is an important source of vitamins, particularly vitamin A, in the West African diet. Its culinary use in West Africa is long established; archaeological evidence suggests that West Africans used palm oil in their cooking some 5,000 to 6,000 years ago.[10] As Barbot noted, it is also used for lighting and as a bodily ointment, while the palm tree itself provides material for building, particularly roof thatching, and for brushes, as well as being the source of palm wine.[11] 'The palm tree', noted Corry in 1807, 'is one of the most useful trees to the African, yielding him meat, drink and rainment.'[12]

From an early date palm oil also found a market overseas. 'There is not another tree in the whole world which produces money with so little expense as this particular crop', stated Morel, and Europeans were quick to grasp its value.[13] As Pacheco Pereira noted, palm oil has been sold to European traders from at least the 1480s.[14] The first recorded English purchase came in 1588 when Capt. Walsh bought a quantity at Benin.[15] As the transatlantic slave trade grew, sales of palm oil to Europeans became more common, the oil being used for provisions on the voyage to the Americas. During the subsequent centuries of the Atlantic slave trade, palm oil exports continued to be used for this purpose; an increasing quantity, however, was traded to Europe. During the eighteenth century Britain imported a small but growing amount of 'oils and fats' from Africa; this increased to an average value of some £6,000–£10,000 per year by its end.[16]

It was in the early nineteenth century, following the abolition of the British slave trade, that palm oil exports from West Africa began to increase significantly. Thereafter, palm oil was to become the quintessential commodity of the era of so-called legitimate trade for large parts of West Africa. In 1807, the year of abolition, Britain imported 2,233 cwt of palm oil from West Africa; by the 1840s this figure had risen to an average of 426,087 cwt p.a.[17] From then on palm oil was to be the most important item British traders bought from West Africa until the end of the century, with imports (from all parts) reaching a peak for the century of 1,262,933 cwt in 1895.[18] The reason for the sharp rise in the trade lay in the increasing industrialisation of Britain during the nineteenth century and the demand this generated for tropical products. Palm oil was used as a lubricant for industrial machinery and railway stock as well as being an essential ingredient in the manufacture of soap and candles. It was valued too as an important source of glycerine and in the processing of tinplate. From the middle of the century this trade in palm oil was joined by trade in palm kernels. British imports of 'nuts and kernels' (of all sorts) from West Africa rose from 592 tons in 1855 to 34,186 tons by 1895.[19] The key factor in the increase in British palm kernel imports was the development of a mass market for cheap margarine; palm kernel oil came to be used extensively in its manufacture, with the residue of the kernels being used as a cattle food.[20]

Palm products were therefore an important, if neglected, aspect of Britain's nineteenth-century industrial history and, as Flint and McDougall point out, the growth in West Africa's legitimate commerce needs to be tied firmly to the development of the Industrial Revolution.[21] The emergence of the palm oil trade thus illustrates the broader development of international commodity trades in the nineteenth century, the place of tropical products in the metropolitan economy, and the growth of a world market in these years. It highlights, too, the integration of the commodity producers of the tropical world into that world market.

Study of the oil trade is also important in illuminating the relationship between Britain and West Africa in the nineteenth century. With the palm oil trade came an increase in the British presence in West Africa, as traders, missionaries, naval officers, and consuls arrived on the coast. For the British, legitimate trade such as that in palm oil was part of a broader attempt to change West Africa through 'commerce, Christianity, and civilisation'. Such trade, it was felt, would renovate West Africa's economy after the ravages of slaving. More than that, it was believed, it would transform West Africans, turning them into model Victorians keen to encourage commerce and to buy British goods. Palm oil trading was at the heart of the vision British policymakers had for remodelling West Africa's economy during the nineteenth century.[22]

The other importance of the growth of the palm oil trade lay in its impact on West Africa's economy, and this is one of the main concerns of this book. For many parts of West Africa, the nineteenth century was the century of palm oil: palm products were the major agricultural export for large parts of the region during most of this period. More specifically, the growth of palm product exports played a central role in the changes in West Africa's economy that followed the decline of the slave trade. While it is important to recognise the limits to the export sector in West Africa's economy, for those West Africans involved in exporting, the transition from slaving to legitimate trade in the first half of the nineteenth century was, on the surface at least, a change of major significance. Precisely what that change was, and what its impact was, has, however, remained an issue of considerable debate among historians.

Though palm oil featured in McPhee's *The Economic Revolution in British West Africa*, published in 1926, the first academic historian to focus specifically on the West African trade in the commodity was Stilliard in his 1938 thesis.[23] However, Stilliard's work – still the only specialist study of the topic – focused very narrowly on the methods of trading utilised by European traders, and on the first half of the century. Subsequent historians considered the oil trade as part of the broader debate about the impact of the transition from slaving on West Africa.[24] During the 1950s and 1960s – though this reflected a much older historiography – a number of historians began to argue that the transition to legitimate trade meant that the ruling elites of West Africa faced a major threat to the basis of their power and wealth. This generated, it was suggested, severe political instability in many parts of the region. Several historians developed this idea, though it was Kenneth Dike, in his *Trade and Politics in the Niger Delta, 1830–1885*, who first directly addressed the role of the palm oil trade in causing these problems.[25] Dike's book was notable on a number of levels, not least for examining the development of the oil trade in depth for the first time and, unlike Stilliard's work, for attempting to place it within the economic history of the Delta states. However, it was the underlying theme of his work that was perhaps its real importance. For Dike, the transition to palm oil trading caused serious political instability within the states of the Niger Delta by encouraging the rise of new social groups, particularly slaves. The resulting internal tensions, he argued, by providing opportunities to intervene which British officials were quick to seize, ultimately facilitated colonial take-over.

In an article published in 1968 that examined late nineteenth-century Yorubaland, Tony Hopkins refined these ideas into the notion of a 'crisis of adaptation' for the elites of the region.[26] The transition, suggested Hopkins, undermined the power of existing ruling elites whose position had hitherto been based on the slave trade, and thereby generated a deep crisis within late nineteenth-century Yorubaland. This crisis, by fuelling the Yoruba wars of this period, eventually prompted British traders to call for political intervention in the interior, and thus contributed to the colonial occupation of this part of West Africa. Hopkins took the idea of a 'crisis of adaptation' a stage further in his *Economic History of West Africa*, arguing that, in contrast to the view that saw colonial rule as the start of 'modernity', the transition from slaving to legitimate trading marked the real beginnings of the modern era in West Africa's economic history.[27] The move to legitimate trading, he argued, was accompanied by the opening of the export economy to a wider sector of society, a shift to smaller-scale units of trading and production, and the spread into the interior of cheap, mass-produced consumer goods from Europe, all of which, he suggested, marked an important break in West Africa's history. Further, the transition to legitimate trade encouraged the commercialisation of labour and land and the development of service industries like transport, and in this way generated a new phase in the growth of the market in the economy of West Africa.

Not all historians of West Africa have been persuaded by the idea that the transition represented a 'crisis' or even a break in the region's history. Critics have stressed the continuities in West Africa's economic history in the nineteenth century, the relatively limited impact of the new trades within the broader structures of the region's economy, and the capacity of the region's elites to maintain power in the face of the challenges that came with the transition.[28] In particular historians of the oil trading states of the coast such as Alagoa and Latham have been sceptical of the idea of the transition causing more than temporary strains, though the issues for the oil producing societies in the interior remain less clear.[29] More broadly, Austen has stressed that the relatively limited development of the West African export economy meant that the region's response to the transition was characterised by flexibility and adaptation rather than any systemic breakdown.[30] For many historians, therefore, it was the changes that followed colonial conquest at the end of the century that remained the critical break in West Africa's economic history. The most recent writer on Africa's economic history to produce an overview, Tiyambe Zeleza, has argued, however, that the real break in West Africa's economic history came not in the early part of the century, but in its middle with the sharp change in the relationship between African and European merchants and a shift towards ideas of monopoly capitalism among the latter thereafter.[31] The debate clearly remains open.

If ultimately the debate about the transition comes down to the familiar argument among historians between proponents of continuity and proponents of change, none the less its significance is in illustrating wider issues in West Africa's economic history and the role of palm oil within it. It would be wrong, however, to see the palm oil trade solely in terms of its place in the transition debate, for the importance of the trade goes far beyond that. Since the early 1970s, historians who have dealt with palm oil in the nineteenth century have concentrated, broadly, on two different spheres of interest. For some historians palm oil's importance has been its place in trade between West Africa and Britain. The topic thus played an important role in several studies produced by Peter Davies, which built on earlier work by C. J. Gertzel.[32] For historians whose primary concern has lain with palm oil's position in trade with Britain, perhaps the most significant issue has been the question of the downturn in prices in the late nineteenth century, a phenomenon that was quite distinct from the transition to legitimate trading.

The fall in prices of West Africa's exports in the 1880s has been examined by a number of historians, most notably by Newbury, and debate has ensued on the causes of the downturn, how far it caused problems for European traders and African suppliers, and the consequences of this for West Africa's trade. Not least, the question has arisen as to its impact on traders' attitudes to colonial expansion. Munro and Austen, in their overviews of this period, have stressed the impact of the price falls of the 1880s but have also noted the importance of keeping this within the perspective of a broader context, in which other commodities might have compensated for the fall in oil prices, and in which price falls were simply part of a much wider change in relationships between Britain and Africa.[33] The exact nature of the crisis – if such it was – of the 1880s and its impact on traders still remains unclear, and work is undoubtedly still needed for specific studies of West Africa's commodity trades to address the important questions thrown up by the price falls of the 1880s. How far in fact did prices fall? What lay behind this fall in prices and why did it take such a severe form – if it did – in West Africa?

Other historians since the early 1970s have examined palm oil in the nineteenth century in terms of its impact on West African agriculture and society, and in terms of its role in generating economic change within the region. Land individuation, labour, and gender relations are all elements that have been examined in recent years as part of this impact, not least – and with immense insight – by Susan Martin.[34] Other scholars have examined production and trading in palm oil or kernels in terms of its place within the economy of a particular society or area: Wilson's work on the Krobo, Oriji's on the Ngwa, and Adam Jones' study of the Galinhas are examples, while both Northrup and G. I. Jones have analysed the impact of oil production more broadly in southeastern Nigeria.[35] In turn these studies have raised the question of what place the export sector took in the wider context of West Africa's economy. The issue at root is whether or not external trade was essentially costless for West Africans. For some scholars, the development of exports in palm oil took place relatively easily and with few costs for West African traders or producers; oil trading was only a part of the wider structure of the region's economy and its development represented a utilisation of underexploited factors of production. For others, stressing the degree to which West Africa became dependent on the world economy, the oil trade brought with it great changes and costs for those societies that became tied to the vagaries of the international economy through it.[36]

Even if one accepts that there was much more to West Africa's economy in the nineteenth century than the export sector, clearly palm oil was not a product of marginal importance to West Africa's history or indeed its historiography. Yet until this present work, no study has tried to integrate these two approaches – of trade and of agriculture – into one specialised study of the history of palm oil. In doing so, I intend to show that palm oil's importance for West Africa is that it illustrates three interrelated questions, or, more strictly, sets of questions. Firstly, did the development of oil trading represent a break in West Africa's economic history? Or, to put it another way, what changes did the development of the palm oil trade in the nineteenth century generate among brokers and producers within West Africa, and did these changes, whatever they may have been, amount to a crisis in some way for West Africa's economy? Secondly, why did the palm oil trade encounter such severe difficulties in the late nineteenth century? What were the factors generating these difficulties and what were their consequences? Thirdly, what light does the trade throw on the economic relationship between West Africa and Britain? How far did changes in the British market have an impact on West Africa? Did the changes in the trade in the nineteenth century occur because of developments in Britain or in West Africa, or from some interrelation between the two?

To study the palm oil trade between West Africa and Britain in the nineteenth century is therefore to address central aspects of nineteenth-century West African history as well as neglected dimensions of the history of British industrialisation. The aim of this study is to throw light on these issues by providing an economic history of the trade in palm products in the widest sense, examining the impact of this trade on producer, broker, and trader alike. By focusing on the economic structures of the commerce, however, the aim is to stress elements that have not received sufficient recognition in earlier studies: the role of technological change and shipping, the growth of the British market, and the development of new managerial techniques within the trade and within the trading firms operating on the coast. In doing so, the study will illuminate the way West Africa adjusted to the ending of the slave trade and how the region adapted to the international economy that emerged during the nineteenth century.

Part I

The development of the palm oil trade in the
first half of the nineteenth century

1 The West African trade in transition

At the start of the nineteenth century the trade in slaves remained the main export activity along much of the West African coast. Britain was the major trader in West African slaves in this period, transporting to the Americas more than two-thirds of the total in the 1790s.[1] The decision of the British Parliament to abolish the trade by British nationals from 1807 therefore posed significant potential problems for African brokers and British traders alike. Moreover, the potential impact of British abolition was exacerbated by the fact that it coincided with other problems for West Africa's external trade. The Anglo-French wars of 1793–1815 caused much dislocation in the Atlantic trade. Privateering, embargoes, and blockades disrupted commerce on the coast and made investing for the future difficult.[2]

This was, in addition, a time of great political instability for parts of the region. In 1806–7 the Asante invaded and conquered the Fante states of the Gold Coast during a period of tension that continued at least until 1830; these years were to see almost continuous clashes on the Gold Coast which were inevitably to affect the trade of the British forts.[3] Not surprisingly, this unrest and instability meant that the Gold Coast's export trade fell into severe decline during the 1810s and large numbers of British traders on the coast went bankrupt.[4]

Similarly, along the Windward Coast between modern Liberia and Senegal, the early years of the century were not ones of prosperity for the export trade. The Anglo-French wars affected the gum trade of Senegambia, for example.[5] The hopes of economic regeneration associated with the settlement of Freetown after 1787 came to little as the town stumbled from one exigency to another. The British government's take-over of the colony from the Sierra Leone Company in 1808 marked a recognition of the bankruptcy of existing arrangements for the settlement.[6] Thereafter the colony's shortage of revenue led to increased customs duties, which in turn generated complaints about their impact on trade; it was not until the late 1810s that the timber trade from this area began to provide a degree of commercial prosperity.[7]

To the east, in the Bights of Benin and Biafra, the prospects for trade in the years around 1807 seemed equally unpropitious. Unlike the area to the west, there were no European settlements here, but the region was of major importance as an exporter of slaves in the late eighteenth and early nineteenth centuries.[8] While a considerable slave trade continued from the Bights for several decades into the nineteenth century, the elimination of the region's main customer for slaves after 1807 raised serious questions for the future, and not least for interior suppliers such as the Oyo Empire and Dahomey. This was to be particularly so once the British, following the ending of the Anglo-French wars in 1815, began to station a naval squadron off the coast to attempt to prevent slave trading by other European nationals.

The impact of abolition can be exaggerated, of course. It was to be many decades after 1807 before the Atlantic slave trade completely ended, and the point is often made that, for many parts of the region, external trade whether in slaves or otherwise was not as important economically as internal trading networks.[9] Yet clearly British abolition had a major impact on West Africa and its export trade as a whole. Eltis and Jennings estimate that Africa's Atlantic exports (effectively, West Africa's) fell from £31.7m in the 1780s to £27.7m in the 1820s (at current prices), while exports and imports combined fell from £50.2m to £38.8m, a fall of nearly 23 per cent.[10] Though many factors played a role in the decrease – not least the fall in prices of imports from Britain – this decline was bound to have important consequences for African producers.

For West African exporters, therefore, the future in 1807 looked difficult indeed. Yet these putative difficulties for the region's export trade did not materialise in fact, for the nineteenth century was to see a dramatic increase in exports from West Africa of agricultural produce. The nineteenth century was to be the century of so-called lawful commerce. From different parts of the coast timber, ivory, gold-dust, groundnuts, rubber, beeswax, gums, and dyewoods were to become major items of export during the century.[11] Perhaps the most important of these was to be palm oil, the product of *elaeis guineensis*.

It was Britain that was to emerge as the major market for West African palm oil after 1807. Palm oil had been imported into Britain from West Africa since at least 1588, though the quantities involved had been small and this was still the case in the eighteenth century.[12] Even for a port like Liverpool with a considerable African produce trade in addition to its slave traffic, palm oil remained low on the list of imports before 1800.[13] However, this was a growing trade, for a marked increase in the value of British imports of oils and fats from Africa, including palm oil, can be noted from as early as the 1760s. British imports of oils and fats from Africa more than

Table 1.1. *Volume of UK palm oil imports from West Africa, 1790–1854*

Year	Cwt	Year	Cwt	Year	Cwt
1790	2,599	1812	11,637	1834	269,907
1791	3,625	1813	NA	1835	256,337
1792	4,609	1814	19,344	1836	276,635
1793	3,071	1815	41,278	1837	223,292
1794	1,584	1816	23,831	1838	281,373
1795	1,350	1817	29,700	1839	343,449
1796	NA	1818	29,310	1840	315,458
1797	2,164	1819	74,049	1841	397,076
1798	3,336	1820	17,456	1842	420,171
1799	4,147	1821	102,490	1843	407,884
1800	4,467	1822	63,754	1844	414,570
1801	3,897	1823	65,402	1845	500,833
1802	7,718	1824	73,989	1846	360,452
1803	9,790	1825	85,366	1847	469,348
1804	6,327	1826	99,068	1848	499,719
1805	4,327	1827	94,246	1849	475,364
1806	7,215	1828	126,553	1850	434,450
1807	2,233	1829	179,922	1851	584,477
1808	11,047	1830	213,467	1852	507,896
1809	14,983	1831	163,288	1853	629,134
1810	25,754	1832	217,804	1854	731,659
1811	23,537	1833	266,991		

Note:
NA: Figure not available.
Source: PP 1845, XLVI (187), 481; *PP* 1854, LXV (296), 726–7; *PP* 1854–5, LI (1999), 399.

tripled in value between the 1750s and 1790s and nearly doubled again between the 1790s and the 1800s.[14]

During the nineteenth century the volume of palm oil imports into Britain from West Africa grew from 2,233 cwt in 1807 to reach a peak of 1,058,989 cwt in 1895.[15] British import volumes increased, albeit inconsistently, throughout the century, with particularly steep rises in the 1850s, in the early 1870s – when the 1 million cwt figure was first reached – and in the early 1890s. In terms of the trade's value, however, sharp increases in the early part of the century, with the £1 million figure being first reached in 1853, were followed by a plateau between the 1850s and early 1870s which can be seen as the trade's heyday, before decline set in. In this period Britain was importing some £1.5m p.a. from West Africa, with the trade's apogee being reached in 1868 when Britain imported £1,873,147 of palm oil from the region. British oil prices followed a similar pattern, reaching a peak in

Table 1.2. *Volume of UK palm oil imports from West Africa, 1795–1854, by quinquennium*

Years	Average imports p.a. (cwt)	% increase from previous quinquennium
1795–9	2,749.3	—
1800–4	6,439.8	134
1805–9	7,961.0	24
1810–14	20,068.0	152
1815–19	39,633.6	97
1820–4	64,618.2	63
1825–9	117,031.0	81
1830–4	226,291.4	93
1835–9	276,217.2	22
1840–4	391,031.8	42
1845–9	461,143.2	18
1850–4	577,523.2	25

Source: *PP* 1845, XLVI (187), 481; *PP* 1854, LXV (296), 726–7; author's calculations.

1854 when a ton of oil cost £48, before levelling off and then falling sharply from the early 1860s. Thereafter prices and, from the early 1870s, the value of the trade declined steeply, to a low point in the late 1880s when prices stood at £19 a ton and the West African trade was worth some £835,967.[16]

Assessing the progress of the trade in palm oil over the century is complicated by the fact that it was joined by a trade in palm kernels from around 1850. Hitherto the kernel at the centre of the palm nut, together with the oil it produced, had been ignored by British traders. However, from the middle of the century Britain began importing quantities of kernels, primarily from the Windward Coast, but later from elsewhere in West Africa: the first exports from the colony of Sierra Leone can be seen in 1846.[17] During the late 1850s and early 1860s the volume of exports of palm kernels to Britain was to increase considerably. In 1855 Britain imported some 592 tons of nuts and kernels; by 1884 the nineteenth-century peak of 43,372 tons was reached, with the trade levelling off thereafter. A similar pattern marks the value of the trade, with British imports of kernels rising to a value of over £0.5m in 1884.[18]

Moreover, other overseas markets for West African palm oil and kernels also developed following abolition, and quantities of palm oil were exported to Germany, the USA, and France. However, these markets did not rival the British until after 1850. Although Germany became the most important European customer for palm kernels, German traders did not enter the major palm oil areas until the second half of the century.[19] Harding's work on Hamburg – the major German port involved in the African trade – suggests that the port was importing quantities of palm oil in the 1840s and early 1850s that remained significantly less than 5 per cent of the British total and usually as low as 1 per cent; this remained broadly true until the late 1870s.[20] Similarly, US traders in the first half of the century did not concentrate on the major palm oil ports of the region, and the quantities of oil that they traded were very small compared to the volumes reaching the British market.[21] France was a more important importer of palm oil in this period, however, with French import figures approaching 20 per cent of the British total in the 1850s; but the figures declined thereafter and France was still never to rival Britain as a market for the commodity.[22] It may be estimated that by the 1850s Britain was the market for around three-quarters of West Africa's exports of palm oil and earlier in the century for much more. Indeed, the Gold Coast was the only important producing area where other markets rivalled the British as a destination for oil exports. For the first years for which reliable figures exist – the 1840s – nearly half of the Gold Coast's exports went to markets other than Britain, but it must be stressed that in terms of the West African trade as a whole this was a relatively small figure.[23] As far as the central areas of the oil trade – the Bights of Benin and Biafra – are concerned, it was clearly the British market that was paramount in the early nineteenth century.[24]

The boom in British imports of palm oil and kernels from West Africa after 1807 meant that the difficulties expected with the abolition of slave trading proved to be short-lived. Indeed, the growth of the British market in the early nineteenth century was dramatic; by 1854 British imports had increased some 300 times over the 1807 figure. By any standards such an increase was a remarkable one, although it needs to be remembered that this took place against a background of a general increase in world trade in this period, within which Africa's share in fact declined right through to the twentieth century.[25] None the less, in absolute terms, West Africa's export trade by 1830 had made up the shortfall that had followed abolition. According to Eltis and Jennings, trade volumes generally between Africa and the Atlantic world may have quintupled between the 1820s and 1860s.[26]

There were to be three periods of sharp increase in the volume of the British oil trade before its heyday was reached in the 1850s: the 1810s, the late 1820s/early 1830s, and the late 1830s/early 1840s. Each of these three periods was significant in establishing the commercial export of palm oil from West Africa. The first, the 1810s, was the decade of the sharpest growth of British imports at any time in the nineteenth century and may be seen as the period of take-off, when the export trade established itself in West Africa. It was at this time, as will be seen, that the trade grew rapidly from Old Calabar, the first port to export in large quantities to Britain and at the heart of the trade in its early decades.

However, the second period of growth – the late 1820s/early 1830s – was perhaps the most significant such span in the century: it saw sharp increases in volume over the decade to 1834 and even greater increases in value; the value of the trade virtually tripled between 1827 and 1832. Remarkably, this growth began at a time when prices remained stagnant, before beginning a steep climb in the early 1830s. As will be seen, a significant change in this period was the entry into the export trade of new areas of the African coast, with the trade moving away from its original sources to become established along the coast.

The third period of growth – the late 1830s and early 1840s – saw less dramatic increases, though 1845 represented the peak for the first half of the century with British imports of palm oil reaching 500,833 cwt. This was accompanied by a fall in prices from their late 1830s high and a levelling-off of the rate of growth in the value of the trade; the increase in volumes in the early 1840s occurred despite steep falls in prices between 1839 and 1844, showing how firmly established the trade was.[27] Moreover, this period was marked by the arrival in the trade of a large number of new British firms which were to be at its heart right through to the end of the century; it was at this time that the patterns and practices of the trade were to be established for the rest of the century.

Hancock sees the years after this third period of increase, namely the 1840s, as a period of stagnation. Rather, after a period of erratic growth in the mid-1840s and decline in the late 1840s, the oil trade entered its heyday in the early 1850s, following abolition of the oil duties in 1845.[28] The 1850s were to see marked increases in British palm oil prices to their nineteenth-century peak in 1854, further expansion in the volumes of British imports, and dramatic rises in the value of the trade. The decade of the 1850s was indeed to be the period when the trade was at its most flourishing and the years traders looked back on as its golden era. By this time Britain had become confirmed as the main world market for palm oil and West Africa the largest supplier.

West Africa's role as the major producer of palm oil in this period was enhanced by the absence of any competitors on the world market. *Elaeis guineensis* was yet to be established in South-East Asia and, in this period at least, the American oil palm contributed very little to the world oil market; small quantities of palm oil from Brazil, the West Indies, and the USA entered Britain in this period, though it is unclear whether these represented indigenous production or, more likely, the re-export of quantities taken across the Atlantic from West Africa. Indeed, although Britain imported palm oil from a variety of sources in this period – included in

British Customs records are imports of palm oil from Belgium, France, Spain, and the Canaries, as well as New York and South Carolina, to name but a few – the quantities were very small and it is clear that in most cases these must represent re-exports of West African palm oil. Between 1820 and 1854 West Africa was overwhelmingly the most important source of palm oil for the British market, producing between 97 and 100 per cent of British imports.[29]

Moreover, by the 1850s palm oil was the major single item traded between West Africa and Britain. The information on this is limited, however, because of problems in the calculation of British official statistics, and any comparisons of the values of commodity imports, at least before the middle of the century, have to be treated with great caution.[30] Inikori, however, has attempted to establish an overall picture of West Africa's exports in this period, using modified official values. According to Inikori, between 1827 and 1850 palm oil accounted for some 54.2 per cent of the value of exports from West Africa to Britain (if the temporary phenomenon of guano exports in the mid-1840s is excluded); this figure is close to the figure for 1815 when already 52 per cent of Liverpool's imports from West Africa comprised palm oil.[31] Though palm oil exports from West Africa were exceeded by continuing slave exports in this period, 'on the whole', Inikori concludes, 'palm oil was by far the most important West African non-slave export by value . . . during the period 1808–50'.[32]

Where were the major sources of palm oil on the West African coast? As table 1.3 suggests, between 1827 and 1845 the area east of the River Volta, covering the Bights to the Cape of Good Hope, provided between 85 and 90 per cent of British imports of palm oil. Given that little oil was exported from south of the Cameroons in this period, clearly the Bights were the heart of the trade. Here, indeed, palm oil came to play a major role in the region's exports, contributing, on Eltis' estimation, 80 per cent of the value of exports from the Bights by the late 1850s.[33] The only other area of any significance to the oil trade was the Gold Coast, which from the 1830s provided some 10 per cent of West Africa's exports of oil to Britain; it is important to note that by the end of this period quantities nearly equal to this were being exported from the Gold Coast to other markets such as the USA. The rest of the coast provided a very minor contribution indeed, with the Windward Coast despatching approximately 2–3 per cent p.a. of British imports and the region 'from Cape Mesurado to Cape Apollonia' (roughly, modern Liberia and the Ivory Coast) even less.

It was the ports of the Bight of Biafra that led the way in the expansion of oil exports after 1807. Old Calabar was the major initial exporter, especially in the years before 1820. Palm oil had been traded from Old Calabar to Britain at least from the 1770s, and undoubtedly from well before this,

Table 1.3. *Origin of UK palm oil imports by region as a % of total palm oil imports from Africa, 1827–1845*

Year	River Gambia to Cape Mesurado	Cape Mesurado to Cape Apollonia	Gold Coast	River Volta to Cape of Good Hope	West Africa not particularly designated[a]	Total
1827	3.2[b]	NA	5.3	91.5		100
1828	3.5	0.3	5.8	90.4		100
1829	1.7	0.2	3.9	94.2		100
1830	0.6	1.6	6.4	91.4		100
1831	1.3	0.5	10.2	88.0		100
1832	2.0	0.0	7.6	90.4		100
1833	1.3	0.8	9.6	88.3		100
1834	2.0	0.7	8.0	89.3		100
1835	2.7	0.0	7.4	89.9		100
1836	1.7	0.8	8.0	86.5	3.0	100
1837	3.7	2.2	9.9	81.5	2.7	100
1838	2.7	2.2	12.7	81.7	0.7	100
1839	3.3	1.7	11.7	83.2	0.1[c]	100
1840	3.3	1.5	14.8	80.4		100
1841	2.4	0.5	10.8	86.3		100
1842	3.6	0.8	9.6	86.0		100
1843	2.4	2.5	15.5	79.6		100
1844	4.3	0.7	12.7	82.3		100
1845	2.7	0.0	8.9	88.4		100

Notes:
[a] This category appeared only in the years 1836–9.
[b] Figure for Sierra Leone only.
[c] Figure for Cape Verde only.
NA: Figure not available.
Source: CUST 5/16–34.

to the ships setting out on the middle passage.[34] It is likely that the port was exporting around 700–800 tons of oil in the years immediately before 1807. By 1812–17, Old Calabar was said to be exporting some 1,200 tons of oil p.a. (though this was a good deal more than total British imports for much of that time), while by 1820 its exports were running at 2,000 tons and by 1833 between 4,000 to 5,000 tons out of total British imports of 13,345.[35] Central to this growth in Old Calabar's oil trade was the role of Duke Ephraim, one-time slave trader and the dominant figure within Old Calabar in the early decades of the century.[36] Old Calabar's exports were to remain at the level of 4,000–5,000 tons p.a. through to the 1850s; but even in 1850 Old Calabar still produced some 20 per cent of Britain's imports and it remained a major exporter right through the century.[37]

Old Calabar may have been the initial centre of the oil trade, but its share of the British market began to drop after 1820. It was then that other ports, most notably Bonny, began to develop as important oil exporting centres in their own right. In the 1812–17 period Bonny exported only some 200 tons, one-sixth of the Old Calabar total, but thereafter it began to increase significantly.[38] Latham argues that the high prices for palm oil in 1818 were the key to the diffusion of the oil trade out of its original centre in Old Calabar. It was at this time that ports like Bonny first joined the oil trade and this is borne out, Latham suggests, by the response to the subsequent price falls. The continuing increase in the volume of palm oil exports to Britain after 1818, as prices fell steeply, can be explained only by the expansion of exports from the new ports attracted into the trade by earlier high prices.[39]

The price rise in the late 1810s clearly did lie behind the emergence of Bonny as a major centre of the trade. John Tobin's younger brother Thomas was, on his own claim at least, the first British trader to develop oil exporting from Bonny, the port he had slave traded from in the 1790s. There is less evidence for Bonny's trade in these years as compared to Old Calabar's, but clearly the port was an important oil exporter by the time Robertson was writing in the late 1810s.[40] According to Stilliard, Bonny's palm oil exports doubled during the years 1831–44; by the late 1840s Bonny had overtaken Old Calabar as the centre of the West African oil trade, with the former exporting around 7,000–8,000 tons of oil compared to the latter's 3,000–5,000 tons.[41] Precisely when Bonny overtook Old Calabar is difficult to establish but it is likely to have been during the sharp growth in British imports in the 1827–33 period or following Duke Ephraim's death in 1834.[42] *Amanyanabo* William Dappa Pepple – who ascended the Bonny throne in 1837 – is remembered as an immensely successful oil trader who opened new inland markets for the oil trade, and clearly his reign, as with Duke Ephraim's in Old Calabar, saw Bonny established as the leading palm oil port of West Africa.[43]

Certainly by the 1840s at the latest Bonny was at the centre of the oil trade. Estimates vary as to the proportion of West African exports that Bonny provided but William Hutton may be close to the mark with his suggestion that Bonny in the early 1840s exported 'as much as all the rest of Africa put together'; however, he put Bonny exports at 15,000–20,000 tons per annum, which is impossibly high and would account for virtually all of Britain's imports at the time.[44] More realistically, from the figures that do exist for the late 1840s, it would seem that Bonny was supplying around 35 per cent of British imports, and possibly as much as half.[45]

Table 1.4. *Sources of Liverpool's palm oil imports 1849–1851*

Origin	1849 (tons)	1850 (tons)	1851 (tons)	Total 1849–51 (tons)	% of Liverpool total	% of UK total from West Coast of Africa
Windward Coast	1,400	962	2,327	4,689	7.8	6.3
Benin	1,160	760	1,065	2,985	4.9	4.0
Rio Bento (Brass)	1,391	694	1,993	4,078	6.8	5.5
Elem Kalabari	2,103	1,617	2,325	6,045	10.1	8.1
Bonny	8,227	6,730	12,421	27,378	45.6	36.6
Old Calabar	2,782	4,260	3,348	10,390	17.3	13.9
Cameroons	1,288	1,796	1,334	4,418	7.4	5.9
Liverpool total				59,983	99.9	80.3

Source: PP 1852, XLIX (284), 453, 461.

Three other ports in the Bight of Biafra were to develop important roles in the trade as it expanded during the 1830s and 1840s. One of these was Brass. There is little evidence of Brass exports during the early years of the century and, according to Alagoa, the oil trade was not of importance for the city-state until the 1850s.[46] By that period, however, Brass was exporting some 2,000–2,500 tons per annum to Britain, perhaps as much as 10 per cent of British imports, and, given that it is unlikely that a trade of this magnitude began from nothing, this suggests that Brass entered the export oil trade during the expansion of the 1840s or earlier.[47] Another such port was Bonny's neighbour, Elem Kalabari. According to Wariboko, Elem Kalabari's export of palm oil remained low until c. 1850, when it began a steady rise. Certainly British oil ships were well established at Elem Kalabari in the 1840s, but much of the port's exports were recorded within Bonny's figures, since it was British traders based at the latter who operated at the former. Given this, it is difficult to determine reliably the size of Elem Kalabari's export trade, though evidence suggests that its production was around a quarter of Bonny's by 1850.[48]

The final exporter of significance for the palm oil trade in the Bight of Biafra in the early years of the century was the Cameroons.[49] The Cameroons had been an exporter of oil since early in the century, though in this period it remained primarily a centre for ivory trading.[50] Robertson,

Table 1.5. *Palm oil exports of the major ports of the Bight of Biafra, 1855*

Port	Tons of palm oil	%
Brass	2,280	9.1
Elem Kalabari and Bonny[a]	16,124	64.3
Old Calabar	4,090	16.3
Bimbia	96	0.4
Cameroons	2,110	8.4
Fernando Po	360	1.4
Total	25,060	99.9

Note:
[a] The figure for Elem Kalabari and Bonny covers the
twelve months from 1 July 1854 to 1 July 1855.
Source: T. J. Hutchinson, *Impressions of Western Africa* (London, 1858), 252.

writing in the late 1810s, referred to 50–60 tons of palm oil exported every year from the Cameroons and Bold predicted in the early 1820s that it was soon going to surpass even Old Calabar. In the 1810s, indeed, the Cameroons had provided some 5 per cent of the British total of oil and, although Bold's hopes were clearly optimistic, its oil exports grew sharply between 1827 and 1834 with the creation of the British settlement on Fernando Po.[51] By the start of the 1850s the Cameroons were exporting between 1,000 and 2,000 tons of oil to Britain p.a., slightly less than 10 per cent of Britain's imports.[52]

The Bight of Biafra ports remained the heart of the trade from its first growth in the 1810s through to the middle of the century and beyond. The relative size of the trade of each port by the 1850s can be seen in tables 1.4 and 1.5. Yet the Bight of Biafra's proportionate contribution to West African exports declined as the expansion of this period brought new ports into the trade, particularly after 1830. Chief among the new areas entering the trade in the 1830s was the Bight of Benin, the area between the Gold Coast and the Niger, which, according to Owen, had contributed very little to West Africa's exports of palm oil as late as 1828. This changed very rapidly thereafter, with the period of high prices after 1830 being the crucial factor in the area's emergence as a major source of oil for export.[53]

The Itsekiri of the Benin River appear to have become significant oil exporters in this period. According to Ikime, the Itsekiri began trading palm oil by the 1820s, though of course quantities of oil had been sold to Europeans from the Benin River since the fifteenth century. Ikime's view is confirmed by the log of the brig *Julian*, which was buying palm oil in exchange for salt on the Benin River in 1829.[54] The turning-point came in 1840 when Robert Jamieson's ship *Ethiope* travelled extensively in the rivers of the Western Delta in search of a route to the Niger; it was subsequent to this, in the late 1840s, that European traders opened factories on the Benin River and its oil exports increased substantially. By the early 1850s the Benin River was contributing some 3–4 per cent of Britain's imports of palm oil.[55]

On the Slave Coast, Lagos remained a slaving centre until the 1850s. The *Julian* found three ships there in 1829, but there is little evidence of any major oil trade from the port until after the British assault of 1851.[56] Rather, it was the ports further west that led the oil trade from the Slave Coast in this period. There were British oil merchants at Little Popo in the late 1820s, for instance, while Thomas Hutton is usually credited with starting the oil trade at Whydah in 1838; the French firm of Régis followed him three years later, while the Hamburg firm of O'Swald could also be found in this area during the 1840s.[57] By the mid-1840s Badagry was an important exporter of oil.[58] Dahomey's part in the oil trade also increased dramatically in this period; according to Reid the late 1830s/early 1840s were the turning-point in the growth of the oil trade from Dahomey with its exports of oil increasing to over 2,000 tons per annum by 1850.[59] Dahomey took to the oil trade relatively easily, with oil and slave exports continuing together at least to the 1850s.[60] Significant in the growth of the oil trade from the Slave Coast was the role of Brazilian slave traders such as Francisco de Souza and in the 1850s, Domingo Martinez; the development of oil exports to Brazil was an important part of this traffic.[61]

If the Bight of Benin followed the Bight of Biafra in developing the oil trade, then the Gold Coast was not far behind. According to Cruickshank, the palm oil trade developed on the Gold Coast in the late 1830s.[62] This is very late, however, for according to Meredith palm oil was being exported from Apollonia and Sekondi, in the west of the Gold Coast, at least by 1812.[63] Indeed, it seems likely that limited palm oil exports from the Gold Coast and certainly from the west of the region were well underway by at least 1810. Exports are recorded from Dixcove, Tantumquery, and Komenda in 1814–15 and 'a substantial quantity' was noted at Anomabu in 1816.[64] Two years later the factor at Dixcove wrote that 'the trade of this place in gold dust and ivory is very trifling . . . [but there] is in the season . . . a good supply of palm oil which fully compensates'. By 1821, with exports of 1,300 puncheons, the palm oil trade was prospering at Anomabu.[65] Thereafter, the Gold Coast's oil exports grew significantly, as

Table 1.6. *Gold Coast palm oil exports to the UK 1827–1845*

Year	Cwt
1827	4,962
1828	7,351
1829	7,002
1830	13,575
1831	16,750
1832	16,544
1833	25,599
1834	21,485
1835	19,008
1836	22,042
1837	21,986
1838	35,673
1839	40,332
1840	46,778
1841	42,745
1842	40,092
1843	63,078
1844	52,593
1845	44,565

Source: PP 1842, XII (551), 496; CUST 5/26–/34.

oil began to be traded from the east of the region from the Krobo and Akuapem areas which were to become major sources of oil by the middle of the century.[66]

The rapid increase from the Gold Coast that accompanied the development of Krobo and Akuapem exports was undoubtedly stimulated by the high prices of the 1830s. Important too was the fact that these years saw a new *modus vivendi* worked out between Britain and Asante and an end to the conflicts that had plagued the area over the previous three decades. Palm oil exports grew rapidly after the 1830 Anglo-Asante settlement to become one of the staples of the Gold Coast's trade and to challenge gold-dust as the major export of the area by 1853. Britain imported some 4,962 cwt of palm oil from 'Cape Coast and the Gold Coast' in 1827; by 1840 this figure had reached 46,778 cwt, with the USA taking around half as much.[67]

By the 1840s the Windward Coast was deeply involved in oil exporting. Evidence for the export of palm oil from Sierra Leone early in the century is scarce. Corry, visiting the area in 1805–6, refers to the production of palm oil, and there are intermittent Customs records of palm oil exports from

1812.[68] In this area, however, the timber trade remained of greater importance until almost the middle of the century, though Sierra Leone ships
were recorded as visiting Old Calabar and Bonny to buy oil in 1811–13.[69]
Official statistics for Sierra Leonian palm oil exports begin in 1824, when
150 tons were exported to the UK and the colony's exports remained of that
order until around 1830; this was only some 4 or 5 per cent of Sierra Leone's
total exports to the UK during this period.[70]

It was only during the 1830s that an increase in Sierra Leone's exports
can be noted: 6,891 cwt was exported to the UK 'from Sierra Leone and
the area between the River Gambia and Cape Mesurado' in 1835 and
10,341 cwt in 1840, with palm oil becoming increasingly important as an
export as the more easily felled forests came to be exhausted.[71] During the
1830s, as oil prices rose, palm oil was Sierra Leone's second largest export
by value and by 1843 it had become the first, though it was to hold this position only briefly; in 1850, however, it was back as the colony's most valuable export.[72] However, as table 1.3 shows, this area provided no more than
3 or 4 per cent of Britain's total imports of palm oil in the 1830s and 1840s.[73]
Similarly Senegal remained of limited importance for the oil trade, while
the River Gambia exported only around £300 to £500 of palm oil in the
1830s and that usually comprised re-exports from outside the colony.[74]

For the area between Sierra Leone and the Gold Coast it is difficult to be
precise about the start of commercial palm oil exports given the lack of
data, but it is clear that palm oil was widely available from early in the
century. Robertson in 1819 noted quantities of palm oil being sold at
various ports along the Windward Coast, while Bold three years later
referred to an 'incredible abundance' of palm oil between Cape Palmas and
Cape Lahou.[75] The American Colonization Society, responsible for the
foundation of Monrovia in 1822, was trading in palm oil along the Liberian
coast a year later. By 1830, the palm oil trade was clearly well established
in this area, but the quantities involved remained minor.[76] The area between
Sierra Leone and the Gold Coast provided only some 2,000 cwt of oil to
the British market in the early and mid-1830s.[77] With the general growth in
the oil trade in the late 1830s export figures for the area between Capes
Mesurado and Apollonia increased to some 4,000–6,000 cwt by around
1840, with a subsequent peak of 10,341 cwt in 1843, but this was no more
than 2.5 per cent of British imports in that year.[78] Such freak years apart,
the Windward Coast was only a limited exporter of palm oil.

The other area to start producing relatively significant exports of oil in
the 1840s lay to the south of the Cameroons, the so-called South Coast.
Once again the high prices of the 1830s had driven traders to seek out new
sources of oil. Gabon had long been an important trading centre in
produce, particularly in ebony and dyewoods, and Bristol traders were very

Table 1.7. *Sierra Leone palm oil
exports to all parts, 1824–1854*

Year	Value (£)
1824	3,817
1825	182
1826	2,874
1827	4,155
1828	4,888
1829	3,476
1830	2,796
1831	3,118
1832	3,731
1833	5,059
1834	5,236
1835	10,735
1836	11,570
1837	5,794
1838	11,343
1839	7,993
1840	11,762
1841	11,844
1842	13,004
1843	29,782
1844	29,295
1845	29,309
1846	24,828
1847	6,891
1848	11,859
1849	43,276
1850	24,970
1851	16,838
1852	29,529
1853	14,289
1854	24,497

Source: CO 272/1–/31.

active in this area by the 1830s.[79] However, little palm oil came from here; Gabon remained an area of mixed trade in dyewoods, ivory, and suchlike, and only limited quantities of palm oil.[80] It was similar further south around Loango and the mouth of the Congo. Little palm oil was exported from this region but it was an area British legitimate traders entered in large numbers in this period, with establishments set up at Loango Bay and Ambriz by the 1840s. Others began to push up the River Congo from 1845.[81] Although the quantities of palm oil exported from this area remained small, none the less this area was not inconsequential to British trade. By the 1850s the South Coast contributed less than 5 per cent of British oil imports, though larger percentages of other products.[82]

It is clear therefore that by the 1830s the heart of the oil trade was the Bight of Biafra, which provided over half of British imports throughout the first half of the century. The Bight of Benin began to contribute considerable quantities from the 1830s – perhaps as much as 30 per cent of British imports by the 1850s – while from the 1840s the Gold Coast was providing around 10 per cent. Elsewhere, the Windward Coast and the South Coast were late to develop and provided less than 5 per cent each by the middle of the century.

What is striking is that this distribution of oil exports is not dissimilar to the distribution of slave exports in the later years of the eighteenth century.[83] In terms of the pattern of exports, little had changed since the slave trade era. This also applies for the British ports that imported palm oil, where too the pattern of the slave trade era continued. Liverpool, the heart of the British slave trade, was to be the centre of the British palm oil trade.[84] The reason for this lay partly in the fact that Lancashire could provide the goods, particularly cloth and salt, needed in the African trade, and partly in the demand for palm oil generated in Liverpool's industrial hinterland, but above all in the fact that Liverpool's traders had the contacts and experience from the slave trade to develop oil trading from the Bights.[85] Continuity was central to Liverpool's African trade. Of the twenty-two ships that left Liverpool for the African trade in 1809, seventeen (or 77 per cent) had earlier been involved in the slave trade; of Liverpool's seventeen African produce traders in that year, all had earlier been slavers.[86] Among the earliest Liverpool oil traders who can be identified were Jonas Bold, John and James Aspinall, and James Penny, all of whom had once been slave traders and all of whom were intimately involved in the early Bights trade; Penny and Bold, along with the ex-slaver John Tobin, were central to the Old Calabar oil trade.[87]

This continuity of personnel allowed Liverpool to retain its position at the centre of Britain's African trade following 1807. Drake suggests that immediately after abolition Liverpool traders concentrated on general African produce trading before turning to the Sierra Leone timber trade during the 1820s. It was only in the late 1820s, when the oil trade expanded, that palm oil became the main interest for Liverpool's African traders. Figures to illustrate this are difficult to come by but the *Customs Bills of Entry,* as seen in table 1.8, give an approximate measure of Liverpool's dominance in the oil trade thereafter. In 1830, Liverpool was clearly the overwhelming leader in Britain's oil trade, importing some 96 per cent of the casks of oil to arrive in Britain. While Liverpool's contribution was to

Table 1.8. *UK palm oil importing ports, 1830–1855*

	Liverpool		London		Bristol	
	Casks of	% of	Casks of	% of	Casks of	% of
Year	palm oil	total	palm oil	total	palm oil	total
1830	26,316	96	660	2	500	2
1835	27,709	89	2,372	8	912	3
1840	30,618	85	2,988	8	2,302	7
1845	42,499	79	4,931	9	6,253	12
1850	30,833	68	6,605	15	7,537	17
1855	59,151	71	11,898	14	12,121	15

Source: Customs Bills of Entry, 1830–55.

decline in the period up to the 1850s, it still remained the major port for Britain's oil trade throughout this period.

The second British port involved in the African trade after 1807 was again the second port of the slave trade era, namely London. London's position derived from its role as the leading commercial and industrial centre of the country and particularly as a major soap producer in this period. As with Bristol, London traders tended to be general traders, trading to the Gold Coast in particular for gold-dust, ivory, and mixed cargoes of African produce.[88] The two best-known examples were the Swanzy family, the progenitor of whom arrived on the Gold Coast as an employee of the Company of African Merchants in 1789, and Matthew Forster of the London firm Forster & Smith.[89]

For a period London was responsible for a significant trade in palm oil. In the first period for which there are data, 1821–4, London accounted for around 20 per cent of British oil imports from West Africa. This figure dropped considerably from 1825; according to the *Customs Bills of Entry* figures, London's share of the trade had fallen to only 2 per cent of British oil imports by 1830, despite this occurring during the second period of the oil trade's expansion. Clearly it was Liverpool traders that were leading the way in the growth of the trade.[90] Thereafter, London's share of the oil trade was to increase, though it was never again to reach the proportion it had held in the early 1820s; it remained on the periphery of the trade for the rest of the century.

The third British port of significance in the early years of the oil trade was Bristol and, again, the continuity with the days of the slave trade is striking.[91] Although Bristol's slave trade had largely died out by the start of the nineteenth century, the port still continued a limited African trade.[92]

Bristol traders developed an increasingly important trade in palm oil from West Africa in the early years of the nineteenth century, though it was not until after 1850 that it reached a significant proportion of the British total. In 1834, the first year for which we have precise statistics, Bristol imported some 5,590 cwt of palm oil, or around 2 per cent of the British total; by 1850, the city imported 53,656 cwt or 12 per cent of the total.[93]

Bristol had a long history of trade with West Africa. Its place in the African trade in this period derived from its role as a soap manufacturing centre as well as its wide range of industries that produced the goods that were in demand in West Africa. The leading oil traders of Bristol were the King family, who, like the Tobins in Liverpool, could trace their mercantile origins back to the slave trade era.[94] These Bristol traders, unlike their Liverpool colleagues, did not specialise in the oil ports of the Bight of Biafra, from which Bristol slave traders had been squeezed out by Liverpool traders earlier in the century. Bristol traders were 'coasting' traders, purchasing general cargoes of African produce rather than special-ising in palm oil. Bristol traders were to be found in areas like Gabon, the Ivory Coast, the Slave Coast, and the Gold Coast, though by the 1850s Bristol traders were to be well established in the oil trade of the Cameroons in the Bight of Biafra.[95]

Just as the Bight of Biafra was at the centre of the African side of the oil trade, clearly it was Liverpool that was at the heart of the British side. The links between Liverpool and the major ports of the Bight of Biafra, espe-cially Old Calabar and Bonny, were vital to the trade in the first half of the nineteenth century. The vast majority of ships in the oil trade operated along this Liverpool–Bight of Biafra nexus: before 1850 well over half of Britain's oil came from the Bight and well over half of Britain's oil was imported through Liverpool, though this is not to suggest that the correla-tion was exact. Yet while Liverpool was at the heart of the British trade, as this period progressed and the trade continued to expand, the port found itself increasingly challenged by rivals better placed to respond to the new demand in the market, with Bristol in particular emerging as its main rival by 1850. Liverpool still remained the overwhelming leader in the trade by the middle of the century, however, with, according to Poole, 75 per cent of all British oil imports (from all parts) going through the port between 1848 and 1852.[96]

The ports in West Africa and in Britain that were involved in oil trading by the 1850s had had to adapt to a staggering increase in palm oil volumes over a relatively short period. What lay behind this growth in the trade was the increased British demand for oil in the early nineteenth century. This increased demand had its origins in changes in the consumption of palm oil in Britain. In the first half of the nineteenth century palm oil was used in

Table 1.9. *UK palm oil prices, 1817–1854 (£ per ton)*

Year	£ per ton	Year	£ per ton
1817	39.25	1836	34.64
1818	63.91	1837	31.16
1819	46.95	1838	41.20
1820	38.83	1839	40.25
1821	33.54	1840	35.37
1822	27.50	1841	33.43
1823	26.20	1842	31.54
1824	25.25	1843	29.70
1825	26.41	1844	26.68
1826	23.62	1845	NA
1827	26.45	1846	32.00
1828	25.66	1847	36.00
1829	25.54	1848	33.00
1830	24.54	1849	32.00
1831	30.69	1850	30.00
1832	33.73	1851	28.00
1833	32.30	1852	29.00
1834	25.95	1853	37.00
1835	26.56	1854	48.00

Note:
NA: Figure not available.
Source: Liverpool Mercury, 1817–44; A. Sauerbeck 'Prices of Commodities and the Precious Metals', *Journal of the Royal Statistical Society* 49 (1886), 641.

the manufacture of candles and soap, as a lubricant for machinery, particularly railway stock, and as a flux in the manufacture of tinplate. The demand for all these products increased significantly in Britain in this period. Rising population and increased industrialisation generated growing demand for tropical products in Britain, a process given added impetus for palm oil with the abolition of duty on it in 1845.[97]

Specifically, technological improvements stimulated increased demand for palm oil. In the mid-1830s, a new technique for bleaching palm oil enabled it to be used more extensively in the manufacture of soap.[98] Similarly in the early 1840s Price's Patent Candle Co. began to utilise a method first developed in France a decade earlier to manufacture stearic candles using palm oil to give a much brighter light than hitherto. With the new stearic candles there was an increased demand for palm oil; this was further stimulated by the abolition of the candle duties in the early 1830s.[99] Similarly, with the spread of industrialisation there was an increasing need

Table 1.10. *UK palm oil prices, 1820–1854, by quinquennium (£ per ton)*

Quinquennium	Average price (£ per ton)
1820–4	30.26
1825–9	25.54
1830–4	29.44
1835–9	34.76
1840–4	31.34
1845–9[a]	33.25
1850–4	34.40

Note:
[a] Average for 1846–9 only.
Source: Calculated from table 1.9.

for lubrication; not least in this development was the role of palm oil as a major component of wagon axle-grease during the great age of railway building in the early nineteenth century.[100]

The spread of new notions of hygiene and cleanliness in Britain equally meant a new demand for soap; soap consumption per head in Britain increased from 3.6 lb in 1801 to 7.1 lb by 1851 and this was given a further boost by the repeal of the soap duties in 1853.[101] Tinplate use grew too, with the increased need for containers, and especially in the second half of the century with the development of food canning. British production of tinplate quadrupled between 1805 and 1837 and then doubled between 1837 and 1850 before doubling every decade thereafter to 1880; over the period 1800–91 British output increased 150 times.[102] Finally in the 1840s glycerine, a byproduct of palm oil, began to be used extensively in medicine.[103]

Palm oil was particularly well placed to respond to this increased demand in the oils and fats market.[104] Until the discovery of mineral oil in the 1850s, its closest competitor was animal tallow; large imports of Australian tallow in the 1840s lay behind the fluctuations in the volumes and prices of palm oil in that period.[105] Usually in this period, however, palm oil had a price advantage of 10s per cwt over tallow and this advantage was reinforced in the early 1850s when the Crimean War disrupted Russian supplies and sent the price of tallow rocketing.[106]

Increased demand alone is not enough to explain the growth in the palm oil trade, however. Equally important was the response of African producers to that demand. Underlying this was the sharp shift in the terms of trade between Europe and Africa in this period. According to Eltis and Jennings,

Table 1.11. *Value of UK palm oil imports from West Africa, 1817–1854*

Year	Value (£)	Year	Value (£)
1817	58,286.25	1836	479,131.82
1818	93,660.11	1837	347,888.94
1819	173,830.03	1838	579,628.38
1820	33,890.82	1839	691,291.74
1821	171,875.73	1840	557,887.47
1822	87,661.75	1841	663,712.53
1823	85,676.62	1842	662,609.67
1824	93,411.11	1843	605,707.74
1825	112,725.80	· 1844	553,036.38
1826	116,999.31	1845	NA
1827	124,640.34	1846	576,723.20
1828	162,367.50	1847	844,826.40
1829	229,760.39	1848	824,536.35
1830	261,924.01	1849	760,582.40
1831	250,565.44	1850	651,675.00
1832	367,326.45	1851	818,267.80
1833	431,190.47	1852	736,449.20
1834	350,204.33	1853	1,163,897.90
1835	340,415.54	1854	1,755,982.60

Note:
NA: Figure not available.
Source: Calculated from tables 1.1 and 1.9.

the terms of trade between Africa and the Atlantic world moved in favour of Africa from around 1680 to 1870, before being followed by a sharp move against African producers in the late nineteenth century.[107] Underlying the move in favour of African producers before 1870 was the decline in the prices of British manufactured goods in this period and the rise in the prices of African commodity exports like palm oil. This process stopped in the 1860s–1870s as prices of African exports began to level off or decline, though prices of British manufactured goods continued their fall. The favourable shift in the terms of trade for producers early in the century made it more and more advantageous for African producers to export and buy British goods in return. This shift in the terms of trade, as Hopkins notes, was central to the establishment of the oil trade in West Africa.[108]

It was for these reasons that the expected problems represented by the British abolition of slave trading in 1807 failed to be more than short-lived. Indeed, the shift from slave trading to oil exporting proved to be remarkably quick along much of the West African coast. This was largely because

Table 1.12. *Value of UK palm oil imports from West Africa, 1820–1854, by quinquennium*

Quinquennium	Average value pa in £	% increase
1820–4	94,503.21	—
1825–9	149,298.67	58
1830–4	332,242.14	123
1835–9	487,671.28	47
1840–4	608,590.76	25
1845–9	752,667.09[a]	24
1850–4	1,025,254.50	36

Note:
[a] Averaged from four years, 1846–9.
Source: Calculated from table 1.11.

of the relationship between the two trades. 'The slave and commodity export trades together formed such a small percentage of total African economic activity', notes Eltis, 'that either could expand without there being any impact on the growth path of the other.'[109] The situation facing African producers and exporters in the early nineteenth century was not one of a stark choice between slaving or oil trading, with the decline of the former pushing them into the latter. Rather the situation was a more complex one whereby slaves and oil were exported together in a symbiotic relationship: as indeed had been the case from the days when palm oil provided the foodstuff for the middle passage. As Northrup has shown, the slave and oil trades in the Bight of Biafra, at least, were 'compatible'.[110] There is no evidence, Northrup suggests, that the slave trade was a restraint on the palm oil trade or that the former's decline was the necessary factor to facilitate the latter's increase. On the contrary, at least as far as the heart of the oil trade – the Bight of Biafra – is concerned, slave exports continued to increase alongside oil exports for several decades after 1807.

This trend explains the growth of the oil trade from West Africa. The reason producers found it so easy to respond to the opportunities provided by the oil trade was precisely because the oil trade did not mark a break with the slave trade. The palm oil trade, indeed, was long established in West Africa: oil had been produced and traded to the coast for centuries before 1807 and was extensively traded within the region. Its growth after 1807 should not be seen as a new phenomenon that occurred at the expense of the slave trade. On the contrary, as Northrup suggests, in the area at the heart of the oil trade, the hinterland of the Bight of Biafra, the oil and slave trades in this period grew together, at least to the 1830s. While Northrup may be right to stress the differences in the inland organisation of these two trades in terms of their export structures, the oil trade grew organically out of the slave trade. As has been seen, the same areas of West Africa were the centres of the oil trade as had been of the slave trade. The same ports in Britain that had been at the centre of the slave trade – Liverpool, Bristol, and London – were at the centre of the oil trade. The same traders who had been involved in the slave trade – the Tobins, the Kings, and others – were the pioneers of oil importing into Britain. Indeed, what is remarkable about the development of the palm oil trade after 1807 is how little of a break with the past it represented; it was because this was so that it could grow so easily in this period.[111] Continuity rather than change was the characteristic of the transition to the West African palm oil trade in the early nineteenth century.

2   African producers and palm oil production

The production of palm oil for the market in the nineteenth century was nothing new for West Africa. Palm oil production for domestic consumption, for local trade, and for provisioning transatlantic slave ships was long established in the region. None the less the great expansion of oil production for export from the 1810s onwards clearly marked a change for West African producers. That this growth could occur so rapidly is a tribute to the enterprise and adaptability of producers in the interior of the region; the story of the massive increase in West Africa's palm oil production in these years is at root the story of the skills and dynamism of West African producers.[1] Yet what is striking about the response of West Africans to this increase in oil exports is the degree to which it occurred within existing structures. Important changes did result from this increase in exports – in the utilisation of labour and in gender relations not least – but as will be seen these developments were accommodated within the continuing productive relationships of the region.

Although palm oil production was widespread throughout the forest regions of West Africa, during the first half of the nineteenth century a number of peoples began to extend their production of oil for export. Clearly underlying this was the shift in the terms of trade in this period which made it so rewarding to increase export production. By itself, however, this does not explain why particular areas turned to oil production on such a large scale. Significant in this were environmental conditions – the distribution of oil palms and access to water communications – together with the availability of labour for production and transport.

The earliest producers to respond to these enlarged opportunities for oil production were those who supplied the ports of the Bight of Biafra, the area which saw the first major increase in palm oil exports from the 1810s. In general, little oil was produced within the coastal entrepôts themselves.[2] Rather it was their hinterland, in what is now southeastern Nigeria, that became the major oil producing area in the early nineteenth century. Here, among the Igbo-speaking peoples, was to be found the most abundant collection of oil palms in Africa, with the area around Owerri described as

34

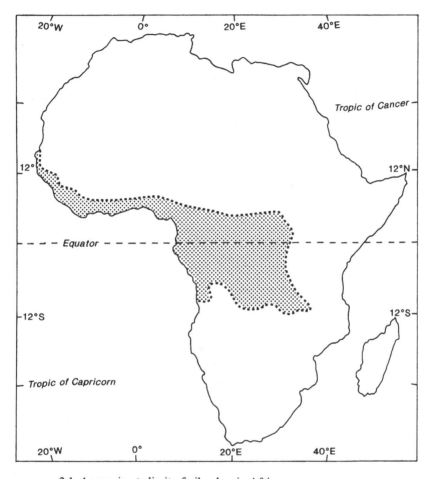

2.1 Approximate limit of oil palms in Africa

the densest grove anywhere on the continent.[3] Not all of Igboland was involved in the production of palm oil for export or indeed was within the oil palm belt, however; few oil palms are to be found north of a line between Onitsha and Afikpo.[4] In addition the problems involved in transporting oil set limits on how far inland oil could be produced for the export market. It was central and southern Igboland, therefore, that were the major sources of palm oil for the ports of the Bight of Biafra in this period.

The east of this area, the Cross River basin, began the initial supply of oil to the export markets of the coast. Igbo and Ibibio farmers up the Cross River and to its west led the way in supplying Old Calabar, the first palm oil entrepôt.[5] Ibibioland, like parts of Igboland, was a particularly densely

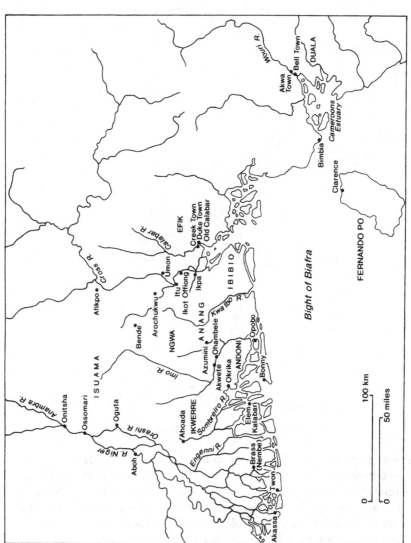

2.2 The Bight of Biafra and its hinterland in the nineteenth century

populated area with an especially high concentration of oil palms; it was also well served with waterways for transporting oil.[6] From the 1810s, large quantities of oil from Ibibio and Igbo producers reached the markets of Umon, Ikpa, Ikot Offiong, and Itu on the Cross River and its tributaries.[7] Beecroft on his visit up the Cross River in 1836 found 'large quantities of palm oil' reaching the river from 'Egbo Syra' (i.e. Ibibioland) and clearly this route was long established.[8] These markets were ones from which the Efik had obtained slaves as well as palm oil for domestic consumption and ship provisioning before the nineteenth century. They were to become the largest centres of the export trade in oil, with Ibibio, particularly Uruan, and Igbo producers bringing the oil in from the hinterland for purchase by intermediaries, such as the Ikpa and Enyong Ibibio, before sale to the Efik traders of Old Calabar.[9] Other quantities of oil reached Old Calabar from the Agwa'aguna further north through Umon.[10]

The rise of Bonny as an entrepôt during the 1820s reflected the development of oil production further west, primarily around markets on the Imo River and in its hinterland.[11] The Ngwa of southern Igboland developed as the main oil producers in this area with their oil being transported to the riverside markets at Ohambele, Akwete, and later Azumini.[12] Bonny also received oil from the Ibibio to the east and from Bende market well to the north; quantities of oil reached it via Bende from as far afield as the Agwa'aguna of the Cross River.[13] The increase in Elem Kalabari exports also in these years resulted from the growth of markets along the Engenni/Orashi, Sombreiro, and New Calabar Rivers, for whom the Ikwerre Igbo and their neighbours were the major suppliers.[14]

Palm oil was also produced from the north of this region. The lower Niger was a major artery for oil supplies with markets at Ossomari, Onitsha, and Aboh collecting oil to trade down the river to Delta ports like Nembe.[15] Oil fed into the Niger trading network from the communities on either side of the river: oil from the Nri–Awka on the Anambra River, for instance, passed into the trading system on the Niger and thence into the Delta; similarly Oguta traders tapped supplies in the west of Igboland before selling to Kalabari brokers who transported it down the Orashi River or the Niger to the Delta.[16]

Throughout the Bight of Biafra hinterland it was the combination of the dense clusters of oil palms with the availability of waterways for transport that was crucial for the development of export oil production in these early years. This applied equally to the hinterland of the Duala of the Cameroons estuary, though oil palms were never as dense here as in Igboland.[17] Although the Duala did settle slaves inland to cultivate oil palms for the market, the bulk of Duala oil exports came from a variety of inland producers such as the Pongo, the Balong, and the Bakundu.[18] Some oil from

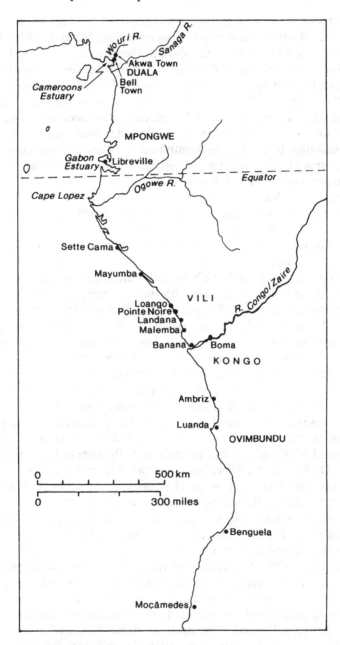

2.3 The South Coast in the nineteenth century

this region was sold to the west. Bold noted that oil from this area reached Old Calabar in the 1810s and Efik traders were active here to late in the century.[19]

If producers in the Bight of Biafra hinterland led the way in beginning production for export, they were followed by farmers on the Gold Coast from the 1820s. The quantities of oil produced here did not compare with east of the Niger, not least because of transportation problems in the absence of navigable waterways such as those the Bight of Biafran producers could utilise, but Fante producers were exporting oil collected from wild palms from a very early date; the oil was headloaded to the coast at Saltpond and neighbouring ports. Fante producers remained an important source of oil to at least the 1860s.[20] However, the Fante were overshadowed by the Krobo, the major Gold Coast producers from the 1820s. Kroboland was, stated Governor Fitzpatrick in the 1840s, 'the neighbourhood . . . [from] which comes almost all the palm oil which is collected between Annamaboe [Anomabu] and Whydah'.[21] Here a thick belt of oil palms could be found stretching between the plains of the coast and the forest of the interior, described by Horton as 'the largest palm plantation I have ever seen'.[22] Krobo producers were particularly adept at exploiting the palms of this area for the export market, with their success lying in the adaptation of their *huza* farming system.[23]

The *huza* was a mechanism whereby a group of farmers would combine to purchase a tract of land to cultivate for a period under an elected leader, the *huzatse*.[24] The tract would then be divided among the individual farmers according to the capital subscribed, with the *huzatse* remaining responsible for settling disputes and defending its members from outside attack. From at least the start of the century Krobo farmers were using the *huza* system as they moved out of Kroboland into the Akuapem foothills to the west in search of land for farming.[25] This 'bloodless conquest' of the region sped up after the defeat of Asante at Katamanso in 1826 and the ensuing Anglo-Asante *modus vivendi*.[26] By this stage *huza* farms were increasingly being used to produce oil, with Krobo farmers planting oil palms for the export market. 'Very diligently [the Krobo] extend the cultivation of oil palm year after year, thus building up oil palm forests', noted one missionary in 1867.[27]

Transport was also a major factor in the success of Krobo producers. The area may have lacked the waterways characteristic of Igboland but the Krobo turned to the River Volta, which became their major export artery.[28] Although some oil was headloaded directly across land to Accra, and some similarly to Anlo, the bulk of Krobo oil was carried to Akuse, Amedica, and Kpong, the Krobo entrepôts along the River Volta, to be bought by Accra, Ada, and other traders and transported by canoe downriver to the

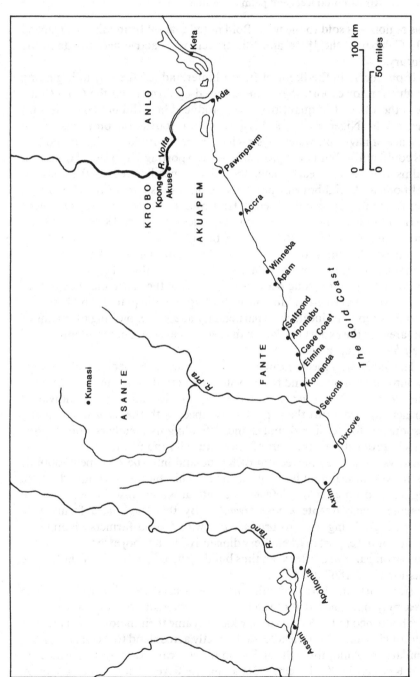

2.4 The Gold Coast in the nineteenth century

coast.[29] Krobo oil production was paradoxically also stimulated by the fine
– to be paid in palm oil – imposed on them by the British following resistance to British taxation in 1858, which, if nothing else, confirmed palm oil
as the cash crop of the area; the fine was initially boycotted by the Krobo,
before eventually being settled in 1866.[30] By this stage Krobo farmers had
reached deep into the Akuapem hills to the Pawmpawm River to the west
and were pushing across it into Akyem land.[31]

The Krobo were joined as producers of palm oil for export from the
1830s by Akuapem farmers and by the 1860s by the Shai to the south, who
developed their own form of the *huza* for palm production.[32] Akuapem production was never on a scale comparable with the Krobo, but they were well
established as oil producers by the 1850s, deliberately planting oil palms
and in turn moving westwards in search of land.[33] 'The oil palm grows here
in quantity', noted a missionary in 1839, 'and is a principal means of live-
lihood to the people. From its fruit they obtain a quantity of oil, which is
sold to the Europeans on the coast and brings much profit to them every
year.'[34] As with the Krobo, their oil was either headloaded or sold down the
Volta to the coast.[35]

The Bight of Biafran hinterland and the Gold Coast led the way in developing production of oil for the export market. However, the 1830s saw oil
production for export extend throughout much of West Africa, with the
steep price rises of the 1830s being a stimulus for this. Prime among the
groups to emerge in this phase were the Urhobo – long-established oil producers – and the Isoko, who began supplying increased quantities of oil for
export to both the Itsekiri of the Benin River and, to a lesser extent, the Ijo
of the Niger Delta.[36] Once again the prevalence of waterways was the key
to this, providing access for Itsekiri brokers to travel into Urhoboland and
transport oil back by canoe.

At around the same time oil production for export began to increase significantly among the Yoruba of what is now southwestern Nigeria.
Yorubaland was the source of the best-quality oil produced in the region
with 'fine Lagos' fetching the highest prices in the market; indeed the Yoruba
were soon to rival the Igbo as producers of palm oil.[37] Initially it was western
Yorubaland and particularly the Egba state of Abeokuta, founded beside
the River Ogun around 1830, which participated in the export of palm oil,
transporting it via Otta to Badagry and by lagoon to Porto Novo.[38] By 1856
the Egba were said to be producing 15,000 tons of oil a year. Other areas to
the west and south of Yorubaland such as Egbado soon followed.[39] Ibadan
also began to produce oil for export in this period, collecting tribute from its
expanding empire in the form of palm oil; by the 1850s Ibadan farmers were
pushing to the north and east of the city into the basin of the Ogun and Osun
Rivers to take over land for cultivating oil palms.[40]

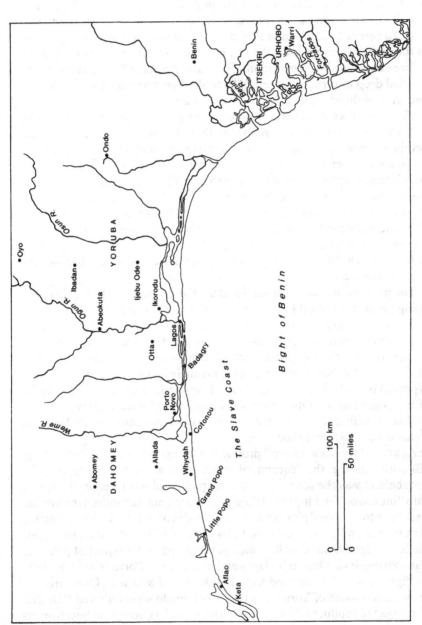

2.5 The Slave Coast in the nineteenth century

Yorubaland had an extensive distribution of oil palms. By 1892, it was claimed, there were some 15 million palm trees in Yorubaland being used to produce oil for export.[41] Initially at least, wild palms were the basis for production among the Yoruba, though in time deliberate cultivation became common.[42] As elsewhere, however, a key factor was the development of mechanisms to transport oil to the coast, for the problem facing Yoruba producers was the lack of a network of waterways comparable to the east of the Niger. The emergence of Lagos in the 1850s as a major entrepôt for oil exports, particularly from Abeokuta and from western and central Yorubaland more generally, helped to overcome this.[43] Simultaneously, Ijebu Ode and Ikorodu developed as important palm oil markets on the land route to Lagos from the interior. Headloading remained important here, but the Ogun River and the coastal lagoons provided a vital artery for transportation by canoe, with some exports for a time continuing along the lagoon to Porto Novo.[44] Although eastern Yorubaland had long been involved in selling oil to Benin, it was not to be until the 1870s, with the opening of the so-called Ondo Road, that producers in eastern Yorubaland made a significant impact in the export market.[45]

Oil exports from Yorubaland were stimulated by the Yoruba wars of this period. Oil was collected as tribute and was sold for arms; oil was used to raise money to pay for retainers or 'warboys'.[46] People captured during wars also provided the slave labour needed for production. Important also was the arrival in Yorubaland from the late 1830s of 'Saros' – freed Yoruba slaves returning from Sierra Leone – who were central to the encouragement of oil trading in this area through their contacts with the wider world; not to be forgotten either were freed slaves from Brazil and the growth of trade links across the Atlantic.[47]

The 1830s also saw exports of palm oil from Dahomey and Whydah accelerate. This oil was produced largely from the area near Whydah and from around Abomey, both areas where particularly dense collections of oil palms could be found.[48] This increase in output was encouraged for fiscal reasons by Gezo, the Dahomean king, who declared the oil palm a 'fetish' in order to protect it.[49] Here oil was produced by small-scale households as well as on larger-scale plantations run by Dahomean and Brazilian merchants using slave labour, such as the ones Forbes noticed near Whydah in 1849.[50] Dahomey indeed is the one instance in West Africa of state plantations being developed; in the mid-1850s Gezo began creating slave plantations on the Abomey plateau to produce palm oil, though this remained largely undeveloped by the time he died in 1858.[51]

The last important group of producers to enter the oil export market in this period were those of the hinterland of the Windward Coast, though the rise in oil prices of the 1830s appears to have had less impact in this area than elsewhere, not least because of the success of the timber trade. Although oil palms were extensive and river transport was available, this region never became a source of oil on the scale of the rest of West Africa. This was because of the small size of the pericarp on the local palm fruit compared to that of oil palms in Igboland and Yorubaland. Thus this region instead saw producers concentrate, with considerable success, on palm kernel exports.[52] Yet quantities of oil were exported from this area from early in the century, particularly from the early 1840s; for a period in the 1850s as the timber trade came to be exhausted, palm oil production was the principal activity for many farmers in the hinterland of Sierra Leone.[53]

Here, as elsewhere in West Africa, it was wild palms that were utilised by producers. Oil palms grew thickly to the south and southeast of what became the Sierra Leone colony, while to the east of Freetown oil palms flourished in the area cleared by the timber trade.[54] Here Temne and Limba producers traded their oil to Freetown along well-established carrier routes via Port Loko or down the Rokel River via Magbele.[55] Greater quantities of oil came from the south and southeast where it was the Sherbro hinterland and the Galinhas areas that were the major exporters of palm products (though mainly palm kernels).[56] Here palm produce originated in and around Mofwe, Pujehun, and Bandasuma from Mende farmers and was brought down the Mano, Moa, Waange, and Bum Rivers to markets on the coast at Mano Salija, Sulima, Lavana, and Bonthe.[57]

The wide range of West Africans who entered production for the export market in the first half of the century is remarkable in itself. That they could do this so rapidly and generate such massive volumes for the export market is indeed testimony to their skills and adaptability. How was it that West Africans were able to increase production so sharply in this period? For many scholars of nineteenth-century West Africa, the explanation is found in the ideas developed by Hla Myint in what has been termed 'vent-for-surplus' theory.[58] Myint attempts to explain the increase in agricultural exports from regions like West Africa by stressing the prevailing underutilisation of factors of production such as land and labour in areas not involved in exporting for the international market; in these areas high transport costs acted as a barrier to export and in effect created the underemployment of labour and its low productivity.[59] With the development of international trade and new transport facilities a 'vent for surplus' emerges which utilises the hitherto surplus factors of underemployed land and labour. The result is the increase in produce exports. This is 'costless', occurring, it is argued, without any significant impact on the existing production of goods and services – not least food output – and without any new capital utilisation or improvements in productivity.[60]

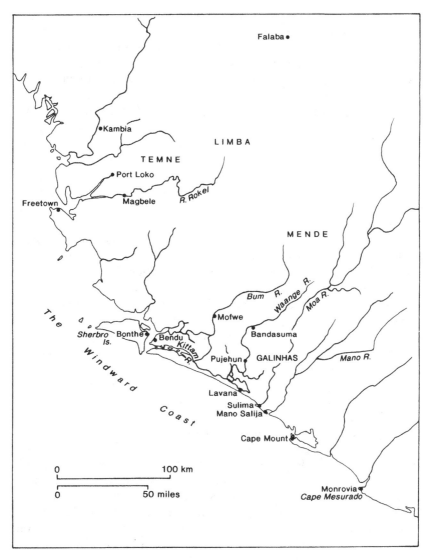

2.6 The Sierra Leone coast in the nineteenth century

The vent-for-surplus theory has been criticised, to a greater or lesser
extent, by several writers who feel that it needs modification: firstly to take
account of costs such as labour migration, the decrease in output of traditional goods and services (such as food production) that accompanied the
'cash crop revolution', as well as the changes in farming practices that
occurred; and secondly to acknowledge the significant role of local

entrepreneurship in encouraging the growth of exports.[61] Many stress that land and labour were never truly underutilised resources before the advent of commodity exporting; increases in commodity exports could occur only through the reallocation of labour from other tasks, a process that was never 'costless'.[62] For Hogendorn, who has attempted to apply the theory specifically to palm oil exporting in the nineteenth century, vent-for-surplus theory, while broadly illuminating, does not give a full explanation of the increase in oil production in West Africa in this period. For one thing, he argues, transport improvements were not critical in the increase in oil exporting in the early nineteenth century. Moreover, Myint's theory ignores two critical factors in the growth of the oil trade, namely the costs that had to be borne through indigenous capital formation in the planting of oil palms, and the high level of African entrepreneurial skill required in the development of oil exports.[63]

To be sure, while vent-for-surplus theory fits the development of palm oil production in West Africa in the nineteenth century in a broad sense, it does need qualification in a number of ways, though these are somewhat different from those suggested by Hogendorn. In practice the expansion of oil production in nineteenth-century West Africa did lead to important changes for West African producers and did have important costs, but these changes were more complex than is sometimes imagined. One can understand this best by looking in turn at the impact of the growth of export oil production in the nineteenth century on the factors of labour and land.

Palm oil production was an immensely labour-intensive activity. The degree of labour intensity depended on the type of oil to be produced. Palm oil in the export market was broadly divided into 'soft' and 'hard' oil, though by the start of the twentieth century it came to be distinguished in four specific categories: edible (the very softest oil), soft, semi-hard, and hard.[64] These oils fetched different prices in the UK market, with 'fine Lagos', the softest, gaining a premium of as much as 20 per cent.[65] Other oils sold for lower prices, with Saltpond known as the source of the hardest oil and fetching the lowest.[66] Old Calabar, Bonny, Opobo, and the Cameroons were regarded as exporters of soft oil; Warri, Nembe, the River Niger itself, Elem Kalabari, the Gold Coast, Sierra Leone, and the Congo were sources of hard oil.[67]

The hardness or softness of palm oil is decided by its free fatty acid (FFA) content, which in turn determined what the oil could be used for in the British market. Soft oil was low in FFA and could be used in soap manufacture, machine lubrication, and, particularly, tinplate processing; it was also high in valuable glycerine. Hard oil was high in FFA and was used in candle manufacture and for certain kinds of soap.[68] Edible oil, such as 'fine Lagos', had a FFA content of no more than 15 per cent by weight – and usually much less – while hard oil had above 45 per cent; Saltpond oil could have a FFA content of 80–90 per cent.[69]

Chemically, palm oil is composed of the glycerides of fatty acids; the production process splits these into glycerol and fatty acids (which thereby become free fatty acids), with the method used determining the proportion and thus its hardness or softness.[70] The aim of the production process is to remove the fleshy pericarp from the kernel of the palm nut and extract the oil from it.[71] The process has several stages: fermentation, boiling in water, pounding, and skimming. How the stages are undertaken, how often they are repeated, and how much time is taken for each determine the FFA content (and thus the hardness or softness) of the resulting oil.[72]

Though some palm fruits might be gleaned by collecting windfalls, in the nineteenth century most were harvested by cutting the bunches of nuts from the tree, a highly skilled and sometimes dangerous task. Most producers relied on their own labour to do this, but in some areas labour would be provided by outside specialists; the Isuama of western Igboland, for example, renowned for their skill in harvesting palm fruits, would travel among neighbouring peoples during the season for this purpose.[73] Harvesting usually began from around the start of the rainy season; for areas in what is now southern Nigeria the season was usually from late February/March through to May/June, with the exact start regulated by custom or by community elders.[74]

The bruising generated when the bunches of fruits fall to the ground starts fermentation. The fruits would be left stored for a period to encourage fermentation and to loosen the nuts from the bunch. This could be in a pit, a heap covered in palm fronds, an upturned canoe or something similar. One of the earliest descriptions of palm oil production, Corry's account from the Windward Coast in 1805–6, notes that the fruits were left in the sun, 'which, by its influence, opens the juices'.[75] Fermentation could also be encouraged by throwing water on the fruits as the Krobo did.[76] Governor Freeling of the Gold Coast noted in 1877 that fruits would be buried in a hole in the ground lined with plantain leaves and covered by palm fronds to decompose: among the Krobo, noted missionaries in 1853, these pits could be twelve feet in diameter and four feet deep.[77]

The duration of fermentation determines the degree of difficulty involved in the rest of the process and thus the labour and fuel inputs that are necessary. The longer the fermentation the less pounding and boiling is required, but the harder the oil. Fermentation releases the enzymes which create the FFA: the longer the fermentation the higher the FFA.[78] Conversely, the less fermentation, the more labour and fuel is required for processing but the softer the oil and the higher the price received.[79]

For producing soft oil, therefore, fermentation would be kept to the minimum, if not avoided altogether, before the palm nuts were removed from the bunch.[80] These would then be boiled in water, the resulting mass pounded in a mortar or similar in order to loosen the pericarp; the pericarp fibre was then separated out by hand and the inner kernel left to one side; discarded kernels from previous operations could be used as fuel for the fire. In several areas, such as parts of Yorubaland, the nuts would be mashed in a canoe by foot, with cold water being added during this process; in other areas the fruits would be crushed in a stone-paved shallow well, or, as Waddell noted in 1851 near Old Calabar, in large wooden troughs.[81] Meredith in 1812 described production in Ahanta with the fruit beaten 'in a hollow wooden cylinder until it is freed from its external and unctuous parts'.[82] According to Sarbah, in the Dukwia River area of Liberia hot stones were added to the pulp to extract the oil.[83] Whichever method was used, the fibre would then be boiled in water, with the oil floating to the surface to be skimmed off.[84] The remaining fibre would be squeezed by hand, sometimes under water, to extract any remaining oil, with the oil being boiled once again to remove impurities.[85]

For hard oil, more time was given over to fermentation in order to ease the production process thereafter. Fermentation could sometimes take as much as three months.[86] This softened the fruits and meant that less time had to be spent on boiling and pounding and that the pericarp fibre could more easily be separated from the kernels. Hutchinson saw an example of hard oil production on Fernando Po in the 1850s:

The nuts are plucked from the cones on which they grow, and then placed in a heap covered with palm leaves till they are verging on putrefaction. They are then pounded in a mortar-shaped hole made in the ground, and paved at the bottom with stones. The pounding operation is sometimes effected with a large stone, frequently with a wooden pestle. When this is finished, the inner kernels are taken out and thrown away. The macerated pulp is placed in a country pot to simmer over the fire, after which the oil is pressed out of it by no more potent agency than the women's hands.[87]

Once processing was completed, the final stage of production was to convey the oil to market. In general this was by headloading in small quantities to local markets where it could be sold to coastal brokers, as with, say, Accra traders on the Volta, or to intermediaries such as the Aro of Igboland.[88] Typically, in this period oil was transported in earthen pots, calabashes, or, as on the Loango Coast, in baskets lined with leaves.[89] Transport would often be in numerous loads of less than one gallon, though each load could be as much as five gallons.[90]

Estimates of the yield of oil produced by these methods vary considerably, not least because of differences between trees; in particular this varied between wild palms and cultivated ones.[91] Estimates suggest differences in yield of an order of 1:5 between the two.[92] Wild palms bear around five bunches of fruit per year, with the weight of fruit thus produced varying between 50 and 150 lb per tree per year.[93] The resultant oil yield again varies significantly, from 5 per cent of the weight being realised in oil to as much as 60 per cent.[94] An estimate made in the early twentieth century was that each tree produced one gallon of oil per year, though other estimates are lower.[95] Differences in the yield of oil could also be due to inefficiency in the production process.[96] Inevitably the methods of production led to impurities such as dirt, clay, and sand entering the oil and quantities being lost in spillage; some estimates speak of between 25 per cent to 50 per cent of oil being lost in the production process.[97]

The yield of the fruit was also affected by rainfall and sunshine. Too little rain decreased the yield but so did too much; lack of sunshine impaired the ripening of the fruit.[98] Drought one year could reduce output the year after. Manning shows a correlation between Lagos' exports and rainfall figures and identifies a nine-year cycle, related to rainfall patterns, in the output figures for the Bight of Benin in the late nineteenth century.[99] Hartley, on the other hand, suggests a cycle of between four and six years in output and this fits the figures for West African exports to Britain in the early nineteenth century.[100]

Why were different methods chosen by different producers? It can be assumed that the soft process was the original method of production since this produces edible oil; Jones suggests it was with the development of the export market in the nineteenth century that the 'hard' oil process emerged.[101] With the increase of exports, producers had to decide whether they wished to concentrate on hard or soft oil. The answer to this would be determined by the availability of labour and other inputs like fuel or water. As noted above, the soft process required higher inputs of labour and fuel than the hard. Estimates in the early twentieth century spoke of the soft process requiring at least three times as much labour as the hard: 420 workdays to produce a ton of soft oil as against 132 workdays for hard.[102] In addition the yield from the processes varied slightly; experiments early in the twentieth century noted that the hard oil process extracted slightly more oil than the soft at a proportion of 21 to 20.[103]

This was further influenced by the price differential available in the market. Thus the decision as to the method of production was determined by a combination of the availability of fuel and labour as against the likely price to be received. This decision was in turn affected by the position of palm oil production in the broader economic life of the producing community: the degree to which there were other demands on labour, the density of population, and the ease of transport of oil to market. The critical factor, however, was the availability of labour to collect fuel and water, pound the fruits, and transport the oil. Thus, as Susan Martin argues, areas with dense populations where there were relatively few other demands on labour, such as Ibibioland and parts of southern Igboland, remained areas of soft oil production in this period.[104] The Krobo are a unique case, not least because of evidence that they followed both methods of production at different times, switching between the two according to circumstances; further research on Krobo oil production is needed to illuminate this pattern.[105] Conversely, areas such as parts of the Niger Delta, the lower Niger, western Igboland, and the Upper Cross River – which were either less densely populated or where there were other demands on labour – were areas of hard production. As Martin suggests, these areas were either relatively thinly populated or experienced heavy demands for labour for canoe transportation or yam production.[106] Similarly, among the Fante, where there were other export activities such as gold mining or the production of gum copal and where the lack of navigable rivers put a high premium on labour for transportation, hard oil was produced.

Clearly the growth in oil production in nineteenth-century West Africa required greatly increased inputs of labour, to harvest palm fruits, to carry the fuel and water required, to pound the nuts, and, not least, to headload or canoe the resulting oil to market. In some areas, such as among the Krobo or in Dahomey, where oil palms were actively cultivated, labour would also have been needed for planting and tending the trees and the clearing away of undergrowth. The development of export production can be assumed therefore to have had important consequences for labour.

To a certain extent the increase in labour utilisation occurred, as Myint suggests, through the taking up of hitherto underutilised labour capacity. Tosh has argued that in the forest zones of West Africa – unlike the savanna – cash crop production could occur within the existing framework of the agricultural year.[107] Farming systems and rainfall patterns in these areas meant that the farming year was long drawn out; labour for oil production could therefore be taken up within the slack periods of the year as they occurred. This meant that oil production could occur without having any significant impact on food production; on this level at least the increase in oil output was 'costless'.

Martin's study of the Ngwa Igbo bears this out. This was a densely populated area, with few other demands on labour besides food production. It was an area, too, where the soft oil process was employed in the nineteenth century, suggesting that, according to Martin, 'providing palm production was the only major commercial activity; it did not impose such major strains on local labour supplies as to provoke the invention of new production methods . . . This is a classic vent-for-surplus picture.'[108] Given the Ngwa agricultural calendar, argues Martin, labour for oil production could be fitted in around existing agricultural tasks. Martin's conclusions are persuasive and can be extended elsewhere among soft oil producers, such as among the Ibibio and the Yoruba. In these areas, clearly, increased output could occur without pressures to change well-established methods of production, though this picture needs, as we will see, to be qualified. Both these areas were relatively densely populated and, until the later decades of the century at least, oil processing remained the major productive activity aside from food production.

One obvious 'cost' for labour of the development of commodity exports would be the reduction in leisure time; if oil production occurred in the slack of the agricultural year then this could only be at the expense of what was hitherto leisure.[109] Equally, the model fails to include the role of migrant labour in oil production such as the Isuama, the Urhobo, and the Aboh Igbo who travelled in southern Igboland harvesting fruits for oil producers.[110] Similarly, there were clearly pressures on areas that turned to hard methods of processing – such as the Fante, the western Igbo, and certain Upper Cross River groups – where the development of oil production for the export market must have generated strains in the utilisation of labour. Northrup, for example, has argued that reports of food shortages in what is now southeastern Nigeria in the 1820s and 1840s suggest that the expansion of oil exports was occurring through the removal of labour from food production.[111]

There is, however, a more significant dimension to the impact of palm oil production on the utilisation of labour in West Africa – the use of slaves. As Lovejoy has shown, in many parts of the region palm oil production for the market was accompanied by a considerable increase in the use of slave labour.[112] The ending of the export of slaves across the Atlantic during the century meant increased numbers were available for the production of commodities within West Africa.[113] The result, suggests Lovejoy, was the marked increase in the use of slave labour within West Africa in the nineteenth century and the extension of a 'slave mode of production' in the region. Slaves were, for example, put to work producing palm oil in Dahomey, where the establishment of oil palm plantations both by local and Brazilian merchants and the ruler himself involved extensive numbers of slaves.[114] Similarly, slave labour on palm oil 'plantations' could also be found on the Windward Coast among the Sherbro and the Mende, claims Lovejoy, though difficulties are attached to the use of the term in this area.[115]

Even where slave plantations to produce palm oil were not established, slave labour became an important dimension of oil production in the nineteenth century. Among the Yoruba, for example, increasing numbers of slaves were used by small-scale cultivators on their farms to produce oil.

Agri notes the increased use of domestic slaves for oil production among the Egba in this period, and by the 1850s slaves were being widely used for agricultural production in Ibadan.[116] Similarly, among the Igbo, though the numbers were fewer and the degree of servitude involved less severe than in some areas, slaves were used by small-scale oil producers across a wide region.[117] Equally, on the Gold Coast, Riis commented in 1842 that 'the labouring people are mostly slaves', with slave labour being used in places to plant oil palms.[118] Indeed, the increase in the internal slave trade in this area in the 1830s and 1840s is undoubtedly tied to the increasing need for labour for agricultural production; Sutton sees the continuation of the Salaga slave trade into the lower Volta basin in the nineteenth century as a result of this demand.[119]

Palm oil production required labour in other ways too. Transportation of palm oil, whether by headloading or canoe, was immensely labour-intensive and this would have increased demands for slave labour. Equally, in some areas, slaves would be needed to produce foodstuffs which could be then traded to those areas heavily involved in oil production. Such was the case among the Yoruba and among the northern Igbo, where intensive yam farming by slave labour occurred to produce exports to southern and central Igbo peoples who supplied oil.[120]

Not all oil producers turned to the use of slaves, or at least not large numbers of slaves. In areas like Ibibioland where population density was high, few slaves were needed and increased export production utilised existing sources of labour.[121] Equally, among the Ngwa and other southern Igbo peoples the use of slaves for oil production in the nineteenth century, while not unknown, remained relatively limited in extent.[122] Among the Krobo the situation is unclear. Sutton stresses the considerable numbers of slaves utilised for palm oil production among the Krobo even as late as the early twentieth century, though Wilson, while accepting that some slaves were undoubtedly used, argues that it was largely family labour that provided the bulk of work on *huza* farms and in transporting oil.[123]

Yet, broadly, the increase in palm oil exporting was accompanied by an increased use of slave labour across West Africa. This is related to another dimension of the impact of increased oil production on labour – namely the issue of gender relations, on which Martin has written with great illumination.[124] In general, production of oil in nineteenth-century West Africa was women's work, and this applied right across the region.[125] This was noted on the Gold Coast in the 1850s, for example, as well as on Fernando Po.[126] It was also the case in Sierra Leone at the end of the century, as Alldridge noted.[127] Johnson wrote that the production of palm oil and palm kernel oil were 'exclusively female industries' in Yorubaland in the late nineteenth century.[128] Repin, a member of the French mission to Dahomey in 1856, noted that 'while their lord drinks, sleeps, or smokes [his women] make the palm oil'.[129]

Men were responsible for the harvesting of fruits by climbing palms and cutting the bunches down, while the processing of the nuts was undertaken by women.[130] Before the commercialisation of the oil trade, it is likely that the production process and the disposal of the resulting oil was left entirely to women. With the growth of nineteenth-century exports, male involvement in oil production increased. During the nineteenth century male labour, probably male slave labour, was increasingly used in the actual pounding of the nuts.[131] At the same time, male rights to the proceeds of the sale of oil were asserted; Martin makes the point that male claims to the profits of the sale of oil were based on the fact that men usually performed the initial harvesting of the fruit.[132] The probability that oil had been produced largely from windfall fruits before the nineteenth century supports this argument.[133] Thus, while there is plenty of evidence that women were responsible for marketing oil, it is likely that it was men who kept the resulting proceeds.[134]

However, it is arguable that women benefited, at least indirectly, from the commercialisation of palm oil.[135] One way, stressed by Martin, was through the waste of the palm oil production process: the kernels. By the second half of the century palm kernels began to be exported in increasing numbers and, Martin suggests, as an increasing percentage of total palm products; the proceeds of this accrued to women.[136] They were regarded as a women's perk and it was women and children who dried the kernels and cracked them.[137] This can be seen amongst the Ibibio and the Ngwa as well as the Krobo, to name but three.[138] A second way women benefited, argues Law, was from the increase in numbers of small-scale units involved in oil production in Yorubaland and Dahomey, at least some of which would have been operated by women capable, potentially at least, to assert their ability to earn money from selling oil; this was also the case among the Krobo.[139] Finally, some women benefited from the new opportunities that developed for the trade in foodstuffs in nineteenth-century West Africa. Among the Krobo, for example, the involvement of men in *huza* agriculture for the export market provided new opportunities for the sale of foodstuffs by women.

Against this, however, it is likely that the increase in oil production led to an overall increase in labour demands on women. As oil processing was women's work, in so far as the increase in production took up slack in the agricultural year, it was women's 'leisure' that suffered. This is Martin's conclusion from her study of the Ngwa.[140] The key issue, she suggests, was population density relative to labour demands. Where population density was low, the demands for increased labour generated by the oil trade

resulted in increased utilisation of slaves to fill that demand. Where population density was great, however, labour demands were filled by an increased
take-up of women's labour. Important in this too was the impact on children who, not least for example among the Krobo, would increasingly be
used as labour in the pounding process or for carrying the water and fuel
required for boiling. Finally it needs to be remembered that the growing
opportunities for the sale of foodstuffs that developed during the period of
increased export production did not necessarily benefit women; nineteenth-
century evidence of who kept the proceeds of such sales is limited.[141]

Thus there is much in the view that the increase in the export of palm oil
in the nineteenth century was accompanied by an assertion of male rights
to women's labour and to the resulting proceeds. As Oriji suggests for the
Ngwa, it was males with access to large numbers of wives who ultimately
were the major beneficiaries of the export palm oil trade.[142] Indeed, in the
increased use of slave labour and in the impact on gender relations, it is
clear that the expansion of oil production in nineteenth-century West
Africa was anything but costless. In this sense, the development of palm oil
exporting in the nineteenth century shows how the vent-for-surplus model
needs modification. A similar conclusion comes from the impact of the
increase in oil exports on the other factor of production, namely land.

According to the vent-for-surplus model, an increase in commodity
exports can be explained by the previous underutilisation of land, which,
following the changes in transport facilities, could be put to productive use.
Was this the case in West Africa? What was the impact of the increase in oil
exports on land use? It is very difficult to generalise about land tenure
across a region as large as West Africa with such a variety of agricultural
systems, but a few tentative points might be made. In general, under customary tenure, land was considered as belonging to the community, though
it was held in trust by the chief or elders.[143] The ruler or elders could assign
rights of usage of land to a particular family and that usage could, theoret-
ically, be inherited, mortgaged, or even sold, though the ownership of the
land remained in the community: customary law did not recognise the sale
of land. Use of 'new' land could be claimed by the first to clear it, though
again with ownership of the land remaining vested in the community as a
whole.[144]

Rights in palm trees were not necessarily co-extensive with rights to the
land on which they stood, though trees, like land, belonged to the community as a whole: usage of oil palms did not necessarily pass with land usage
rights, but in many areas was allocated separately.[145] Much depends on the
category of tree involved. The rights to usage of what can be termed 'household' palms – those growing adjacent to a particular compound – would be
seen over time to be vested in the particular family that tended them.[146]

'Wild' palms on the other hand, were open to all, though in practice customary use over a period would mean that a particular farmer would have rights to certain groves recognised by the community.[147]

How far did the development of the export oil trade in the nineteenth century lead to the individuation of land tenure or palm ownership? To understand this, it is necessary first to examine the means whereby oil palms were cultivated. For producers before the nineteenth century a reliance on wild palms for obtaining their oil remained the norm. Little planting of palms was required. Oil palms spread with the development of intensive agriculture in the forests of West Africa. So-called slash-and-burn agriculture, by clearing the forest, helped propagate oil palms in the less dense secondary growth that ensued. It was on this process that most producers relied for propagating their palms.[148] This is not to say palms were never deliberately planted, especially close to settlements, to provide oil for household consumption, and deliberate tending of young palms by clearing, trimming, and such activities also occurred, but in general producers relied on wild palms to provide the oil they required.

This remained largely true for most producers even with the increase in exports in the early nineteenth century. There is little evidence for widespread deliberate plantation building or individuation of ownership. Among the Ibibio and Igbo, for example, oil palms remained a communal resource with only those palms categorised as 'household' palms passing into, effectively, individual family 'ownership'.[149] Plantations were unknown in this area in this period. For most Igbo it continued to be the case that wild palms remained the source of their oil. However, exploitation of such wild palms became more tightly regulated by the community during the century and access to palms passed increasingly to lineage control in many parts of Igboland.[150]

Yet, clearly the reliance on wild palms to produce oil began to change in some parts of West Africa after 1800. Deliberate planting and cultivating of oil palms – farming in a systematic sense – did become common in some areas.[151] Problems exist in defining terms such as 'farming' and 'plantations', especially as used by nineteenth-century observers, and it would be wrong to see a strict dichotomy between 'farmed' and wild palms; rather, one should see the exploitation of the oil palm in nineteenth-century West Africa as characterised by a continuum from the use of untended palms through various degrees of tending and cultivation – whereby 'wild' palms came to be recognised as 'belonging' to a particular producer – to large-scale plantations.[152] None the less, from the early nineteenth century a number of areas in West Africa began to turn to the systematic planting and cultivation of oil palms, with oil palm 'farming' becoming increasingly common.

Such farming developed, for example, in Dahomey where both large- and small-scale plantations did appear, helped by the prevalence of slave labour. Equally, the Krobo, through their *huza* farms, developed a system of cultivating palms that was based on an effective combination of communal and individual tenure: the *huza* was purchased as a whole from neighbouring peoples by a group of farmers and was immediately divided between individual subscribers. *Huza* farmers remained under the authority of the *huzatse*, but farmed their own individual plots, the usage of which could be sold or inherited by their successors.[153] This pattern of individual land tenure was not widespread, however, throughout West Africa for the farming of oil palms, though Jones does see increased individuation of tree-owning among the Igbo, and a similar development can be identified among the Yoruba, though it was by no means extensive.[154]

What is striking, however, is how restricted this process was. A similar pattern emerges for the production of palm oil. Production of oil generally remained focused on the small unit, usually the family, since this was a trade that was easy to enter.[155] The reason for this was that, as Hopkins suggests, there were few economies of scale in palm oil production.[156] Oil could be successfully marketed in relatively small units; while it could also be produced on large-scale plantations as in Dahomey, there was little scope to achieve economies of scale in production, not least since trees grew wild.

Apart from the large-scale plantations of Dahomey where special factors operated, it was, therefore, the household unit that processed the fruits and that became the basis of oil production throughout West Africa. This can be seen across Igboland where oil was produced in small quantities by numerous small units of production.[157] Equally, in Yorubaland, where the power of lineage heads remained considerable, oil production was still essentially an activity of the individual family unit.[158] Among the Krobo this was similarly the case and even in Dahomey, besides the large-scale plantations owned by the king and wealthy merchants, production was dispersed among numerous small-scale family producers.[159] This reflected a broader trend in 'legitimate' commodities, seen not least in the sharp increase in imports of cowries into West Africa in the middle decades of the nineteenth century.[160] William Hutton stressed in the 1840s that oil could be sold in minute quantities and this had broader consequences; Francis Swanzy noted on the Gold Coast in 1842 that 'wealth [was] more diffused' compared to the slave trade era.[161]

This shift to individual units of production has been seen by scholars as marking the start of 'modernity' in West Africa's economic history.[162] Not only did the production of 'legitimate' commodities encourage an emphasis on small-scale production units, but it also generated linkages that spread widely in the interior. Land and labour were increasingly commercialised; cheap mass-produced imports spread widely in the region. Central to this was the fact that many individuals could enter the export trade for the first time: given that trees grew wild, there were few barriers of entry into producing oil for the export market.

There is much in the argument that the great increase in oil production in the nineteenth century marked a break in West Africa's economic history. One can see this among the Fante where oil production for the export market in the early nineteenth century, Sanders argues, led to major changes.[163] Mass-produced imports became accessible to large numbers of producers, wealth was more dispersed than had been the case in the eighteenth century, increasing social stratification occurred, and a money economy developed. Wilson argues that for the Krobo the introduction of palm oil exporting 'transformed every aspect of . . . society', leading to the development of wage labour, upward mobility for domestic slaves, immense benefits to women, and the wide accessibility of Western luxuries for Krobo farmers.[164] Reynolds draws a picture for the Gold Coast more broadly that reflects this process.[165]

Clearly this was a period of important changes in palm oil production. But how far did these changes add up to a significant break in West Africa's history? It has been argued by many, from observers in the nineteenth century through to recent historians, that the transition from slave 'producing' to oil production brought with it a 'crisis of adaptation' for many parts of West Africa.[166] This has been most clearly spelt out for nineteenth-century Yorubaland by Hopkins, who argues that the ending of the slave trade produced a crisis for those Yoruba elites hitherto dependent on it as the basis of their power, and who came up against the emergence of numerous small-scale oil producers able to compete effectively in the market. Faced with the shift in economic power to these new producers, the old elites attempted a variety of economic and political responses to maintain their power; these responses encouraged the political instability and warfare that characterised much of Yorubaland in this period and which ultimately prompted British intervention.[167] The economic changes associated with the transition to palm oil production were thus accompanied by political tensions that threatened the elites of parts of West Africa.

This debate over the 'crisis of adaptation' has been focused around the separate issues of production and trading; in so far as these functions can be disaggregated, it is the former that concerns us here. It is certainly true, as has been seen, that the development of palm oil exports in the nineteenth century brought with it many changes for producers, not least in the way it was accompanied by the emergence of numerous small-scale units of production, able to enter the export market for the first time. With this came the spread of western goods deep into the interior to stimulate this expansion. It has been seen, too, that with it came a move towards individuation of land tenure and ownership of palms in parts of the region.

However, this argument needs to be qualified. The issue is whether these changes created new productive or social structures and amounted to a 'crisis'. One factor to be stressed is that for many areas oil production was an incidental activity, carried out only in order to buy luxury goods.[168] Within the overall context of the changes resulting from oil production by small-scale units, the factors reflecting continuity need to be remembered. As has been noted, the production of palm oil for an export market was nothing new in the nineteenth century, given the long-established provisioning trade, while the slave trade took several decades to die out, even from those parts of West Africa where palm oil production for export was quickest to establish itself.[169] This was far from an abrupt break and the length of the transition between the two must have eased the experience for many areas.

Equally, the increase in export oil production, while facilitating the emergence of small-scale producers, did not necessarily result in a shift in economic and political power in their favour. There were two reasons for this. On the economic side, large-scale units of production were by no means disadvantaged by the shift to the oil trade, as the utilisation of large-scale plantations in Dahomey shows.[170] Access to labour, whether slave labour or the labour of women, allowed the previous 'producers' of slaves to switch very effectively into oil production. Moreover, there clearly were some economies of scale to be gained in oil transporting and marketing, where the use of slave labour in transporting oil to market gave an advantage to those producers able to call on extra inputs of labour. Large canoes could transport large quantities of oil to market more efficiently than small ones or than porters headloading oil to the coast. Law has stressed that the costs of transporting oil were higher than for transporting slaves in the slave trade era; this suggests that there were economies of scale available for large-scale units in transporting oil to the coast.[171] 'The real profits were to be made', says Isichei, 'by those responsible for bulking and transport', an argument reflected in Jones' view that despite the emergence of numerous small-scale producers, the major profits went to those able to handle oil in bulk.[172] Overall, indeed, control over the marketing of palm oil provided a very effective way for large-scale producers to continue to benefit from their control over access to slave labour, as Berry has argued for Yorubaland.[173] Hence, too, the continuing power of trading intermediaries like the Aro in southeastern Nigeria.[174]

Similarly on the political side, it would be wrong to assume that the development of export oil production necessarily led to the emergence of new social strata and a shift in political power towards small-scale producers. As scholars have suggested, the old elites of West Africa were able to use control over access to palm trees to assert their influence over oil production; while palm trees may have grown wild, this did not necessarily imply that there were no barriers to entry into the market.[175] The elites of West Africa were able to use political means to attempt to control access to palms during the nineteenth century, a process which reinforced their attempts to restrict marketing of oil. Northrup makes the point that the management of access to palms by communal elders in southeastern Nigeria during the nineteenth century increased, while Martin stresses that among the Ngwa the management of land rights by lineage heads meant that these figures were able to regulate access to palms, and that this process in fact tightened during the nineteenth century.[176]

Indeed, it seems clear that, while the transition to export oil production was marked by a shift to small-scale units, the longer-established elites of West Africa were still able to assert their powers over the trade. Far from new social strata emerging, it was in fact 'big' men, rather than 'new' men, who were the chief beneficiaries of these changes. This is the argument of Isichei, who stresses that the wealth that resulted from oil production in Igboland was 'not a prosperity that was widely distributed or shared'; rather it mainly accrued to those – the 'Ogaranya' or wealthy – able to utilise slaves, wives, or clients.[177] Oriji argues that, among the Ngwa, while 'the common man' benefited, it was lineage and village heads who gained most from the transition to oil exporting with production of the new commodity 'tending to strengthen the authority of the heads of various communities'.[178] The reason, he suggests, was that those able to call on extra labour – whether slave or free labour from within the community – were able to benefit most. In short, far from being egalitarian in its impact, oil production reinforced existing social differentiation.

Thus, while the development of oil production for the market did lead to important changes among producers, this neither amounted to a crisis nor led to a fundamental break. These changes occurred within existing relationships rather than in creating new ones, and they must be seen in a broader context of the continuing structures of West African society. This was no revolutionary break in West Africa's economic history. Rather, it was precisely because oil production was so long established in West Africa's economic life, and fitted so easily into existing patterns of social differentiation, that the great increase in output for the export market could occur as it did in the nineteenth century.

3   African brokers and the growth of the palm oil trade

Continuity characterised the broking networks of the West African trade in the years before 1850. Here the structures and practices that had evolved in the slave trade era continued to determine the trade in palm oil. It was precisely this that allowed the great increase in exports of oil to occur as it did in these years. The figures involved in these trades – the coastal brokers who bought the oil from the inland markets – were as central to the rapid growth of exports in this era as the numerous producers who processed oil in the interior.

The success of such brokers in the transporting and marketing of palm oil can be seen in the way African brokers – in this period at least – largely determined the practices of the trade with the Europeans. 'Whether they liked it or not', notes Jones, 'European traders had . . . to conform to the African trading organisation.'[1] It was the very efficiency of the African broking system that lay behind this. So effective were the methods used for transporting palm oil to the coast that European traders, in this period, had little desire to penetrate inland to the markets of the producers. Thus the methods of trading that had marked the slave trade era continued virtually unchanged for the 'legitimate' trade of the first half of the nineteenth century.

The continuity in palm oil broking structures was reinforced by the fact that the oil trade was already well established before 1800, in the form of the provisioning trade for slave ships and for local consumption. The long existence of this provisioning trade meant that, as Northrup has suggested for the Bight of Biafra hinterland but which applies more broadly, the slave trade and the palm oil trade were 'compatible' in the demands they made on producers and brokers. Contrary to the view at the time that the slave and oil trades could not operate together, in much of West Africa the two co-existed successfully. Thus output of slaves and oil from areas like the Bight of Biafra grew 'in tandem' in the early nineteenth century, and the export of slaves from oil producing areas continued to increase through to the 1840s.[2]

The reason for this was not, as Northrup suggests, that the slave trade and the oil trade relied on different broking organisations inland, allowing the one to expand without interfering with the other, but rather because, as Latham argues, they relied on the same. It was the fact that oil and slave trading were to a degree peripheral to the economy which was behind this; capacity was thus available to allow both palm oil and slaves to be brokered using the same trading networks.[3] Differences between the two trades clearly existed, but they lay in the initial marketing of oil and slaves. Once palm oil reached the market, it was to be traded along essentially the same networks that the slave trade had relied on.[4]

How then was palm oil brokered between the producers of the interior and the European traders on the coast? It was rare for oil producers in West Africa to sell directly to Europeans, just as it was rare for brokers to produce palm oil themselves; only Dahomey of the major oil exporters was an exception to this. Rather, the trading system for palm oil in this period operated around a number of major states on the West African coast which became specialised brokers. In most cases these oil broking states were those that had emerged as major slave exporters before 1800, and were to continue as such through much of this period.

It was in the Niger Delta and neighbouring areas that the major palm oil broking states of West Africa emerged and their brokers will be the primary focus of this chapter. The two major oil broking states of the early nine-teenth century were Old Calabar and Bonny, and both had long been estab-lished in the overseas trade. As Old Calabar produced virtually no oil itself, local brokers relied on an elaborate trading network up the Cross River to buy palm oil from the Ibibio and other peoples of the interior.[5] Along the river and its tributaries a series of markets such as Ikpa, Umon, Ikot Offiong, and Itu provided oil for purchase by Efik brokers; to these markets fleets of canoes would be sent from Old Calabar to collect palm oil during the season. This trading network was nothing new, as Northrup stresses: 'in forging or renewing these trading links the Efik of Old Calabar did not depart in any dramatic way from the techniques of the slave trade and the provisioning trade'.[6]

Old Calabar's oil trade was operated by the mercantile oligopoly which had emerged in the slave trading era.[7] These men dominated Efik society and the trade between the interior and the Europeans; indeed, by the 1830s one such broker who had risen to power with the slave trade, Duke Ephraim (Efiom Edem), had effectively created a monopoly of the oil trade in his own hands, simultaneously controlling 'comey', a tax the Europeans paid, and holding the two major offices of Old Calabar, that of *Eyamba* and *Obong*.[8] Duke Ephraim remained the most successful palm oil broker of Old Calabar until his death in 1834. Thereafter other Efik traders from the various wards of Old Calabar were able to flourish in the oil trade in their own right: Latham identifies around ten major Efik traders dominating the oil trade by the late 1840s.[9]

Bonny operated a trading network similar in scope and complexity to that of Old Calabar. Like Old Calabar, it produced virtually no palm oil itself: its major source of oil lay in the markets of the lower Imo River, such as Akwete and Ohambele, which tapped hinterland suppliers among the Ngwa and Ibibio, though some oil came from as far north as Bende and the Upper Cross River; Bonny traders could also be found obtaining oil far to the west, from Aboh on the River Niger.[10] Bonny continued to export slaves right through to the 1840s.[11] Its success in adapting to the palm oil trade lay in its ability to utilise pre-existing broking networks for the export of oil. This was done relatively quickly during the 1820s and 1830s, for the waterways of the Eastern Delta provided the water transport that was ideal for conveying oil from the interior.

At the heart of the trading system Bonny established to obtain its oil was the canoe house. The canoe house had emerged out of the lineage system of Bonny during the slave trade era. It was essentially a more compact version of the lineage, transformed for trading, military, and political purposes; at its simplest it was a house able to maintain a war canoe. In the process of this transformation the original lineage definition of the house became blurred and trading merit and political ability replaced the original descent criteria for seniority within it. Non-lineage members – more particularly, slaves – were thus able to be absorbed within the house and to rise within its seniority system on the strength of their abilities.[12]

Though Bonny had been exporting palm oil from an early date, the great increase in its trade coincided with the emergence of William Dappa Pepple as *Amanyanabo* (loosely translated as 'king') of Bonny after 1837. William Dappa Pepple – whose mother came from Bile on the northern margins of the Delta – was responsible for opening new oil markets inland and no doubt his kin ties were important in this.[13] His first period as *Amanyanabo* (1837–54) was marked by the great increase in oil exports from the port, but also by great rivalry between the two major canoe house groups that had emerged within it, Manilla Pepple House and Anna Pepple House, and between them and himself. The tension was exacerbated by William Dappa Pepple's use of his position as *Amanyanabo* to attempt to control contact with the European traders and in particular access to the credit, or 'trust', the traders offered. Equally, he abrogated to himself the comey the Europeans paid, as well as the subsidies offered by the British government from 1848 in return for Bonny's abolition of the slave trade.[14]

The Old Calabar and Bonny broking networks had much in common, not simply a shared derivation from the slave trade era. They both utilised what might be termed intermediate levels of brokers between themselves and the producers in the provision of their oil. The best known of these were the Aro, who had spread widely across Igboland during the slave trade era and had established scattered communities of traders involved in transporting slaves to the coast.[15] The development of the export oil trade in the nineteenth century posed difficulties for the Aro, but they were to continue to play an important role in the export economy of the area. Aro traders continued to purchase oil and were an important source for Bonny in particular; for example, they were behind the diversion of Agwa'aguna oil from the Upper Cross River to Bonny sometime before the 1840s.[16]

Old Calabar and Bonny were the most successful broking states of the early nineteenth century, but other coastal peoples of the Delta region developed broking networks up the creeks and rivers of the interior that were similar. The Itsekiri, for instance, established camps among their Urhobo suppliers from which they transported oil by canoe to the Benin River; by the 1850s Olomu, *Gofine* or governor of the Benin River from 1879, had emerged as one of the most successful traders of the area.[17] Oil traders from Elem Kalabari could be found in a 'trading diaspora' along the Sombreiro and Orashi Rivers as well as up the River Niger as far as Oguta by the middle decades of the century; Kalabari traders would acquire land in these markets to establish cask houses for storing oil while they negotiated prices with Europeans on the coast.[18] Perhaps the 'quintessential precolonial middlemen' were the Duala of the Wouri estuary.[19] Their ability to prevent contact between the sea and the hinterland and their control over the provision of trust from the former to the latter was the key to their power. 'Kings' Bell and Akwa had emerged by the nineteenth century as the major trading brokers of the area with their own separate towns in the estuary; from these they organised their trade up the Wouri, Dibombe, and Mungo Rivers into the interior to collect oil.[20]

The main oil broking network to rival those of the Niger Delta area for sophistication and the ability to move large quantities of produce was located further west on the River Volta, reaching from the coast to the Krobo oil markets of the interior. Here the long-established salt trade from the coast lay in the hands of Ada traders whose canoes penetrated up the Volta to Akuse and Odumase. Salt was traded for oil. From these markets Ada traders returned to the coast with their canoes laden with Krobo palm oil.[21] This network was nothing new, having a long history for exporting slaves. Similarly, to the west of the Volta, the palm oil trade fitted into the existing broking system based on the slaving forts of the Gold Coast, where during the first half of the nineteenth century Fante producers brought their oil to sell to the Europeans.[22] The main feature of this area was the development of an increasingly large number of independent African oil brokers from the community around the forts.[23]

Dahomey was a case where both production and the broking of oil lay within one state. King Gezo (1818–58) was not directly involved in oil trading, but relied on taxing the new trade as it developed.[24] Rather, a number of traders – the *mercaders*, some Brazilian, some local – developed as major oil brokers in Whydah from around 1840, selling to European traders like Hutton and Régis and combining this oil trade with the continuing slave trade from the area.[25] The dominant figure in this until his death in 1849 was Francisco Felix de Souza, a Brazilian trader and the *Chacha* (chief) of Whydah. By the late 1840s Domingo Martinez, another Brazilian merchant, had emerged as one of the largest oil brokers of this area, while still continuing a clandestine slave trade.[26] Elsewhere on the Slave Coast brokers in Porto Novo and Badagry relied on suppliers among the Yoruba of the interior to bring oil through a series of markets to the coast.[27]

Palm oil was less important as an export commodity on the so-called South Coast between Gabon and Angola; only around Loango and the mouth of the River Congo did exports of palm oil reach any significant level.[28] Here, as elsewhere in West Africa, a number of broking states had developed during the slave trade era which were able to continue their role into the era of legitimate commerce. Indeed, the continuing slave trade from this region meant there was a considerable demand for oil in the provisioning trade until late in the century. Landana, Pointe Noire, and Banana were to become the main palm oil broking centres by the middle of the century.[29] Europeans did not push inland in this area, though factories became common as they established themselves on shore from early in the century.[30] Central to the broking systems in the major states along this coast was the office of *Mafouk*, which had emerged during the slave trade as the royal official responsible for regulating trade with the Europeans; he appointed the brokers (*markedores*) who received the caravans bringing produce from the interior. This system moved seamlessly into the produce trade of these years.[31]

Around Sierra Leone a long-established trading network existed whereby Temne, Limba, and Mende traders brought produce to the coast. This system operated around 'landlord/stranger' relationships whereby brokers on the coast would provide hospitality for traders arriving from the interior.[32] By the middle of the century, however, the broking system had begun to change as Krio traders from Freetown became more settled in markets in the interior, replacing indigenous brokers in the produce, and not least oil, trade of this area.[33] From these markets they purchased oil and other commodities from producers, and shipped it in canoes to the coast or to Freetown. By the middle of the century they were well established in Sherbro and up the Bagru, Bum, and Kittam Rivers, in each case pushing up the rivers to the heads of navigation, and were buying palm products from the Galinhas to the south. Although this Krio diaspora marked a change in the trading system of this area, these Krio fitted into pre-existing trade networks, such as that focused on Magbele on the Rokel River, where interior suppliers brought their produce to the river markets to sell to coastal traders.[34]

In these areas, the broking networks that moved such vast quantities of oil in the early nineteenth century were all based on slave trading foundations. So too were the techniques used by brokers to maintain their position in the oil trade. At the simplest level, coastal brokers had to ensure that interior suppliers and European traders were kept apart: this was the key to their position as oil brokers, as it had been in slave trading times. The few attempts by European traders and others to penetrate the interior in this period were firmly and successfully controlled. When Beecroft attempted to ascend the Cross River in 1841 he faced persistent Efik objections.[35] A missionary noted in 1872 that the Efik prevented any other traders having contact with the European ships 'under pain of death' and resolutely opposed mission attempts to penetrate the interior.[36] Various attempts by British traders to open trade up the River Niger in this period similarly met with resistance, often violent, while Jackson reported 'King Pepple' stopping trade in Bonny in retaliation for Capt. Vidal's attempt to survey up the Rio Real in 1826.[37]

There was much more to the brokers' position than simply keeping producer and buyer apart. Their skill lay in their ability to handle two sets of relationships simultaneously: that with interior suppliers and that with the Europeans. This they managed to do very successfully in these years, as they had done in the slave trading era. It was their control of transport, labour, and credit that was at the heart of this. Transport in particular was vital, if such large quantities of oil were to be moved efficiently to the coast. 'The problem of transport', notes Jones, 'was the determining factor in the expansion of the palm oil trade.'[38] Unlike slaves, palm oil could not transport itself. Its high weight-to-value ratio in a region without pack animals, together with the limited belt within which the oil palm could ideally flourish, meant that palm oil tended to come from an area within relatively easy reach of the coast.[39] The most successful brokers for the palm oil trade were thus those able to rely on water transportation; the major oil broking states in West Africa were all located on or beside waterways. Such was the case with Old Calabar and the various Niger Delta states, as well as Lagos and the Cameroons, not to mention the River Volta; in Sierra Leone river transport became central to 'legitimate' trade generally and palm products trading in particular.[40]

This was nothing new for the West African trade, for even slaves, where possible, were transported by canoe.[41] 'The palm oil trade made use of an existing transport system', writes Latham of the Cross River; 'it did not create a new one.'[42] The canoes used by oil brokers for transportation were immense, with the largest carrying up to eight or nine tons or 2,400 gallons in twelve casks/puncheons of oil at a time; indeed, de Cardi describes canoes in Nembe carrying fifteen puncheons.[43] Moreover, the numbers of canoes required were considerable. Massive fleets of canoes, each requiring up to forty paddlers or 'pullerboys', would set out from Bonny up the creeks of the interior to visit the oil markets.[44] King Eyo of Old Calabar was said to have 400 canoes in his fleet in 1847, the king of Aboh 300 in 1841.[45] As Latham notes, these canoes represented huge capital expenditure for the brokers involved; not least of the consequences was that the oil trade generated a large canoe manufacturing industry in the region.[46]

Where water transport was not available, headloading provided the means of conveying oil to the coast.[47] The typical headload for a porter was said to be around forty or fifty lb or about five gallons of oil, though loads of sixty lb were not uncommon.[48] Given this, the numbers of porters involved must have been considerable. Caravans of porters would carry oil through Yorubaland to Lagos, for example.[49] The Aro continued to transport oil by headloading in this period.[50] Headloading was common on the Gold Coast where navigable rivers were lacking; cask rolling developed here and in Dahomey as a means to transport oil to the coast.[51]

Headloading was expensive, however, and time-consuming. Van der Laan estimates that it was twenty times as expensive as water transport in the Sierra Leone area.[52] The amount of labour it required drew resources away from production and imposed limits on the quantity and quality of exports.[53] Thus, although most of the oil broking networks did rely on headloading for at least part of the way to the coast, water transport would be used wherever possible. Typical was Krobo oil which was headloaded some distance to the markets on the Volta before being canoed downriver. Similarly, in Sierra Leone, oil would be carried to riverside markets or 'factories' to be sold to Krio brokers; the producers then travelled overland to Freetown to spend their earnings while the oil was transported by canoe there or to other coastal entrepôts like Sulima or Sherbro.[54] Producers would assess opportunity costs to decide which method of transport to use: some Krobo suppliers would headload to the Volta to sell their oil into the river broking network, for instance, while others would go directly overland to the coast.[55]

Whichever method of transport was used required labour. Slave labour underpinned the palm oil broking networks of West Africa, just as it did the producing structures. The numbers of porters required to carry oil in Yorubaland or the Gold Coast or of pullerboys to paddle the massive canoe fleets of the Niger Delta area required huge inputs of slave labour.[56] While the export slave trade continued, slaves would be used to carry oil to the coast before being sold themselves.[57] Bindloss at the end of the century estimated that two-thirds of the oil exported from the River Niger was transported to European traders by slave labour; this figure is probably an underestimate and certainly earlier in the century would have been higher.[58]

Slave labour was central to success in broking oil. While the trading of oil may well have been open to anyone able to purchase even the smallest quantity, it was those who owned slaves who benefited most from it. Given the vast distances such broking networks covered, slaves were necessary for brokers who wished to expand their operations beyond the immediate hinterland of a port. A wealthy chief in nineteenth-century Elem Kalabari could have up to 500 slaves working as pullerboys transporting oil by canoe.[59] Among the Itsekiri, ownership of slaves was necessary if a trader was to have any chance of succeeding in the oil trade. Olomu owned, according to various estimates, between 1,000 and 4,000 slaves.[60] Large numbers of slaves conveyed status and could also be used to produce food to enable brokers to concentrate on trading; such agricultural slaves were settled on farms outside Old Calabar, Bonny, and the Duala towns.[61]

Slaves were also involved in the trading of oil on behalf of their owners. Slaves were sent inland with trade goods to buy oil; others would be based in interior markets to collect oil over a period. Such so-called trade slaves were very different in status from those used in agricultural production or in transportation. Many held highly responsible posts in the broking networks of the Niger Delta area, and rose to important positions of power. The best known of these was Jaja, of Igbo slave origin, who rose to head Anna Pepple House in Bonny and eventually established his own state, Opobo. Only slightly less distinguished were other brokers of slave descent such as Oko Jumbo in Bonny, George Amachree of Elem Kalabari, Charlie Deido (Eyum Ebele) in the Cameroons, and Black Davis in Old Calabar.[62]

Success in the broking system also required credit. This brokers obtained, as they had in the slave trade, from European traders on the coast. Goods would be advanced to brokers by European traders; brokers would then use these goods to purchase oil in the interior markets before returning to redeem their credit with the oil they had obtained. Such 'trust', as it was termed, was a central mechanism throughout the West African trade in the nineteenth century and without it the trade could never have grown to the levels it did.[63]

Trust was long established in the West African trade.[64] It was certainly present in the Old Calabar slave trade at least from the eighteenth century, but its origins lie much earlier.[65] By the nineteenth century the advancing of credit by European traders was widespread throughout West Africa, being found as far apart as Senegal and the Congo. Bold, describing it as 'a great evil', noted that it was essential in order to trade in Old Calabar while Adams commented that the brokers of Bonny obtained 'very extensive credits' from European traders.[66] It was clearly widespread throughout the Delta by the middle of the nineteenth century and underpinned the oil trade in Lagos and Dahomey and on the Gold Coast.[67]

Large sums of credit could be involved in trust. Crow reported that he gave out trust of between £600 and £800 a time in Bonny; Andrew Swanzy observed that the king of Dahomey owed him between £200 and £400 in the early 1870s.[68] Old Calabar was an area where trust appears to have become particularly inflated: over £200,000 was owed in trust in 1851 and reportedly over £400,000 by 1857.[69] Yet, without this, the system could hardly operate. At the heart of the oil broking system was access to trust. Obtaining trust from European traders was essential if a broker was to succeed. Trade goods and specie were necessary to buy oil from the inland markets; without such goods a broker could not hope to trade in the interior. Gaining access to such goods from the European traders on the coast was therefore the key to success or failure in the broking system. The broking elites of West Africa were thus keen to restrict access to trust as far as possible. In Bonny, for example, *Amanyanabo* William Dappa Pepple attempted to concentrate trust in his own hands, allowing other brokers to receive it only on his recommendation.[70] Similarly, in Old Calabar, Duke Ephraim's success lay in his ability to control who received trust from the Europeans and who did not.[71]

Trust was given in the form of 'trade goods'. The type of trade goods demanded varied from area to area. West African brokers and producers were extremely particular in this. Bold noted how precise was the choice of goods that West African brokers would accept for their palm oil: what would sell in one river would not necessarily be acceptable in another.[72] Equally, the idea that consumers necessarily preferred European and American imports to local production was by no means always true at least early in the century, as Laird noted in 1843. 'The natives of the interior would not look at our cottons, preferring their own stronger goods.'[73] The fall in the real price of imported manufactures, however, did allow such goods to make increasing inroads into the local market over the century; over time the make-up of imports into West Africa was characterised by a shift towards finished manufactures.[74]

Salt, textiles, tobacco, alcohol, and firearms were the main trade goods used in trust for palm oil. Salt held an important place in the early years of the palm oil trade. Adams, Bold, and Robertson all noted that it was vital for trading at Old Calabar and Cameroons; Crow stressed its importance in trade on the Benin River.[75] Old Calabar was the major salt importing port in West Africa in this period and the Efik were successful in creating a salt monopoly over a wide area: salt imports via Old Calabar may have reached as far north as the Benue.[76] Salt imports remained a staple of the African trade right through to the second half of the century, but increasingly came to be replaced in importance by textiles.[77] According to Inikori, textiles composed up to 50 per cent of all West African imports from Britain between 1808 and 1850.[78] Early in the oil trade, it was Indian cloth that was in demand in the ports of West Africa.[79] From the 1830s on the Gold Coast and from the 1840s in Old Calabar and then elsewhere the balance shifted towards cloth from Lancashire, though this still remained a luxury item.[80]

Tobacco and alcohol became increasingly important for buying palm oil in this period. Imports of Brazilian tobacco were significant from an early date in establishing the influence of Brazilian traders along the Slave Coast, just as imports of cheap US tobacco helped establish American oil traders on the Gold Coast.[81] Inikori calculates that alcohol rose to over 10 per cent of total West African imports by the middle of the century, with the area of modern Nigeria being the largest importer at around 1 million gallons of spirits, mainly rum, per annum in the 1840s.[82] By the later part of the century gin was preferred in Yorubaland and in ports like Nembe and Old Calabar; thereafter Schiedam Schnapps became the staple of the oil trade.[83] Firearms and gunpowder were also vital. The second-hand arms trade, particularly after 1815, flooded large numbers of cheap weapons into the West African market. Jones suggests that virtually every male in the Bight of Biafra hinterland had a firearm by the late nineteenth century and identifies a 'gun frontier', coinciding with involvement in the palm oil trade, across what is now southern Nigeria.[84]

Many of these items – salt, cloth, and gin – were used as trade currencies by oil brokers.[85] The iron bar was extensively used as a currency, particularly in the interior of Bonny, though its value depreciated sharply during the century due to cheap imports from Britain.[86] Manillas, at one time common across much of the coast, were by the second half of the century restricted to the Eastern Delta and parts of the Ivory Coast; one was worth around 3d, though unlike most currencies in the Delta area, its value appears to have appreciated over the century.[87] On the Cross River the copper rod or 'copper' – usually by the nineteenth century made of brass – was the accepted currency, though it too was subject to depreciation over the century, falling in value from 1s in 1805 to 2d–3d by the 1840s.[88]

During the nineteenth century coins from outside the region such as the US dollar, Latin American (particularly Mexican) dollars, and Spanish doubloons and dollars became established on the coast, with the best known of these being the Maria Theresa dollar of 1780.[89] Such coins were particularly utilised in the illicit slave trade with Latin America but were used by palm oil traders too: traders unable to fill their oil cargo would sell their goods to slave traders on the coast in return for such specie to carry home.[90]

Of all the currencies used in West Africa, however, the one most intimately involved with palm oil broking was the cowrie shell. Its advantage was that it could be used to express small units of value and thus could be used to buy small quantities of palm oil, or make the ubiquitous payments and dashes that were needed to keep the broking system flowing; its corresponding disadvantage was that for larger units it was immensely bulky. The increasing use of cowries in parts of West Africa in the nineteenth century, particularly after c. 1820, was closely tied to the growth of the oil trade.[91] It was particularly common on the Gold Coast, where in parts palm oil could not be bought except with cowries.[92] Cowries also became well established in the Dahomey oil trade and in Yorubaland, on the Benin River and on the Niger.[93] Only in the Eastern Delta and Cross River areas, where manillas, iron bars, and coppers were already established, were cowries not extensively used. For the rest of West Africa, problems set in with 'the great cowrie inflation' from the middle of the century, when European traders started to import cowries directly from the Indian Ocean, which led to a decline in their use.[94] A 'head' of cowries (2,000) in Lagos in 1851 bought three gallons of palm oil; by 1861–2 it bought one gallon.[95]

Brokers' control of transport, labour and trust was their chief technique in managing oil supplies from the interior, but other measures were needed to maintain these broking networks. These could vary from planting villages or farms with dependants in the interior, such as the Efik farms Walker noted up the Cross, Calabar, and Kwa Rivers in the 1870s (a practice also used around Bonny, Cabinda, and the Wouri estuary), to the appointing of resident agents to be semi-permanently based in inland markets.[96] Many peoples, such as the Duala of the Cameroons, developed marriage ties with interior suppliers, with the offspring of such unions being used to trade more effectively in the interior; as mentioned above, William Dappa Pepple's success in the oil trade was undoubtedly helped by his family ties in the Bonny hinterland.[97] The use of religious sanctions such as the swearing of oaths to cement trading ties was common too. Cookey notes that Bonny traders would swear blood covenants (*ogbugbandu*) with influential figures in the interior in order to protect trade. Jaja was said to have used a 'fetish' to prevent producers on the Kwa Ibo from contacting European traders, a technique used also by Duala brokers.[98] Above all, the generous use of 'dashes' or gifts by brokers to maintain goodwill was necessary, with this extending to hospitality and feasting as appropriate.[99]

However, disputes in the interior broking networks could degenerate into violence at great cost for brokers, as in Bonny's war with Andoni in the 1840s or the series of wars in the Eastern Delta between 1869 and 1881.[100] Such disputes had to be resolved, and this might mean the utilisation of mediators, such as the Efik's use of Beecroft on the Cross River in the dispute with 'Ecricok' (Ikot Offiong) in 1836, Beecroft's involvement in resolving the dispute between Umon and Agwa'aguna in 1842, or Bonny's use of British traders in its dispute with Andoni in the 1840s.[101] More widely, the Arochukwu oracle was consulted throughout the Biafran hinterland for the settlement of all kinds of disputes.[102]

Yet such breakdowns were not common. Rather, these broking systems were networks of mutual advantage. When they worked successfully, which was usually, they were lucrative, too. However, the profitability of the oil trade remains unclear. Law suggests that the costs of oil broking were significantly higher than that of the slave trade; the cost of transporting slaves in the Niger Delta in the 1830s was some fifty times lower than that of an equivalent value of oil conveyed by headloading. Even where water transport could be used to cut costs, says Law, the transportation of oil cost three times more in terms of subsistence costs than that of slaves of an equivalent value.[103] None the less, the profitability of broking remains difficult to unravel. Much depended on the ability of brokers to influence prices paid in the interior, coupled with their capacity to resist price cuts from European traders, issues about which data are lacking. Certainly the prices of European goods were falling in this period and the terms of trade were moving in favour of African suppliers, but in the absence of fuller data it is difficult to assess the exact profitability of brokers.

Yet it is clear that the brokers of West Africa cut impressive figures. This was deliberate, as this was the image that brokers needed to portray to European traders with trust to distribute. Jackson described himself as 'astonished' at the wealth of 'King Pepple' in 1826. Duke Ephraim was another figure of obviously immense financial standing, while someone like King Eyo of Creek Town who could put 400 canoes to water was clearly a wealthy figure by oil trade standards.[104] Whatever the exact profitability of broking, clearly the leading figures of the trade made huge sums from their skills in transporting large volumes smoothly and efficiently to the coast.

If the nexus between brokers and interior suppliers was vital to the former's position in the oil trade, so too was their relationship with the European traders on the coast. Here, too, oil trading between African broker and European trader continued to rely on the established formalities of the slave trade. The purpose of these conventions was to maintain a close relationship of mutual self-interest between broker and trader, based around, in this period at least, European conformity to African practices.

A variety of trading systems could be found along the West African coast, with the precise practices of the trade depending on whether the European trader had gained a foothold on shore. On the Gold Coast and around the Congo, where traders had established themselves onland, a 'factory trade' relying on permanent shore bases had developed. Where Europeans had not succeeded in moving on land, as in the Niger Delta, the trade remained an essentially shipboard process, or 'floating trade' as it was termed. A third and older practice of a 'coasting trade', where canoes traded between a coastal entrepôt and a passing ship, continued in areas such as much of the Windward or Slave Coasts where there were few safe anchorages inshore.

It was the 'floating trade' of the Niger Delta area that was at the heart of the oil trade. The rivers of this area, once the bar at their mouth had been crossed, offered safe anchorages where the European traders' ships could wait out the palm oil season. In these rivers, trade took place on board ship and coastal brokers were keen to maintain this trading frontier between themselves and the Europeans. The only exception to this came as traders established cask houses on shore to store the casks in which palm oil was transported.[105] Analogous to the barracoons used in the slave trade, these cask houses, for which traders paid a rent, were prevalent from an early date in the oil trade and certainly existed in Old Calabar from the start of the century.[106]

The start of trade between European trader and African oil broker in the Delta rivers was surrounded with much formality. Adams refers to the need to fire a gun salute as a mark of respect on arrival in the Bonny River – as also in Old Calabar – while Jackson describes the ceremony of 'breaking trade' in 1826, which required the *Amanyanabo* to break eggs against the hull of the ship, followed by a ceremonial meal on board before trade could begin.[107] Ceremonial was stressed not only because brokers insisted on a recognition of their sovereignty – though they certainly did – but also because it reflected deeper issues about who was allowed to trade with the Europeans. These ceremonies allowed the king to introduce the major brokers to the European traders and thereby determine who would receive trust. No one could trade in Bonny, noted Jackson, until 'King Pepple' said so.[108]

This ceremonial also reflected the capacity of brokers to control the way the oil trade operated. This could be seen in the insistence on the use of pilots, with both Old Calabar and Bonny demanding payment for the use of a pilot to enter the river, whether one was used or not.[109] A similar practice was comey, or port dues – long established from the slave trade – which the broking states required all European traders to pay before they could trade. In the middle of the nineteenth century this was calculated in a variety of ways, from two puncheons of oil per ship's mast in Nembe to 20 coppers per registered ton in Old Calabar.[110] Adams calculated that a ship would have to pay around £150 comey in Bonny early in the century and £250 in Old Calabar, while de Cardi at the end of the century estimated the average cost of comey as 2s 6d per ton of oil.[111]

There were other charges that brokers insisted on. Most important was the 'shakehands' paid to the king and major chiefs by a trader on arrival.[112] Dashes were mandatory; regular and liberal dashing and entertaining was necessary to maintain goodwill, particularly on completion of a deal.[113] Cowan early in the twentieth century estimated that dashes could cost 1s per puncheon for the 'boy' involved in bringing oil to the ship and 4s for the broker. De Cardi similarly refers to the 'boys' dash' of a piece of cloth and a cap and the 'gentleman's dash' of two pieces of cloth expected in Bonny.[114] In addition there were various extra charges such as the 'custom bar' or 'bar comey' of one bar for every puncheon of oil and the 'work bar' of one bar for every twenty puncheons to be paid to the broker, though these were eventually abolished and replaced by 'topping' or 'topside', a charge of 20–30 per cent on top of the price of the oil.[115]

In the Delta area, the trading itself relied on barter and the use of trust. As in the slave trade era, to facilitate this a 'unit of account' was used to calculate values: a quantity of goods would be advanced to a broker and the palm oil owed in return calculated in terms of the unit. During the seventeenth and eighteenth centuries the 'ounce' had developed on the Gold Coast and the western Slave Coast as the unit of account in the slave trade, and this continued into the nineteenth century; in the Niger Delta area other units came to be used for palm oil, such as the bar in Bonny and the copper in Old Calabar.[116]

The continuation of these slave trade practices reflected the fact that African brokers remained the determinants of the trading relationship with Europeans in this period. They decided the oil trade's methods and where the frontier between broker and trader lay; European traders conformed to the patterns established by brokers over trust, barter, charges and even anchorages, though it would be wrong to see this as being at the expense of European interests.[117] The oil trade in the Delta involved a close relationship of mutuality between brokers and traders that was recognised as benefiting both. At its heart was the relationship between the individual African broker and individual European trader, best summed up by the very name 'trust'. At its heart was indeed trust: trust that the broker would return his trade goods in oil and trust that the trader would continue to support that broker. Reputation was important in this: Duke Ephraim was said never to have reneged on a deal; King Eyo Honesty's name reflected the image he wished to portray.[118] Thus the closeness that developed between Duke Ephraim and John Tobin in the 1810s and 1820s was typical of the relationship aimed for in the oil trade. Like Tobin, European traders would attempt to find a particularly enterprising broker who could ensure regular supplies of oil and would then build 'a trading alliance' with him to mutual benefit.

Various mechanisms developed to cement these ties. One such was the very language used in the trade, namely 'pidgin', a modified form of English, though many brokers in fact spoke English to a high standard, as Adams pointed out.[119] It was not uncommon for brokers to send a son to Britain in the care of a trader to be educated.[120] Also significant were the various 'marriages' that European traders developed with local women. These were common throughout the Delta area.[121] Or there was the use of pawns – sometimes one of the broker's wives or sons – given by a broker to a trader to guarantee the repayment of trust. This practice was utilised by Bristol traders along the Ivory Coast even late in the century and was common too on the South Coast.[122] Also common was the traders' practice of buying local chieftaincy titles in order to maintain ties and ensure the repayment of debts; a considerable number of British traders in Old Calabar bought such titles in order to use Ekpe sanctions to get debts repaid.[123]

None of these practices was new to this period, and all were ways whereby traders and brokers could ensure that debts were honoured and relationships sustained. Comey was central to this relationship because it came to be seen by European traders as implying a right to 'protection'. Above all – and this lay at the heart of the web of mutuality that benefited both trader and broker – it ensured that no one would be allowed to trade who had not paid comey, thereby keeping European interlopers out of the river trade.[124]

The Delta area states like Old Calabar and Bonny were the most sophisticated brokers of the oil trade. Elsewhere in West Africa the basic methods used in the trade differed little from those elaborated in the Niger Delta area. On much of the Windward Coast and the western Slave Coast, for example, not to mention the many hundreds of small-scale entrepôts along the Ivory Coast, brokers emerged who provided oil for coasting ships which called in for only brief stops for produce. In these areas there were few natural harbours with the result that ships remained at sea beyond the surf and the long stop-overs common in the Niger Delta area did not develop. Trade took place over a shorter period of time and was less formalised, but in other ways mirrored the mechanisms that had developed in the Niger Delta area.

Bold noted that European traders 'coasting' along the Windward and Ivory Coasts would fire their cannon and raise colours when they approached an entrepôt as a sign that they were looking for trade.[125] Local brokers would canoe out across the surf and bargaining would begin. In some instances direct barter would be used, with palm oil being exchanged directly for the trade goods the traders brought. In others trust was used, though on a much more limited scale than in the Niger Delta: small quantities of trust would be distributed, with the oil being collected on the ship's return along the coast. As in the Delta, trade would be calculated by use of a unit of account such as the iron bar or, in places, the 'round'.[126] As elsewhere, a liberal use of dashes would be used to maintain contacts and keep trade flowing.

The 'factory trade' that characterised those areas in which Europeans had become established on land during the slave trading era shared many of the features of the floating trade. On the Gold Coast European traders had long set up on shore. Elsewhere the late eighteenth and early nineteenth centuries saw European 'legitimate' traders set up factories in Freetown, around the Congo, and, from 1838, at Whydah. Around these factories emerged groups of Eurafrican trading intermediaries such as the Krio of Sierra Leone, Brazilian traders like Domingo Martinez, or the local traders of the Gold Coast.[127] Trade was based on the use of trust, often advanced from commission houses in London or from Brazil.[128] In turn such credit would be advanced to local brokers who bought oil from the interior markets. As elsewhere in the oil trade, barter, and the use of a unit of account – the 'ounce' or the 'slave' on the Gold Coast, 'longs', 'pieces', and 'bundles' around the Congo – remained the basis of commerce.[129]

Although European traders established themselves on land in these areas, as in the Delta they continued to adhere to African customs and practices. Although the term 'comey' was not always used, taxes were imposed by local rulers – Gezo claimed one gallon for every eighteen exported from Whydah – and rent was paid for the factories on the South Coast.[130] On parts of the South Coast trade remained in the hands of the *Mafouk*, a powerful figure who decided when trade would be opened and who would be allowed to trade.[131]

Whichever method of trading operated, the broking structures of West Africa were immensely flexible and adaptable, given the massive increase in exports of oil handled between the 1800s and the 1850s. This is not to say that there were no problems in the trade. The trade in this period as much as any was marked by disputes and 'palavers' between African broker and European trader. These disputes had a number of causes, from clashes over prices to allegations of pilfering from cask houses. More often they were over adulteration of oil or short measure of European goods.[132]

The main source of palavers in the early nineteenth-century trade, however, lay in trust. Non-repayment of trust by brokers could have a number of causes. Sometimes it might be due to a broker being unable to obtain oil from inland producers, possibly because of a stoppage of trade in the interior; such problems affected output from Old Calabar in 1850, for example.[133] Alternatively it might be due to European traders forwarding trust to a broker who was patently unfit to trade or, more generally, granting more trade to a port than it could ever possibly expect to return in a season.[134]

Once such a situation arose, there were various responses open to a broker. The most common was to choose whose trust to repay, repaying some traders but not others. For those who went unpaid such a situation caused great difficulties. As the oil season ended, he had the unpalatable choice between returning to Britain with an empty hold and attempting to reclaim his trust the following year, or remaining on the coast over the out-season with all the dangers of disease and loss thereby encountered.[135] Alternatively a trader might 'chop oil', that is, seize by violence the amount of oil that was owed irrespective of whether the person it was seized from was the original debtor or not.[136] For the broking state the response was to stop trade altogether and boycott the European traders. Such disputes could result in violence, as in the events which led to the death of Capt. Kirtley in Bonny in 1847.[137]

Such disputes had to be settled. In this period the process involved consensus and discussion to establish an agreement that satisfied all parties. The local ruler was recognised as being responsible for ensuring the resolution of such disputes, and it was in his interest to find a settlement acceptable to all if trade was to be kept flowing. Recognising this mutual self-interest, the long-established European traders were prepared, in this as in other aspects of the trade, to accept the authority of local rulers in finding such consensus, at least in this period.[138] Thus, serious disputes were the exception, at least until the middle of the century. In general trade flowed freely and the mechanisms that had evolved to settle palavers were effective in keeping it operating. The success of the system can be seen in the fact that few wished to change its methods in this period, and that relatively few European traders – and certainly few of those in the heart of the trade in the Delta rivers – were interested in pushing inland to interior markets in these years. The coastal brokers were recognised as the essential basis of the oil trade.

What was the impact on brokers of the great increase in oil exports in the years before 1850? What, in particular, was the effect on the broking societies at the heart of the oil trade, namely in the Niger Delta and surrounding areas? As far as the relationship between broking states was concerned, the oil trade might be said to have accompanied many changes. A number of broking states rose to considerable prosperity and prominence on the basis of the palm oil trade. As has been seen, first Old Calabar, then Bonny emerged as the major palm oil broking state of this region in the first half of the nineteenth century. Equally, this period saw a struggle for control of oil markets in the interior between the various oil exporting states of the area which often degenerated into violence. During the 1840s Bonny, for example, exerted its power over the Andoni, blocking their access to the Europeans and asserting its influence over Andoni trade.[139] Old Calabar attempted to increase its power up the Cross River by asserting its hold on intermediate traders inland. Equally, the Itsekiri were prepared as necessary to use force to maintain their trading interests over the Urhobo, while Nembe was prepared to fight Elem Kalabari for markets on the Engenni and Orashi Rivers in the 1860s and 1870s.[140]

Yet this was hardly novel. Indeed, what is striking about the Delta area is how little it changed in terms of state structures and market patterns in the early nineteenth century. The major oil broking states of the Niger Delta area were long established and the struggle for interior markets was far from a new development. Even the Duala towns of the Cameroons, perhaps the 'newest' brokers to emerge to prominence in the early part of the century, had already been developing in this way before the oil trade began to expand.[141] The only example of a state that might be said to have owed its existence to palm oil was Opobo in 1869, but even its emergence can not be attributed to the oil trade alone.

If the development of the oil trade cannot be said to have fundamentally altered relationships between states in the Delta area, what was its impact within these societies? A number of observers at the time suggested that the trade in palm oil – because it could be exchanged in small quantities – encouraged small-scale traders and that the transition to oil trading therefore paved the way for new elements within the politics of the broking states. As Hutton reported at the time, 'all classes' could pursue the oil trade because it could be traded in quantities as small as a pot.[142] This idea was taken up in the twentieth century by Dike, but can be seen in the work of several historians of the area. For these historians the transition to the oil trade saw the emergence of 'new men' whose power underlay the endemic instability of the Delta states in this period: more specifically Dike identified what he saw as 'slave risings' in the nineteenth century as being the result of the transition to oil exporting.[143]

Certainly the nineteenth century was a period of instability within the states of the Delta region: Bonny saw the overthrow of William Dappa Pepple in 1854 before splitting in two in 1869; the Itsekiri were without a ruler for many years after the death of Olu Akengbuwa in 1848; Elem Kalabari saw Will Braid's challenge to *Amanyanabo* Princewill Amachree during the 1870s before it split into three in the 1880s; the Duala towns experienced increasing disorder and a 'slave rising' in the 1850s; and Old

Calabar was affected by intense rivalry for the offices of *Eyamba* and *Obong*, as well as, in Dike's view, a 'slave rising' in 1851. Did the transition to the oil trade cause such tensions in the broking states of the Delta? Can one identify here a 'crisis of adaptation' derived from the transition to oil trading that mirrors the one postulated for the producers of West Africa?

At the heart of such views has been the idea of the rise of slaves within the Delta area states. Certainly slaves and figures of slave descent such as Jaja, Charlie Deido, and others achieved important positions in broking states in this period. Equally, the Delta area states were clearly experiencing intense political struggles during the early decades of the century. Yet it would be wrong to see this phenomenon as simply the result of the growth of the oil trade. As Alagoa has shown, the problems of Delta states in this period had intensely complex causes that were deeply rooted into the structures of these societies; these were not the result of the rising power of slaves or new social strata.[144] Latham similarly stresses that Dike's so-called Bloodmen slave rising of 1851 in Old Calabar needs to be seen in the context of the long-term factional struggles within the Efik state.[145] The tensions in Bonny owed more to long-established cleavages between houses within the Bonny state than the 'rise' of slaves to positions of power, while the 1850s problems in the Cameroons were relatively easily contained.[146]

The degree to which the oil trade generated new opportunities for women is difficult to assess, and research is needed to modify the generalisations impressionistically suggested here. Certainly women can be found trading in oil in many of the broking networks of the Delta area as well as up the Niger in these years. Laird and Oldfield encountered a woman trader on the Niger who owned 200 slaves and several canoes 'which she employed trading on the River', and, though the evidence is limited, the likelihood is that this was more widespread than might be assumed.[147] Certainly by the early colonial period in the Delta women brokers were common.[148] Yet the significance of this is difficult to determine, given that it remains unclear how far these women traded on their own account. Indeed, the major role played by women in the oil trade of the Delta states at least in the early part of the century may have remained their long vital function in maintaining trade networks as marriage partners with interior suppliers and with European traders. Indeed, there is no evidence from the Delta area of women selling oil in bulk to European traders, at least in the early part of the century.[149] Wealthy women traders were common in late nineteenth-century Lagos, but there appear to be no examples in the Delta comparable with Madame Tinubu's career, at least until further research considers this question; the reason for this difference remains unclear.[150]

Rather, women's role in the Delta oil trade in the early nineteenth century may have been restricted to the trade in foodstuffs and in small quantities of palm oil, primarily for provisioning. This was long established, of course, though as the century progressed the increasing presence of European traders and their crews for long periods in the Delta rivers presumably provided opportunities for women to expand this trade. Equally, the involvement of large numbers of brokers and slaves in the interior oil trade – though similar patterns existed in the slave trade era – may have created increased demand for provisioning. At least before 1850, continuity rather than change appears to have been the chief characteristic of gender roles within the trade.

This was the case more broadly for the political structures of the Delta area states. Jones and others have suggested that the expansion of the oil trade led to the growth of the canoe houses of the Delta states into larger canoe house groups which in turn generated further tensions.[151] The ensuing rivalry split states like Bonny in half. In Old Calabar the rivalry between wards for control of the trade led to intense political struggle, while in the Cameroons this period saw the various Duala towns pitted against each other in competition for supremacy in the oil trade. In this sense, the argument here is that the transition to oil trade exacerbated existing political divisions. Central to this in many parts of the Delta area was the issue of comey and who received it. Increasingly comey came to be concentrated into one person's hands, with tensions thus developing over the status and standing of figures like the *Amanyanabo*. In Old Calabar, Duke Ephraim succeeded in concentrating comey in his hands; in Bonny, William Dappa Pepple attempted to do the same, while simultaneously retaining the subsidies paid by the British for the ending of slave trading.[152]

This is certainly the pattern in many states of the Delta area. But this does not imply that the oil trade created these tensions or that they were new to the nineteenth century. Political instability was certainly a feature of the nineteenth-century history of these states, but historians have been wary of seeing these crises as being derived primarily from the development of the oil trade or representing the emergence of individualistic new traders. Rather these tensions arose from pre-existing factional divisions. Indeed, what is remarkable is how far the established elites of these states were able to maintain their positions during the transition to the oil trade, a process seen most notably in the case of Old Calabar.[153] This is not to argue that the transition did not cause difficulties for these polities, but it is hard to see it causing a political 'crisis' that undermined the ruling elites of the broking states. On the contrary, these elites were in practice well able to maintain their power in the new era of 'legitimate' trade.

The reason for this lay in the capacity of these oligarchies to control entry into the palm oil trade. They did this in two ways. Firstly, they were able to use political weapons to shore up their position in the export trade.

Latham's work on Old Calabar shows how successful the ruling oligarchy of Old Calabar was in employing institutions like the Ekpe society to do this. Far from being overwhelmed by new, small-scale brokers, the existing brokers of Old Calabar were able to use Ekpe regulations to stop the sale of oil in small quantities in 1862 and again against the sale of kernels in 1869; similar regulations were utilised by chiefs in Brass in 1867, while Hargreaves has shown that the transition in Bonny was accompanied by house heads reinforcing their control over the market through the use of intra-house sanctions.[154]

Moreover, brokers' long-established ties with European traders meant that the community of interest between the two groups made the latter eager to maintain the one advantage they had against their own competitors, namely their relationship with the existing brokers of the Delta states.[155] This was reinforced by British consuls who, fearing instability and disruption in the trade, were keen in the various treaties they signed with Delta rulers to reinforce the power of traditional political authorities over access to the trade and particularly access to trust.

Secondly, there were economic reasons for this continued dominance by the large-scale coastal brokers. The capital required to enter the oil trade was too great for small-scale traders effectively to challenge the existing oligarchy of brokers. Economies of scale, especially concerning transport from the interior, were to give large-scale brokers a considerable advantage vis-à-vis smaller-scale ones; the advantage would continue to lie with those brokers who could utilise large canoes and large numbers of slaves to transport their oil.[156] Transport remained the major barrier to entry on the African side of the trade. Moreover, the key issue in the oil trade was access to trust. Those who received trust from the Europeans were able to exploit economies of scale and it remained in the interest of European traders to ensure that trust went to large-scale brokers whose credit was well established.

The result was that it was the existing elites of the area – once again 'big men' rather than 'new men' – who dominated the oil trade in the early nineteenth century. This was precisely because the oil trade did not represent a break with the slave trade. Indeed, it was because the oil trade's structures and practices were a continuation of the old that it grew so rapidly in the early nineteenth century. The institution of trust was at the centre of this, for it generated a network of common interest between European trader and African broker which facilitated, initially at least, a continuance of the status quo. This web of mutuality, based on the acceptance of long-established African practices in the operation of the trade, was of benefit to both, not least because it kept interlopers out. Tensions and disputes most certainly occurred, but while the broking mechanisms worked so efficiently neither side had any interest in changing them.

In this, European trader recognised the skill and thus paramountcy of African broker. The broking system that handled the palm oil trade in its early years was extremely efficient. It was a long-established system that had evolved over the years of the slave trade, and had emerged to fit the needs of both broker and trader and the determinants of West African geography. It was accepted by both sides and kept both broker and trader in roles of mutual convenience. European traders did not, by and large, attempt to push inland to make contact with the major interior oil suppliers in this period. They did not wish to do so and, when they did try, they were successfully resisted. A boundary, acceptable to both, was drawn firmly along the coast. This *modus vivendi* remained largely unchallenged to the middle of the century.

4   British traders, British ports, and the expansion of the palm oil trade

The final link in the passage of palm oil from the oil palm to the processor in Europe was provided by the trader. In the early nineteenth century these were largely British traders, though a number of French and German firms played a significant role in the trade by the middle of the century. The importance of this early generation of traders cannot be exaggerated. Their role in opening a market for palm oil in Britain was crucial for the development of the trade, and yet has largely been ignored in previous studies.[1]

For Britain's African traders, the abolition of the British slave trade in 1807 posed a potential threat. One major British slaving firm, Aspinalls, expressed concern on 'not knowing how to employ either our time or capital to advantage' in the face of abolition.[2] More generally it was feared that abolition would leave Liverpool, the leading port of Britain's African trade, devastated. Prophets of doom 'sprung [sic] up in every street . . . and the whole [Liverpool] community was terror stricken', wrote Gomer Williams of the prospect of abolition.[3]

In practice, however, abolition had only a limited impact and any crisis in Liverpool's African trade was short-lived. Drake suggests that 'continuity and flexibility' rather than a sharp break marked the experience of abolition for most Liverpool African traders. He sees Liverpool's trade with Africa as characterised by a process of evolution over these years, rather than as two distinct trades, one replacing the other after 1807. 'There was', he states, 'an essential continuity in the African export trade [with Liverpool] of the periods before and after Abolition.'[4]

Drake's argument for continuity in Liverpool's trade carries conviction for Britain's commerce with Africa more broadly. Indeed, the degree of continuity over the period of abolition is striking. This applies whether we look at the traders involved, the ports they came from, or the techniques of trading they used. There were two reasons for this. Firstly, abolition had been on the horizon for so long that Liverpool traders were able to re-deploy their shipping well in advance. Slave traders did not renew their fleets as ships aged, or diversified them into other trades, particularly the direct West Indies trade. Moreover, Drake suggests that the fact that slave trading, while clearly important, was not of crucial significance for the fortunes of the port as a whole by the end of the eighteenth century made this transition easier than it might have been: in 1791, for example, only 3 per cent of Liverpool shipping was involved in the African trade.[5]

Secondly, Liverpool's 'legitimate' African commerce, far from being suddenly born with abolition, was an integral part of the slave trade before 1807. 'In the last years of the slave trade few slave ships returned to Liverpool without some African cargo on board', notes Drake. As much as 20–30 per cent of net profits on a slave voyage in the last years of the slave trade came from produce imports. This was not least because the Dolben Act of 1788 had restricted the numbers of slaves that could be carried on board ship, pushing slavers towards produce trading. 'Slaving and legitimate trading on the West African coast', argues Drake, 'were inextricably inter-related' and had long been so. Thus, abolition did not lead to the crisis in Liverpool that the prophets of doom anticipated. 'By 1809', writes Drake, 'the port had shaken off the effects of abolition – such as they were.'[6]

Thus Liverpool African traders found it relatively easy to develop a 'legitimate' trade – first in timber, then in palm oil – after 1807. It was ex-slavers who were responsible for this, not newcomers to the trade or to the African coast. These ex-slave traders had long been buying palm oil both for provisions during the Atlantic crossing and for the British market. Indeed, most of the prominent Liverpool 'legitimate' traders in the early nineteenth century owed their origins to the slave trade.[7]

James Penny, one of the leaders of Liverpool's opposition to abolition, was an early pioneer in oil imports from Old Calabar, importing 750 casks of oil into Liverpool in 1813, for instance.[8] Jonas Bold was another ex-slaver to develop oil trading from Old Calabar.[9] His firm, run at this time by Isaac Oldham Bold, was the largest African firm in Liverpool in 1820 and still one of the top five palm oil businesses in 1840.[10] George Case, another ex-slaver involved in the Old Calabar oil trade, and the Aspinall family, major slave traders of Liverpool in the 1790s, were other prominent oil pioneers of these years.[11]

The best known of the ex-slavers who developed the oil trade in these early years was John Tobin. He was originally a Liverpool slave ship captain, working for George Case and others in the Angola trade, who soon established a successful slaving firm of his own, John Tobin & Co. He was to pioneer the Old Calabar oil trade after 1807, and by the 1830s was probably the biggest importer of palm oil in Britain.[12] His brother Thomas Tobin similarly began his career as a master in the slave trade in the 1790s sailing between Bonny and Jamaica for Aspinalls before turning to palm oil, particularly from Bonny, after 1807.[13] He was one of the largest palm oil traders in Britain over a long period; even as late as 1852 he was the fifth largest importer of palm oil into Liverpool.[14]

Charles Horsfall was another early Liverpool palm oil trader who owed his business origins to the slave trade. His fortune was made in commerce with the West Indies, though he denied involvement in slaving itself.[15] From the 1810s Charles Horsfall & Sons began to specialise in the African trade in partnership with Thomas Tobin, while continuing to trade with India and the West Indies. By the middle of the century Horsfalls, run by Charles' son Thomas, were the largest palm oil importers in Britain, with in 1852 more than double the imports of any other firm.[16]

Traders from Bristol – the leading British slaving port in the early eighteenth century – also were involved in developing the oil trade in this period, with a pattern very similar to that of Liverpool. Thomas King of Bristol was a sailing master who developed a trade with West Africa in the 1790s; from the 1810s he was a major African trader, operating along the Gabon and Ivory Coasts and trading in a variety of commodities. When in 1833 he handed his firm over to his sons, Richard and William King, it was a significant importer of palm oil and was soon to be one of the largest oil firms in Britain.[17]

This continuity in traders reflects the continuity in the ports they operated from. Liverpool was the port at the centre of Britain's African trade throughout these years. With the exception of Thomas King and his sons, the pioneers of the palm oil trade in the early nineteenth century were all from Liverpool. As the leading slavers in Britain they were the traders most acutely threatened by abolition. Their central role in developing the new commerce meant that Liverpool remained at the heart of Britain's African trade after 1807. While reliable figures are difficult to come by, it is clear that Liverpool was responsible for importing around three-quarters – and possibly more – of Britain's palm oil throughout the first half of the century. Bristol and London were responsible for the rest, with London being the second port in Britain for palm oil at least to the 1820s and Bristol emerging to replace it by the 1850s.[18]

These three ports had been at the centre of Britain's slave trade in the eighteenth century; they were able to continue in the African trade after 1807 for three reasons. Firstly, traders from these ports had the experience, contacts, and knowledge of West African commerce needed to develop the oil trade.[19] Secondly, the hinterlands of these ports were major suppliers of the goods and commodities required in the African trade. Liverpool's great advantage for the oil trade was its proximity to the saltfields of Cheshire, salt being central to the early years of the oil trade.[20] Although Indian textiles were the major textiles in demand in the early years of the nineteenth century, Lancashire was soon to replace India as the major source of cloth for the African trade, with 'Manchester goods' generally becoming central to the development of the new commerce.[21] London was the nation's premier manufacturing city; it was also the centre of Britain's East Indian trade, and procured the Indian textiles in demand in West Africa in these years. Bristol was an important centre for metalware, particularly brass wire and copper, as well as gunpowder and lead shot. It was particularly important as a centre of manilla manufacture in the early nineteenth century, and had close links to the Midlands for supplies of metalware generally.[22]

Thirdly, and perhaps most importantly, the hinterlands of these ports were major centres of consumption of palm oil. London was – as it had been for centuries – a major soap producing centre.[23] A. & F. Pears was established in 1835 in London and, with John Knight (established 1817), produced soap for the high-quality end of the market. The situation was similar for candle manufacturers: Price's Patent Candle Co. (established early in the century and registered as a joint stock company as E. Price & Co. from 1847) operated from Battersea in this period.[24]

There were a number of factors which contributed to Liverpool's prominence for palm oil consumption. Merseyside was a centre of candle manufacturing and, given its industrial hinterland, ideally sited to supply lubricants for the factories and railways of Northwest England. The textile industry of Lancashire required oils for wool and soap for the cotton and calico industry. Liverpool, too, was well situated to supply the tinplate industry of Staffordshire.[25]

Most importantly, however, Liverpool was the major soap producer in Britain, replacing London by the 1820s.[26] Liverpool had grown as a soap producer during the eighteenth century, using Irish and Scottish kelp, but it was in the nineteenth century that it reached its pre-eminence. The reasons for this lay partly in the demand for soap from the industrial cities of the hinterland of Liverpool, partly in the proximity of the salt deposits of Cheshire, and partly in the port's access to palm oil supplies. While London soap producers in this period relied on expensive imported Spanish barilla for their alkali and tallow for their fat, Liverpool benefited from the introduction of the Leblanc process, which allowed its soap manufacturers to use Cheshire salt for cheap caustic soda, which combined well with palm oil to produce cheap soap.[27] Liverpool thus became the largest single centre of soap output in the early nineteenth century. Together Liverpool, Runcorn, and Warrington produced 37 per cent of Britain's total production of hard soap in 1837 and 67 per cent of soft.[28] Liverpool also was noted as the major centre for the export of soap, with the bulk of British exports coming from the port by the 1850s. As one London soap maker commented in 1835, 'Liverpool is the great market now for the export of soap . . . and almost all the soap for exportation . . . is made from palm oil exclusively.'[29]

The early and middle years of the nineteenth century were thus a period of significant growth for soap producers on Merseyside, many of which went on to become household names. Joseph Crosfield & Sons were established in Warrington in 1815, while Thomas Hazelhurst started soap making in Runcorn in 1816 and William Gossage in Widnes in 1855. These were later joined by the two best-known soap manufacturers, R. S. Hudson which moved to Liverpool in the 1870s, and William Lever's business which began on Merseyside in 1885.[30]

Bristol was the other major palm oil importing port, and again there were clear reasons for this in the development of the processing industry. Bristol was a soap manufacturing centre of great antiquity; by the early nineteenth century its major soap firms were Fry, Fripp, & Co. (est. 1771) and Thomas Thomas (est. 1824), later to merge as Thomas, Fripp, and Thomas, and later still to appear as Christopher Thomas & Bros., the largest soap firm in the West of England.[31] Bristol was well placed for the West Midlands where industrial growth provided a continuing demand for lubricants. The Great Western Railway reached Bristol in 1841, while its major engineering works were opened in Swindon in 1843. Most important for Bristol was its location adjacent to the tinplate industry of South Wales – the largest in the world until late in the century.[32]

The techniques of commerce with Africa pursued by traders from the three British oil ports varied. This was conditioned partly by history and partly by the geographical area of West Africa in which the traders of a particular port had developed a market. As in the slave trade era, London was the home of the factory-based trade of the Gold Coast, as well as being the port used by traders operating from the new entrepôt of Freetown.[33] London's African traders tended to be very small-scale in their operations: they were general produce traders who imported palm oil as part of a broad spectrum of African imports from the Gold and Windward Coasts, often remaining in the African trade only for a short period before moving on; John Nicholls, an ex-slaver who operated from the 1790s to 1828, and George Redman, who traded on the Windward Coast for around thirty years, were exceptions to this.[34] The cargoes of oil imported through London thus tended to be small, with only a few dozen casks per trader per voyage early in the period and an average for London traders of only 270 casks per voyage as late as 1855.[35]

The Gold Coast remained the main source of palm oil for London traders, though attempts were made during the 1810s, 1820s, and early 1830s to break into the burgeoning Delta oil trade by exploiting the geographical proximity of the island of Fernando Po. First G. A. Robertson, then the Gold Coast Mining and Trading Co. in 1825, then Richard Dillon, and finally the West African Company, all of London, developed ultimately abortive schemes to use the island as their trading depot for the Delta region.[36]

These London traders operating on the West African coast were usually reliant on commission houses for their credit. Commission houses were well known in Britain's overseas commerce, not least the West Indies trade, but only in the late 1810s did they begin to enter palm oil importing. Commission houses bought goods in Britain which they would forward to traders based on the West African coast at a commission; they would then sell the resulting produce on behalf of the trader, also at a commission, thus enabling small-scale merchants to operate without the costs of maintaining an establishment in Britain.[37]

The best-known commission house in the palm oil trade was Forster & Smith of London, run by Matthew Forster, MP for Berwick-on-Tweed.[38] Matthew Forster appears to have entered the African trade around the end of the French wars, and was certainly operating in the gum trade in the Senegambia from c. 1816, where William Forster, his brother, was established until 1849.[39] The origins of the Forster & Smith partnership are unclear and there is no clear evidence as to who the 'Smith' was; the firm appears under that name from 1826.[40] Forster & Smith had sixteen ships operating to West Africa in 1845, the largest fleet in the African trade. They traded in a variety of produce and became particularly well established in the Gambia and on the Gold Coast where the indomitable Brodie Cruickshank was their agent.[41]

The other major London traders of this period were W. B. Hutton & Sons, founded in the late eighteenth century by William Bernard Hutton, and which following his death in 1822 was taken over by his son, William Mackintosh Hutton.[42] They developed into major traders in African produce: by 1835 they were among the ten largest palm oil firms in Britain and were certainly the largest oil importers in London.[43] Huttons were unusual among London traders in operating extensively not only on the Gold and Slave Coasts but also attempting to enter the Bonny trade, though they had little success in this. More significant was William M. Hutton's nephew, Thomas Hutton, who based himself at Cape Coast and was the first to open a factory for oil at Whydah, in 1838.[44] Although they remained among the ten largest importers of oil in Britain, the firm was wound up in 1851 on the death of William M. Hutton.[45]

Bristol was the home of the coasting trade in this period. There were few merchants from Bristol involved in the African trade in the early years of the century. Apart from Thomas King, the only other firm until the middle of the century was Lucas Bros. These Bristol firms involved in the African trade, like those of London, tended to be general produce importers, importing palm oil among a wide variety of African products. Compared to London traders, however, they imported much larger quantities of oil; the average Bristol cargo of oil by 1855 was 505 casks per voyage.[46]

Bristol traders tended to specialise on an area of the West African coast different from those utilised by London and Liverpool traders. One such area was the Ivory Coast, which came to be called the 'Bristol Coast' for this reason; Bristol traders were also prevalent on the Slave Coast, in the Cameroons, and to the south. They could also be found trading to a limited extent on the Gold Coast.[47] With the exception of the Gold Coast, these were largely areas without established shore factories, and this determined the trading techniques these traders followed. While in the Cameroons and Gabon Bristol traders relied on the 'river trade', elsewhere along the West African coast they utilised the long-established mechanism of 'coasting', that is trading by sailing along the coast, buying small quantities of commodities or giving out small amounts of trust and then laboriously returning along the coast against the wind to redeem it.[48] Often the process would have to be undertaken twice or more before a full cargo could be obtained. This method, which went back to the very earliest days of the slave trade, had the advantage of spreading risk and was necessary for areas, such as parts of the Windward Coast, where no deep-water ports existed. It continued to be used by Bristol traders until very late in the century.[49]

Thomas King led the way in this Bristol trade. He opened up the Ivory Coast and the Gabon to British 'legitimate' trade from around 1810. These were not palm oil areas, however, and Thomas King clearly saw himself as a general produce merchant, for he traded too with areas outside Africa; it was his sons Richard and William, after they took over the firm in 1833, who were to concentrate their energies exclusively on West Africa. They moved into the Gold Coast and Slave Coast oil trade and began operating from the Cameroons. While the brothers continued to trade in a variety of produce, they increasingly focused on palm oil, and their decision to do so was instrumental in the significant growth of the firm during the 1830s.[50]

Liverpool traders followed a technique of trading different from those pursued by their London and Bristol competitors. Initially after 1807 Liverpool traders dealt in general African produce – with a particular emphasis on the timber trade of Sierra Leone – with only a few, like John Tobin, specialising in palm oil. As the palm oil trade grew in the 1820s and 1830s, however, Liverpool increasingly became the home of palm oil specialists who concentrated on what was termed 'the river trade', that is, trade with the rivers of the Niger Delta area.[51] These were the rivers that had been at the heart of the Liverpool slave trade before 1807; the success of Liverpool in the new trade was due to the dominant position the port's traders succeeded in establishing here just at the moment they were to prove to be the most valuable entrepôts of the oil trade. As this trade grew, it became more specialised. Thus Liverpool's oil trade by the 1830s was characterised by the single voyage to a single port in the Delta returning with a cargo exclusively of palm oil; by the 1850s at least half of all voyages to Africa from Liverpool fitted this pattern.[52]

Despite London traders' abortive attempts to use Fernando Po to break into the Delta oil trade, the Delta remained the Liverpool traders' preserve. These were the larger firms in the trade; the average oil cargo for a Liverpool voyage was 857 casks by 1855. Liverpool was also the home of the majority of British oil traders from 1830 through to 1850 and, while London came close to challenging this in terms of numbers, its oil firms remained small in size in comparison to those of Liverpool.[53] Liverpool firms were thus the largest importers of palm oil in Britain each year, with this position usually being held by Charles Horsfall or John Tobin in the period up to 1850.[54]

Whichever technique was followed by British firms – factory trading, coasting, or river trading – the figure responsible for its success was the master or supercargo of the ship. In the early years of the trade both the voyage and the trading on the coast were entirely in the hands of the ship's master.[55] Over time, however, traders divided responsibilities between a sailing master and a supercargo responsible for trading; if long delays were involved in Delta rivers it was often the case for the supercargo to remain on the coast with the ship while the master returned home with another of the firm's vessels. This developed in some cases into a relay system.[56] Rather than a ship waiting until 'its' oil was ready, oil was sent back as it became available on any vessel belonging to that firm, almost immediately upon the ship's arrival; a few remaining ships would then wait out the season on the coast with the supercargoes, presaging the later development of permanent trading bases in the Delta rivers.[57]

In this period, these masters gained their reputation as 'palm oil ruffians'; and they quickly resorted to violence in cases of dispute. They were, in Whitford's words later in the century, 'rude, uneducated men, who prided themselves upon coming in at the "hawse-hole and going out at the cabin windows"'.[58] Col. Edward Nicolls spoke for many when he complained of 'the total want of principle amongst the greater part' of the trading masters he came into contact with: 'there is no infamy or enormity that some of these Liverpool commanders will stop at'.[59] The epitome of the palm oil ruffian was Capt. John Lilley, who shot and killed an African in a dispute over a debt in Bimbia in 1834 and who settled as a trader in the Cameroons to the 1860s.[60]

Yet such reputations should not obscure the fact that the West African trade was a difficult one that required considerable experience and skill from its practitioners, concerning not just sailing conditions along the coast but also trading techniques and the risks involved in assessing credit. A mistake over trust could ruin a voyage and an experienced master or supercargo was thus essential for success in the trade. Moreover, the problems of disease along the coast meant that a 'seasoned' master, who had survived at least one season in the trade, was a major advantage. The death of a master while trading in West Africa not only caused serious delays for a voyage while a replacement was obtained, but could result in the loss of that master's trust. Experienced masters would therefore be retained over a long period by a particular trader: examples of such included Reuben Hemingway, who was employed by Thomas Tobin and Tobin & Horsfall during the 1820s and 1830s, and Ralph Dawson who worked for Wilson & Clegg between 1827 and 1839.[61]

Indeed, the palm oil traders as a whole relied on a relatively small group of masters who were employed over many years and who spent their entire careers in the African trade. Many worked their way up in the trade, such as Capt. Henry Dring who climbed from cabin boy to master between 1818 and 1842.[62] One consequence of this was that it enabled masters over the long term to set up as traders on their own account.[63] Such was the case of course, with John and Thomas Tobin and Thomas King, but also with Reuben Hemingway, who was trading on his own account by the late 1840s and went on to become a major Liverpool trader.[64]

The importance of the master derived from the length of the trading voyage. The voyage to West Africa and back, including the time taken to collect a cargo, could take up to a year, though much depended on where the cargo was collected. Of thirty-five ships sent to the coast by Huttons between 1836 and 1842, the average time away from Britain was just over eleven months; the longest return voyage was twenty-five months.[65] Some ships could be delayed even longer on the coast, though Drake's study of Liverpool ships carrying palm oil cargoes in 1820, 1830, and 1840 suggests an average length of voyage of around forty-eight weeks.[66]

Of this time only seven or eight weeks might cover the voyage out to the coast; Jackson took fifty-seven days to Bonny from Liverpool in 1826 and noted that another ship's 42-day passage was 'quick'.[67] How long was spent on the coast depended whether the ship was coasting or trading directly with the rivers of the Delta area. The palm oil 'season' in the Delta area began from around March, meaning that ships engaged in the river trade would leave Britain early in the year to spend the 'season' in the Delta rivers collecting oil, before returning home towards the end of the year.[68] 'Turn-around times' were vital in determining the success of a voyage and such pressures lay behind the ready resort to violence in this period. Jackson, typically, spent some seven months in Bonny in 1826 between January and August, though this was on board two ships, while Capt. Ralph Dawson spoke of spending up to six months to fill a cargo at Bonny.[69]

The voyage to the coast from Britain did not go directly to a Delta river. This was because the oil trade relied on the use of casks to store the palm oil. These were usually sent out stacked as shooks, to give space for the trade goods carried on board, and then assembled once the ship had arrived.[70] Such casks lasted only a handful of voyages, sometimes as few as two or three. For many firms these casks were collected from France, suggesting that wine trade casks were being used. Ships would then call at Cape Coast or Accra in order to collect coopers, trained by mission schools, to assemble the casks once the ship reached the Delta.[71]

The other major call on the voyage out was the Kru coast where labour was collected for work on loading and unloading in the Delta rivers.[72] Kru labourers had many advantages, in addition to their long seafaring experience. Kru labour was less susceptible to the health hazards of the Delta and was cheaper than British labour.[73] This practice allowed ships to rely on British crews solely for the voyage out and back, with crews returning home on another ship almost immediately after they had arrived on the coast. Kru labour would be returned to the Kru coast once trading was completed, sometimes on board a man-of-war, though many were carried to the long-established Kru community in Liverpool.[74]

Once the coast had been reached, trading could begin. For ships on the coasting system such trade would be undertaken in many different ports as the ship proceeded along the coast and back; one trader noted that a ship could have its anchor 'up and down ten times a day'.[75] When 'Jerry' was involved in the coasting trade in the 1880s, his ship passed three times along the coast in one fourteen-month voyage.[76] For ships sailing to the factories of the Gold Coast, trade was an easier process, though given the small quantities of oil available there such ships would expect to coast along the Slave Coast as well.

For the river trade to the Delta area ports the main problem was the long delays that could ensue waiting for trust to be redeemed. It was not until around 1850 that hulks – that is, old, unseaworthy ships that were towed to West Africa to be left to rot while being used as traders' depots – began to appear in the Delta rivers.[77] Before the use of hulks, trade would occur on board the sailing ship. On arrival in a Delta river a ship would be dismasted and its decks would be thatched with leaves or mats for shade: it would be on deck under this thatch that trading would take place.[78] The reassembled casks would be stored in a cask house on shore; such facilities represented the only instance whereby trade might be said to have moved on shore in this period.[79] One end of the ship would be partitioned off to become a store/shop, with oil passed down a hose to the hold below once it had been bought and tested for adulteration.[80]

Once the required ceremonies had been completed and the relevant fees and charges paid, trade could begin. It would then continue from dawn to dusk.[81] 'Jerry' later in the century complained of 'oil, oil from morning to evening'.[82] The ships concerned would become hives of activity. Waddell on his arrival in Old Calabar in 1846 vividly described the scene he met:

an oil ship . . . is covered from stem to stern with a roof of which the rafters are bamboo and the covering palm branches . . . [which] effectually keeps out both the sun and rain. On deck there is much business going forward, making or tightning [sic] oil puncheons, boiling or straining oil, and as there are both the white crew and the black crew probably forty in number and all employed it is a scene of great industry especially when the oil is coming quickly in. Indeed so many large ships in the river with their boats and the native canoes always coming and going, the chanting of the people as they paddle along and the sound of the coopers hammers resounding . . . make on the whole a lively scene, while the numerous oil puncheons in enclosures along the beach and the people employed about them give an appearance of business that one would scarcely expect.[83]

The semi-permanent communities of expatriates that developed in the Delta area rivers during the oil season would involve considerable numbers of Europeans and Africans from elsewhere along the coast. Each ship might involve forty to fifty crew in total and a port like Bonny might have eight or nine ships anchored there at a time by the middle of the century. Certainly there would have been several hundred whites in the Delta area rivers at the height of the season by the 1850s.[84] Life for traders who would spend an entire season waiting for oil could be a difficult experience. Disease was a constant fear and for this reason crews preferred what was seen as the healthier coasting voyage at sea to spending long periods in Delta rivers.[85] Periodic epidemics, such as the Yellow Fever outbreaks of 1823, 1829, and 1862–3, swept through the trading communities of the coast. Even without such epidemics there was the constant threat of malaria and the other illnesses that affected visitors to West Africa.[86] Deaths from disease could be numerous on a trading voyage. Jackson noted thirty-two deaths of sailors over a period of six months in Bonny, while one master spoke of losing 25 per cent of his crew every voyage.[87] Ships would carry a surgeon – Jackson discharged the duties for Tobin & Horsfall in Bonny – though the surgeons in the African trade were often unqualified or inexperienced and used treatments that left much to be desired. From the 1840s the Association of African Traders employed a doctor for each of the main Delta trading rivers for the duration of the oil season.[88]

Disease was only one of the dangers that traders in the Delta rivers faced. Others were fire – particularly given the dangers inherent in thatching ships

– and explosion from the large quantities of gunpowder carried on board for trade. Such an explosion caused the destruction of the *Martha* and the *Saracen* in Bonny in 1856.[89] Equally, thefts both by the crew and by outsiders were a constant problem for masters, quite apart from the usual difficulties of the maritime life: fights, desertions, mutinies, and such like. The British administration on Fernando Po between 1827 and 1834 provided a magistrate's court where many of the more intractable of these disputes ended up.[90] Crew discontent, given the long periods some spent in the rivers, was common, with complaints about food and conditions inevitable; hence the preference of some traders to send crews home soon after arrival.[91]

Shipboard life would have been monotonous for a trader based in a Delta port for the best part of a year and would have been leavened only by the round of entertaining that developed among the traders and with the local chiefs.[92] Alcohol, no doubt, would have been a solace for many.[93] Some shooting and hunting occurred, though this was restricted by the refusal of local authorities to allow traders inland. Boat racing between crews was popular among masters, though it is debatable if the enthusiasm was shared by their men.[94]

Little information exists on sexual liaisons between ship and shore. Certainly, liaisons with local women were far from unknown among masters.[95] There is little evidence of the extent to which this occurred among ordinary British sailors, however, though there were numerous problems over relations between Kru men and local women in the Delta rivers in this period. The palm wine-drinking dens for sailors that developed on Fernando Po in this period no doubt also functioned as brothels, and presumably were not unique to that island.[96]

The sheer tedium of the trading life undoubtedly contributed to the numerous acts of violence that came to be so prevalent in the expatriate communities of the rivers. Attempts were made to 'improve' the social life of traders though it was not until hulks became common that much came of this. The arrival of the missions in the Delta area from the 1840s also had an impact, though not always a welcome one; traders resented the missionaries' interference, as it was considered, in trading practices and most particularly their insistence on sabbatarianism.[97]

The expatriate presence on shore was carefully regulated by local rulers in this period. Few masters appear to have developed much interest in the local community, though publications by Jackson and others show that some at least took an interest, albeit limited in its insight, in their surroundings.[98] For most masters, however, their only aim was to complete their trade profitably and quickly. Yet relationships with local brokers and involvement in local communities that went beyond the purely mundane could and did develop, as with John Tobin in Old Calabar; traders who gained titles in so-called secret societies clearly had a close connection with the communities they did business with.[99]

For many, though, departure could not come quickly enough. Return to Britain for Delta ships, however, did not involve returning along the coast. The northeast trade winds that, together with the Guinea current, carried ships out to the Delta meant that returning along the coast would require laborious beating against the wind, as Bristol coasters found. It was usual therefore for ships in the Delta trade to sail south for their return in order to catch the southeast trade winds in the Atlantic for the voyage back to Britain.[100]

This pattern for the return voyage also enabled oil ships to call at the island of Fernando Po.[101] Fernando Po played a major role in the oil trade in the first half of the century. Between 1827 and 1834 the British settlement at Clarence on the northern end of the island became a port for ships to call at for repairs, for medical care, and to utilise the facilities of the British administration.[102] For a period in the late 1820s traders sent their larger ships, which were unable to cross the bars of some Delta rivers, to the island while smaller tenders collected oil from the mainland.[103] Other traders became permanently resident on the island, collecting oil from the Bubi of the interior and from the neighbouring ports on the coast.[104] Above all the island was a major port of call for ships to collect provisions and water for the journey home.[105] It also developed Kru settlements which allowed ships to drop off or collect Kru labour and avoid the Kru coast if necessary.[106] It thus became the regular point of departure from West Africa for oil ships leaving the Delta.

These methods of organising the African commerce showed little change from the patterns that had characterised the slave trade era. Such continuity can also be seen in the structure of the firms involved. For the most part these firms were organised around the enterprise of an individual trader. In the early years of the trade these figures emerged, as we have seen, from earlier careers in the slaving era; others were long-serving sailing masters like Reuben Hemingway, while yet others based careers on windfall profits earned from privateering during the French wars.[107]

The firms that resulted were relatively unsophisticated businesses, as had been the case in the slave trade. The high risks of the African trade and especially the shipping risks were the reason for this. In the early years of the century it was common, as during the slaving era, for partnerships to be formed simply for one voyage, with new partnerships for each subsequent venture.[108] Such a system was immensely flexible, allowing firms to respond quickly to opportunities as they arose, but provided little stability over a longer period.

The firms that survived longest in this period were family-based ones –
like the Tobin, Horsfall, and King undertakings – where the business could
be handed on to a relative and where the necessary capital came from
savings within the family. Marriage with another family was often important in this raising of capital, as with the marriage of John Tobin into the
Aspinall family.[109] Thus typical firms in the oil trade in this early period
were Thomas King with his sons, Richard and William, John Tobin and
Sons, Jamieson Bros., R. & G. Benn, or the brothers W. A. & G. Maxwell.
Only a few long-established firms in the first three decades of the century
were partnerships between two or more traders. Tobin & Horsfall – the
partnership between Thomas Tobin and Charles Horsfall – is one that did
survive. By and large, however, such partnerships were not common in the
oil trade until the 1840s and after. Rather, the family basis of a firm had
many advantages. It ensured profits could be kept within the family and
ploughed back into the firm; it enabled the firm to continue once the
founder had died or retired, and it provided a supply of staff. Thus traders
would use relatives as their agents on the coast, as in William Hutton's
reliance on his nephew on the Slave Coast in the 1830s and 1840s.

Though these were mainly family-based firms the range of their operations was anything but small-scale. A number of them were general merchants, whose trade in West African palm oil was merely one part of a
broader trading operation. Such were Jamieson Bros., which did considerable trade with China and South America. Similar were Zwilchenbarts of
Liverpool, which traded widely with Africa as well as with the USA and
Lebanon for cotton.[110] This pattern of trade in several commodities was of
course the norm for the African trade immediately after 1807, before palm
oil became established as the major item exported from the coast. However,
even those which might be termed palm oil specialists after the 1820s still
traded with other areas and in other commodities. Both John Tobin and
Horsfall & Sons traded with India, buying cloth for use in the African oil
trade. Both continued to trade with the West Indies after 1807, buying
sugar and particularly rum, with the latter clearly for use in the oil trade.
The Tobin family also owned a factory in Ireland to produce gunpowder
for the African trade.[111]

In general, most firms in the oil trade in the early part of the century, and
particularly the Liverpool ones, tended to own or charter their own shipping; there were no specialist freighters operating in the oil trade in the
period before 1852, though captains returning home with cargo space
would be willing to fill this by freighting for rival firms at a charge.[112] This
integration of shipping and trading stood out against the trend in Britain's
wider trade in this period towards the specialisation of the two functions.[113]
The risks reputedly involved in the African commerce undoubtedly explain

this feature of the African trade. Only rarely was a firm of agents used: this was clearly the case for Huttons which used Parnells of Jersey, and for the other London firm in the oil trade, Forster & Smith, which continued to run Forster & Sons – to provide the shipping for the firm – as a separate business.[114] This shipping generally came from the three British ports involved. Ships were small in this period compared to later in the century. The largest ship used in the trade in 1830 had a registered tonnage of 455 and most were substantially smaller with an average tonnage that year of 242; by 1855 the largest ship was 1,240 tons and the average was 344 tons.[115]

The profitability of the oil trade for these firms is difficult to assess precisely given the absence of documentation. This issue has indeed been subject to much debate. At the time there was talk of 'colossal fortunes' being derived from the oil trade.[116] Most notably, Consul Livingstone in 1866 commented on the 'enormous profits' made by oil traders in the early nineteenth century.[117] The mark-up between the price paid for oil in West Africa and that obtained by a trader in Britain was certainly large: conventionally this has been put at 100 per cent and in some instances as high as 300 per cent. However, Latham has suggested that such massive profits were largely 'a myth', and this view has been echoed by others.[118] The high costs involved in the trade, together with the high risks, meant that large, long-term profits were unlikely.

Certainly it is difficult to provide definitive figures for profit levels in the oil trade, partly because of problems about defining levels of profitability, and partly because of lack of data. The costs were certainly great. Quite apart from the cost of the trade goods to be sold these included insurance – usually at 5–7 per cent of the value of the goods – casks, sailing expenses including wages and the fees and commission of the master, as well as the various charges such as comey to be paid in West Africa.[119] Underlying this was the high capital cost of shipping and the costs incurred by the length of time between the capitalisation of a voyage and the realisation of that capital in the form of casks of oil delivered back in Liverpool, perhaps a year later. Important too was the cost of wear and tear on a ship in the difficult period spent on the coast.

Data derived from W. A. & G. Maxwell & Co. of Liverpool for seven voyages in the period 1835 and 1840, however, suggest that Maxwells were obtaining net profits on their palm oil trade varying between 50 and 300 per cent a voyage.[120] It needs to be stressed that these are net operating profits on the trade goods provided for the voyages concerned and do not include start-up costs, but they do suggest that, once established, a typical firm (such as Maxwells) could make, at least in this period, substantial profits. What is also notable from the figures is that the economies of scale in the oil trade were such that the largest ships employed by Maxwells were the ones to return with the highest percentage of net profits.

But how typical was this period? Were Maxwells' substantial profits due to particular circumstances operating in the late 1830s? Certainly profit margins would have varied over time with prices, but it seems unlikely that these figures were unique or abnormal. Indeed, the late 1810s saw large windfall profits for British traders, given the sharp rise in oil prices in Britain in 1818. John Tobin, Latham suggests, benefited from this.[121] In contrast, the 1820s saw sharply falling oil prices in the British market, but this must have been counteracted by the increasing overall value of the trade in the 1820s and particularly by the falling cost of exports to West Africa throughout this period. The late 1830s saw sharp increases in oil prices in Britain and in the value of the trade, thus producing the profit figures that Maxwells enjoyed. While prices in Britain fell in the 1840s, partly because of Australian tallow imports, squeezing profit margins once again, the value of the trade continued to increase in this period; given falling costs of exports to West Africa, profit margins may well have held up.[122] Over the period as a whole, substantial profits could clearly be made.

What was the market structure of the British side of the trade? The oil trade comprised a handful of what might be termed 'major' traders at its heart and a larger number of 'minor' traders at its margins. The major traders tended to be oil specialists, had several voyages to the coast each year, and remained in the trade over a considerable number of years; minor traders tended to see palm oil as merely part of a broader pattern of their business, had only one or two voyages to the coast each year, and stayed in the trade for only a relatively short period.[123]

The major traders at the heart of the palm oil trade consisted of the older generation, like the Tobins and Charles Horsfall, who had been responsible for the growth of the commerce in the years immediately after 1807. Generally they were Liverpool-based – except for Huttons, Forster & Smith, and Kings – and they remained the firms at the oil trade's heart during the first four decades of the century. Other long-established Liverpool traders who, while not so well known, held a similar position in this period included Isaac Bold and Hamilton, Jackson, & Co.[124] Few were to survive long, though W. A. & G. Maxwell, general produce merchants established in 1808 and involved in the African trade from at least 1830, did thrive into the twentieth century.[125] Calculations based on the *Customs Bills of Entry* show that by the 1830s these major firms numbered about a dozen or so and imported between them well over half of the casks of palm oil arriving in Britain.[126]

With success in the oil trade went success in local politics. It is well known

Table 4.1. *Major British palm oil firms, 1830*

	Port of operation	Number of cargoes per year	Casks of palm oil imported per year	% of total
Horsfall & Co.	Liverpool	10	11,189	40.7
G. Quayle	Liverpool	7	6,746	24.6
H. Laffer	Liverpool	5	2,887	10.5
I. O. Bold	Liverpool	2	1,734	6.3
Maxwell & Rotherham	Liverpool	4	1,689	6.1
J. J. Hamilton	Liverpool	2	1,000	3.6
G. Wilson	Liverpool	1	704	2.6
King & Sons	Bristol	4	494	1.8
Henderson & Co.	Liverpool	1	353	1.3

Notes:
Total number of firms: 21.
Total casks: 27,476.
Source: Customs Bills of Entry, 1830. The firms included are those which import over 1 per cent of the UK total in 1830.

that Liverpool's African traders played an important role in the borough's politics before 1807. It is often forgotten, however, that African traders continued to play such a role after that date. George, John, and Thomas Case, Sir John and James Tobin, Thomas Littledale, Charles, George, and Thomas Horsfall – all African traders – sat at various times on the Liverpool Council.[127] In the period before the 1835 Municipal Corporations Act, African trading and Tory interests were closely intertwined on the Liverpool Common Council – as Whig critics repeatedly pointed out.[128] John Aspinall, Thomas Case, Sir John Tobin, Thomas Littledale, Charles Horsfall, Thomas Horsfall, and James Tobin were elected mayors of Liverpool; all were African traders and many were related by marriage. Thomas Horsfall also sat as Tory MP for the borough for twenty-one years from 1857.[129] The Tobins and the Horsfalls were at the heart of this network, but judicious intermarriage ensured that the ties among Liverpool's major African traders remained close. A very similar picture can be drawn for the African traders of Bristol.[130]

As the trade expanded during the 1830s and 1840s the composition of this group of major firms at the centre of the commerce began to change.

Around 1840 a number of new firms entered the trade, in what might be termed an '1840s generation'. Thomas Harrison & Co. (established 1837), Stuart & Douglas (established 1843), Wilson & Dawson (established by 1830), and Hatton & Cookson (established 1838) were but the most prominent of these; others included R. & G. Benn, Lucas Bros., and Tyson, Richmond, & Co., the soap manufacturers.[131] With the exception of Lucas Bros., these were all Liverpool firms, confirming that port's role as the heart of the trade. It should be noted, too, that the 1830s and 1840s were to see a number of French and German firms such as Victor Régis of Marseilles and O'Swald & Co. of Hamburg begin operations in West Africa.[132]

It should be stressed that these new firms remained relatively small-scale in the 1840s, but they were to develop into major oil enterprises with the boom of the 1850s. They were to be prominent in the Association of African Traders formed in 1843 and in the Liverpool Chamber of Commerce after 1850. Stuart & Douglas were one such firm. By 1850 they were among the ten largest importers of palm oil in Britain and were the second largest two years later. The firm was established by Peter Stuart, a Liverpool cooper, and Peter Douglas, a one-time surgeon for Maxwells. Through their agent, C. J. S. Jackson, they began opening up the Brass trade in the mid-1840s and that port remained central to their success in this period; they also traded with the East and West Indies as well as Australia.[133]

Hatton & Cookson, another of these new firms, were to prove to be one of the longest lasting. They were formed out of the ironmongers' and anchorsmiths' firm established in Liverpool c. 1800 by James Hatton. His son, Edward Hatton, and son-in-law, Thomas Worthington Cookson, moved into the West African trade in 1840, though they too traded with India and the Americas. By 1854 they had fifty-four ships operating under their name and were among the six largest importers of palm oil by 1850. Their success lay in their opening up of the 'South Coast'.[134] As with Stuart & Douglas, Lucas Bros. of Bristol were probably derived from a late eighteenth-century cooperage firm. The firm grew substantially under the leadership of Edward Thomas Lucas and his brother John and was involved in the African trade by the late 1840s, usually operating in partnership with another Bristol firm, Edward Gwyer & Son, as Lucas, Gwyer, & Co.[135] Perhaps the biggest of the new firms was to be Thomas Harrison, though there is little information on the firm. Thomas Harrison was primarily a ship-owner in partnership with James Baines, and owned shares in the Black Ball line; undoubtedly he must have been involved in chartering ships to the oil trade before deciding to enter it himself. By 1845 Harrisons were the fifth largest importer of palm oil into Britain and the third largest five years later.[136] Not least of the reasons for the firm's success was its opening up of the Benin River trade from the late 1840s.[137]

There were two reasons why this '1840s generation' emerged when it did. Firstly it was due to generational change as the older, former slavers reached retirement. As with any family-based firm, these firms faced problems of transition. While the Tobin, Horsfall, and King businesses continued, their principals retired in the 1830s and 1840s: Thomas King in 1833, John Tobin in the early 1840s, and Charles Horsfall probably in the late 1830s. Other firms like that of Isaac Bold, which left the trade in the 1840s, and James Penny, disappeared in these years.[138] This process created gaps in the market to be filled. Secondly, the high oil prices of the late 1830s and early 1840s and the continuing increase in the value of the trade in this period offered opportunities for new firms to seize, just as new producers within West Africa were doing simultaneously. As the trade expanded, openings emerged for these new firms, which were additionally encouraged by the high profits, such as those gained by Maxwells, promised by the high prices of this period.

Yet the importance of this new generation needs to be kept in perspective, at least before 1850. They entered the trade at this time, but their major success was to occur in the second half of the century. At least before 1850, it was still the older generation of firms – Horsfalls, Tobins, and Kings above all – which remained at the centre of the commerce. While new firms were emerging, what is remarkable is how far the old order continued to survive. The commercial patterns and trading techniques established in the slaving era continued to characterise the trade through to the middle of the century.

This was indeed still a trade based on the techniques and structures of the slave trade. Above all, it was still marked by the lack of specialisation of function between shipper and trader that had characterised the African trade since its earliest years. It was this continuing central fact that determined the market structure of the trade. At its heart were the dozen or so major traders like Horsfalls, Kings, or Harrisons which imported five or so sizeable cargoes of oil per year and which were responsible for over half the oil imports into Britain. These were Liverpool- or (in the case of Kings) Bristol-based firms. Outside this group were a more transient collection of a dozen and a half or so minor, largely London-based firms involved in only one or two voyages to West Africa and which remained in the trade for a very short period. Their transitory involvement can be seen in the fact that, of the thirty London firms noted in the trade between 1830 and 1855 (at five-yearly intervals), only eight appear more than once in the *Customs Bills of Entry*.[139]

To what extent did this pattern represent some form of oligarchy?[140] Certainly the trade was a dangerous one with high risks, which created a high turnover of firms, particularly those outside its heart in the Delta.

Only five firms appear every year in analysis of the *Customs Bills of Entry* between 1830 and 1855: Tobin, Horsfall, Wilson & Dawson, R. & W. King, and Forster & Smith. Yet it is also clear that the major half-dozen Delta firms did control over half of the market each year and did survive over a long period. At the heart of the oil trade before 1850 was a small oligarchy that enjoyed high profits and considerable longevity of operation.

This pattern suggests a degree of imperfect competition. The reasons for this lay in the barriers to entry into the trade which derived from the way it was structured. Firstly, it required expert knowledge and experience of the African market if a trader was to succeed, given the highly differentiated nature of that market from river to river along the coast. Secondly, the shipping and trust requirements involved represented formidable capital barriers. As Newbury says, this was a trade 'characterised by large outlay of capital and a lengthy seasonal turnover'.[141] The capital costs of outfitting a ship and maintaining it over a long voyage (especially if it practised coasting), together with the risks and cost of trust that could take up to a year to be redeemed, were all major barriers to entry for small-scale firms. Trust in particular remained a key way existing traders were able to maintain their hold over the trade: the great increase in the quantity of trust noted in the second half of the century reflects this. These capital costs of entry were high enough to keep out all but the most determined or the most well capitalised of interlopers from entry into the group of major firms at the trade's heart.

These barriers reinforced existing oligarchic tendencies. It was only in the period from c. 1840 when the trade was expanding substantially that a new generation – whose members had gained experience of the trade in other capacities – was able to overcome these barriers to enter it. Even so, this was a formidable undertaking. By 1850, indeed, the trade still remained, as it had been for decades, one dominated by a handful of major merchants able to rely on the traditional techniques of trading to keep out rivals. These techniques went back to the slave trade era and were at the heart of the continuity between the slave and the palm oil trades from West Africa before the 1850s.

Part II

The restructuring of the palm products trade
in the second half of the nineteenth century

5 Technological change, the British market, and African producers

The 1850s marked the heyday of the palm oil trade. In 1854 the British price of palm oil reached, according to some calculations, £48 a ton, a price it would not touch again in the nineteenth century.[1] Similarly in the 1855–9 quinquennium, the value of British imports passed the £1.5 million p.a. mark, a level that they were to stay at or around until the mid-1870s. Observers, indeed, spoke of the 1850s as the golden age of the trade. Heddle, in 1857, commented on 'the marvellous progress of the present palm oil trade' and predicted an ever increasing future.[2] Profits appeared to be growing; it was at this time that observers spoke of the 'colossal fortunes' to be made in the trade.[3] It was the Crimean War of 1854–6, disrupting as it did Russian tallow supplies, that underlay this period of prosperity, but developments in the British market appeared to suggest that this expansion in the trade was here to stay. Changes in soap and candle processing were expanding the oil market; equally the growth of the tinplate industry provided increasing demand for the commodity. Richard King reflected the confidence of many in the trade when he described palm oil in 1853 as 'one of the most valuable articles of the present age'.[4] The difficulties facing the Africa trade at the time of abolition had clearly been overcome.

The optimism of the 1850s for the future of the oil trade was reinforced by the commencement, in 1852, of a regular steamship service between Britain and West Africa. In August of that year the African Steam Ship Co. was incorporated by royal charter to undertake the contract awarded by the British government to carry mail by steamship to West Africa.[5] In September the company's first steamship, the *Forerunner*, set out from London. This was to mark the establishment of steam as the new transport technology in the African trade and was to have major consequences both for how the trade was organised and for relations between Britain and the peoples of West Africa. For the rest of the century, steam, and the ramifications of its introduction, was to dominate the history of the palm oil trade.

The impact of technological change on the relations between Africa and the wider world, particularly for the nineteenth century, has only recently begun to be studied in any depth.[6] Technological change in the spheres of transport, communications generally, medicine, and weaponry in the middle and later decades of the nineteenth century were indeed to have a major impact on the relationship between Africa and Europe and were to underpin the development of imperial rule. This can be seen particularly in the changes in the palm oil trade that followed the introduction of steam. The establishment of palm oil as the major commodity traded between West Africa and Britain had required little or no change in the technology – particularly sailing technology – used in the African trade. Although the vessels in the African trade had become significantly larger over the first half of the century, little had changed in ship design or in the means of ship propulsion since the slaving era. This was still the case in the early 1850s.

Early attempts at using steam in West Africa – such as the Niger expeditions of 1832 and 1841 or Beecroft's use of the *Ethiope* on the Niger, the Gabon, and the Cross between 1839 and 1847 – had come to little. Either the ships used were unsuitable for the task or problems such as disease had prevented a full appreciation of their potentialities. Indeed, throughout the world, the spread of steam in place of sail was a good deal slower than might have been expected. Problems with fuel efficiency together with improvements in sailing ship design meant that for long voyages with regular winds sail retained a significant economic advantage over steam until late in the century.[7] However, the ultimate triumph of steam was not to be denied. A regular transatlantic steamer service was in operation by 1840 and thereafter the British government's mail contracts provided a major stimulus for steam shipping. By 1842 the mail contract to India had been awarded and the West African contract was soon to follow.[8]

The technological breakthrough for steam power came with the development of the high-pressure compound engine around 1860 and then the triple expansion engine in 1881, both of which increased fuel efficiency and cut costs significantly. Alongside these innovations came the triumph of screw propulsion over paddle and the development of condensers to allow the utilisation of fresh water in place of brine. With these changes came the use of iron hulls which allowed an increase in ship size over the effective limit of 2,000 tons or so imposed by wooden hulls. By 1875 a steamship was said to be comparable to three sailing ships of similar tonnage. This showed the triumph of steam over sail and, during the 1870s, steam passed the 50 per cent mark for tonnage entered and cleared in UK ports.[9]

From 1852, steam was to become successfully established in the West African trade. For many British observers at the time the introduction of a steamship service to the west coast seemed like the start of a new era in relations between Africa and the wider world. The possibilities developed by steam communication, not least for the palm oil trade, seemed immense. The steamship marked the dawn of a new era of prosperity for the trade between Africa and Britain, for not only would it allow the coastal trade to expand, but by allowing the penetration of the interior of the continent it would finally open up the full trading potential of West Africa. Others stressed that steam would finally extinguish the slave trade, the one thing, it was believed, that was holding back Africa's commercial development and the expansion of its trade.[10]

Many reflected the optimism that this marked a new era for the African trade. Given the Victorian belief in the relationship between trade and 'civilisation', the moral consequences of this technological revolution were emphasised. The *Colonial Magazine and East India Review* in 1850 described steam as 'the true civiliser' and stressed that 'we are at the commencement of a new era in the progress of human affairs', suggesting that steam shipping would lead to great changes within Africa itself.[11] The governor of Sierra Leone in 1851 echoed this when he stated that a steam-ship service with Britain would lead to 'a marked change for the better in the state of affairs, moral, mercantile, and political' on the coast, while Laird and Oldfield asked in 1837, 'can there be a nobler or more profitable application of [steam], than employing it to open up Central Africa? . . . it might have been created for the purpose'.[12]

The stimulus for the establishment of the steamship service to the west coast was the British government's 1852 mail contract which the African Steam Ship Co. won, beating Charles Horsfall & Sons among others in the competition. The contract was worth an average of £21,250 p.a. and involved the provision of twelve services a year for ten years.[13] Macgregor Laird, a member of the Birkenhead ship building family and the man responsible for the first attempt to use steam power in West Africa on the 1832 Niger expedition, was the figure behind the firm and was to be its managing director until 1855.[14]

The African Steam Ship Co. made its headquarters in London and its early voyages began from there and called at Plymouth before heading for West Africa; from 1856 it switched its home port to Liverpool. Initially the firm had five steamships, all screw steamers of between 400 and 1,062 tons.[15] Although the *Forerunner* was dismasted on its way to West Africa, its first voyage was completed successfully and the company's fortunes rapidly grew. In its *Annual Report for 1853* the firm noted that 'the number of ship-pers by the company's Steamers is increasing rapidly, new branches of trade are opening out' and went on to hope for 'a great stimulus to the trade'. In its first results it declared a net profit of £1,929 18s 3d on six months' opera-tions and a dividend of 2s 6d per share.[16] Following fresh negotiations with the government, it was awarded a new mail contract in 1858 and was to con-tinue to hold it until 1872.[17]

The African Steam Ship Co. was joined in the West African trade in 1869 by a second shipping firm, the Glasgow-based British & African Steam Navigation Co., which operated initially from Liverpool and Glasgow, and by 1874 from Liverpool alone. In 1870 the two shipping firms agreed to fix freight rates and sailing dates and their relationship thereafter remained close; from 1872 they shared the government mail contract between them. By 1875 they were together operating seventeen ships to West Africa. In 1891 Elder Dempster & Co., the shipping agents for the British & African since 1869, effectively took over the management of both firms.[18]

Through these two firms Elder Dempster controlled the West African trade into the next century. Other shipping firms that attempted to enter the West African trade – such as the West African Steam Navigation Co. in 1881, the Prince Line in 1891–2, the General Steam Navigation Co. in 1894–5, and Furness Withy & Co. in 1895 – were soon seen off.[19] The figure behind Elder Dempster, Alfred Jones, had by the 1890s emerged as the dominant figure in the West African shipping trade and remained so until 1909. Through Elder Dempster he controlled the British & African and by 1900 he had bought a controlling interest in the African Steam Ship Co. Jones' interests stretched beyond Elder Dempster to the control of the surf boats used to unload the steamers at the various ports along the coast, cold stores, hotels, and the Bank of British West Africa.[20]

Competition also came from shipping firms outside Britain which attempted to enter the West African trade in this period. The best known was the Woermann Line of Hamburg, though Portuguese steamers also operated to Angola for a period after 1858 and again from 1881, and French shippers like the Fabre–Fraissinet line of Marseilles began operating along the coast in 1889.[21] Portuguese and French interests posed little threat to the British lines, though Woermanns, operating to the same parts of West Africa, clearly did. Such a situation led to the establishment in 1895 of the West African shipping conference between the two British lines and Woermanns, which utilised a deferred rebate system to encourage traders to use the conference's ships. Traders who gave all their cargo to conference ships over an agreed period received a rebate on their freight rates at the end of that time.[22] As a result Jones effectively drove out any competing shipping from the West African trade by the late 1890s; moreover, the geography of the West African coast and the nature of the trade meant that tramp steamers were never an effective alternative.[23]

There were two routes used by the two British shipping companies. Both had a service to the Niger Delta, terminating at Old Calabar, the Cameroons, and Fernando Po, and calling at all the major ports on the coast between there and Liverpool. In addition, starting from the early 1870s, both had a service to Angola, terminating at Luanda or Moçâmedes and calling at eight to ten ports between there and the Delta before returning to Liverpool. Initially, during the 1850s and 1860s, the African Steam Ship Co. offered only a monthly service to the coast but by the 1880s this had increased to a weekly service to the Delta operated alternately by the firms, and a monthly one by each firm to Angola.[24] The time taken by such voyages varied depending on the number of ports called at, but in the 1850s and 1860s was expected to take around ten weeks, including stoppages, from Liverpool to the Delta and back, compared to between five and eight months for sail; by the 1880s, Bonny to Liverpool took around four weeks by steam.[25]

Freight rates for the African Steam Ship Co. in the early 1850s were £5 per ton gross of palm oil. These rates were higher than those in sailing ships from the coast at this time – which stood at approximately £4 per ton of oil – but steam's speed gave it the advantage.[26] Thereafter rates fell significantly and by 1881 stood at £2 10s per ton of oil and £1 15s per ton of kernels for the voyage between Lagos and Liverpool.[27]

The advantages of steam over sail for those in the African trade were manifest. Firstly and most obviously, steam transport was far quicker. This had several ramifications – especially once the telegraph reached the Delta in 1886 – but above all meant that traders could maintain lower inventories on the coast and thus reduce costs.[28] It also increased the speed of turnover and meant that palm oil could be converted to capital much more quickly. For a trade based on credit this represented a significant reduction in costs. As one trader, Harry Cotterell, who worked in the Delta in the 1860s, recorded:

We found that our system of working the trade by steamers answered well, as compared with the old-fashioned way followed by other merchants of sending sailing ships out and keeping them waiting several months in the River until they were loaded, as in addition to our advantage of getting out fresh goods by each steamer, we also had the advantage of sending our produce home by them, thus getting it to market and the proceeds converted into goods two or three times while the other merchants had theirs waiting until their ships arrived home. By this means the trade became revolutionised and all the merchants in turn had to dispose of their sailing ships.[29]

Secondly, ships could become bigger, with a corresponding increase in cargo capacity. The average size of ship operating in the oil trade in 1850 was 255 tons. By 1880 the average size was 822 tons; within five years the average ship had passed 1,000 tons.[30] This increase in ship size meant that unit costs were reduced and freight rates fell further, to around £2 per ton of oil by the start of the new century.[31] This cost advantage was reinforced by the reduction in wage bills, insurance, interest charges, and so forth that ensued when traders abandoned their sailing ships.

Thirdly, steamers were more flexible in their routes which meant that new

Table 5.1. *Shipping in the palm oil trade, 1850–1890*

Year	No. of palm oil voyages	No. of steamship voyages	Total tonnage (A)	Total steamship tonnage (B)	B as a % of A
1850	85	0	21,650	0	—
1855	137	9[a]	47,113	3,073[a]	6.5
1860	141	12[a]	45,786	8,127[a]	17.7
1865	161	12[a]	51,192	8,060[a]	15.7
1870[b]	172	43	58,775	32,561	55.4
1875	137	58	72,744	55,401	76.2
1880	109	77	89,550	80,301	89.7
1885	90	79	90,196	87,048	96.5
1890	80	76	89,841	88,768	98.8

Notes:
[a] Precise total unclear from the *Bills*.
[b] The 1870 *Bills* include eleven ships which are entered twice, at Glasgow and Liverpool; these have been counted once in these figures.
Source: Customs Bills of Entry, 1850–1890.

ports could be integrated into the export trade. The steamship services were able to call at numerous ports on the coast both on the way out and on return; steam avoided the difficulties with beating against the prevailing wind which encouraged traders using sailing ships to the Delta to concentrate on one port. This enabled the Delta traders in particular to operate at several ports in different parts of West Africa and spread their operations along the coast, thereby reducing risk and, ultimately, costs. All traders, in a sense, could become coasting traders once the steamer services arrived.

Faster, cheaper, and more flexible: these advantages meant that, once introduced, steam very quickly came to replace sail in the West African trade. Livingstone in 1870 noted that 'the number of sailing ships is rapidly diminishing in consequence of steam navigation'.[32] The crucial decade in the transition was the 1860s: by 1870 the shipping tonnage in the palm oil trade that was steam-driven had reached 55.4 per cent; by 1880 the move from sail to steam was effectively complete.[33] It represented the first major change in the organisation and practices of the oil trade since its commencement in the slave trade era. Indeed, it marked the first major break in the techniques of West Africa's external trade since the arrival of the Portuguese.

What was the impact of these transport changes on West Africa's exports of palm oil in the second half of the century? Did steam have the effect that the enthusiasts of the 1850s had expected? Did the introduction of steam from 1852 lead on, as had been expected, to ever greater prosperity for the oil trade? In the event these hopes were not borne out. Far from being the start of a golden age of the oil trade, the 1850s were its apogee and the second half of the century was to see the trade entering a period of increasing difficulty. This can be seen above all in the British price of palm oil which began to fall from the mid-1850s through to the early 1890s.

The extent of the fall in British prices of palm oil depends to a degree on the price series used. There are a number of series covering this period of which Sauerbeck's and that given in the *Parliamentary Papers* are the most reliable.[34] These two differ only slightly, with Sauerbeck's figures being approximately 5–10 per cent higher than the *Parliamentary Papers* series. However, the trends in both series over the second half of the century are the same and, given the improved reliability of the official series after the 1850s, the *Parliamentary Papers* figures have been used here for the latter decades of the century.

UK prices for palm oil reached a peak in 1854. With the exception of the years 1818–19, this year saw the highest price palm oil reached during the century. Prices remained on a rough plateau just above £40 a ton from 1854 until 1861 but then began to fall; there was a sharp fall in the early 1860s followed by another in the mid-1870s before a major slump in prices began in the late 1880s with a trough in the years 1887–8. By 1887 the price of palm oil had fallen to less than half its 1861 price and stood at £19 a ton, the lowest recorded price for the century. It was to recover only slightly thereafter.

The volume of British palm oil imports grew over this period but the increase was not to be sufficient to compensate for the fall in prices. British imports of palm oil from West Africa rose from 780,599 cwt in 1855 to 1,058,989 cwt in 1895, with the latter year marking the nineteenth-century peak in the volume of the trade.[35] This growth, while certainly not as spectacular as the increases noted in the early nineteenth century, was none the less sustained to the 1890s, with bursts noted in the early 1870s and the late 1880s–early 1890s.[36]

However, although the second half of the century saw continuing growth in the volume of the oil trade between West Africa and Britain, these increases in volumes did not compensate for the fall in prices of this period. Figures for the value of British imports show an approximate plateau for the trade between the 1850s and the 1870s, followed by sharp decline as difficulties set in.[37] The value of British imports of palm oil fell over the period from £1,697,803 in 1855 to £872,588 in 1899, with particularly steep falls in the late 1870s, the late 1890s, and, above all, the late 1880s. The late 1880s and specifically the years 1887–8 marked the lowest point of the trade since 1855. Between 1884 and 1887, the value of the trade fell sharply by

Table 5.2. *UK price of palm oil, 1855–1897 (£ per ton)*

Year	£ per ton	Year	£ per ton
1855	43.50	1877	35.62
1856	43.00	1878	34.80
1857	43.75	1879	30.52
1858	38.83	1880	29.43
1859	45.08	1881	29.09
1860	44.67	1882	30.49
1861	42.68	1883	35.11
1862	39.83	1884	33.50
1863	35.93	1885	26.90
1864	33.65	1886	20.92
1865	36.32	1887	19.48
1866	40.21	1888	19.83
1867	38.62	1889	21.17
1868	39.41	1890	22.90
1869	38.89	1891	22.30
1870	36.48	1892	22.10
1871	34.75	1893	24.94
1872	35.87	1894	21.75
1873	33.67	1895	20.91
1874	33.57	1896	21.02
1875	33.35	1897	20.58
1876	34.77		

Source: PP 1866, LXXIII (3675), 32–3; 1880, LXVII (2484), 74–5; 1890–1, LXXXIX (6457), 134–5; 1898, C (8992), 148–9.

Table 5.3. *UK price of palm oil, 1855–1894, by quinquennium (£ per ton)*

Quinquennium	Average price (£ per ton)
1855–9	42.83
1860–4	39.35
1865–9	38.69
1870–4	34.87
1875–9	33.81
1880–4	31.52
1885–9	21.66
1890–4	22.80

Source: Calculated from table 5.2.

Table 5.4. *Volume of UK palm oil imports from West Africa, 1855–1899*

Year	Cwt	Year	Cwt
1855	780,599	1878	663,243
1856	772,825	1879	875,132
1857	825,790	1880	1,016,551
1858	773,008	1881	816,172
1859	659,682	1882	782,775
1860	784,588	1883	706,132
1861	713,378	1884	819,781
1862	844,602	1885	872,272
1863	773,287	1886	926,309
1864	656,867	1887	858,283
1865	793,895	1888	871,449
1866	785,761	1889	893,084
1867	781,671	1890	768,717
1868	950,595	1891	904,430
1869	796,407	1892	903,476
1870	833,273	1893	962,789
1871	1,018,600	1894	975,849
1872	991,882	1895	1,058,989
1873	1,009,975	1896	907,700
1874	1,057,574	1897	848,396
1875	891,669	1898	784,914
1876	867,472	1899	804,393
1877	882,018		

Source: CUST 5/52–/162.

Table 5.5. *Volume of UK palm oil imports from West Africa, 1855–1899, by quinquennium*

Quinquennium	Average cwt
1855–9	762,380.8
1860–4	754,544.4
1865–9	821,665.8
1870–4	982,260.8
1875–9	835,906.8
1880–4	828,282.2
1885–9	884,279.4
1890–4	903,052.2
1895–9	880,878.4

Source: Calculated from table 5.4.

Table 5.6. *Value of UK palm oil imports from West Africa, 1855–1899*

Year	Value (£)	Year	Value (£)
1855	1,697,802.83	1878	1,154,042.82
1856	1,661,573.75	1879	1,335,451.43
1857	1,806,415.63	1880	1,495,854.80
1858	1,500,795.03	1881	1,187,122.17
1859	1,486,923.23	1882	1,193,340.49
1860	1,752,377.30	1883	1,239,614.73
1861	1,522,348.65	1884	1,373,133.18
1862	1,682,024.88	1885	1,173,205.84
1863	1,389,210.10	1886	968,919.21
1864	1,105,178.73	1887	835,967.64
1865	1,441,713.32	1888	864,041.68
1866	1,579,772.49	1889	945,329.41
1867	1,509,406.70	1890	880,180.97
1868	1,873,147.45	1891	1,008,439.45
1869	1,548,613.41	1892	998,340.98
1870	1,519,889.95	1893	1,200,597.88
1871	1,769,817.50	1894	1,061,235.79
1872	1,778,940.37	1895	1,107,173.00
1873	1,700,292.91	1896	953,992.70
1874	1,775,137.96	1897	872,999.48
1875	1,486,858.06	1898[a]	834,617.00
1876	1,508,100.07	1899[a]	872,588.00
1877	1,570,874.06		

Note:
[a] CUST 5/159 and /162.
Source: Calculated from tables 5.2 and 5.4.

nearly 40 per cent, making this the severest period of difficulty in the trade in the second half of the century, though the slump in the late 1890s was little better. In 1887, at the trough of the late 1880s slump, the value of the British trade was half what it had been in 1855.

Clearly the British market for palm oil was experiencing serious difficulties in the second half of the century. It is true that, in contrast, the value of US and German imports of palm oil from West Africa increased in this period, but, as far as palm oil is concerned, these markets did not represent more than a small proportion compared to the British and their increase was not sufficient to take up the shortfall caused by its decline. In any case, the value of German imports of palm oil followed a similar trend to that of the British figures, with serious difficulties setting in from the mid-1880s.

Far from being the start of a new era of continuing growth, as many had

Table 5.7. *Value of UK palm oil imports from West Africa, 1855–1899, by quinquennium*

Years	Average value pa in £	% change
1855–9	1,630,702.09	—
1860–4	1,490,227.93	−8.6
1865–9	1,590,530.67	+6.7
1870–4	1,708,815.74	+7.4
1875–9	1,411,065.29	−17.4
1880–4	1,297,813.07	−8.0
1885–9	957,492.76	−26.2
1890–4	1,029,759.01	+7.5
1895–9	928,274.04	−9.9

Source: Calculated from table 5.6.

hoped, the middle decades of the century were the peak of the oil trade before it entered a period of problems to the end of the century. Why did the palm oil trade experience such difficulties after the 1850s? The answer to this lay in the very factor that had been expected in the 1850s to inaugurate a new era of prosperity, the steamship. The changes that followed the introduction of the steamship were to have major consequences for the palm oil trade.

The impact of the introduction of the steamship service into the African trade lay in its division of the functions of trading and shipping. It was no longer necessary for a trader to own or charter shipping to participate in the oil trade: trading and shipping were now two separate activities. Traders could now use the steamship services and thus avoid the high start-up capital costs of buying or chartering their own shipping. Thus the African trade caught up with the trend elsewhere in nineteenth-century British commerce where such functional specialisation had long been established.[38] This development was a blow to the larger-scale traders in palm oil in particular. The high capital cost of shipping had been one of the main ways they had maintained their 'oligopoly' in the African trade and kept out competitors before 1852. The introduction of the new freight services meant that any trader who wished to could charter space in one of the steamers and begin trading in West Africa.

This had significant consequences, in that it opened the oil trade to new traders and increased competition within it. New British firms were able to enter the trade without the costs of setting up expensive establishments on the coast or buying or chartering ships. Equally, small-scale African traders – Krio or Gold Coast merchants, for example – were able to enter the trade by using the steamship. Even African brokers and coastal chiefs could, in principle at least, charter cargo space to trade directly with Britain and bypass the established firms. The steamship, in short, opened the market to new sources of competition and knocked away the oligarchic conditions on which the established firms had relied. The palm oil trade was thus a far more competitive trade in the second half of the century than it had ever been in the first half and the tensions that ensued contributed significantly to the downward pressure on prices in this period.[39]

The steamship thus played an important role in the difficulties traders faced in the oil trade in the second half of the century. But there was more to the problems the trade faced than this. Other technological changes within the British market for oils and fats were to have major ramifications for the West African palm oil trade, driving down prices. On the one hand, competing oils, hitherto limited in or absent from the British market, significantly increased their presence in the market, while on the other, changes in the processing industry were to lead to a sharp decline in the demand for palm oil.

Technological change lay behind the increased competition from other oils. Partly this too was the result of the steamship. The communications revolution, of which the steamship was but a part, enabled oils and fats from other areas of the world to enter the British market from the middle of the century.[40] As steam shipping spread to Asia and freight rates began to fall, Indian oils and fats became competitors to African palm oil in Britain; existing competitors like Australian tallow significantly improved their position in the market. This process was reinforced as the time taken for the voyage from Asia dropped significantly with the opening of the Suez canal in 1869.[41] While falling freight rates benefited palm oil also, the problem was that it was facing increased competition from new supplies of oils and fats.

Moreover, from 1876, systematic attempts were begun in Labuan, and thereafter elsewhere in South-East Asia, to cultivate *elaeis guineensis* and produce palm oil.[42] Indeed, sporadic attempts at cultivation had been made in the Dutch East Indies from as early as 1850.[43] Although the attempts were initially of limited success, South-East Asia did export small quantities of palm oil to Britain in the 1880s and 1890s and was, from the early twentieth century, to develop as a significant producer.[44] Even if this represented a potential rather than an immediate threat to West African suppliers, West Africa clearly was no longer the only source of palm oil for the world market and the first expressions of concern for the future of the industry were being heard.[45]

However, perhaps the main threat on the supply side came from the discovery of major sources of mineral oil – petroleum – in Pennsylvania in

1859. This was to have major ramifications throughout the oils and fats market in the USA and, eventually, elsewhere.[46] Petroleum, together with its derivative kerosene, was rapidly to replace other oils in the illumination and lubrication market and its sharp fall in price – from 36 cents a gallon in 1863 to 8 cents by 1885 – reinforced this.[47] By 1895 the USA alone was producing 100 million barrels of petroleum p.a. and this was clearly to be the commodity at the centre of the oils and fats market in future.[48]

This increase in supplies of competing oils was matched by a decrease in the demand for palm oil in the British market. On one level this was part of the general phenomenon sometimes known as the 'Great Depression' which set in from around 1873 and which led to a decline in British demand for a variety of commodities.[49] But there were also more specific changes in the oils and fats market during the second half of the century which affected palm oil particularly. In the lubricants market, clearly, mineral oil came to replace palm oil as the main oil used for machinery and railway lubrication from the 1860s. In the illumination market, the spread of electricity from the 1880s and of coal gas, kerosene, and paraffin meant that the demand for candles was to be checked. Equally, in the soap industry, new processes meant that palm oil was in less demand; cotton oil came increasingly to replace palm oil in cheaper domestic soaps over time.[50] The development of the hydrogenation process at the end of the century – whereby hydrogen was added to harden liquid oils – meant that cheaper oils hitherto unsuitable for soap manufacture could increasingly be substituted for palm oil.[51]

However, perhaps the change that most emphatically illustrated how technological development was altering the market for palm oil came with the case of British tinplate manufacture, where the demand for palm oil was hit partly by the impact of US tariff policies in the 1890s – which had a major effect on the British tinplate industry – but above all by the introduction of zinc chloride as a cheap and effective flux for tinning during the 1880s.[52] The decline in demand for palm oil in the South Wales tinplate industry marked the *coup de grâce* for Bristol's palm oil trade.

The ensuing fall in world prices for palm oil after the 1850s posed major problems for producers, brokers, and traders. However, the effects of these problems were partly compensated for by the development of the palm kernels trade. The palm kernel was what was left once the pericarp had been removed from the palm fruit; the inner nut was then cracked to produce the kernel.[53] Oil was obtained by crushing and grinding the kernel and then adding water or, later, carbon bisulphide. The result was a colourless, translucent oil that had the same properties as coconut oil.[54]

Palm kernel oil was initially used in soap manufacture. It produced a hard soap which was very soluble and quick to lather; it was cheaper than coconut oil, had better keeping qualities, and was ideal for the mass market for soap that was developing in Britain.[55] Palm kernel oil was used thus from the middle of the century but the key development in this process was William Lever's use of palm kernel oil as the major component of his immensely successful 'Sunlight Self-Washer' soap, patented in 1884.[56] This was the first soap to establish a mass market in Britain. 'Sunlight' was ideal for the hard-water cities of Northern England and Lever's use of advertising and his stress on brand identity marked a revolution in soap marketing that left the older soap firms in his wake. 'Sunlight' was a runaway success and, with the building of Port Sunlight on the Wirral from 1888, Lever had established himself as the major soap producer of Britain.[57] Ironically, this affected palm oil imports, since the success of 'Sunlight' stimulated the use of palm kernel oil in preference, rather than in addition, to palm oil in the soap market.[58]

Soap manufacture was the main use for palm kernel oil before the end of the century, though it was also used in nitroglycerine production, and the residue of the kernels, once the oil had been extracted, was a valuable component of cattle cake and was used extensively by farmers.[59] Its other value, however, at least by the end of the century, was in the manufacture of margarine. Margarine – or 'butterine' as it was initially called – was invented by the French chemist Hippolyte Mège Mouriès in 1869.[60] Originally margarine was composed of a mixture of animal, dairy, and vegetable fats, with beef tallow being the major component, and was designed as a substitute for lard in the working-class diet. From the 1880s, margarine increasingly came to be made from vegetable oils, including palm kernel oil, and this was given a further boost with the development of the hydrogenation process at the turn of the century which not only prevented the oils in margarine from going rancid but also allowed more and more liquid vegetable oil, and particularly palm kernel oil, to be utilised in its manufacture.[61] Palm kernel oil proved to be perfect for margarine, and became a major component of the product, with some types of margarine being composed of as much as 70 per cent palm kernel oil.[62]

World margarine production quadrupled between 1875 and 1900. Dutch producers, especially the family firms of Jurgens and Van den Bergh, were at the forefront in developing margarine in the 1870s before it was taken up by German producers and then, from 1889, was produced in Britain. Initially at least, it was the British market and particularly the British mass urban market, that was the focus of Dutch and German production, though Germany itself developed as an important source of demand. By the end of the century margarine had become firmly established in the working-class diet in Britain and Germany.[63]

Hitherto palm kernels had been largely ignored as an export commodity by West African producers and brokers because of a lack of demand from

Table 5.8. *Volume and value of UK imports from West Africa of nuts and kernels 'commonly used for expressing oil', 1871–1895*

Year	Volume (tons)	Value (£)
1871	27,123	356,330
1872	23,170	274,524
1873	13,993	183,734
1874	22,225	308,158
1875	26,884	374,491
1876	23,836	333,687
1877	23,244	323,150
1878	23,821	332,544
1879	24,043	323,659
1880	34,786	471,754
1881	24,061	286,911
1882	41,885	484,309
1883[a]	39,036	491,348
1884	43,372	599,708
1885	34,507	406,856
1886	29,901	299,289
1887	33,537	322,659
1888	36,212	358,398
1889	36,789	370,840
1890	27,873	320,145
1891	31,769	365,334
1892	31,063	348,918
1893	38,809	428,045
1894	43,111	439,232
1895	34,186	339,236

Note:
[a] Figures for 1883 not complete.
Source: Annual Statement of the Trade and Navigation of the UK in *Parliamentary Papers*.

European traders, but from the middle of the century these new uses for kernels meant that the trade began to increase rapidly. Statistics of British imports are difficult to come by for this trade since palm kernels were grouped together with other nuts and kernels in British Customs records. However, the first records of exports from West Africa to Britain date from 1846 when £48 worth were traded from Sierra Leone.[64] Sierra Leone led the way in exporting palm kernels from the west coast though the amounts involved remained very limited until the 1850s. Thereafter, the increase in Sierra Leone's exports was rapid, though it was not until 1861 that Sierra

Table 5.9. *Average value of UK imports from West Africa of nuts and kernels, 1870–1894, by quinquennium*

Quinquennium	Average value (£)
1870–4[a]	280,686.50
1875–9	337,506.20
1880–4	466,806.00
1885–9	351,608.40
1890–4	380,334.80

Note:
[a] Average calculated from years 1871–4.
Source: Calculated from table 5.8.

Leone's exports (to all parts) passed £30,000.[65] Other areas of the coast appear to have been much slower to export palm kernels; Lagos' first recorded exports were in 1862, though Campbell reported Egba exports through the port in 1856, and the Gold Coast's first significant exports occurred in 1868.[66] Data for other parts of the coast, particularly the Niger Delta, are scarce, but the general point that this was a trade that saw its effective beginnings in the 1850s holds true.[67] Manning estimates that the 'Nigerian' export of palm kernels to Britain reached a nineteenth-century peak of 27,500 tons in 1896.[68]

Britain was by no means the only market for palm kernels from West Africa. The French market was also significant, though figures are hard to come by, while the USA received some imports of palm kernels from the Gold Coast after 1868.[69] Germany, however, with Hamburg and Emmerich as the major crushing centres in Europe, was the major importer of kernels and is estimated as taking as much as 90 per cent of West Africa's exports by the early twentieth century.[70] The earliest figures for Hamburg imports of palm kernels from West Africa date from 1861; by 1900 the entrepôt imported 124,187,600 kg (2,444,638 cwt) from West Africa.[71]

The degree to which the increase in the kernels trade compensated for the decline in oil figures in these years is difficult to assess. For German traders these were clearly boom years and the sustained growth of kernel imports into Hamburg at the very least cushioned – though did not remove – the worst effects of the late 1880s slump.[72] For British traders, on the other hand, this was not the case. Overall, by 1895 total British imports of *all* nuts and kernels stood at £339,236, which did not make up for the shortfall caused by the decline in the value of the oil trade since 1855.[73] Moreover, in terms of the slump of the late 1880s and 1890s, traders still faced consider-

Table 5.10. *UK price of nuts and kernels used for expressing oil, 1876–1897 (£ per ton)*

Year	£ per ton
1876	14.91
1877	14.83
1878	15.77
1879	15.18
1880	15.09
1881	13.33
1882	12.53
1883	14.24
1884	14.81
1885	13.09
1886	11.32
1887	11.00
1888	11.33
1889	11.07
1890	12.70
1891	13.15
1892	12.19
1893	12.19
1894	11.41
1895	11.27
1896	10.63
1897	10.90

Source: PP 1890–1, LXXXIX (6457), 134–5; *PP* 1898, C (8992), 148–9.

able pressures, even when importing kernels to make up for falls in oil figures. The volume of 'Nigerian' exports of palm kernels fell sharply in the late 1880s, as did the value of British imports of all nuts and kernels.[74] Newbury shows that palm kernel export values from West Africa to the UK passed through difficulties in the 1880s, falling from an index of 100 in 1875 to 71 in 1887.[75] Palm kernel prices, for which information is sparse for the early years of this period, reflect this fall, with the Lagos price of kernels falling from £11.70 a ton in 1880 to £6.89 by 1896.[76]

Despite the growth of the palm kernels trade, therefore, these years were clearly a period of considerable difficulty for British palm oil traders in West Africa. Newbury, indeed, quantifies the long-term fall in palm oil and kernel prices in the late nineteenth century as culminating in a recession in the late 1880s with 'a sharp fall of about 20 per cent in traded values'.[77] Both oil and kernels were at the heart of this slump.

What underlay these changes was the fact that palm oil, which had so suited the needs of processors in the first half of the century, was facing a market that, because of technological change after 1850, was becoming more and more specialised. Whether in the soap, lubrication, or illumination markets, palm oil was meeting growing pressure from competing oils and fats that more specifically suited the needs of that particular market; in the case of tinplate manufacture, for example, it was zinc chloride that was the more appropriate commodity. This was the heart of the problem. The consequence of technological change meant that what might be termed an all-purpose oil like palm oil, which had initially suited several markets, was no longer appropriate in a situation where more specialised oils were required; market specialisation was to the detriment of palm oil. Technological improvements in the processing industry thus ensured that palm oil did not inherit the glittering future in the British market that had seemed so apparent in the 1850s.

What was the impact of this on African producers? The changes in the market for oils and fats in the late nineteenth century generated considerable difficulties for producers. Moreover, the fall in UK palm oil prices from 1862 and in palm kernel prices from 1880 was part of a serious deterioration in the terms of trade for West Africa generally.[78] Though the precise movements in the terms of trade for West Africa in the nineteenth century are difficult to establish given the paucity of data, the work of Eltis and others suggests that, in broad terms, the gross barter terms of trade between Britain and Africa, having shifted markedly in favour of Africa from around 1817 onwards largely due to the falling cost of British manufactures, began to reverse in the later years of the century. Exactly when this adverse move began is a matter of dispute, though Eltis and Jennings suggest that a deterioration in the gross barter terms of trade can be seen from around 1870. From then to the end of the century, African oil and kernel exporters faced the levelling off of the fall in prices of British manufactures and declining prices for their own products.[79]

These pressures had important effects on palm producers, squeezing their incomes and obliging farmers to develop new strategies to deal with them. From around 1870 a tightening 'staple trap' was emerging for palm producers. Prices for their products were falling and the terms of trade were moving sharply against them. The impact of these changes hit different areas in different ways. Much depended on the balance between oil and kernel production in a particular area, with changes in the relationship of prices for these two commodities affecting areas unevenly. As Manning suggests, for example, producers in what became eastern Nigeria suffered more than those to the west because of their greater dependence on oil over kernel production at a time when oil prices fell faster than the price of kernels.[80] Also important were the opportunities available for producers to turn to other commodities. Thus some suppliers in the Gold Coast and Yorubaland moved into other products such as cocoa or rubber during the oil price slump of the 1880s and 1890s, with these years seeing a rubber boom and the start of significant cocoa cultivation on the Gold Coast.[81] This was facilitated by the fact that other crops could be planted by clearing land between oil palms without losing the products of the palm in the process. Not all producers chose this option or indeed could do so; environmental conditions in areas like Igboland, for example, meant that irrespective of price movements, palm production remained the most appropriate pursuit for farmers throughout this period.[82]

For those producers who remained in palm oil exporting there were a number of possible responses to the price problems of the late nineteenth century. The initial response was to increase the output of palm oil. At least as far as the UK figures suggest, up to the 1870–4 quinquennium this succeeded in continuing to increase the value of the trade and thus to maintain returns to producers. From the mid-1870s, however, increased output failed to compensate producers for falling oil prices and the value of the returns to West African oil producers fell sharply through to the late 1880s. Based on the figures for UK imports, West African producers between 1860–4 and 1890–4 increased their oil output by 20 per cent but received 31 per cent lower returns.[83]

Even exporting to other European markets did not provide an escape for these producers. German imports of palm oil increased markedly in volume over this period, with a particular increase in the 1880s as the slump in prices began to bite. Yet until the 1890s the volumes involved remained less than a sixth of British imports and were not large enough to compensate for falling prices in the British market. Overall, increasing the output of palm oil was not an adequate response to the problem of falling prices facing African producers in the late nineteenth century.

A second response by palm producers to these problems was to attempt to find economies of production; however, there were few economies of scale that could be exploited by producers.[84] Increasing the density of palms per acre would have had little effect given that few producers systematically cultivated trees and palms take several years to fruit, though one response to these problems might be seen in the various injunctions against felling oil palms to produce palm wine seen in parts of West Africa from this period.[85] Susan Martin suggests that economies of production could be achieved by moving the processing of fruits nearer to the tree or nearer to waterways in order to reduce labour costs and gain economies of transport, though the latter at least would not have been an opportunity available to all and there were limits to the former set by the distribution of trees.[86] That apart, given the technology available in this period – such crushing mills that were introduced into the region proved very ineffective before 1900 – there were few if any changes that could be made in the techniques of cultivation of palms or processing of palm oil that would alleviate the problems facing producers.[87]

A third response for West African palm producers was to turn to palm kernel exporting, in order to use the increased returns from kernels to compensate for the fall in value of oil exports outlined above. Indeed, given that hitherto the kernel had been regarded as a waste product from the production of palm oil, its increasing use for export in this period might be regarded as an economy of production. Production of the kernels was relatively straightforward, albeit time-consuming. Instead of being disposed of as waste, the nut left once the pericarp of the fruit had been removed was dried in the sun and then cracked between stones to remove the kernel, with the husks then being used as fuel to help process palm oil. This was an extremely laborious process, however; one estimate suggested that to obtain 1 lb of kernels required cracking 400 nuts.[88] Given that the production of kernels was regarded as female work – as indeed in parts of Sierra Leone was the trade in kernels – it was women and children who carried the burden of this increase in output.[89]

As we have seen, as the European market for kernels developed in the late nineteenth century so exports from West Africa increased. The value of West African palm kernel exports to Britain rose until the 1880s while the German equivalent grew right through to the end of the century. In the British case, kernels never reached more than a small proportion of the values that palm oil imports did in this period, but for Germany kernel import values outstripped those of palm oil from the early 1880s.[90] Estimates for total West African exports of kernels are elusive but Manning suggests that 'Nigerian' exports to all parts stood at around 80,000 tons p.a. by the early 1890s, and Dahomey exports of kernels at 24,062 tons in 1894; Sierra Leone exports of kernels to all parts stood at 21,042 tons in 1895 and Gold Coast exports at 15,559 tons.[91] West Africa may be estimated as exporting at least 140,000 tons p.a. by the early 1890s.

In general palm kernels were produced by the same peoples who provided palm oil and were to be exported from virtually the entire coastline of the region. Some producers became particularly associated with the export of kernels. This was the case on the Windward Coast where the fruits of *elaeis guineensis* were characterised by thin pericarps and the exporting of kernels was thus especially appropriate; from 1861 the value of palm kernel exports substantially outstripped that of palm oil for Sierra Leone and this continued to the end of the century, with kernels ranking first in the colony's export values for most of this period.[92] Here the Galinhas country and the Sherbro hinterland became major centres for kernel exports.[93] On the Gold Coast, kernels never achieved the predominance they held in Sierra Leone, though Krobo and Akuapem producers developed considerable kernel exports from the late 1860s and some quantities were exported from Ahanta to the west.[94] In Dahomey, the value of palm kernel exports overtook oil in the 1880s, and grew by an average of 4 per cent p.a. until World War I; according to Manning the rapid increase in kernel exports was due to the faster increase in world prices of kernels over oil in this period.[95]

For the area of modern Nigeria, where the oil trade had its centre, kernel export values were slower to overtake oil exports, but had done so by 1900.[96] However, this fact masks important variations between producers. The major producers of kernels in the Nigeria area were the Yoruba, and Customs statistics for Lagos show the value of kernel exports exceeding palm oil from as early as 1867.[97] Here Yoruba producers, particularly in western Yorubaland, utilised slave labour to develop kernel exports from an early date; Ekiti producers also began to send kernels to the coast along the 'Ondo Road' from the 1870s.[98] To the east of the Niger, kernels were certainly being exported from the Delta from at least the 1860s and possibly earlier.[99] For the 1890s, the value of Delta palm kernel exports remained substantially lower than oil exports with producers clearly preferring to export oil over kernels; Latham calculates that the ratio of oil to kernel exports in the late 1880s stood at 1:1.4 tons at Old Calabar, compared to 1:2.7 at Lagos, though Martin stresses that in the Delta area in this period the proportion of kernels to oil exports continued to rise over time.[100]

This raises the question of why Igbo and Ibibio producers in what became eastern Nigeria saw advantages in concentrating their efforts, at least in this period, on oil rather than kernel exporting. Latham suggests that the higher ratio of kernels in Lagos exports might be accounted for by greater domestic consumption of oil among the Yoruba than among the suppliers of Old Calabar.[101] Martin stresses the availability of labour, and for kernels particularly female labour, as the vital factor; areas where such labour capacity was available were able to develop kernel exports more quickly than those without it. In the latter areas, kernel production could occur only at the expense of some other activity. The degree to which there was spare labour capacity would be determined by issues of competing demands for labour, the availability of transport, the availability of alternative supplies of foodstuffs, and the degree to which an area already concentrated on labour-intensive soft – as opposed to hard – oil production. These points are illuminating, but also of importance in explaining this phenomenon, at least initially, was the higher proportion of oil to be obtained from the fruit of oil palms east of the Niger compared to Yorubaland.[102]

The degree to which increasing kernel output compensated for the fall in oil prices for producers in the later decades of the century is difficult to assess with any precision, given the data. The trends in the export of oil and kernels between, say, 1870–4 and 1890–4, suggest that the increase in kernel output failed to compensate for falling prices. Comparing these two periods is difficult given the paucity of data, but it can be estimated that the overall trade in oil and kernels to Europe and the USA in the 1870–4 period was of a value of approximately £3m p.a., while for 1890–4 exports are unlikely to be much above £2.75m p.a.[103] These figures are broad estimates, but they suggest that palm kernel exports clearly helped to moderate the worst effects of the decline in prices for producers in the 1880s though they did little more. Overall, the increase in the value of palm kernel exports from West Africa after 1870 failed to compensate for the decline in returns from palm oil.

Moreover, this broad trend covered more particular difficulties for specific producers. Increasing kernel production was not costless, and Susan Martin stresses that the growth of kernel production had important implications for women in particular. Given that kernel production was regarded throughout the region as women's work, increased kernel output must have impinged severely on women's time for other activities. While this might have been alleviated by the fact that, unlike oil, palm kernels do not go rancid and can be stored to be processed at will, at the very least women's 'leisure' would have suffered. It is true that returns from kernel sales may have accrued to women and, if so, that the rise in kernel output would have offset the impact on women of the late nineteenth-century fall of prices – with by implication a corresponding increase in the impact of falling oil prices on men – but much depends on the degree to which women were able to keep the income from kernel sales for themselves. This no doubt varied from area to area and requires detailed local research; equally, information is required on how far men would have been able to insist on the priority of oil production at the expense of kernel output in this period. In short, while kernel production may have enabled some female producers to avoid the worst of the slump, kernel output would not necessarily have alleviated the pressures of this period for women.[104]

Clearly, therefore, the three reactions to falling prices taken by producers in the late nineteenth century helped lessen the worst effects of the slump, but did not eradicate them entirely. It can be suggested that the problems generated by the shift in the terms of trade facing West Africa from the 1870s onwards meant that this would have been a difficult time for palm producers and would have been reflected in increased pressures on labour to expand output, whether of oil or kernels or both. There was little way out of this trap for palm producers unless other crops could be substituted. Farmers would have worked longer and harder; women in particular would have faced increased burdens; and, as Lovejoy suggests, increased utilisation of slave labour would have been a major feature of these years. Even the production of palm kernels, while utilising a waste product and bringing in new returns for producers, was not costless. At the very least, kernel production would have impinged on producers' 'leisure' time and, at worst, could have happened only at the cost of some other activity or output. Thus, just at the moment that palm exports had become firmly established in the region's economy, producers faced major difficulties, with few easy ways out of these problems. Far from the technological changes epitomised by the arrival of the steamship inaugurating a new era of prosperity, the latter decades of the nineteenth century were a period of increasing strain for the palm products trade.

6   British traders and the restructuring of the palm products trade

The development of the steamship services between Britain and West Africa after 1852 led to major changes on the British side of the palm oil trade. These changes amounted to a major restructuring; it was at this time, as Zeleza suggests, that the old slaving organisation of the West African trade was abandoned.[1] As we have seen, this was a time of increasing difficulties for the trade. From the early 1860s oil prices began to fall, while from the mid-1870s the value of the trade began to decline, a process that culminated in the crisis of the 1880s. As the market shrank, this became a time of marked competitiveness for palm oil traders. This process was exacerbated by the changes in the trade generated by the establishment of the steamship services. The combination of price falls with the impact of the steamers meant that the late nineteenth century was to be a time of great stress for the oil trade; for established British traders in particular, it was to be a period of immense change and difficulty.

The reorganisation of the trade derived ultimately from the introduction of the steamship services. The steamers set in motion many changes, not least of which arose from their impact on British ports in the oil trade. On a general level, the steamship services concentrated the trade on Liverpool. As has been seen, Liverpool's pre-eminence in the African trade had come to be challenged by the emergence of traders from Bristol and London during the 1830s and 1840s; Liverpool's share of palm oil imports, calculated in terms of casks of oil, dropped from 96 per cent in 1830 to 68 per cent by 1850, albeit within a trade that was expanding overall.[2] Liverpool's relative decline continued after 1850, not least because the African Steam Ship Co. initially operated its services from London; London, Bristol, and, once the British & African began operating from there in 1869, Glasgow held significant shares of the trade to the 1870s. Even after the African Steam Ship Co. moved its operations from London in 1856, these ports retained an important share of imports; the years c. 1840–c. 1870, when the British palm oil market was expanding most rapidly, can be seen as the heyday of the satellite ports of London, Bristol, and Glasgow.[3]

Thereafter, however, the impact of the steamship services in the face of falling oil prices prompted a return to the older pattern of an African trade largely centred on Liverpool. By 1890, indeed, the oil trade was virtually entirely Merseyside-based. Glasgow was the first to disappear, with Glasgow firms like Taylor, Laughland, & Co. and William Couper & Co. moving their trade to Liverpool once the British & African ceased to operate from the Scottish port in 1874. London was next to go, in the early 1880s. Bristol, however, remained a palm oil port for much longer; indeed, Bristol remained the most important British oil port after Liverpool throughout these years, with its soap manufacturing and the South Wales tinplate industry continuing to flourish until the last decades of the century. However, by 1890 even Bristol had virtually disappeared from the trade, with R. & W. King, for example, operating increasingly from Liverpool as the century went on.[4] Only in the 1880s, with the development of palm oil imports into Hull, did this picture of the trade's concentration on Liverpool change; Hull's imports, however, remained small and may be assumed to be re-exports from Hamburg.[5]

The reason for the disappearance of the satellite ports from the 1870s lay, of course, in the decision of the two steamship companies to operate exclusively from Liverpool. The rationale for this move in turn lay in the demand for palm oil from Liverpool's industrial hinterland, but also important were the quicker turn-around times on Merseyside following the dock improvements of the middle of the century and the impact of changes in railway communications within Britain; the latter allowed palm oil to be transported relatively cheaply across the country. Critical, however, was the impact of falling prices on traders based outside Liverpool; as profit margins contracted, traders were driven to cut costs by exploiting the freight rate efficiencies of the steamship services from Liverpool.

This return to an older trend of British imports was not accompanied by a reversion to the early nineteenth-century pattern of Liverpool's African traders specialising in palm oil alone. Here too the steamship brought change. It was still the case that Liverpool remained the home of the palm oil specialist, while London and Bristol traders dealt in a variety of African products of which palm oil was but one, as late as 1855. However, once the steamship service began to operate from Liverpool, Merseyside traders were able to move away from their earlier specialisation in palm oil to trade in a variety of products. By 1880, only 6.3 per cent of Liverpool's voyages fitted the older palm oil specialisation, and the port's African traders had become what London's and Bristol's had always been – general African merchants.[6]

These changes were reinforced by shifts in sources of palm oil in West Africa. In the first half of the century, the bulk of Liverpool's oil came from the Niger Delta area. As table 6.2 suggests, however, the steamship services opened up the whole coast to Liverpool traders, so by 1880 Liverpool's oil

Table 6.1. *British palm oil importing ports, 1850–1890*

Year	Liverpool			London			Bristol			Glasgow		
	Number of voyages	Number of casks of oil	% of total casks	Number of voyages	Number of casks of oil	% of total casks	Number of voyages	Number of casks of oil	% of total casks	Number of voyages	Number of casks of oil	% of total casks
1850	45	30,833	68.6	25	6,605	14.7	15	7,537	16.8	—	—	—
1855	69	59,151	71.1	44	11,898	14.3	24	12,121	14.6	—	—	—
1860	75	42,959	64.0	47	11,057	16.5	18	12,377	18.5	1	680	1.0
1865	96	59,697	70.4	40	9,381	11.1	16	10,878	12.8	9	4,793	5.7
1870	97	48,788	72.3	62	6,514	9.7	12	8,829	13.1	12	3,350	5.0
1875	91	63,740	85.7	36	3,417	4.6	10	7,231	9.7	—	—	—
1880	79	71,447	83.0	16	5,221	6.1	14	9,459	11.0	—	—	—
1885	84	64,073	94.4	1[a]	0	0	5	3,767	5.6	—	—	—
1890	79	68,392	99.4	—	—	—	1	415	0.6	—	—	—

Note:
[a] Cargo not expressed in casks of oil.
Source: Customs Bills of Entry, 1850–90.

Table 6.2. *African origin of cargoes and casks of palm oil, by British port, 1880*

Origin	Liverpool		London		Bristol	
	Number of cargoes	% of Liverpool casks	Number of cargoes	% of London casks	Number of cargoes	% of Bristol casks
'Africa'	0	0.0	0	0.0	3	18.7
Windward and Ivory Coasts	198	8.5	1	0.1	4	33.2
Gold Coast	397	26.5	26	50.7	0	0.0
Slave Coast	163	11.9	15	28.1	0	0.0
Niger Delta	284	48.3	5	4.8	4	31.5
Cameroons – Angola	71	4.1	14	16.4	2	16.6
Miscellaneous[a]	5	0.7	0	0.0	0	0.0

Note:
[a] Cargoes from the Canary Islands.
Source: Customs Bills of Entry, 1850–90.

was coming from a much wider range of sources. Liverpool's traders still largely relied on the Delta, London's on the Gold Coast, and Bristol's on the Windward, Ivory, and South Coasts, but the older pattern was clearly changing, with Liverpool's traders now operating widely along the West African coast.

The concentration of Britain's palm oil trade on Liverpool was part of a wider trend that resulted from the establishment of the steamer services. The impact of the steamers was to eradicate alternative methods of organising the trade and mould it into a uniform pattern determined by the cost efficiencies of the steamship. By introducing a freight service and thereby divorcing shipping from trading on the coast for the first time, the steamship services brought the West African trade into line with the rest of Liverpool's commerce in the late nineteenth century.[7] But this meant that the methods of organisation that Britain's African traders had relied on since slaving – based on the integration of shipping and trading and using the single voyage to the coast executed by the trader himself – had become obsolete. New methods of organisation had to evolve and new techniques of trading for oil on the coast were necessary. In the long term this had serious implications for the way trading firms structured themselves.

At its simplest, the consequence of the introduction of the steamship was to generate a move 'from ship to shore' in the African trade.[8] The cost efficiencies resulting from the steamship services were most apparent where traders could base themselves in a land depot, bulk their oil to await the arrival of the steamer, and then send it to Britain as part of a regular service. The several systems of trading that had operated within the West African oil trade hitherto – ranging from the factory trade to coasting to the river trading of the Delta – were thus to disappear. The change had least impact on the factory trade, since this system of shore entrepôts where produce could be bulked on land in advance was precisely the one that suited the needs of the steamship most closely. Thus little changed on the Gold Coast where traders were able to send produce back to commission houses in Britain as they had always done. Equally, once Lagos – perhaps the most important new oil entrepôt of the second half of the century – expanded its oil trade after 1851, it developed an essentially factory system, with European and Krio traders establishing depots in the town.[9]

Coasting, however, saw important changes. Some traders, particularly those based outside Liverpool, continued for some time after the 1850s to utilise coasting for their oil trade. Coasting made sense for traders not prepared or able to operate through Liverpool and particularly for those trading in areas like the Ivory or Slave Coasts where deep-water ports were lacking. The most important of these coasters remained Bristol traders such as R. & W. King, who had utilised this method over many decades and had established themselves as the major British traders on the Ivory and Slave Coasts by the middle of the century.[10] It was clearly an effective technique even in the age of steam; 'Jerry' Langdon's evocative description of his coasting voyages in Kings' ships dates from the early 1880s, when the technique was clearly still a viable way of trading.[11] Indeed, as late as the 1890s, such Bristol traders had an important presence along the Ivory Coast and their 'floating factories' remained a major feature of the maritime scene in this region.[12] Yet, clearly for the long term there was little future in ignoring the advantages of steam. As the steamer service extended its number of ports of call and as permanent loading and unloading facilities came to be established along the coast, coasting traders found themselves being squeezed out of the oil trade. While local coasting networks, such as on the Liberian coastline where Americo-Liberian firms like McGill Bros. collected small quantities of oil to send to Europe on the steamships from Monrovia, did survive, by the end of the century coasting had entirely died out among British palm oil traders.[13]

The main impact of the steamship services lay in the heart of the oil trade, in the river trading system of the Niger Delta area. Here major changes not just in the organisation but also in the techniques of the oil trade were to be generated by the steamer services. The central result was the forcing of trade on to land during the third quarter of the century. By the end of the century trade in this area fitted closely the factory pattern to be found elsewhere in West Africa.

During these years, three institutions – none of them new to the trade – which particularly suited the efficiencies of the steamer services began to take on a central role in trading organisation in the Delta.[14] The first of these was the hulk. Once the steamer services removed the need for firms to use their own shipping, an alternative operating base to store oil and accommodate staff had to be found. While African authorities remained reluctant to allow European traders to take up residence on land, the answer lay in hulks. Hulks were obsolete ships towed out to West Africa to be moored in a river, dismasted, and covered over by thatch, or later zinc, roofing, and used as the base of operations for a firm for that river, 'like jaded horses unfit for service . . . turned out here to serve as amphibious stores till they can hold together no longer', in Crowther's words.[15] These could then act as combined residence, store, and trading depot, and on them oil could be bulked while waiting for the steamers.

Hulks had occasionally been used in the oil trade before the middle of the century, but by the mid-1850s they had become central to the organisation of the trade and could be found right across the Delta area and the Cameroons.[16] By the 1870s there were fourteen or fifteen in Bonny alone and another ten or eleven in neighbouring Elem Kalabari.[17] Nor were they limited to the Delta; hulks could be found right along the West African coast in the second half of the century and were to be the defining feature of the oil trade in these years.[18] 'It is a huge vessel', noted Whitford of one he visited in Bonny in 1873, 'very like an exaggerated Noah's-ark, anchored in the swift current, and it swings with the tide . . . the old-fashioned grand cabins, once the temporary homes of admirals, princes, and fair ladies . . . are now occupied by white carpenters, coopers, and junior clerks. Beneath the quarter-deck is the spacious old saloon, now converted into a trading hall.'[19]

The use of hulks was linked to a second change in the way oil traders operated in the Delta. Hitherto trading firms had relied on the ship's master or a supercargo to undertake their trade in West Africa. Again, the arrival of the steamer service ended this. In place of the supercargo attached to a single voyage firms appointed resident agents, accompanied by clerks, to be based on their hulks in the Delta, and to be responsible for all their trade in a river; when the agent returned to Britain at the end of the trading season a clerk would be left in charge of the hulk until the next year.[20] Resident agents were hardly new in the West African trade and had been used for centuries in areas like the Gold Coast where European traders had been able to become established on land. In the oil trade itself they existed in areas like the Cameroons and on Fernando Po from early on, but they remained very much the exception in the Delta before 1852. The arrival of the steamship services, however, made such resident agents the norm for the trade from the 1860s onwards.[21]

These figures were responsible for a firm's operations in a river; they were usually titled 'Captain' and acted with the powers of that post. Some became well known in the trade, such as Alexander Cowan, agent for Miller Bros. in Opobo in the 1880s, or Capt. R. B. N. Walker, agent for Hatton & Cookson on the South Coast in the 1860s.[22] They could often be very young; Harry Cotterell was twenty-three when he became agent for Tysons in Bonny in the 1860s.[23] Work for these agents involved a long day in the season, from 5.00 am to 6.00 pm each day.[24] King Eyo in 1855 complained 'that the white man bothered him too much, that he had no peace from them day or night from their repeated calls on him for oil'.[25] Observers stressed the monotony and boredom of work in the trade, with the sheer grind to find oil often generating the drunken and violent outbreaks to which such agents seemed prone.[26]

The development of the resident agent system markedly changed the character of the oil trade in the Delta. Most striking was the increase in numbers of Europeans compared to, say, the 1830s; Burton estimated that there were up to 1,000 Europeans living in the Delta in 1864, and probably a quarter of that stayed in the rivers out of season – another new departure.[27] Important in this was the development of malaria prophylaxis after 1854, which allowed Europeans to live in the Delta rivers without the high mortality rates that had hitherto restricted their numbers on the coast; also important was the steamers' capacity to repatriate sick employees as necessary.[28]

The reputation of these agents was certainly mixed. To one observer in 1868 they were 'the worst of drunkards, liars, whoremongers, gamblers, etc.', a view echoed in the complaint of one Bonny man in 1861 that 'white man come here, no teach we anything but rogue, they squeeze oil from we'.[29] For Johnston, the whites in the trade were 'drunken swine . . . utterly unscrupulous scoundrels', and 'ignorant, brutal men with a crew of ruffians who when drunk were like dangerous beasts'.[30] Yet for every R. B. N. Walker who flogged an African to death in Gabon in 1869, there were no doubt others who were models of sobriety and who regularly attended the mission churches that began springing up in Delta rivers in these years.[31]

Certainly by the later decades of the century, as life for traders in the Delta took on a degree of permanence, it did change in tone with references to libraries, billiard rooms, and even tennis courts, though the 'Calabar Literary Association' of 1864 may have existed only in Burton's imagination. Indeed, firms tried to look after their agents' comforts, with stewards, servants, and cooks provided, and 'Palm Oil Doctors', as they were termed, appointed to each river.[32] By the 1870s there were cases of agents bringing their wives out from Britain for the season.[33]

Yet while large communities of white traders were becoming permanent in the Delta rivers in these years the social distance between white and black was, if anything, increasing; as the steamers brought traders closer to Britain, they also drew traders away from African society. No doubt sexual liaisons across that distance continued as before but, as the white communities became larger, not least due to the presence of missionaries, and as occasional families joined agents on the coast, traders were less interested in building social relationships with Africans; this process was reinforced by the spread of racist attitudes within British society in these years. In this way the move from ship to shore was accompanied by the white trading community drawing in on itself. In the second half of the century there was to be no equivalent of John Tobin's relationship with Duke Ephraim.

From the development of hulks and consequently of resident agents, it was but a short step towards the third change in the Delta generated by the steamers, namely the development of on-shore factories. These had hitherto been rare in the Delta area but here too the river trade was brought into line with the rest of the coast.[34] Only in the Western Delta, where Horsfalls and Harrisons had factories on the Benin River, could they be found by the 1850s.[35] African authorities in the Delta remained reluctant to allow such factories on land; when one trader attempted to settle on land in Old Calabar in 1862 he was firmly resisted.[36] Yet cask houses had long been permitted and these increased in size with the growth of the trade as numbers of traders and their staffs proliferated; and as mission stations became established on shore, resistance to trading factories on land began to be eroded.[37] By the 1880s such resistance had virtually disappeared.

These factories were the homes of the staff of the trading firms and thus became centres of large expatriate African communities. These were the Kru, Krio, and Gold Coast populations that accompanied the oil traders and which were estimated to number some 2,000–3,000 in the Delta area in 1871.[38] Kru labour had long been used in the oil trade; from the middle of the century they were joined by coopers, carpenters, and cooks from the Gold Coast, trained in the Basle mission school in Accra and by increasing numbers of low-waged Krio employed as clerks to traders.[39] Kru were indispensable to the trade and in addition to the heavy labouring work they had always undertaken they became increasingly important as crew for traders' steam launches.[40] Fernando Po remained a major recruiting ground for these Kru, though the establishment of the steamer services meant that a regular supply of labourers could be obtained direct from the Kru coast.[41]

In practice the move from hulk to factory took place almost seamlessly as these trading communities became increasingly permanent over time. Hulks were de facto factories and were beached when they became particularly rotten, to become on-land stores and in time, shore bases for traders.[42] From this it was but a short step to building permanent factories. The 1870s marked the start of the move on to land for white traders in much of the Delta; in 1875 Dandeson Crowther noted in Brass 'specks of factories built in a row at nearly equal distances one from the other and each surrounded by well white-washed and decently kept cask houses . . . The Europeans trading here live . . . in storied houses substantially built and furnished.'[43] Elsewhere this took longer; though a number of traders were living on land in Old Calabar by the 1870s, in that river the move occurred in the 1880s.[44] By the 1890s, said Cowan, only half a dozen hulks were left in the Delta, and factories were everywhere to be found: eight in Old Calabar alone in 1890.[45]

By this time the organisation of the oil trade conformed to a broadly similar pattern along the whole West African coast. Clearly the steamship services had generated major changes in the organisation of the trade, and above all in the Niger Delta. Yet the move from ship to shore had little immediate impact on the techniques and practices of trading itself in the Delta. Initially, at least, the established system of using trust and barter and of relying on miscellaneous dashes to facilitate personal contacts survived.[46] Trust, in particular, despite several attempts to stamp it out by the consul, continued to be the bedrock of the trade until the 1880s.[47] As before the 1850s, the trade was still characterised by delays and disputes over debts, and traders still used local institutions like the Ekpe society in Old Calabar to regain their trust.[48]

Yet changes did come eventually as a result of the steamship service. Over the longer term the steamer services led to a regularising of the practices of the trade just as they had with the ways the trade was organised. For one thing, comey had to be recalculated because of the steamers; the old methods of charging comey according to tonnage of ship or number of masts clearly no longer could apply when one steamer carried oil for a plethora of traders; instead the trade moved towards applying a standardised charge on each puncheon of oil. By 1869 this had been set at half a crown for each ton of oil in Old Calabar.[49] Equally, the dashes and other charges traders were expected to pay to African brokers became increasingly regularised under the impact of the steamship.[50] The trade was moving away from its earlier unsophisticated nature.

A similar change came with the currencies used in the trade. The second half of the century saw considerable inflation in trade currencies, most particularly the cowries used in the Bight of Benin and on the Gold Coast, and in the iron bars used elsewhere. This inflation was due to the falling cost of supplying these currencies, not least because of the steamship services; in time, as well as causing problems in calculating comey due to depreciation in the bar, this began to undermine the barter system on which the oil trade had been based.[51] The result was a steady growth of cash payments. The turning-point in this came in 1880 when the British colonies in West Africa demonetised the silver dollar because of its depreciation in value; in 1889, the African Association, the largest oil firm, banned the use of barter and insisted on using cash transactions only in future.[52] The oil trade thus increasingly came to rely on paper receipts, or 'book', which the African broker would receive in lieu of his oil to redeem for goods at leisure.[53] In time traders turned to the use of British coins to pay for oil; hence the great increase in imports of coinage into the West African colonies in the 1880s and 1890s.[54] This was part of a wider move towards the ending of trust, which, with the move to a direct cash trade by the end of the century virtually, though by no means completely, died out.

The impact of the move from ship to shore generated by the steamship services can hardly be exaggerated. By the late 1890s the organisation and techniques of the oil trade fitted a broadly similar pattern right along the West African coast. This had wider implications for those operating in the palm oil trade, particularly the established, large-scale Liverpool traders. In themselves these changes in organisation and techniques caused difficulties and increased costs, by forcing traders to adapt their practices to stay abreast of a rapidly changing commerce. But more importantly, these changes eroded the advantages that the large-scale traders had hitherto relied on to restrict access to oil trading, in particular the capital barriers of shipping and trust which had helped these traders keep interlopers out. These barriers to entry disappeared quickly under the impact of the steamship services. Indeed, the elimination of such barriers was the major single consequence of the establishment of the steamship services. The result was that the 1850s–1870s saw an influx of new, smaller-scale traders, particularly into the trade's heart in the Niger Delta.

The steamship services opened the oil trade to these smaller-scale traders in a number of ways. Firstly, by providing freight space they meant traders no longer had to own, or charter, their own ships and the major capital barrier to participation in the trade had been removed at a stroke. Secondly, the speed of the steamer services meant turn-around times for a trader's capital were cut, meaning that smaller stocks could be held, thereby allowing smaller-scale traders to enter a trade where hitherto considerable capital sums in the form of goods and oil had had to be held for eighteen months or more. Thirdly, by calling at many more ports the services facilitated coast-wise trade, particularly for those traders prepared to operate at low margins on the periphery of the trade. Fourthly, by eroding the trust system and encouraging the move to a cash-based trade, they removed a further capital barrier; trust inflation had allowed established traders to keep rivals out of a river. Finally, traders no longer needed to be involved in importing goods in order to trade, and could specialise simply in exporting oil; small-scale traders benefited particularly from this ending of the vertical integration of operations that had hitherto been necessary to trade in oil.[55]

Central to this was the institution of the commission house, long established in parts of West Africa. Its role had been to enable small-scale traders without the resources to open establishments in Britain to enter the trade.[56] These commission houses found the steamships ideal in facilitating their business. Large numbers of commission houses began to operate in Lagos, and then in the Delta, as smaller-scale traders began to spread along the coast, using the steamer services to despatch their produce to Britain.[57] Numerous commission houses entered the palm oil trade in this period, of which Irvine & Woodward (later James Irvine & Co.) of Liverpool, John Holt's suppliers between 1867 and 1875, and John Walkden & Co. of Manchester, prominent in the 1870s and 1880s, were among the most notable.[58] Even long-established firms like Tobins felt the pull of this trend: it became a commission house, the Company of African Merchants, in 1863.[59]

The increase in numbers of commission houses was simply a symptom of the emergence of smaller-scale palm oil traders that occurred during the third quarter of the century. This influx was dramatic.[60] Immediately before the establishment of the steamship services there had been some twenty to twenty-five British traders involved in the palm oil trade, divided between the ten or so major firms which specialised in palm oil and the larger number of small-scale firms that entered the trade for short periods and which remained very much on its margins. As can be seen from table 6.3, the number of traders importing palm oil into Britain jumped markedly after 1852, with a particular increase in the late 1860s once the British & African began its operations. By 1880 the number of firms in the trade had increased by at least four-fold.[61]

A large number of these newcomers who emerged in the 1850s–1870s had just one or two cargoes of oil p.a. and were of limited importance for the trade. Others, however, such as A. & M. Herschell of Liverpool (established 1865), Banner Bros. & Co., Pinto Leite & Nephew, Lintott & Co., Brunnschweiller & Co., W. B. MacIver & Co., Pickering & Berthoud (established in Lagos in 1886), or Isaac Zagury, while remaining small-scale in their operations – usually only a dozen or so small cargoes of palm oil p.a. – became well-known names.[62] Many, indeed, went on to become major

Table 6.3. *Number of palm oil traders per British port, 1830–1880*

Year	Liverpool	London	Bristol	Glasgow	Total[a]
1830	10	9	2	—	21
1835	14	11	1	—	26
1840	16	11	2	—	29
1845	21	5	2	—	28
1850	12	11	3	—	26
1855	15	65	8	—	88
1860	78	42	7	1	106
1865	94	42	5	4	117
1870	135	28	4	6	150
1875	65	12	3	—	72
1880	64	66	3	—	105

Note:
[a] Traders operating from more than one port are counted only once.
Source: Customs Bills of Entry, 1830–80.

participants in the trade. They included Miller Bros. of Glasgow, which entered the African trade in the late 1860s, developed an important trade in Brass and Opobo and up the Niger during the 1870s, and were to become one of the largest palm oil firms of all, and John Holt & Co., which grew out of John Holt's store on Fernando Po in the 1860s and made its initial breakthrough by developing the South Coast trade before it, in association with George Watts, successfully made inroads into the Delta trade in the 1870s.[63] Other firms to emerge in these years and to go on to bigger things included Couper, Johnstone, & Co. of Glasgow, established in 1879 out of a number of Scottish firms trying to trade in the Delta and which made important inroads in Opobo in the 1880s; Taylor, Laughland, & Co. also of Glasgow, formed from businesses operating in the Delta, the Gold and Windward Coasts, and on the Congo in the 1850s and early 1860s; and G. B. Ollivant of Manchester, which began operating through Lagos in 1880 and Freetown shortly thereafter.[64]

A longer-established firm which began a very considerable expansion using the steamer services was F. & A. Swanzy, formed in the late 1840s though based on an existing trading enterprise on the Gold Coast, and, through its agent William Cleaver, very active in developing its trade along the Gold, Slave, and Ivory Coasts during the 1850s–1870s. Steam was central to its success, with the firm quick to use the steamship services and being one of the first to use steam launches, in its case to develop trade on the lagoons of the Ivory Coast.[65]

Many of the newcomers to the palm oil trade in these years were Sierra

Leonian Krio. 'Steam has also developed a goodly number of black traders', noted an observer in 1874.[66] These Krio were able to utilise the steamships and the commission houses to spread down the coast as traders during the 1850s and 1860s. 'Ever since the mail steamers were established, in 1852', noted one writer, 'they [educated blacks from Sierra Leone and Liberia] have availed themselves freely of the facilities thus offered, to trade at the various places on the coast at which the steamers call. As many as 150 per month of these native traders pass in the mail steamers between the different stations.'[67]

This Krio diaspora had a long history, of course, but with the steamship it took on a new momentum during the 1850s and 1860s. Lagos was an early destination, given the Yoruba origins of many Krio; so too was Old Calabar, where the first Krio arrived in 1854.[68] By the 1860s all the main Delta rivers as well as the Cameroons had Krio traders settled in them.[69] There were large numbers up the River Niger from the 1860s, with over forty Krio traders from Lagos still on the river in 1885.[70] Others could be found on the Slave Coast to the west of Lagos: S. B. Rhodes began his career at Agoué in the 1870s, while G. B. Williams was established at Danoe in 1875.[71] By the 1870s Krio palm oil traders could be found all along the West African coast.

Without this Krio presence the oil trade could not have expanded in the way it did in the 1850s and 1860s. Many Krio acted as clerical staff in the Delta for the big oil firms. Others became sub-agents for such firms, particularly in difficult areas such as the River Niger, where few European staff could be persuaded to operate. But the main role of Krio in the oil trade was as traders in their own right. Some were very small-scale, trading in only minute quantities, but many were prominent in the import–export sector as well as the retail trade of Lagos and Freetown. Solomon Macfoy, J. P. L. Davies, J. S. Leigh, Mohammed Shitta Bey, and Richard Blaize were but a few of the most prominent Krio oil traders.[72] Many owned steam launches for collecting produce, such as Leigh on the River Niger or Macfoy along the Sierra Leone coast, while John Ezzidio was involved in an abortive attempt in 1867 to establish a 'Niger Steam Ship Co.'.[73]

The steamship services provided an opportunity which the Krio were quick to exploit in the Delta area. In 1855, Peter Nicholls of Freetown was using the steamers to send oil from Old Calabar to Britain; a year later Daniel Hedd and John Robinson were doing the same, followed after another year by William Hazeley.[74] By this period a considerable number of Krio were involved in exporting oil on the steamers from the Delta area.[75] In the 1860s they were trading at Bonny; several then followed Jaja into Opobo in the 1870s.[76] On Fernando Po and from the Cameroons in the 1850s Krio were despatching oil by steamer; this was still the case in the

1880s.[77] Even as late as the 1880s, Krio were attempting to utilise the steamer services, and in so doing were helping African rulers to do so; S. B. Rhodes assisted Jaja in these years. Both Moses Ledlum and J. S. Leigh were still sending oil from Delta rivers to Britain in the early 1880s.[78]

Krio oil traders could be found elsewhere on the coast in the 1850s to 1870s. Lagos was a major centre of Krio enterprise in the oil trade; large numbers of Krio names appear in a list of Lagos exporters of palm oil as early as 1855. Krio in Lagos were giving credit to the Egba to collect oil from the interior that year and one Macaulay had a brig waiting in the port to collect palm oil to send to Freetown for onward despatch.[79] Richard Blaize was but one of the larger Krio traders trading in palm oil from Lagos by the 1870s; J. S. Leigh had a notable trade bringing oil from the Niger to Lagos in these years.[80] Numerous other Krio oil traders could be found on the Slave Coast, in Liberia, and on the Ivory Coast by this time.

The other group to attempt to exploit the steamer services from 1852 was the African merchant community of the Gold Coast. Dumett estimates that this group of traders numbered around twenty-five or so.[81] Such figures included William Ocansey, trading at Ada from the middle of the century, buying oil from the Lower Volta and selling to Millers and F. & A. Swanzy. He also shipped direct to Liverpool, using the steamers and a commission house, Hickson & Sykes. His attempt to obtain his own steam launch from Merseyside in the 1880s ended in failure.[82] Or there was Robert Ghartey of Winneba, Apam, and Anomabu, who developed an important trade in oil, and particularly kernels, in the 1860s and 1870s.[83] Similar were Robert Hutchinson of Cape Coast, George Blankson of Anomabu who traded through Forster & Smith, and Joseph Smith who also used Forster & Smith as his commission house until he went bankrupt in 1861.[84] Perhaps the most prominent in the 1860s and 1870s was John Sarbah, who had several stations along the coast, and developed a major trade in kernels using J. F. Hutton & Co. of Manchester and later Grimswade & Ridley as his commission houses.[85] At least in the 1850s–1870s, as the trade expanded, this group enjoyed considerable success.

Another group which increased their presence in the palm oil trade in the second half of the century – though this was only indirectly due to the British steamships – came from France and Germany. When Burton undertook his survey of the Delta area rivers in 1864 he found only one Spanish and one Dutch firm challenging the British traders.[86] Yet things were changing. Régis, Aîné, & Co. of Marseilles – formerly Victor et Louis Régis – had long been prominent on the Slave and Ivory Coasts, but now expanded their operations. By the mid-1850s they were well established in Lagos and by the 1860s around the Congo mouth.[87] They were soon joined on the coast by Daumas, Lartigue, & Co., and Augustin Fabre of Marseilles.[88] The key moment came when C. A. Verminck, prominent on the Windward Coast, moved into the Delta oil trade in the early 1880s.[89] These firms were quick to utilise the Fabre–Fraissinet steamship service from Marseilles after 1889.[90] French traders were joined by German oil firms. Woermanns of Hamburg – which began their steamer service to the coast in 1886 – were operating in the Cameroons by 1868, and Jantzen & Thormählen of Hamburg by 1875.[91] Similarly, Wilhelm O'Swald & Co. of Hamburg was central to the oil trade of Lagos from 1853; in 1869 it was taken over by G. L. Gaiser. Seven years later Witt & Busch had arrived in Lagos.[92] Nor should Dutch firms be ignored. Pincoffs & Kerdyk and the Afrikaansche Handels Vereeniging were prominent on the South Coast by the 1860s.[93]

The steamship services, in short, opened up the palm oil trade to the influx of new traders that occurred during the expansion of the 1850s through to the 1870s. The effect of this irruption was to increase competition, itself both the cause and the consequence of the fall in oil prices that set in from the 1860s. It was the longer-established traders who had the most to lose from this increased competition. As Boyle suggested in 1874 for the Gold Coast, the steamers 'worked mischief with the . . . leviathans'.[94] Livingstone noted as early as 1866 that the older firms which had developed the oil trade were in difficulties:

their large capital in ships, goods and experience gave them a monopoly of the trade . . . The monthly line of mail steamers has broken up the monopoly of the large traders . . . Business formerly was conducted on the principle of large profits and slow returns, but since the steamers furnished such facilities, great numbers of small black traders have sprung up whose motto evidently is small profits and speedy sales, many being satisfied with only 5 per cent profit.

'Steam has brought new firms and a keen competition', he added seven years later, noting that 'there are too many traders . . . for the yield of oil'.[95]

Warnings of the consequences of this competition could be seen as early as the 1850s on the Gold Coast where one observer spoke of how the steamship service was pushing profits down; Burton in 1864 made the same point for the Niger Delta.[96] The *African Times* spoke in 1862 of how 'competition there has, we are assured, already so reduced the profits that the West Coast is not . . . the Eldorado it once was'.[97] Further complaints referred to 'the insane competition' of the Niger trade in 1875.[98]

The fortunes of Krio traders in the 'savage trade war' of the 1860s–1880s reflect this competitive atmosphere.[99] From the start the Krio faced what can be termed 'the European trader's counterattack', with the seizure of their oil in Old Calabar in 1855, followed by the 1856 Court of Equity regulation which required all traders at Old Calabar to pay 20,000 coppers to be allowed to trade; this was a clear attempt, when added to the sharp increase in trust quantities in these years, to squeeze small-scale Krio

traders out of the river.[100] As Hedd noted, 'it appears to be the determination of all the supercargoes . . . in this river that none shall trade but such
as are able to do so with large vessels'.[101] Crowther recognised the implications. 'A Sierra Leone merchant hardly gets a place in Bonny, New Calabar,
and Brass', he wrote, 'they must prepare to encounter difficulties . . . their
opponents will try to undersell them so as to involve them in losses and so
drive them out of the river . . . the hatred borne against them is imaginable
. . . the Sierra Leone merchants will have much to do to maintain their
ground in these new fields.'[102]

Krio none the less did well in the 1850s and 1860s, but their success ebbed
as the trade began to be squeezed from the 1870s. One small-scale African
trader in Old Calabar, admittedly not a Krio, complained in 1871 that
supercargoes 'do not allow us, African traders, to ship our palm oil by
steamers to England. We see the steamers coming out and going home; but
alas, we find that they were not built for us . . . but for the use of the supercargoes.' 'A Voice from Calabar Beach' stressed that European traders were
trying to drive the Krio out of the river in 1874; Krio could not join the
Court of Equity, they were physically attacked by traders, their cargoes
were delayed by the steamers, and the native authorities were bribed to
expel them. The *African Times* spoke in 1874 of supercargoes 'frustrating
as far as possible every effort of Sierra Leone traders to purchase oil and
ship it to England'; Krio were 'altogether excluded from the advantages of
steam communication'.[103] Moses Ledlum complained at his oil being seized
in 1882 by Couper, Johnstone, & Co.'s agent in Bonny, while S. B. Rhodes
complained at his trade in Opobo being stopped by the consul in 1887.[104]
On the Niger the establishment of the Royal Niger Co. in 1886 and its introduction of a trading licence system meant the end of the Krio traders there.
There had been forty Krio traders on the Niger in 1885; ten years later,
noted MacDonald, there was 'not one single outside trader'.[105] The final
blow came with the creation of the Elder Dempster–Woermanns shipping
ring and the deferred rebate system of 1895 which tied up small-scale
traders' capital for several months in an interest-free loan to the shipping
companies. It was a system that clearly discriminated against Krio in favour
of the large-scale traders.[106]

Yet it would be wrong to see this counterattack as the only cause of the
difficulties Krio traders faced. On the contrary, as was the case on the Gold
Coast where the African trading community flourished to the 1870s, Krio
could and did succeed despite the assaults from supercargoes. What
affected the Krio, however, was the contraction of the trade from the mid-
1870s and more particularly the sharp deterioration in the 1880s. Small-
scale traders, without access to capital reserves, found it difficult to survive
through this crisis. Thus many Krio were driven out of the trade and were

reduced to becoming clerks for European firms or petty merchandise traders in their own right.[107] Similar experiences faced African traders on the Gold Coast, who by the 1870s were also being relegated to 'petty traders and agents to large European firms'.[108] Indeed, even those Gold Coast African traders who did survive managed it while being driven out of the direct trade between Africa and Britain to become, in effect, brokers, collecting oil from producers inland to sell to locally based European firms to despatch to Liverpool.[109]

Such intense competition caused difficulties for all in the trade but by and large these could be accommodated as the value of the oil trade continued to grow. The problems, however, set in from the late 1870s as values plunged. It was at this time that the competition initiated by the steamer services combined with the slump in the trade to cause significant difficulties for all traders and set in motion major changes in business organisation and the structure of the trade. This could be seen particularly with the impact on the larger oil firms.

It was the 'leviathans' which had faced the greatest changes with the influx of newcomers after 1852. The biggest eight Liverpool firms had provided around 62 per cent of Britain's palm oil imports in 1850; if Kings of Bristol, the other major importers, are included, the total provided by this group reaches 74 per cent.[110] The threat posed by the opening up of the trade represented a serious challenge, made worse once the value of the trade began to contract from the 1870s. These firms faced, in Newbury's words, 'a search for commercial security'.[111] 'It is not a trade for nervous people to be engaged in', wrote Holt of palm oil, and for the major firms like Horsfalls, Harrisons, and Stuart & Douglas, which had dominated the trade from the days of sail, these were difficult times indeed.[112]

The increased competition after 1852 meant that the large-scale firms had to change if they were to survive. The obvious response for these firms was to cut costs. Hence the numerous attempts from the 1860s to reduce prices paid to Africans for palm oil, often by stopping trade, but which led to violence in return. Similarly they attacked adulteration, particularly by the 1880s, devising new ways of detecting pollutants in oil and among kernels and urging the colonial government to act where it could.[113] But such measures were limited in effect and, as Holt noted, prices could hardly be driven lower by the late 1880s.[114]

Another way to cut costs after 1852 was to use the steamship services. Yet this was not as easy as it appeared, not least because these traders owned long-established sailing fleets. What was to happen to these ships? Some of the older firms continued to rely on sail for their transport. Bristol traders, for example, still used sail in the 1880s for coasting and even on river voyages to the Cameroons. Sail indeed still made sense for low-value coarse and bulky goods, and even in the Delta it continued to be used by oil traders as late as the 1870s. One firm, Harrisons, still used some sailing ships for their trade as late as 1888.[115]

Other firms tried to develop their own steamship fleets rather than rely on the steamer services; Hatton & Cookson bought their first steamship in 1871 and abandoned sail over the next six years.[116] Harrisons moved into operating their own steamships too, as did Miller Bros.[117] Other firms chartered steamers on an individual basis, like Taylor, Laughland, & Co.[118] One attempt to develop a rival steamship service by oil traders came with John Holt's moves in the mid-1890s.[119] In practice, however, the savings to be gained by using the steamer services were such that few established oil traders could afford to ignore them in the long term. Harrisons sold their fleet in 1890, followed by Hatton & Cookson in 1891.[120] By the 1890s virtually all the large-scale oil firms were reliant to a greater or lesser extent on the steamship services.[121]

Yet relying on the steamer services had important costs, for it necessitated the established firms changing their operations in West Africa accordingly; the savings in shipping costs were followed by increased investment in shore facilities. Moreover, using the steamer services meant of course that they lost many of the competitive advantages they had hitherto relied on in the oil trade vis-à-vis smaller-scale interlopers. While still having economies of scale, they were now effectively trading on an equal basis with these smaller-scale traders, who, operating on smaller profit margins, based perhaps in only one port on the coast, reliant on close knowledge of the local market, and using the steamer services, faced fewer risks. In short, using the steamer services was not a means of maintaining the status quo and still meant major changes for the established firms.

The alternative response for the 'leviathans' in face of the competition after 1852 was to increase returns by increasing the volume of their trade. Thus these firms ceased to specialise in palm oil alone but became traders in a variety of African produce. Hatton & Cookson is a good example of a firm that flourished by developing an extensive trade in a variety of produce from the South Coast in these years.[122] Where Tyson, Richmond, & Jones, a palm oil specialist, had been typical of the 1840s and 1850s, Hatton & Cookson, general merchants, were to be so for the 1870s, 1880s, and later.

This meant looking outside the Delta. Thus the established traders began to consider new areas of the coast as a source of oil and of produce more generally as prices began to fall. Partly this generated a more intensive utilisation of existing but less important areas in the trade, as in attempts to develop the Volta in the 1870s.[123] It also involved developing new areas like the South Coast where Horsfalls and Hatton & Cookson were joined in the 1860s and 1870s by a number of large-scale traders like Stuart & Douglas,

Taylor, Laughland, & Co., James Irvine & Co., and others; John Holt was perhaps the best-known trader operating on the South Coast in these years.[124] Monteiro saw the consequence of this when he noted the numerous Liverpool factories on the South Coast in 1873.[125]

With the move to open new sources of oil came the use of steam launches to open up creeks and rivers. Possibly the first traders to use steam in this way on a regular basis were Harrisons, which were using a launch on the Benin River as early as 1856.[126] Thereafter more and more firms began to invest in these launches, particularly from the 1870s as the technology became more reliable. James Pinnock was using one in the Western Delta in 1870.[127] Taylor, Laughland, & Co. were using steam launches right across the Delta by that year.[128] By 1873 so were Miller Bros.; their *Sultan of Socatoo* was being used for establishing factories in 'unfrequented localities'.[129] Steam launches were particularly common on the Niger by this time while George Watts used a steam launch to open up the Kwa Ibo River in the 1880s to great effect.[130] Launches were also used extensively on the South Coast by Hatton & Cookson by the 1880s, particularly up the Congo and Ogowe, and by Swanzy on the Ivory Coast.[131]

Yet the changes in trading techniques that were pursued by the established British traders after 1852 were not cost-free. New parts of the coast required additional investment in shore facilities and steam launches, fresh contacts to be developed, and further risks to be taken. This was required at a time of falling prices and a contracting market. Nor did these changes solve the problems facing the established traders, for prices continued to fall and from the late 1870s the trade began to contract severely.

Newbury's estimate that the slump of the 1880s resulted in a fall in trade values of some 20 per cent was reflected in concerns expressed in the coastal press in the early 1880s and in references by individual traders to a 'crisis'.[132] Profit margins were being sharply squeezed as the trade contracted during the 1880s in the face of these competitive tensions.[133] As one observer in Sierra Leone noted in 1885, 'the fair profits of the good old days can never return', because, he argued, there were too many firms in the trade.[134] 'It is a pitiful sight to see merchants squabbling and fighting over a trade which is at the lowest point on record, worthless at the moment to any man', wrote Holt in 1886.[135] By the 1880s profit margins were falling sharply; for oil firms the slump of the 1880s represented a major crisis.

For the established British traders, this decline was a turning-point in the way they traded for oil in West Africa. The methods that they had followed to deal with the increased competition since the coming of the steamship were no longer sufficient in the face of this crisis. They would have to pursue major changes in trading techniques and in business organisation if they were to stay in the trade. The attempts by European firms at price cutting, removing adulteration, finding new supplies, and utilising steam launches all proved inadequate in the face of this slump. More radical measures had to be found. These pressures drove the European firms to major changes in their trading organisation.

It would be wrong to suggest that all of the established firms faced the abyss in the 1880s. Some did well in this period, but all had to adapt their methods and organisation to survive. Hatton & Cookson, for example, were to survive this period through to the 1920s, but did so because of their rigorous development of the South Coast trade; they also benefited from the emergence of the new generation, Thomas and Edward Cookson, who took over the firm in the late 1860s.[136] Stuart & Douglas were another firm that had emerged in the first half of the century. They had six factories across the Delta by 1884 and were the second largest traders in the area by 1889. Their success lay in their early move to Opobo and their rapid development of the oil trade from that port.[137] These were firms prepared to innovate and whose operations were characterised by enterprise and a willingness to take risks.

What the palm oil firms were facing by the 1880s was the obsolescence of the older, family-based business structures with which the pioneers had developed the trade in the first half of the century. The family structure had many advantages, not least in the ability to utilise savings from family members. However, in the face of the problems of the 1880s, the changes in trading techniques and the sharp fall in prices, palm oil firms needed to raise considerable sums of capital to invest in order to survive; families were not always best placed for this. Horsfalls, one of the very creators of the palm oil trade, had shown the limitations of the family structure in the 1870s. They had tried to keep up with the changes in the trade during these years but found the costs so great that they left the African trade in 1875.[138]

Other firms were driven from the trade by the pressures of these years. R. & G. Benn, Wilson & Dawson, and Tyson, Richmond, & Jones were but some of the long-established names that disappeared in this period. For many firms this withdrawal was the result of inevitable generational change in a trade that relied heavily on the individual trader's experience and knowledge; as traders retired their businesses were sold. Other firms left the trade for more obvious reasons, going bankrupt or being taken over in the face of the depression. Such failures of firms were nothing new. Forster & Smith had left the trade in the 1860s, with the impact of the steamer services given the blame.[139] The Company of African Merchants was another to go, becoming part of the British & Continental African Co. Ltd in 1873.[140] But as the trade contracted from the mid-1870s, a shake-out of palm oil firms occurred. John Capper & Co. failed in 1880 and Irvine & Woodward in 1881, while Isaac Zagury was taken over by Henry Tyrer in

1883 and F. & A. Swanzy by Millers in 1894.[141] Moritz Herschell went
bankrupt in 1886, and the British Congo Co. in 1888–9, with perhaps the
most significant failure of these years being Taylor, Laughland, & Co. in
1896; four years later W. B. MacIver followed them.[142]

These pressures led some traders to establish joint stock companies as a
way of raising capital. The Tobin family had been one of the earliest to do
this. In 1863, when the younger brother, Thomas, died, the Tobin business
was merged with several others, including the Huth, Gruning, and
Castellain businesses, as the Company of African Merchants, with James
Tobin, Thomas' son, as managing director.[143] The new firm tried to develop
the South Coast trade and act as commission house for the Krio in the
trade. The 1860s saw several other joint stock companies emerge in the
trade, such as the London & African Trading Co. Ltd, and the West African
Company Ltd.[144] These became more common as time went on. The British
& Continental African Co. Ltd, which took over the Company of African
Merchants, was another, as was the United African Co. Ltd, created in
1879, and Couper, Johnstone, & Co. Ltd also formed in 1879, out of several
Glasgow firms.[145] The year 1885 saw the British Congo Co. Ltd launched,
while Hatton & Cookson became a private limited liability company in
1901.[146]

The move towards joint stock companies reflected the ongoing changes
in the palm oil trade and the need to raise capital to adapt to them. The
years from the late 1870s were clearly a difficult time for oil traders and
those that remained in the trade faced, in Newbury's words, 'a crisis in commercial organisation' if they were to survive the slump.[147] Not only were
firms being driven away from the unsophisticated, family-based structures
that had characterised the trade in its early years, but they were also being
impelled towards combinations and amalgamations.

Pooling and price fixing agreements were the first step along this road.
Under these agreements all the produce in a particular river was pooled and
the proceeds divided out by agreed shares; this thereby removed price
competition and enabled British traders to force down the prices paid to
African brokers. An early attempt at establishing such an arrangement in
Old Calabar in 1874 failed.[148] The 1880s saw further efforts including one
in Opobo.[149] Another attempt at Old Calabar in 1883 between the six major
traders in the river was successful, at least initially, and survived for a
number of years. As with all such combinations, however, it proved difficult
to maintain in the face of a firm determined to break it; the 1883 scheme
broke down in 1887 due to Harrisons' withdrawal and the arrival of Miller
Bros. in the river.[150] Further attempts at pooling in the Delta area were tried
in 1895 and 1900.[151]

The limited effectiveness of pooling pushed the larger traders towards the more radical step of amalgamation. Following the emergence of the United African Co. on the Niger in 1879, amalgamations were being urged for the Delta from the early 1880s, particularly by John Holt and George Miller.[152] For Holt and Miller the logic of the contraction of the market made some form of amalgamation inevitable. Plans were suggested for a merger of the major oil firms with the Royal Niger Co. in the late 1880s but these collapsed, not least because of the opposition of the shipping services orchestrated by A. L. Jones.[153] Instead, in 1889 the nine largest firms in the Delta area – Thomas Harrison & Co., the British & Continental African Co., Couper, Johnstone, & Co., Hatton & Cookson, Holt & Cotterell, R. & W. King, Stuart & Douglas, Taylor, Laughland, & Co., and George Watts – merged their businesses to form the African Association Ltd of Liverpool with nominal capital of £2m.[154] Harrisons, the largest firm in terms of produce traded in the Niger Delta at amalgamation, were the effective centre of the company and nominated the chairman of the new enterprise, Stanley Rogerson.[155]

This merger encompassed only their Delta area businesses, but the African Association was to be the giant in the oil trade after 1889 and one of the very biggest players in the African trade as a whole. Its only real rival after 1889 was the Royal Niger Co. on the Niger, but it had a stranglehold over the Delta oil trade with twenty-seven factories in 1890. Only Miller Bros., of major Delta oil firms, stood outside it.[156] Besides Millers, only a few very minor, small-scale firms like Ditchfield or Pinnock survived in the Delta, and Pinnock's Delta business was to be taken over by the Association in 1906, while Ditchfield went bankrupt in 1893. With these exceptions the African Association remained the dominant firm in the palm products trade; its success marked the degree to which the trade had become concentrated, and centred in particular on Liverpool. The company was to go on to become one of the major components of the African & Eastern Trade Corporation in 1919 and the United Africa Co. after 1929.[157] The slump of the 1880s had shaken out the firms in the oil trade.

The amalgamation of the African Association in 1889 was the inevitable result of the pressures that had been generated by the changes in the oil trade by the establishment of the steamship services and the slump of the 1880s. Its creation marked the end of an era, dominated by the family-based firms that had pioneered the oil trade in the early decades of the century. It represented a major restructuring of the trade. Clearly the trade had gone through major changes following the arrival of steam, of which the establishment of the African Association was but the culmination. The trade that emerged at the end of this period, in which the joint stock company was common and the African Association dominant, was a very different one indeed to that which had existed in 1850. The opening of the trade and the ensuing competitive tensions had set in motion deep-seated changes in its commercial structure. These changes led to a transformation of the organisation, methods, and business structures of the oil trade. The trade in which the African Association was the dominant force after 1889 was a very different one to that which John Tobin and other ex-slavers had developed after 1807.

7   African brokers and the struggle for the palm products trade

The second half of the nineteenth century was to be a difficult time for the brokers of the palm oil trade. If the early part of the century was a period of growth and prosperity for brokers, the later decades were to be much more mixed. Partly these difficulties were due to the impact of the fall in oil prices after 1861 but partly, too, they were due to the changes generated in the organisation of the trade by the steamship services. The commencement of the steamship services in 1852 brought as many changes on the African side of the export trade as it had on the British. While facilitating the expansion of oil exports across much of the region and thereby confirming palm oil's place in West Africa's economy, the steamer services also set in motion changes that raised questions about the future structure of the trade and the place Africans were to hold in it.

As we have seen, these were years of considerable growth in the volume – and until the mid-1870s, the value – of palm oil exports from West Africa. This growth in exports must have had an important impact on those sectors of West Africa involved in the export trade in the second half of the century. While there is little precise evidence to show price levels on the coast, it can be suggested that incomes of palm producers and brokers would be likely to have grown while the values of the trade continued to expand. This can be seen reflected in the corresponding growth in import values for West Africa in this period. Again, reliable figures are difficult to come by, but Eltis and Jennings calculate an increase in Africa's Atlantic imports between the 1820s and 1860s from £10.6m to £41.3m – a remarkable jump, though less than the increase in world trade in this period.[1] Equivalent estimates are not available for the period after the 1860s, but some measure of the rise in import values for West Africa can be seen in the increase in the value of Lagos' imports from £77,933 in 1862 to £500,828 by 1890.[2] While Eltis and Jennings' conclusion that in 1860 'most Africans were feeding, clothing, and sheltering themselves . . . without overseas economic exchange' carries much weight even for later in the century, clearly the growth in import values for West Africa by 1900 shows that large parts of the region had become increasingly integrated into the international economy.[3]

Table 7.1. *Origin of British palm oil imports, 1850–1890 (% of total casks)*

Year	'Africa'	Windward and Ivory Coasts	Gold Coast	Slave Coast	Niger Delta	Cameroons – Angola
1850	31.6	2.6	10.5	1.5	51.9	1.8
1855	17.7	3.9	6.1	8.3	59.6	4.5
1860	15.9	4.6	3.6	15.4	56.8	3.7
1865	15.5	3.6	5.1	8.6	63.3	3.9
1870	16.8	3.8	8.9	9.1	56.0	5.3
1875	10.9	6.3	18.1	6.7	55.6	2.4
1880	2.1	10.7	25.3	11.7	43.9	6.2
1885	2.4	10.5	19.6	16.3	43.4	7.8
1890	0.6	13.6	18.3	17.3	43.3	6.9

Source: Customs Bills of Entry, 1850–90.

Underlying this was the centrality of palm oil production and exporting to the economy of large parts of West Africa. This can be seen in the fact that the increase in palm product exports in the second half of the century was accompanied by changes in the distribution of the trade in West Africa. Firstly, there was a considerable expansion in the number of ports exporting palm oil. By calling at numerous ports on their voyage along the coast, the steamship services facilitated the opening up of new areas to palm oil exporting: the number of ports exporting oil to Britain rose from 14 in 1850 to 133 by 1885, with the major increase coming after the introduction of the British & African's services in 1869.[4] This is contrary to the view that stresses that the economics of the steamship services led to a concentration of the trade on to a small number of ports; this clearly happened, but not until the turn of the century. Given that many of these new ports were producing small quantities, this remains only a superficial measure of the change in the trade but it is still clear that a wider area of West Africa was participating in the oil trade in the second half of the century than had been the case before 1850.

Secondly, this was accompanied by changes in the relative distribution of exports. As noted above, the Niger Delta area had hitherto been the heart of the palm oil trade, at one time producing up to 90 per cent of British imports.[5] In the second half of the century as the steamship services became fully operational, this changed. As table 7.1 suggests, the Delta area remained the major source of oil after 1850, producing around half of Britain's supplies, but its share was clearly reduced from the predominance it once held, as other parts of the region like the Windward and Ivory

Table 7.2. *Casks of palm oil from selected Niger Delta area ports,*
1850–1890 (% of total British imports)

	1850	1855	1860	1865	1870	1875	1880	1885	1890
Fernando Po	1.1	8.6	0.5	0.8	2.9	0.9	0.6	0.7	0.6
Old Calabar	17.4	10.7	6.9	12.3	16.2	9.8	10.0	8.6	6.4
Opobo	—	—	—	—	1.2	4.5	8.5	6.5	10.2
Bonny	24.7	30.2	34.3	30.0	26.1	28.8	10.5	5.8	4.6
Elem Kalabari	2.4	2.3	4.9	5.0	0.7	1.4	3.4	4.4	1.9
Akassa	—	—	—	—	—	0.3	4.5	6.9	3.5
Brass	—	5.0	4.1	7.2	2.7	2.4	2.3	2.3	1.7
Benin	3.3	2.8	5.5	8.0	5.6	5.1	4.0	5.3	3.9

Source: Customs Bills of Entry, 1850–90.

Coasts became increasingly important. Indeed, for British imports, the Delta was the only area to decline in relative terms in the second half of the century, while other areas increased, in the case of the Slave Coast quite spectacularly.

Even within the Delta area, there were important changes in the distribution of palm oil exports. Table 7.2 shows that Bonny remained the major single supplier for Britain until around 1880. The secession of Opobo in 1869 clearly did not have much of an immediate effect on Bonny's position, at least until the late 1870s.[6] It was only thereafter that Bonny went into sharp decline – in terms of its proportion of British imports – to be replaced by Opobo, Akassa, Elem Kalabari, and elsewhere, though none of these ports was to achieve the position within the British trade once held by their predecessor.[7]

These changes in the relative importance of West African ports were related to the emergence of new oil producers within the region during these years. This was, for example, the period in which the Galinhas country on the Windward Coast was fully drawn into 'legitimate' trade and emerged as a major exporter of palm produce from the Moa and Mano Rivers; the increase in exports from the Windward and Ivory Coasts after 1850 noted in table 7.1 was to a considerable extent accounted for by the Galinhas. Palm produce exports also sharply increased from the Sherbro area from the middle of the century, where the spread of Krio traders facilitated the bringing of produce down the rivers of its hinterland.[8] On the Slave Coast, it was the period from around 1850 that saw Dahomey fully established as a major exporter of palm products as Fon producers turned increasingly to the trade, while the British attack on Lagos in 1851 coincided with the growth of significant exports of palm produce from Yoruba farmers of the interior.[9] Similarly, along the South Coast, the trading frontier in this period was pushed deep inland as palm products began to be produced increasingly for the export market, even from the River Congo. On the Loango coast specifically, the period from around 1860 saw the ending of the slave trade and the rapid growth of oil exports with the arrival of the steamer services and of American, British, and particularly Dutch firms. Palm oil began to be collected from the Vili of the Loango plain and from Bungu and Kakongo villages near the Chiloango River from where it was transported to Landana, the major palm export port of this area after 1860.[10]

In area after area, it was the second half of the century that saw palm production for export firmly established at the centre of the economy of West Africa. Eltis and Jennings estimate that palm product and groundnut exports amounted to three-quarters of the value of all African exports to the Atlantic world in 1860, with the value of palm oil equal to the value of the slave trade at its peak.[11] Even as late as 1900, when West Africa's exports had become much more diversified, palm products accounted for 73 per cent of the value of Nigeria's exports to all parts, 50 per cent of Sierra Leone's, and 38 per cent of the Gold Coast's.[12]

On the face of it, therefore, the second half of the century was a flourishing period for those West Africans involved in the palm products trade. Yet despite the apparent prosperity, this was a time of considerable strain for the established brokers of the West African coast. Given the lack of evidence of the prices and profit margins on which brokers operated – which makes it difficult to establish how far they were able to pass on price cuts to their suppliers – it has to be assumed that the fall in value of the palm products trade after the mid-1870s would have hit brokers' incomes significantly. Moreover, this period, as has been seen, was one of major change in the organisation of the European side of the oil trade and the ramifications of this were to reach deep into the broking structures of West Africa. The long-term consequence of the arrival of the steamship services was to undermine the role of the established coastal broker. On the one hand, the steamship service helped speed the opening up of the coast to new groups, like the Krio, who implicitly posed a challenge to the existing brokers' position in the trade. On the other, the move 'from ship to shore' generated a greater European trading presence on land and raised basic questions about whether there was any need for a broking network at all. This threatened the place of the brokers of West Africa. Would this group survive to become the capitalist class that would transform West Africa's economy?[13] Or would they disappear under the challenges they faced? For how long

could their so-called middleman role survive in the face of the technological and economic changes that accompanied the increased British presence
on the coast after 1852?

Coastal brokers faced these threats to their role in the trade at the same
time as they coped with the massive expansion in the volume of oil and
kernel exports from West Africa that occurred in this period. This expansion posed its own problems of organisation and adjustment; the point has
often been made that the capacity of coastal brokers to handle these huge
quantities of oil and kernels after 1850 – and manage the labour and transport these required – is a major tribute to their skill and enterprise. That
they were able to do this while simultaneously facing fundamental challenges to their very role as brokers is even more a sign of the sophistication
of the trading structures they had developed over the previous two centuries.

For the broking system of West Africa this was a period of great changes.
The steamship services widened access to the market and thereby threatened all those – broker as much as trader – who had prospered from existing commercial relationships. In a number of areas, such as Lagos, the Gold
Coast, Sierra Leone, and the Niger Delta, new groups were to seize the
opportunities provided by steam to establish themselves as brokers in palm
produce. In Lagos the expansion of oil and kernel exports in these years was
related to the quickening influx of Krio into the port after the British attack
in 1851. These groups were the 'Saros', returned Yoruba freed slaves from
Sierra Leone, and the 'Amaro', returned Yoruba from Brazil, both of which
had been arriving in Lagos since at least the 1840s. Within a matter of years
these newcomers were prospering in the oil trade; by the last quarter of the
century several, such as J. S. Leigh, J. W. Cole, Mohammed Shitta Bey, or
R. B. Blaize, were wealthy entrepreneurs running successful businesses.[14]

These Krio entrepreneurs initially entered the direct export trade to
Europe, using the steamship services to transport and commission houses
to sell their oil and kernels. Such Krio played a central role in the growth
of the palm produce trade from Lagos from the 1850s and flourished in the
third quarter of the century. Their success was based on contacts among the
Yoruba of the interior, from whom they bought palm oil and kernels. This
palm produce was purchased in the markets of Ikorodu, Epe, Leckie,
Artijere, Ejinrin, and others located just outside Lagos and which sat at the
termini of the trade routes via Abeokuta or Ijebu Ode from the interior;
other Krio moved westwards to buy palm produce in the markets of
Badagry, Addo, and Porto Novo.[15] Yet others developed an important
trade with the River Niger until 1886, in the case of figures like Leigh,
through the use of steam launches; others brought oil overland from the
river.[16]

Table 7.3. *Lagos, Gold Coast, and Sierra Leone palm kernel exports to all parts, 1855–1895*

Values in £, figures rounded to the nearest £.

Year	Lagos	Gold Coast	Sierra Leone	Year	Lagos	Gold Coast	Sierra Leone
1855	NA	11	10,935	1876	331,854	67,645	87,075
1856	NA	—	15,831	1877	358,592	62,625	145,280
1857	NA	—	10,010	1878	317,951	48,706	112,676
1858	NA	—	11,320	1879	319,445	53,115	113,993
1859	NA	—	8,057	1880	346,147	101,666	107,221
1860	NA	18	27,065	1881	221,633	47,508	104,941
1861	NA	—	34,106	1882	261,184	50,317	101,164
1862	70	—	36,367	1883	278,303	61,543	81,578
1863	25,274	—	48,035	1884[a]	327,347	403,876	68,377
1864	NA	—	17,544	1885[a]	282,293	335,117	76,802
1865	19,150	—	28,586	1886	255,422	47,830	86,365
1866	61,685	—	48,234	1887	266,940	41,613	76,884
1867	221,304	—	37,764	1888	314,885	68,525	97,177
1868	240,692	7,355	97,453[b]	1889	239,987	62,542	105,963
1869	324,414	38,881	107,342	1890	319,286	78,432	107,827
1870	215,300	22,035	50,052	1891	341,349	89,589	157,457
1871	288,622	7,323	112,239	1892	260,109	103,295	141,492
1872	223,712	5,874	69,152	1893	436,056	183,910	147,676
1873	193,720	NA	104,765	1894	440,066	112,373	154,138
1874	273,719	NA	86,143	1895	320,434	93,385	155,605
1875	287,111	47,252	90,905				

Notes:
[a] Gold Coast figures for these years include Lagos.
[b] Sierra Leone figures from 1868 include exports from Sherbro and Isles de Los but exclude exports between these ports and Freetown.
NA: Figures not available.
Source: CO 100/11–/45; CO 151/1–/33; CO 272/32–/72.

The 1860s, says Gertzel, were the heyday for the Krio, but thereafter they were increasingly squeezed out of the export trade.[17] This was particularly so during the 1880s when the fall in prices hit profit margins, concentrated the trade in the hands of a few European firms, and drove the smaller-scale traders out of business; by 1886, said Moloney, only Williams Bros. of the Lagos Krio traders still dealt directly with Liverpool.[18] Yet the Krio did not disappear; many turned to the retail business, as the flourishing Krio community in Lagos in the early twentieth century testified. Others who left the direct export trade concentrated instead on their role as brokers supplying produce to the European firms which moved into Lagos. This role was nothing new, since Krio had been operating as brokers to European firms since the 1850s. Nor was it just Krio who were involved, as numerous indigenous Lagos entrepreneurs moved into this niche as well. These barracooners, as they were known, were produce brokers who purchased oil and kernels from the inland markets to bulk and clean before selling to the European firms in Lagos for export.[19] By the 1880s it was this function that Krio and Lagosian increasingly successfully exploited and on which the European firms in the port depended for their supplies of produce. Taiwo Olowo was a good example of such a broker. He developed links with the German firm, G. L. Gaiser, in the 1860s and the credit he received he forwarded inland to markets like Ikorodu, Ejinrin, and Abeokuta, or to Badagry and Porto Novo, to purchase oil and kernels. The produce thus obtained was then forwarded to Gaiser for export.[20] The development of such brokers as Taiwo, operating between the Yoruba palm produce markets and the British and German traders in Lagos, was the central feature of the economy of the Slave Coast after 1850.

Similar processes can be identified on the Gold Coast. Here by the second half of the century a community of African merchants had emerged as the brokers of the palm – and other – produce trade. Figures like William Ocansey of Ada and John Sarbah of Anomabu had established powerful positions between the palm producers of the interior and the markets of Europe. The success of these African merchants was rooted in their ability to tap the inland oil markets. They gave credit to smaller-scale traders who pushed into the interior to buy palm oil and transport it to their stores on the coast; alternatively these traders established their own operations inland, sending agents and labour to buy oil and kernels directly. Ocansey worked a successful operation up the Volta, reaching upriver to the markets where Krobo oil was sold.[21] Sarbah was also successful at getting inland directly to the oil markets, particularly in the hinterland between Winneba and Cape Coast, thereby cutting out European firms on the coast.[22]

These merchants were also able to retain a position in the direct export trade with Europe, at least until the 1890s. Once again the use of the steamship services and commission houses was the reason for this, with Ocansey particularly successful in developing his trade with Germany through Donner & Callenberg and Wolber & Bröhm, both of Hamburg.[23] Yet for all these African traders the 1880s and 1890s were difficult times as oil prices fell. Credit from commission houses dried up and the rebate system operated by the steamship lines from the mid-1890s hit such figures, who had only small capital reserves, hard.[24] Moreover, European firms moved in to the Gold Coast during the 1880s–1890s, not least because of the rubber boom of this period, and began cornering the produce trade.[25] One such firm, F. & A. Swanzy, had long been established in the Gold Coast, of course, but they were joined by numbers of other firms, not least Miller Bros. and, by the mid-1890s, the African Association as well.[26]

Many of the African merchants on the Gold Coast, with their low capital reserves, faced great difficulties in this situation. J. H. Caesar of Ada was a case in point. His business (J. H. Caesar & Sons) in the Volta trade had been built up sending produce to commission houses like Pickering & Berthoud of Manchester during the 1880s, but came under intense competition from the European firms during the 1890s. By 1899 he was complaining that his business was in serious trouble because there were too many European firms in Ada.[27] Clearly all the African merchants faced similar problems. Yet they did not disappear in the face of these pressures. Increasingly squeezed out of the direct export trade with Europe, they focused instead, as did the Krio of Lagos, on their broking businesses, and retained a niche buying produce inland to sell to the European companies on the coast. Again Caesar was a case in point, continuing to buy oil and kernels during the 1890s to sell to a European firm, Chevalier & Co. in Ada.[28]

In Lagos and on the Gold Coast, the arrival of the steamships provided broking opportunities which groups like the Krio and the African merchants were quick to exploit. Such developments could be seen elsewhere on the West African coast. In the Sierra Leone area, the second half of the century was to see Krio and other entrepreneurs thrive as brokers in the palm produce trade in the Sherbro hinterland and the Galinhas. Krio from Freetown – and increasing numbers of women traders by the 1870s – bought produce inland to take downriver to the European firms in Bonthe.[29] Others brought palm produce to Freetown for onward dispatch to Europe. In the Galinhas, John Harris at Sulima was the major palm broker by the 1860s, giving out credit inland to get palm produce brought to his factories on the coast.[30] Similarly on the South Coast around the Congo, the steamship facilitated changes in the broking system. In this area, numerous Portuguese and Afro-Portuguese traders had established themselves up creeks to carry on a small-scale trade, based on credit they had received from the British, American, and Dutch firms on the coast, to which they sold oil, kernels, and other commodities from inland producers.[31]

In all these cases it was the existing brokers of the area who were squeezed by the changes in broking patterns developing as a result of the steamship services. Similar pressures were experienced in the states of the Niger Delta, the major broking states of the palm produce trade in the second half of the century. The steamships brought changes here too. Here, as elsewhere, the steamers opened access to the market and the ensuing fluidity of trading relationships threatened the position of Delta brokers. These years were by no means easy ones for Delta brokers, as they attempted to adjust to a rapidly altering commerce, yet what is remarkable here, unlike elsewhere on the coast, is just how successful these figures were in retaining their position in the trade. That this would result was by no means certain, since here, too, particularly with the move 'from ship to shore' in the frontier between European trader and African broker after 1850, a major struggle over commercial roles was to occur.

It was the steamship services that were responsible for these changes. One of the major consequences of the move 'from ship to shore' was the erosion of many of the practices brokers had hitherto used to control the operation of the trade. This could be seen symbolically in the problems that developed over pilotage. The steamship services laid buoys in several of the Delta rivers, a process which removed the need to rely on Delta pilots and eroded the way local authorities could control the entry and exit of traders and their ships. Similarly, the ending of trading on board individual sailing ships ended the practice of Delta rulers visiting a ship to 'open' commerce through ceremonial ritual, with no one being allowed to begin business until receiving permission. This had deeper significance. Pilotage and 'opening' had confirmed the power of existing brokers and authorities; by adhering to these practices on arrival, traders were acknowledging the authority of the broking oligarchies of the Delta rivers. The ending of these practices represented a broader erosion of broking power. In the short term, the disappearance of the old methods threatened existing brokers' capability to regulate the trade. In the longer term, it raised the question of whether there was any need for brokers at all.

Such questions initially came to focus around the issue of brokers' access to the new steamship services. The arrival of the steamers offered opportunities for brokers to adjust the trading system in their own favour, bypassing the Europeans and exporting their oil directly to Britain. The best-known example of this was in Old Calabar where King Eyo II (or Eyo Honesty) of Creek Town began sending oil directly to Britain on the steamer service between 1855 and 1857 using Krio and others as his agents.[32] The significance of this African–Krio 'alliance' can hardly be exaggerated, for it threatened to restructure the trade in its entirety and if Eyo had succeeded it would have meant the end, not of the coastal brokers, but of the role of Europeans in the Delta trade.

The reaction of the British supercargoes in Old Calabar to Eyo's scheme was predictable. Seizures of Eyo's oil on the grounds that this represented unpaid debts were accompanied by successful appeals to the British government for help to stamp out a practice which, if it became widespread, would have seriously affected the position of European traders.[33] Eyo was not to be gainsaid, however, and his attempt to utilise the steamer services was followed between 1857 and 1858 by his chartering of a brig from Liverpool, the *Olinda*, to ship oil directly to Britain in his own name.[34]

British traders responded by once again claiming that the oil involved represented unpaid debts, blaming the Scottish Presbyterian missionaries for encouraging Eyo and calling in the British consul for assistance. In particular, they objected to Eyo not having to pay comey on his oil and threatened to sue the mission for any losses.[35]

In the event King Eyo's scheme failed in the face of this combined consular and trading opposition. Other brokers did try to emulate him in exploiting the potentialities of steam though it is unclear how successful they were. Bonny brokers appeared to have contemplated the possibility but little seems to have come of the idea.[36] A number of African brokers did try to buy steam launches in this period, but these were small vessels suitable for use only in interior creeks and not viable for the sea voyage between West Africa and Britain.[37]

The defeat of King Eyo's attempt to use the steamers in the late 1850s marked the failure of the most significant attempt to use the steamship services to reorganise the structure of the oil trade in favour of the coastal brokers until Jaja's renewed efforts in 1885–7. Eyo's failure meant that the frontier between African brokers and European traders was clearly to remain firmly in West Africa and the role of brokers was to remain circumscribed; as Hargreaves points out, Africans were not to be allowed to get a footing in the oceanic trade of these years.[38] The brokers of West Africa were not to become the capitalist class that would transform the region's economy.

On the contrary, not only were Delta brokers not able to use the steamers to trade directly to Britain, but they had to cope with a number of significant threats to their position posed by the opening of the trade after 1852. Delta brokers were to face a threefold challenge after 1852 from Krio, from British traders, and from within their own societies. Not least of these was the arrival of the Krio, who posed a threat to the large-scale British traders – and thus offered an important opportunity to bypass these traders, which King Eyo tried to utilise – but who also provided potential difficulties for brokers. The African–Krio 'alliance' that Eyo tried to establish was designed to benefit the existing broking system. Yet it also posed a potential threat. If allowed access to interior markets, these Krio could challenge the very position of the coastal brokers. Crucially, the Krio insistence that they were subject to British jurisdiction rather than local law raised important implications for the broking states' control over them. Hence, in Old Calabar, where considerable numbers of Krio settled from the early 1850s, local authorities moved quickly to assert their rights over these newcomers and the Gold Coasters who accompanied them. In 1858 King Duke of Duke Town instructed the consul concerning the Krio to 'tell man come . . . live here that he live for my country law, when he live here'.

In 1876, indeed, Efik authorities attempted to expel the Krio by force, with King Archibong III insisting that 'those who will not abide by my Country law must leave my Country'.[39] The Krio did not leave, but the Efik were successful in keeping them out of trade with the interior. Krio were welcome, but on brokers' terms only.

Containing the threat posed by the Krio was one thing, but that posed by British traders was even greater. The years from the 1850s were to see British traders increasingly threaten the brokers' position in the trade; the result was that the relationship between African broker and European trader in the Delta area was one that became more turbulent after 1850. 'Quarrels and misunderstandings' between broker and trader were not new in the oil trade of the Delta.[40] They had been prevalent in the 1840s, as seen in the clashes between British traders and Bonny brokers in the middle of the decade that left several dead; such conflicts helped prompt the creation of a British consulate for the Bights of Benin and Biafra in 1849.[41] But from the early 1850s, as the trade began to change under the impact of the steamer services, violent clashes between British trader and African broker became much more common.

There were a number of reasons for this. Important was the increased presence of Britons in the Delta area after 1852. With the development of hulks, resident agents, and, eventually, factories came the greatly increased numbers of British traders and their employees in Delta rivers; in itself this raised serious questions about legal jurisdictions.[42] Moreover, the Europeans who moved into the Delta trade in this period were a very different breed of individuals to the sailing masters and supercargoes who had hitherto operated in the trade. They may not have been 'ruffians', but these new traders were less tied to established trading conventions and, unlike, say, John Tobin who had built a business around his personal relationship with Duke Ephraim, were much less supportive of existing broking oligarchies. As Wilmot noted of the Delta trade in 1864, the 'constant disturbances' were to 'be attributed to the youth and inexperience' of these new traders.[43] These were employees of firms based in Britain, concerned with short-term success and immediate returns. They were ready to trade with anyone on the African side in the search for profits – whether established chief or interloper – and were willing to bypass the existing brokers of the coastal states or challenge existing oligarchies if necessary. The implications of the move from 'ship to shore' and the arrival of the new traders were that the relationship between British trader and African broker in the Delta would come under increasing strain.

Moreover, these new traders were arriving in the trade at a time when, due to the steamer, the existing conventions and practices acceptable to both sides that had hitherto regulated the commerce were breaking down.

Disputes were generated by the new methods of trading that were emerging with the steamship; such disputes could no longer be settled by reference to custom. Not least of these clashes were those over how comey should be calculated. Hitherto comey had been relatively easy to assess, but once the steamer service with its multiple cargoes for numerous traders replaced the sailing ship chartered to one trader, the question arose as to how, in future, comey would be calculated, a problem that was made worse by the depreciation in the iron bars used to calculate the sum.[44] Similar disputes were generated over the anchorage of hulks, the paying of what were effectively redundant pilots, the positioning of cask houses and factories on shore, whose jurisdiction would apply to these new factories, and so forth.

All this was happening at a time when the trade was becoming increasingly competitive. The problem was that the opening up of the trade destabilised the relationships between all those involved in it. Thus established trader fought with British newcomer, and Krio trader fought with both. This then had a knock-on effect on relations with brokers, as could be seen in the operation of the trust system. The major single cause of disputes in the trade in the 1850s and 1860s lay in the great increase in amounts of trust given out by British traders in order to squeeze out their Krio rivals; sums far in excess of what a river could produce in oil were forwarded, with inevitable clashes following once brokers proved unable to deliver. Such was the case in Old Calabar in 1856, where, in response to the Krio threat, two and a half years' produce was pledged to Liverpool traders.[45] Inevitably such sums could not be redeemed easily, with predictable results for the trader–broker relationship.

Thus, while it was competition between European traders that lay at the root of these problems, it was traders' relationships with African brokers which felt the strain. Traders increasingly took the law into their own hands to keep control over supplies of oil or, after 1861, to force prices down. The two weapons most often resorted to by British traders in this were the trade stoppage to force down prices, and 'chopping' of oil to ensure the repayment of trust. Stoppages, whereby brokers in a port enforced a complete cessation of trade with the Europeans, sometimes lasting for several months or even years, were difficult to maintain because of the problem of keeping unity among British traders in such a competitive era; it required only one firm to break ranks for the effort to be sabotaged. One such stoppage occurred in the Benin River in 1870, where agents unsuccessfully tried to reduce the price of oil, culminating in a three months' hiatus.[46] More serious was the stoppage in Brass between 1867 and 1869 in which Liverpool traders tried to push prices down, accompanied by an attempt to force Brass brokers to trade at Brass itself rather than in the Nun River; the Liverpool traders' aim in this was to squeeze out the

West African Co.'s trade on the Nun.[47] An allied weapon was the refusal to pay comey, as occurred among agents at Brass in 1867–9 and on the Benin River in 1868; such actions had a limited effect, however, and only sparked retaliation.[48]

Chopping oil – seizing oil irrespective of whether it belonged to the broker owing the debt – could be accompanied by considerable violence, as Livingstone noted in his complaint that traders were too prone to taking the law into their own hands in such matters.[49] This could be seen in the well-known clash on the Benin River in 1861 when Richard Henry, agent for Harrisons, seized fourteen puncheons of palm oil over an alleged debt, and then chained the broker who owed it.[50] Such behaviour was also common in Old Calabar, where Hutchinson noted that it had a long history and where Burton in 1862 complained of the prevalence of 'the rule of the revolver'.[51]

The 1850s and 1860s therefore were a deeply unstable time in the Delta trade as it adjusted to the new competitive strains following the arrival of steam. These clashes led British traders increasingly to appeal to the consul – appointed almost coincidentally with the steamer services – with demands to resolve the difficulties; pressures were building for the consul to become responsible for regulating the trade. Burton complained in 1862 at the way traders 'seem to consider the consul their bailiff, whose duty is to collect their debts'.[52] This stopped well short of an agenda to take over the Delta, but traders were clearly becoming willing to urge political intervention in trading matters from the middle of the century.

Traders had an ambivalent attitude to the consul and recognised that his presence could be a two-edged sword. On his side the consul was far from impressed by traders' treatment of brokers. Livingstone observed in 1867 that 'not without cause do the British agents dislike visits from Consuls'.[53] 'Loud is the call for the immediate presence of the consul in a man-of-war to punish the lawlessness of the black goose, but not the lawlessness of the white gander', he added later, while Wylde noted in 1868 'our agents are ready enough to demand protection and to insist upon the native Chiefs performing their part . . . but they will shirk their liabilities if they have an opportunity and still claim to be protected'.[54]

None the less from the early 1850s oil traders increasingly appealed to the consul for help against brokers, urging him to make more frequent visits to the Cameroons, for example, in order to break brokers' capacity to operate trade stoppages against them.[55] They were even ready to urge him to intervene to solve an inland trade dispute on the Cross River in 1856.[56] A year later traders called on the consul to act in the Benin River to ensure the payment of debts, and similarly nine years later in Bonny and Elem Kalabari.[57] Firm actions by brokers to defend themselves against traders' aggression prompted agents to appeal to the consul for protection, as in the Nun River in 1866, and the Benin River two years later.[58]

Thus British traders were increasingly ready to welcome consular attempts to regularise the palm oil trade in the Delta area by treaty. The motives of consular policy are not the concern here, but between 1850 and 1862 the several consuls dealing with the Delta area signed a series of commercial treaties with Delta area states covering the procedures of the palm oil trade, beginning with Elem Kalabari and Bonny in 1850 and continuing to the treaties Burton signed with Old Calabar and the Cameroons in 1862, with further additions to these agreements being signed thereafter.[59] These treaties were followed by attempts to establish Courts of Equity in each river, comprising the major traders and brokers under a British chairman, and intended to enforce treaty provisions; appeals from the Courts were to go to the consul.[60]

The treaties of 1850–62 were designed to bring a degree of regulation to the practices of an oil trade that had been changing rapidly. They covered issues such as how comey was to be calculated and paid, the placing of anchorages for hulks, procedures in cases of fire on board ship, protection of cask houses, size of casks, charges for trading, and so forth. These replaced the ad hoc arrangements, settled by long-established custom between all concerned, that had prevailed in the trade when there had been relatively few traders.

British traders were ready to welcome these treaties and the consular regime that went with them. But their support for the consular treaties needs to be seen in context. The treaties were not seen as the first step to the take-over of the Delta; traders recognised that brokers' control of labour and transport was essential to the effective supply of oil and kernels. The treaties represented a desire to control brokers, certainly – not least by emphasising that existing authorities were responsible for the smooth operation of the trade – but they were also designed to control access to the British side of the commerce. Included in a number of these treaties were provisions about paying substantial charges in advance in order to be allowed to trade, which were specifically designed to squeeze out small-scale interlopers; such provisions were soon rescinded by the Foreign Office, but even so, the large-scale British traders continued to see the consul as their ally against the influx of newcomers.[61] This was particularly the case with the Courts of Equity, which were simply ignored by African brokers and which soon evolved into exclusively white institutions dealing with disputes between British traders, and specifically barred to small-scale traders like the Krio.

Using the consular regime to control access to the British side of the trade had broader implications, of course, for this was a way of trying to influence prices and, in turn, African brokers' access to the market. With their support of these treaties and courts, British traders were hoping to achieve a degree of economic leverage over brokers. What motivated traders was the fact that the trade was changing rapidly due to steam. British traders were attempting to reassert the control over access to the trade that had been eroded by its opening up resulting from the steamship services. They were thus calling on political intervention in order to restore the status quo ante 1852.

On one level this policy was relatively successful. By the 1870s the violence that had disfigured the relationship between trader and broker in the previous two decades in the Delta was in decline and a degree of stability had been re-established. Yet on another level, the policy of trying to control Delta brokers was of limited success, at least before the 1880s, because they were never passive in the face of the consular regime. Indeed, the constant need to amend the treaties, the repeated attempts at re-establishing Courts of Equity, and the consul's continued complaints at his powerlessness vis-à-vis Delta states showed that brokers largely ignored these treaties where they conflicted with their own interests, boycotted the Courts of Equity, and continued to encourage newcomers – such as Jaja's encouragement of Millers – where this was to their advantage. In this resistance brokers were largely successful. It would be wrong to assume that before the 1880s British traders, consuls, or Courts of Equity chairmen had established any significant degree of control over Delta oil brokers.

Indeed, up to the 1880s, Delta area brokers remained essentially successful in their attempt to maintain their position in the trade relative to traders. The weapons available to brokers to resist British interference remained potent. Their main method in this struggle with traders was the trade stoppage. In Old Calabar in 1855, ten ships had been waiting an average of nine and a half months for a cargo.[62] This could be backed up by other sanctions, as with the case, outside the Delta area, at Batanga in 1865 where brokers cut off water supplies to European traders, or at Brass in 1867 where food supplies were cut.[63] In particular brokers reacted firmly to attempts at price cutting by British traders from the early 1860s.[64] This lay behind the major stoppage at Old Calabar in 1862, in the Cameroons in the same year, the twelve-month stoppage on the Benin River between 1863 and 1864, and again in 1870, as well as several stoppages in Brass in the late 1860s.[65]

The potency of the trade stoppage for African brokers lay in the institution of trust and their ability to play off one European trader against another concerning its repayment. Livingstone, complaining about a dispute on the Benin River in 1870, noted that 'native traders are united and almost always win', because of their ability to manipulate divisions among British traders.[66] Given the large quantities of credit given out to brokers in the form of trust, by stopping trade brokers were hitting European traders hard and thereby forcing their ships to return home empty or remain rotting over several years in a Delta river. One of Wilson & Dawson's ships remained over two years in Old Calabar in the late 1850s, for example, and this was by no means uncommon; trade stoppages were also frequently used by Jaja of Opobo in the early 1870s.[67] Stopping trade was, however, a weapon of last resort and ultimately was in no one's interests, for it meant a drastic reduction in brokers' incomes as much as anything else. Yet it was a weapon brokers utilised on numerous occasions in this period, and increasingly once prices began to fall from the early 1860s.[68]

A further response to traders' pressure could be found in the adulteration of oil and kernels. This was certainly considered an increasing problem by British traders in the late nineteenth century, though their own adulteration through the sale of short-measure cloth or the watering of spirits received less comment.[69] The most common method of adulteration of oil was the addition of water or dirt which sank to the bottom of the container, while the weight of kernels could be increased by the addition of stones, dirt, or the shells of the nut; soaking of kernels in water had the same effect. Adulteration certainly increased in this period and provoked elaborate countermeasures by European traders, but not all instances were necessarily deliberate; kernels for example would often be soaked by rainfall in transit.[70] In any case adulteration could be of only short-term value in responding to traders' pressure and had the inevitable consequence of provoking retaliation.

Where brokers felt their vital interests under attack, violence was their weapon of last resort. Certainly violent retaliation was not uncommon, particularly during the 1850s and 1860s. This could be seen in the several attacks on British traders in the Benin River during the 1860s, and the assaults on supercargoes in Old Calabar in the late 1850s, though these incidents, not being in brokers' interests, were never the unprovoked assaults that European traders liked to suggest they were.[71]

Delta brokers were particularly prepared to resort to violence to resist British traders' attempts to penetrate the interior. Preventing British traders moving inland was at the heart of their trading position. The best-known examples of this came with the various attacks on European traders attempting to open trade on the lower Niger during the 1860s; numerous assaults were launched during this period, allegedly at the instigation of Brass brokers determined to maintain their hold over the markets of the area.[72] Traders were still being shot at in this area in the late 1870s. Miller Bros. led the way in using steam launches to penetrate inland markets in the 1870s; Brass traders forced out Miller Bros. in 1878 when their agent found a new route to the Niger.[73]

Similarly, Efik attempts to prevent missionary penetration of Old Calabar's trading hinterland are well known.[74] The people of the interior were, reported one missionary, banned from contact with Europeans 'under pain of death'.[75] When Burton tried to open interior markets up the Cross River in 1862 he too was turned back by a show of force.[76] Three years later an attempt at trading between interior producers and British traders on the Cross River was forcibly stopped by Duke Town chiefs.[77] This policy was vigorously maintained elsewhere by others. Bonny brokers firmly resisted British attempts to contact Andoni and other suppliers such as on the Ikomtoro River in the 1860s and 1870s.[78] Elem Kalabari was equally persistent in its efforts to prevent British traders reaching Okrika in the 1870s.[79]

Whatever method Delta area brokers used, what is striking is that they were generally successful before the 1880s in maintaining their position within the broking system vis-à-vis the British, just as they had vis-à-vis the Krio. They were also successful in dealing with the final threat they faced to their broking position, that is from within. From the 1850s groups within the broking states of the Delta area did attempt to enter the trade as smaller-scale traders by utilising the increased European presence. Brokers were well aware of the potential danger of such threats from within and moved quickly to retain their control over access to European traders. Thus in Old Calabar the broking elite was quick to use Ekpe regulations to stop sale of oil to Europeans in small quantities in 1862 and to control the sale of kernels in 1872; similar regulations were used by chiefs in Brass in 1867.[80] The trade of Old Calabar, notes Latham, remained securely in the hands of the Efik oligarchy throughout this period.[81] In Elem Kalabari, too, merchant chiefs were able to keep interlopers out of the trade by imposing swingeing fees to enter interior oil markets.[82] In Bonny the ruling elite was less united given the divisions within it that culminated in the secession of Jaja in 1869, but even here there were few signs of individual oil traders successfully challenging the position of house heads. Not least, the survival of 'topping' or 'topside', the substantial charge house heads insisted traders paid to them on any oil bought from smaller-scale brokers, ensured the reinforcement of the larger-scale brokers' position within the trade.[83] In the Benin River, merchant princes like Olomu or Nana were well able to maintain their authority against smaller-scale interlopers.[84] While the Cameroons estuary towns went through deep internal crises in this period, with serious disputes breaking out over access to credit, there is little evidence, before 1880, of broking elites losing control over the trade to smaller-scale interlopers from within. It was not until the establishment of colonial rule over the Delta that this picture substantially changed.[85]

The reason that existing broking oligarchies were able to maintain their position in the oil trade of the Delta area, whether in relation to Krio, to Britons, or to internal rivals, was because of their control over interior markets. Here, to a greater extent than in other parts of West Africa, coastal brokers maintained control over the trade routes inland. Indeed, the volume of oil and kernels traded made coastal brokers' ability to provide labour and transport essential for the operation of these networks. Indeed, it was the very longevity of these structures that was crucial to this and that allowed these brokers to maintain their position through the transition and afterwards.

In this period, indeed, control was stepped up, with coastal broking states moving to eradicate intermediate middlemen in order to get direct access to interior markets. Such a case occurred in the Cameroons, where by the early 1880s Duala traders had pushed inland along the Mungo River to make direct contact with Balong and Bakundu suppliers, circumventing intermediate middlemen in the process.[86] Similarly Jaja's secession to Opobo in 1869 represented a strengthening of his control over Kwa Ibo markets and he was ready to use force whenever necessary thereafter to maintain this hold.[87] The most successful brokers in this regard, however, remained the Efik of Old Calabar, who, while unable to push inland to the markets beyond Umon, acted decisively against rival middlemen to secure their control over Cross River markets in this period.[88]

Moreover, though the evidence is slight, brokers must have utilised economic measures to maintain their position in the inland trade by exploiting what cost economies they could, particularly as prices began to fall and the terms of trade turned against suppliers from the 1870s. The most obvious economy came in transport, and one can see the move of Jaja to Opobo and attempts by other Delta brokers to relocate inland as measures to get nearer to oil markets in ways which would have had a sound economic – quite apart from political – rationale. Equally, the use of larger canoes to transport oil and kernels could produce significant savings; such a trend to the use of larger canoes, however, is difficult to identify specifically in this period and one must assume that such large canoes were already being utilised wherever possible by brokers.[89]

Other economies of transport could be achieved by investing in new technology, and the last quarter of the century saw a move by brokers to purchase steam launches from Europe for collection of oil and kernels from the interior; George Pepple of Bonny tried in 1877, and William Ocansey of Ada in the early 1880s, while Chief Coco Bassey of Old Calabar bought the steam launch *Progress* from the African Association in 1894.[90] In general, however, these attempts were not as successful as they might have been. Few brokers could raise the capital to purchase launches and the problems of maintenance, fuel, and spare parts would undoubtedly have restricted the boats' effectiveness. None the less, such transport efficiencies as brokers could gain must have played their part in maintaining interior networks.

However, this assertion of brokers' influence over inland oil suppliers in the late nineteenth century was by no means a smooth process. Not least it generated open warfare between rival Delta broking states for access to inland markets. Some historians have seen the Yoruba wars of the second half of the century in these terms, though this has been a controversial issue. Less attention has been given to the Eastern Delta wars of the mid-1860s to mid-1880s where, although deeper religious and kin ties played their part in the causes of the conflict, control of oil markets was certainly the central aim of military operations.[91] For much of the time this struggle to control inland markets simply generated intermittent skirmishing and raids on rival trading canoes, but between 1867 and 1869, 1871 and 1873, and 1876 and 1881 this struggle broke into outright warfare between Elem Kalabari and its neighbours, Bonny, Nembe, and Okrika.

Control of the oil trade was indeed at the heart of these Delta wars. It was attacks on Kalabari canoes trying to get to markets inland, particularly on the Engenni–Orashi River, that sparked the start of the war in 1867. Attempts by the British consul to achieve a settlement in 1871 by allocating markets between the protagonists – following a failed attempt to refer the dispute to the Arochukwu oracle – was of little success as were attempts by local rulers to arbitrate.[92] Further violence over markets followed in the mid-1870s, which spilled over into civil war within Elem Kalabari after 1879 and continued until the split of the state in 1883–4 and its relocation into the towns of Bakana, Abonnema, Degema, and Buguma.[93]

It was not only Elem Kalabari that split under these pressures. The struggle for hinterland markets also became entangled with the internal problems within Bonny in this period, which culminated in the secession of Jaja and Anna Pepple House in 1869 and the establishment of a new state at Opobo.[94] One of the factors behind Jaja's decision to secede was his desire to get closer to the oil markets on the Imo River; and, while it took time for Jaja to build up this trade, by the 1880s Opobo was clearly the leading exporter of oil from the Eastern Delta area with its influence very effectively established over the markets of the lower Imo.

Yet despite the wars and secessions of this period, Delta area brokers were generally successful in maintaining their inland broking networks, at least to the 1880s. Broking oligarchies had flexibly and effectively adapted to the new trading conditions developing from the 1850s onwards. Certainly their position was coming under pressure from consular interference, from some European traders being willing to try to push inland, from elements emerging within Delta states as potential rivals, and from difficulties ensuing from the rivalry between states for interior markets, yet the existing broking oligarchies of this area had essentially maintained their position within the palm products trade by the 1880s. The emergence of Opobo in 1869 and its success thereafter is symbolic of the degree to which traditional trading structures and broking methods continued to thrive in the Delta.

However, for brokers generally in West Africa, the 1880s were to see changing fortunes. In particular the severe fall in produce prices and the adverse shift in the terms of trade of the 1880s and 1890s were a new kind of threat and were seriously to affect brokers' incomes. The years after 1880 were ones of severe strain for brokers.[95] By the late 1880s, as prices fell to their lowest since the middle of the century, things would have become increasingly tight, with few options available to alleviate the worst of the difficulties. Indeed, it was the narrowing range of options facing brokers that prompted a number to attempt to use the steamer service once again to ship direct to Britain and cut out the European trader, as King Eyo had tried in the 1850s. Attempts were made by brokers in Bonny and Brass in this period, and, most famously, by King Jaja of Opobo between 1885 and 1887. These efforts brought into sharp focus once more the issue of the place of Delta brokers in the palm products trade. The reaction that developed over Jaja's attempt, coinciding as it did with the quickening pace of colonial occupation in West Africa, was to bring to a head a deep crisis over the future structure and organisation of the palm products trade. This crisis, as will be seen, was to culminate in the eventual elimination of the coastal broker.

For established palm produce brokers generally, the second half of the century was a period of immense change. In some areas, like Lagos or the Gold Coast, new groups emerged to take up a position between the inland producers and the European traders. In the Delta, the heart of the trade, coastal brokers faced immense challenges to their position. Yet what is striking in the Delta is that, despite all the changes in commercial practices that had occurred since 1852, by the 1880s brokers still remained essentially in control of the trade. Undoubtedly the very success of Delta brokers in developing the trade during the early decades of the century explains their success compared to their colleagues elsewhere on the coast. There were clearly problems on the horizon that were to have a serious impact on their role, but up to the slump of the 1880s, at least, brokers remained the essential and necessary key to the palm products trade. If nothing else, this was testimony to the remarkable vibrancy of the broking networks that had evolved in West Africa over the previous 300 years.

8   The coming of colonial rule and the ending of legitimate trade

The opening of the palm oil trade from 1852, followed by the subsequent contraction of the British oil market, had by the 1880s culminated in major problems for all those involved in the palm products trade. This had important implications for Anglo-West African relations. This is no place to examine either British imperial policy or proconsular practice in West Africa, but it is important to look at the way the restructuring of the trade in the second half of the century led to changes in the relationship between British palm product traders and their African suppliers, and particularly to changes in the attitudes of British traders towards political intervention on the west coast. By the 1880s earlier attitudes that had been largely indifferent to ideas of political expansion had begun to change among Liverpool firms, moving towards support for political intervention in those areas – particularly the Niger Delta – that lay at the heart of the palm products trade. Some traders at least had by the 1880s come to see political intervention as a solution to the economic problems facing the trade. This was to have major long-term implications for the future of the coastal palm products brokers.

This change in attitudes was in fact a long time coming. In the period up to c. 1880 British palm products traders – and particularly the established Liverpool firms like Harrisons, Horsfalls, and Hatton & Cookson – had remained largely neutral to notions of British political annexations in West Africa or of removing the brokers of the coast.[1] Those who supported territorial expansion or contemplated moves inland were either newcomers to the trade who wished to undermine the position of the established firms, or Krio traders who saw British influence, with themselves at its centre, as the key to the future of the region and a necessary defence against assault from supercargoes.[2] The established British traders, by contrast, while willing to see consular intervention to resolve local difficulties in their favour in the Delta or elsewhere, remained committed to free trade and the status quo regarding political structures in West Africa. Most would have echoed the views of Andrew Swanzy in 1874 that governmental annexations simply led to increased taxes which traders had to pay: a process that, Swanzy argued, drove firms to trade outside British territory, not least in order to avoid restrictions concerning the sale of arms.[3]

This was to change after c. 1880. From that time, and particularly from 1885, Liverpool traders' attitudes became much more interventionist. On the one hand they began to move towards supporting calls for political annexations in the region, while on the other they began to urge strong action against some of the brokers of the Delta area, and to contemplate pushing inland to reach the oil markets of the interior. These moves were to culminate in calls for a charter over the Delta for the African Association Ltd and ultimately in the erosion of the power of the coastal brokers.

The background to these developments was the broader change in African–European relations that was occurring in the 1880s. The wider causes of the developing partition of West Africa in the 1880s lie beyond the scope of this work, but clearly the expansion of European colonial interests on the coast, and the rivalries this generated, was becoming marked by the early 1880s. From 1880 a French firm, the Compagnie française de l'Afrique Equatoriale – soon followed by Verminck's Compagnie du Sénégal – became active on the Niger, supported by Capt. Mattei as French consular agent; in 1883 French warships arrived in the Delta.[4] In the same year, the French seized Porto Novo on the Slave Coast. Disputes over the boundary of the French territories on the Ivory Coast with the Gold Coast in the early 1880s developed into piecemeal French expansion from 1886. Similarly the acclamation that de Brazza received from the Paris Chamber of Deputies in 1882 for the treaties he had earlier signed in the Congo region implied increased French interest in West-Central Africa, a threat that echoed King Leopold of Belgium's burgeoning ambitions to the Congo basin.[5] Significantly, in July 1884, Germany marked its presence in West Africa by declaring protectorates over Togoland and the Cameroons.[6] A scramble for West Africa was beginning which would soon lead to the crisis over the Congo and the Berlin West African conference of 1884–5.[7]

Whatever may have been the cause of these moves, their effects clearly changed the political situation along the coast. They also changed the general tenor of British traders' attitudes towards political intervention in West Africa. Traders in Britain, whether Bristol traders operating on the Ivory Coast, Manchester traders connected with the South Coast, or Liverpool traders in the Niger Delta, began to react to what they saw as a potential threat to their interests. While oil traders no longer held positions of local political power comparable to individuals like Sir John Tobin, Thomas Horsfall, or Richard King in the past, such traders were now organised in bodies to articulate their views to government and the public. Chambers of Commerce had been established in Bristol in 1823 (reconstituted in 1850) and Liverpool in 1850, to name but two; since 1843 there had been the African Association (distinct from the later trading company) representing the interests of oil traders in Liverpool. In 1884, in response to this growing crisis, the Liverpool Chamber established an African trade section and the London Chamber a West African section.

German or French rule in itself was not necessarily a problem for British traders, but these moves appeared to be accompanied by the threat of discriminatory tariffs. This possibility loomed from the French colony of Senegal from 1881 and became increasingly apparent by the middle of the decade.[8] The key was the Congo, where Anglo-Portuguese negotiations in the early 1880s, culminating in the unratified Anglo-Portuguese treaty of February 1884, threatened to endorse Portuguese tariff policies in Africa by extending the Mozambique tariff, and generated great unrest among British traders. The news that Portugal might impose tariffs on the Congo, noted the Bristol Chamber of Commerce in 1885, was 'vexatious in the extreme' and other Chambers as well as the trade press joined in a vociferous campaign against the treaty; the Birmingham Chamber, showing the co-ordination that was occurring between the protesters, attacked the 'vexatious' Mozambique tariff.[9]

The Congo campaign showed that the central principle of British traders in West Africa was still a commitment to free trade and that this remained true to a very late date.[10] The response of British traders to these French, German, and other moves was not to demand that Britain should seize territory, but rather to urge guarantees against discriminatory tariffs.[11] The African Association, for example, were willing to consider the neutralisation of the Congo basin, if necessary through the acceptance of Leopold's claims – at least until his reversion agreement with France – in the hope that this would guarantee free trade.[12] Similarly the German occupation of the Cameroons in 1884 prompted demands by British traders for free trade guarantees rather than annexations in retaliation.[13] Bristol traders, who were the British traders with most to lose, petitioned Granville, the foreign secretary, that 'your memorialists are apprehensive that in course of time the Germans will be levying differential dues'.[14] Equally, when Peter Stuart led the African Association in protesting to Granville on the German move into the Cameroons in 1884, it was the French differential duty at Gabon that seemed his real fear.[15] Until the mid-1880s, in short, British traders were less interested in demanding that Britain join in this developing scramble than stressing the need for equal rights for British traders with their French and German rivals.

The British government's decision to declare a protectorate over the Delta area with the Niger Districts Protectorate in 1885 and to grant a charter to the National African Company in 1886 to protect British interests on the lower and middle Niger satisfied many firms that British trade in these areas was being safeguarded, even though neither action involved the government in establishing administration.[16] For many Delta traders this was sufficient. Few were committed to moving inland in this period, given the potential costs, and in this sense the declaration of the Niger Districts Protectorate was welcomed less as a move to expand the British presence than as an attempt to maintain the status quo.

Yet clearly changes in the general tone of traders' attitudes towards British political action on the west coast were beginning to become apparent from the middle of the decade. From the mid-1880s, demands began for political action by the British government on a broad canvas, beginning with the Manchester Chamber's call for action over the Delta in 1884 and continuing with traders urging the government to occupy the Slave Coast in 1885, asking for moves into the interior of the Gold Coast in 1886 and for measures to establish 'law and order' and peaceful conditions for trade in the interior generally; this was also urged specifically for the Gold Coast from 1888 by the Liverpool Chamber.[17] A year earlier the London Chamber had urged moves inland to open the roads for the merchant on the Gold Coast.[18] News of the French move towards Abeokuta in 1888 prompted vociferous protests from the Liverpool Chamber; similarly the French occupation of parts of the Ivory Coast after 1886 provoked protests from the Bristol Chamber of Commerce in 1889 to Salisbury against 'the prohibitive French tariff' and explicit demands that Britain should annex the western Ivory Coast including Cape Lahou, the major Bristol trading centre.[19]

In making these protests, commercial interests were going beyond calls for the preservation of free trade to demand active political intervention by the government. This change in emphasis was reflected in the trade press which urged the expansion of the Gold Coast in 1882, the occupation of 'the Trans-Volta Districts' also in 1882, the Galinhas in 1884, and, more generally, annexations along the west coast in 1883; in 1885 the *African Times*, no longer the house-magazine of the Krio trader, supported calls for government action concerning the slump in the African trade to prevent the trade being lost to Hamburg and Marseilles.[20] The *Lagos Times* urged intervention to settle the Yoruba wars in 1881 and 1882, as did the *Lagos Observer* in 1882.[21] By 1888 the *African Times* was supporting proposals for a widespread occupation of the Ivory Coast, the Slave Coast, and elsewhere.[22]

It would be wrong to suggest that by the middle of the decade all British traders had begun to support political expansion by the government into West Africa. Yet clearly the general attitudes of traders towards political expansion by Britain were shifting and what had been rejected out of hand earlier was, from c. 1885, becoming increasingly acceptable. Were these changing general attitudes reflected specifically in the palm products trade? The difficulty in answering this is that oil and kernel traders had become so diversified in their trading by the 1880s that only in relatively restricted areas of the coast, such as the Niger Delta, could they still be described as oil and kernel specialists. But one sign that these changing attitudes were permeating the palm products trade was oil traders' greater willingness to call on governmental action in stamping out adulteration of oil and kernels by the 1880s. Adulteration had long been a problem in the trade, but had been resolved by mutual agreement. What was new from the mid-1880s was the way traders increasingly saw measures to deal with it as the government's responsibility. Hence the calls for stern action by the Lagos government to deal with adulteration in 1888–9.[23] Equally, in the Delta, by 1894 governmental regulation had replaced the earlier practice whereby claims of adulteration were settled by agreement between broker and trader.[24]

Changing attitudes among oil and kernel traders towards the role of governmental intervention can be seen too in calls for expansion in those areas of the coast where palm oil and kernels were the major items traded. Pressures from traders based in Lagos began developing from the late 1880s for governmental moves inland into Yorubaland and westwards towards Porto Novo, exacerbated by fears of French intervention. These calls from traders in Lagos were repeated by the Liverpool and Manchester Chambers, and culminated in the British attack on Ijebu Ode in 1892.[25] Equally, traders in Freetown were not averse to demanding annexations during the depression of the 1880s, blaming the wars of the interior for the slump in oil and kernel trading.[26] John Harris, the largest trader at Sulima, complained at the way wars on the upper Kittam River were disrupting his trade in 1880; moves by the Liberian government into his trading sphere similarly generated protests to the Freetown government.[27] Other traders in Sherbro in 1888 also complained at the impact of interior unrest on their palm products trade.[28]

The main change in attitudes occurred, however, in the heart of the palm products trade, the Niger Delta area. Here the general move of traders during the 1880s towards welcoming a greater political presence became marked. Certainly much depends on what is meant by 'trader'; established firms from Liverpool and Bristol need to be distinguished from the relative newcomers like Miller Bros. or John Holt who had different perspectives on the trade and their position within it. Equally, a distinction needs to be drawn between those simply seeking to push inland, as Holt did from an early date, and those urging political annexation. In general, the established traders tended to be happier with the status quo and less interested in supporting moves inland or political annexations, while the newcomers were more willing to attempt to open the interior and to welcome any political changes that might create new opportunities for them to exploit. None the less, while there were varying degrees of enthusiasm for political action between these groups, both were clearly moving towards a much keener support for British territorial expansion in West Africa from 1885.

Gertzel has argued that the Liverpool oil firms remained committed to the status quo in the Delta until a very late date.[29] They were, she argues, reluctant to remove the palm brokers; in effect, Liverpool traders had an unwritten 'alliance' with the coastal brokers and saw their control of transport and labour as essential for the smooth functioning of the trade. No British firm in this period could hope to match this investment. On the contrary, Liverpool palm oil traders were content to maintain their traditional commercial organisation on the coast and this in turn required the continuation of the brokers' networks in the Delta. Hence Hewett's 1888 description of 'the rest content-where-we-are policy' of the Liverpool firms.[30] These attitudes survived, Gertzel argues, until at least 1900, if not later. There is much of value in this argument. Yet it is also true that Liverpool oil traders' views were beginning to change from 1885 onwards, towards a much more qualified view of the role of the Delta oil brokers; brokers had a continuing role in the trade, as Gertzel suggests, certainly, but this was a role that was to be controlled and determined by European trading needs. This meant the assertion of some form of colonial rule. The survival of a role for brokers in the trade did not preclude support for imperial rule more generally over the Delta area. Nor did a recognition of the brokers' role in the short term prevent support for opening up the interior by the government in the future.

At the centre of the changing attitudes of the Liverpool oil firms in the mid-1880s was the continuing competition within the trade at a time of falling prices. These were difficult years for the oil trade. As prices fell and the value of the trade shrank to its trough in 1886–7, the big oil firms faced major difficulties. It is true that not all British oil importers were doing badly in this period; those that had diversified into other commodities such as rubber or ivory, for example – both of which did well in these years – experienced very different conditions to the palm oil specialists of the Delta.[31] None the less, for those firms, like Harrisons or Stuart & Douglas, which specialised in the Delta trade, the problems were growing. A general air of crisis and difficulty pervaded this trade by the 1880s. George Miller spoke of 'this insane competition' in 1887 while others complained of the decline in profit margins.[32] As the decade proceeded the search for some solution took on an increasingly urgent character. The *Lagos Times* in the early 1880s spoke of 'an anxious crisis' in the trade while Holt predicted in 1886 that 'the end of the palm oil trade for all of us will soon be reached'.

Two years later that point seemed near when he described the situation facing traders as 'a distinct crisis'.[33]

Pooling agreements and similar arrangements, while of temporary success in some cases, were very fragile and clearly were not a long-term answer to these problems. Equally, amalgamations, such as occurred with the formation of the African Association Ltd in 1889, were not enough in themselves to solve the problems of the traders unless they included all those involved in a particular area. In the event Miller Bros. refused to join the African Association Ltd in 1889 and the amalgamation did not, in itself, give the large-scale traders the monopoly they sought over the Delta oil trade.

Moreover, so long as the Royal Niger Company remained a separate entity on the Niger, the oil firms would face a formidable competitor, because of its encroachment on the markets of the interior of the Delta. With the buying out of its French rivals and the gaining of a charter in 1886, it became a major force within the palm products trade. Moreover, disappointing returns in its early years prompted it to push south into the Delta in order to tap the oil trade of the interior markets.[34] Its encroachment on oil markets squeezed the coastal brokers, particularly those of Brass, and had an important effect on the supplies of oil reaching the Liverpool firms on the coast after 1886.

Although the terms of its charter, and indeed the agreements settled at Berlin, stated that the company could not establish a monopoly on the Niger, to all intents and purposes it did. As Flint notes, the policy of the company was 'to lay down the greatest possible impediments to the trade of competitors'.[35] It forced traders on the Niger, whether Liverpool, Krio, or 'native', to pass through its customs posts, or ports of entry, and pay the duties it imposed; it charged substantial licence fees of £100, later reduced to £50, before a trader could operate within its territories, with a further £100 licence to trade in spirits. Very quickly it drove most of its competitors off the Niger.[36]

These actions provoked considerable complaints, by the brokers of the Delta, by the Liverpool firms which bought oil from them, and by those Krio and Lagos traders like J. S. Leigh who still operated on the river in 1886.[37] Brass brokers protested in particular: given their location it was their oil markets that were most affected by the Royal Niger Company's operations. Indeed, most of the big Liverpool firms – Harrisons being the exception – abandoned Brass after 1886, though they continued to complain to Whitehall on the Brass brokers' behalf.[38] Even Consul Hewett admitted the deleterious effect the company was having. By 1888 the Royal Niger Co. was encroaching on Itsekiri–Urhobo oil markets on the Forcados and Ramos Rivers in the Western Delta as well, provoking

further complaints from brokers and Liverpool firms.[39] Soon it was Elem
Kalabari's turn to be affected, with Kalabari brokers being forced out of
Oguta markets in 1887.[40]

The Liverpool firms retaliated with a press campaign, with numerous
meetings and protests, and by entering the Royal Niger Company's territories and deliberately trading at a loss.[41] The Liverpool firms were prominent
in the late 1880s in complaining at the impact of the company on their
trade.[42] Harrisons were particularly involved in this. Their agent at Brass,
A. A. Whitehouse, led complaints at the Brass brokers' loss of oil markets
to the company in the late 1880s; Harrisons' exports from Brass had been
halved, he claimed, between the granting of the charter and 1889. It was,
he said, impossible to compete with the Royal Niger Company in these circumstances.[43] The final straw came when the company established a
customs post at Idu in 1888, outside its territory and clearly threatening the
oil markets of Elem Kalabari.[44]

The other problem for the Liverpool oil firms in the mid-1880s came
within the Delta trade itself. While the small-scale interlopers had largely
been squeezed out of the trade by the late 1880s, this was still an intensely
competitive business. The established firms found it difficult to co-operate,
as the failure of various pooling agreements showed, and attempts at
forcing prices down often foundered on the ability of brokers to find individual firms willing to break any putative price rings. One such was Miller
Bros., under George Miller, which remained in many ways a maverick firm,
uneasy at prospects of co-operation with their longer-established competitors. Millers had been active opening trade on the Niger until bought out
by the United African Co. in 1879; thereafter, Millers turned to develop
their business in the Delta, and became particularly prominent in Opobo,
helping Jaja to break the price ring of the Liverpool firms in 1885.[45]

Or there was John Holt for another, who, as a relative newcomer, having
entered the Delta trade only in the 1870s, was from the first keen to push
inland behind the established firms to get to the oil markets of the interior.
He urged moves inland on the South Coast in 1888 and into Yorubaland
from 1892 and encouraged George Watts to move into the Kwa Ibo after
1880. In 1886 Holt was urging moves inland beyond Opobo to bypass
Jaja.[46] He constantly urged governmental action to remove 'recalcitrant'
brokers and to support the opening of the interior to traders more generally.[47]

Clearly, by the mid-1880s, the main Liverpool firms still faced major
difficulties in the Delta oil trade. Competition from Millers and Holt and
the encroachments of the Royal Niger Co. all threatened the future of the
trade. George Miller spoke in 1887 of 'a fierce and ruinous war of prices';
others feared the end of the trade.[48] Clearly palm oil trading would not in

fact come to an end, but what was at issue here was its future commercial structure. Who would dominate this trade in future? Was there a place in the trade for individual firms, or just one large-scale amalgamation? Perhaps most importantly, was there a place in the trade for African brokers, or could British traders dispense with their services and push inland direct to the producers? The slump of the 1880s was raising fundamental questions about the future organisation and structure of the trade.

It was the brokers of the Delta who were at the receiving end of these changing attitudes to political intervention by British traders. These were difficult years for Delta brokers. In the 1880s and 1890s brokers faced a fall in oil prices and an adverse shift in the terms of trade that was seriously to affect their economic position. Equally, they faced increasing political pressure on their place in the trade from European traders, with sustained attempts to push inland or remove brokers who stood resolutely against European interference. Initially at least, brokers remained very effective at resisting any European push inland. Attempts by George Watts and Harry Hartje to penetrate the Cross River with a steam launch in 1883 were abandoned due to fears of the likely Efik reaction.[49] Equally the Duala insisted on a clause in their 1884 treaty with the Germans to prevent German traders trading inland with 'Bushmen'.[50] Bonny traders, suggests Hargreaves, were very effective in retaining, even expanding, their influence over interior oil markets in this period.[51]

Moreover, this resolution in resisting European traders' penetration of interior oil markets was matched by a new attempt by brokers to use the steamer services to trade directly with Europe. A number of attempts to do this were made in the 1880s. One was by James Spiff of Brass, who began operating through Fenn & Ellis in 1883 though his efforts were soon blocked by consular intervention.[52] Another was by Squiss Banigo of Bonny in 1887–8.[53] The most significant was the case of King Jaja.

Since his secession from Bonny in 1869 and subsequent establishment of the Opobo state, Jaja had proved himself one of the most consummate oil brokers of the Delta area. At the heart of his success was his successful preservation of access to the interior oil markets of the Imo and Kwa Ibo Rivers from European traders. When Watts, with Holt's backing, tried to enter the Kwa Ibo in 1881, Jaja moved quickly to prevent him gaining a foothold. At this stage the main Liverpool firms supported Jaja against this interloper and remained content to maintain the status quo in the Opobo broking networks; only Holt took a much harder line and pressed for movement inland.[54] However, when the five oil traders at Opobo – the British & Continental, Taylor, Laughland, & Co., Harrisons, Couper, Johnstone, & Co., and Stuart & Douglas – tried to operate a price ring against Jaja to force prices down in 1885, matters reached a crisis. Millers, through their agent David Farquhar, broke the ring and gained access to Opobo's trade for the next two years; in 1885 Jaja tried to ship oil direct to Britain 'in large quantities', using S. B. Rhodes, a Krio.[55]

In retaliation the agents wished to penetrate the oil markets at Essene and Ohambele up the Imo River, but this was impossible given the strength of Jaja's influence. By this point, however, the consul was involved.[56] Hewett fined Jaja in early 1886 for not letting the traders move inland and shortly thereafter stopped the payment of comey; Jaja on his side referred to the 1873 Anglo-Opobo treaty which acknowledged his control over access to these markets.[57] The British traders continued to attempt to open upriver. Using steam launches, Taylor, Laughland and Couper, Johnstone both tried to open at Essene, Couper, Johnstone at Azumini, and Stuart & Douglas at Ohambele. Yet this was all of little effect and Jaja's influence was too strong to be broken. It marked the final collapse of relations.[58] When Acting Consul Johnston arrived in July 1887, he tried to enter the interior markets himself, to no avail, and responded by banning Jaja from trading.[59] The British traders involved urged the removal of Jaja. The agents protested to the consul and a delegation of representatives of the traders visited the Foreign Office in August 1887 to demand action against Jaja. Only Millers objected, claiming the crisis was purely motivated by attempted price cutting on the part of the aggrieved traders; clearly, too, fears about Jaja's use of the steamers to export direct to Britain played a part.[60] The result was Johnston's notorious deportation of Jaja in September 1887.[61]

Jaja was removed, ultimately, because of competition between the European oil traders. His fate was significant because it showed how much the oil firms were willing to urge the use of governmental intervention against the power of the brokers. The consul may well have had his own motives, but for the Liverpool firms the issue was Jaja's success in using Miller Bros. to break their attempted price ring. There were specific causes operating in the Opobo case but this was clearly more than just a single instance; attitudes were changing among the oil traders of the Delta, towards supporting a more assertive role for the political arm in resolving trade disputes.

The full implications of these new attitudes to political intervention in the 1880s could be seen with the campaign by the major oil firms for a charter to cover the Delta area. The aim was to obtain a charter similar to that of the Royal Niger Company's, allowing the oil firms to administer the area. It would necessitate an amalgamation amongst the firms, hence ending competition, and, as on the Niger, would give the chartered company the ability to squeeze competitors out, particularly small-scale traders from Lagos.[62] Through elimination of competition, the new company would be able to force down the prices for oil and kernels that it paid to brokers. It was the clearest indication yet that the oil firms were being driven by the slump in oil prices during the 1880s towards political action to support economic ends.

The idea of a charter to cover the Delta area first emerged in 1883. Watts, Holt, and George Miller were among the earliest proponents. For Holt this was a way of removing harmful competition and enabling oil traders to push inland; Holt was explicit that the value of a charter was that it would keep out interlopers.[63] But this would clearly have major implications for the future of the coastal brokers, who would end up facing a united combine to buy their oil and which would be in an immensely powerful position to dictate prices. Brokers might well still survive in such a trade, but their room for manoeuvre would be sharply curtailed. Moreover, such a charter would include the oil markets of the hinterland, which would thus be exposed to the new company's operations. If successful, the charter campaign would thus have effectively broken the power of the coastal brokers in the oil trade.

Clearly such a charter would first require the amalgamation of the major Delta palm product traders if it was to be acceptable to the government. However, in the early 1880s, the major Liverpool traders remained doubtful of the benefits of amalgamation. In particular, Harrisons, probably the largest firm in the Delta by the 1880s, refused to go along with the scheme, and they were soon joined by Stuart & Douglas, the second largest.[64] Inevitably such firms would be the ones with most to lose by any amalgamation and the scheme ground to a halt. Protests also developed among smaller traders like G. A. Moore, who clearly saw the danger such a conglomerate would pose to their interests.[65] Miller tried to push on but divisions, particularly between Miller Bros. and the established Liverpool firms, led to the plan for amalgamation breaking down. Without an amalgamation, a charter was impossible, and by 1885 the proposal had stalled.

A second proposal for a charter to cover the Delta area emerged in 1887, following the granting of one to the Royal Niger Company the previous year.[66] Holt and Miller again led the way. The plan was for what was termed fusion – that is the merger of all the Delta firms, including Millers, with the Royal Niger Co. – leading to the extension of the Niger charter over the Delta.[67] Millers were keen and Goldie was interested. The Foreign Office, too, given the potential costs of administering the Niger Districts Protectorate, was prepared to take the proposal seriously and it looked as if the scheme would succeed. By November 1888 the oil firms were close to agreement, with the putative company to be known as the 'Royal African Co.'.[68] But the proposal ground to a halt, with difficulties developing between Millers and others because of the legacy of the Opobo struggle.[69]

With the delay the news of the plan leaked out, prompting a reaction against it organised by A. L. Jones and the shipping firms, but including opposition from Lagos traders, among others.[70] The shippers feared the plans because, if successful, the new organisation would be so powerful as to be able to dictate shipping rates or even develop its own line.[71] But the Foreign Office too developed cold feet over the scheme, not least because of German objections and the general protests against it prompted the government to delay. Instead, in December 1888, it sent Major Claude MacDonald to examine the situation in the Delta and on the Niger and to look at the future administration of the region. The fusion scheme collapsed.[72]

A third attempt was made in 1889, but this time a separate charter was called for, for the oil firms in the Delta only.[73] The amalgamation of the firms as the African Association Ltd was achieved and in January 1890 the new company petitioned for a charter over the oil rivers.[74] The proposal, however, came to nothing. The MacDonald report came out against a charter for the oil rivers, not least because of the opposition of the oil brokers of the Delta, who realised its implications for their bargaining power and complained vigorously.[75] Opposition came also from Miller Bros., which had not joined the amalgamation of 1889.[76] Lagos traders objected too, as did their commission houses, because of their fear that the proposed charter would keep them out of the trade of the area. Smaller-scale traders, in particular, urged the establishment of direct colonial government rather than rule by the African Association. The fiercest opposition came once again from Jones and the steamship lines, using the Liverpool Chamber of Commerce (largely made up of small commission houses) to articulate their concerns.[77] The meeting of the Liverpool Chamber in March 1890 which came out against the proposal marked the end of any realistic chance of it going ahead.[78] The Foreign Office rejected the scheme and decided instead, as MacDonald had recommended, to inaugurate a colonial administration in the form of the Oil Rivers Protectorate.[79]

In 1891 the Oil Rivers Protectorate (from 1893 the Niger Coast Protectorate) was established, with its headquarters at Old Calabar and with MacDonald as the first consul-general and commissioner. The protectorate marked the failure of the oil traders' plans for a charter, but also reflected the determination of the British government to consolidate its control over the Delta area and its hinterland. Among its first actions were to set duties on imports into the protectorate and to abolish comey, replacing it by subsidies to chiefs.[80] Over the next couple of years administration was extended into the interior with government stations established at Akwete, Degema, Sapele, Warri, and elsewhere and visits made to Benin, into Urhobo country, and up the Cross River. By 1895 colonial administration was pushing deep inland.

How did the African Association Ltd fare in the new conditions of the palm products trade following colonial take-over? The early 1890s proved to be difficult for the African Association, and not least because of the disputes that broke out within the company. Partly these had their origin in personality differences – particularly between John Holt, chairman from 1894, and Harry Cotterell – and partly they were over business strategy. Should the African Association compete against the Royal Niger Co. and Millers, as Holt urged, or not? Should they take on the steamship services – from 1895 operating a shipping ring with Woermanns – by running their own shipping? In the tight trading conditions of these years, a trade war was a very difficult proposition, as Cotterell recognised, and ultimately, in 1896, the African Association sold its fleet to A. L. Jones and came to terms with its rivals, prompting Holt to resign from the board.[81] There was even a last, vain attempt at a fusion with the Royal Niger Company and Millers in 1895–6.[82] Yet such proposals did little to help the firm. The differences within it were exacerbated by the fact that the combination of 1889 had not meant a merger of the individual businesses that made up the company but only their Delta plant; this was further complicated by disputes concerning the valuation of the capital handed over at the time of amalgamation. Serious losses were incurred in 1892 and 1895.[83]

With the failure of the charter proposals and the establishment of rudimentary colonial rule, the issue facing oil traders like the African Association was how far they would move inland themselves. Would Hewett's description of their 'rest content' policy remain true? Or would political expansion be followed by the move of the trading frontier inland? Initially the response was to move inland, at least for the Opobo and Bonny markets. With the overthrow of Jaja in 1887 traders had moved up the Imo River. Taylor, Laughland, & Co. started to open factories in markets at Ohambele, Akwete, Essene, and elsewhere. Millers too moved into the market at Akwete in 1888, while Harrisons set up in Ohambele and Stuart & Douglas in Obaku. The African Association itself moved into Akwete in 1891.[84]

However, despite early optimism, these traders did little business. The move behind Opobo was not successful, noted the *African Times* as early as 1888. 'A heavy expenditure on steam launches, lighters, stores, building materials, etc., has been incurred in connexion with these up-country branches and the result of the experiment is said to have given rise to keen disappointment.'[85] Little palm oil was obtained, particularly in markets such as Ohambele, where trade slowly ground to a halt during 1888 in the face of continuing Opobo opposition.[86] Soon firms began pulling out, not least once attacks began, as on Millers' Akwete factory in 1891.[87]

The result was the 'retreat' of 1893. In 1892 the African Association sent Hampden Jackson, the company secretary, to West Africa to examine the firm's operations.[88] His decision was to evacuate the Opobo markets, which occurred in early 1893. The African Association's inland factories were sold off to the Opobo brokers for £7,000 and the company retreated back to the status quo of 1887; it remained in Opobo and received oil as before from the local broking network.[89] It was a salutary experience. In many ways Gertzel's view is correct, that the traders found it impossible to match the investment of the oil brokers in labour and transport. But the key point was that this retreat was not through choice; the choice of the firms that made up the company had been clear in their move inland in 1887. Rather, they had been defeated by the continuing power of the brokers, who had shown their capacity to use extra-economic forces, whether religious or political, to prevent producers trading with the British traders. It was the brokers' power that the African Association was compelled to recognise in 1893.

The company was forced to face reality on the River Niger too. Here the problem was not the power of brokers but the position of the Royal Niger Co. Fierce competition against the Royal Niger Co. continued after 1889, with the African Association trying to operate on the river during the early 1890s. A price war on the Niger ensued, developing into disputes over the boundaries with the company in the Warri area, and also concerning the customs post at Idu, during 1891–2.[90] Further protests erupted from the Liverpool Chamber and a challenge to the terms of the Royal Niger Company's charter was made. But here too the African Association had to recognise the power of its rival and pull out, selling its Niger business in July 1893.[91]

The retreat of 1893 marked the end, at least for the moment, of the African Association's policy of trying to move into the oil markets of the Opobo interior and the Niger. However, their retreat needs to be kept in perspective, at least in the Delta. It was a withdrawal from Opobo markets; it did not mean a retreat by all oil firms everywhere in the Delta area. Elsewhere, the establishment of colonial administration after 1891 was followed by moves inland by traders. In 1892, for example, several firms were looking to move in to the Forcados trade in order to cut out Itsekiri brokers.[92] John Harford was doing well in the Kwa Ibo by the early 1890s.[93] In 1895 Millers and the Oil Rivers Trading Co. moved back into Akwete.[94] The African Association itself still considered going up the Cross River in 1893, and bought property in Sapele in the Western Delta in the same year, showing its growing interest in the other two major markets for palm products in the region.[95] It was still doing extremely well in the markets of the Kwa Ibo in 1893.[96] Indeed, it even drew up plans to move into Asante at the end of that year.[97] The African Association's defeat by Opobo brokers in 1893 marked the loss of a skirmish rather than the end of a campaign.

Moreover, the retreat of the African Association in 1893 was followed by continuing pressure for governmental action in other ways. Thus the early 1890s saw a stepping up of demands by traders for the three 'R's, that is the opening of roads, rivers, and railways inland.[98] This could be seen right across the region. On the Gold Coast there was a clear push from c. 1890 for the building of new roads and railways, while Alldridge's mission into the interior of Sierra Leone in 1890 was marked by his stress on the need for road clearing.[99] From as early as 1880 the *African Times* was urging railway construction for the Gold Coast and Lagos.[100] In Yorubaland, Liverpool firms objected to the warfare that closed routes inland from Lagos and, in 1892, supported by Chambers of Commerce all over Britain, urged an attack on the Ijebu.[101] Holt welcomed MacDonald's safeguarding of routes in the Delta area in 1893.[102] Three years later Holt was urging further action to move inland in the Delta: 'a strong arm' was necessary, he suggested, adding, '[but] no killing of our customers'.[103]

Moreover, oil traders began urging intervention elsewhere in the Delta area. Strong-arm measures with very little tact began to be exerted by the British up the Cross River, with shelling of villages in 1895.[104] Similar action occurred in the Western Delta, where the British met fierce resistance, led by Nana, the *Gofine* or governor of the Benin River since 1883. Vice-Consul Gallwey toured Urhobo oil markets in 1891, described the Itsekiri as opponents of free trade and blamed Nana.[105] The picture he drew was echoed by Pinnock's agent on the Benin River, who urged an attack on Nana in July 1894; it would produce better trade, he said, 'and more profitable too'.[106] The result was the attack on Ebrohimi in 1894, and the trial and deportation of Nana.[107]

The fate of Nana, and indeed of Jaja before him, showed the future for brokers in the new conditions surrounding the palm products trade after 1880. Yet perhaps the clearest illustration of these changes came with the Akassa Raid of January 1895, launched by the people of Brass in the face of the steady deterioration of their trading position because of the Royal Niger Company's stranglehold over lower Niger markets.[108] The attack by Brass on the Royal Niger Company's main depot at Akassa was a final despairing gesture by Delta brokers against the erosion of their position in the trade. The inevitable result was the sacking of Nembe in February 1895.[109]

In practice the move inland by British traders was to be several years coming, and coastal brokers survived and in some cases prospered in the Delta palm products trade into the first decade of the twentieth century. It was not until then that the Cross River trade was entered by Thomas Welsh or the Orashi River by John Holt, to give but two examples.[110] The final blow to the brokers' role came from the impact of other developments introduced by the British colonial administration to remodel the practices of the trade. These measures included the eradication of trust, the imposition of British currency, and the abolition of comey, trade dashes, and such like – practices that had been at the heart of the trade. It was the subsequent introduction of the pedal cycle, the four-gallon kerosene tin, and then the building of railways – as in the completion of the Port Harcourt–Enugu line in 1916 – that finally finished off the coastal brokers of the Delta area. With the arrival of the lorry after World War I, these developments reached a conclusion. This did not mean an end to brokers; many turned to providing water carriage for British firms, at least until the railway arrived – broking labour and canoes rather than oil and kernels – while others found niches in collecting oil and kernels to sell to the inland trading stations or in providing lorry transport.[111] But this was a very different niche from that which their coastal predecessors had occupied during the nineteenth century.

The Akassa Raid and the subsequent sacking of Nembe marked the effective end of the Delta states' role as independent brokers in the palm products trade. It was the end of an era in the oil trade. The oil firms of the Delta continued to use the brokers' transport and labour to obtain oil and kernels until the new century, certainly.[112] But the seizure of Jaja in 1887, the take-over of Old Calabar in 1891, the deportation of Nana after 1894, and finally the sacking of Nembe in 1895 all represented the British removal of the political capacity that these states and leaders had hitherto relied on to defend their broking position. Brokers remained in place, but their independence had been destroyed. The implications of this for the future of the trade were clear. The aim of the oil firms in the 1890s in the Delta area was not to remove brokers, at least not yet, but to establish a degree of control over them and thereby to eradicate their capacity for independent action. A charter, as proposed during the 1880s, would have served this purpose. In its absence, the colonial authorities acted as a substitute to break the power of the broking states. With the establishment of colonial administration in the Delta after 1891, the capacity of brokers for independent action in the trade had been removed and their economic position emasculated.

This had wider implications, for the commercial and political assault on the Delta brokers represented the ending of their role more generally in the trade. In Yorubaland, the Gold Coast, and Sierra Leone, this transition may not have been as dramatic, since such powerful broking states had not developed in the oil and kernels trade of these areas. But the trend was the same. Whether it was Krio traders or British firms which moved inland, the turn of the century saw the ending of the independence of indigenous brokers in oil and kernels.

The imposition of colonial administration – British, French, and German – in the coastal regions of West Africa during the 1890s marked the end of an economic era. While it would take several years before coastal brokers finally disappeared, it was the end of their role in the oil trade. The clearing of creeks, the arrival of the railway, and the building of roads that accompanied the establishment of colonial rule meant that there was little need in the future organisation of the trade for the great broking states of the coast. Colonial conquest thus marked the end of a process of change in the oil trade that had begun with the introduction of the steamer services in 1852. The coastal trading system, with its accompanying structures and practices that went back to the slave trade and which had survived the transition to 'legitimate' trade in the first half of the century little changed, was disappearing. By colonial conquest, the Europeans had decided to transform this system come what may. It would take some years for this process to be completed, but the palm products trade as it had existed for a century and as it had been known to Duke Ephraim, William Dappa Pepple, Eyo Honesty, Jaja, and Nana was effectively at an end.

Conclusion

It may be facile to speak of individual centuries as if they represent a distinct period in historical reality, yet the nineteenth century has a unity in the history of West Africa's export trade. Slaving continued for several decades after 1807 across the Atlantic – and for even longer across the Sahara – but in terms of West Africa's economic history this was the century of legitimate trade. Until the destruction of the coastal brokers' powers at the end of the century, this was a period when West Africans produced agricultural commodities for the world market, and transported, bulked, and brokered those commodities within their own independent states and societies.

Of the agricultural commodities that West Africans produced for the world market in the nineteenth century, palm oil and kernels were by far the most important for large parts of the region. When one considers the numbers of farmers, specialist palm climbers, oil processors, kernel crackers, porters, canoemen, brokers, pilots, and labourers involved – not to mention those producing the foodstuffs, canoes, mortars, baskets, calabashes, and other products required to facilitate the trade – it is clear that the production and trade of palm produce played a major role in West Africa's export economy. Equally, this trade had an important, if too often ignored, impact on the population of Britain. The products of West Africa's palm oil industry spread deep into the households of industrial Britain in the nineteenth century. With items such as Price's candles, 'Sunlight' soap, and Van den Bergh's margarine, there can have been few, if any, British households that did not receive the produce of West Africans' labour in these years. Similarly, railway carriages greased by palm oil carried members of the British public on their journeys, factory machinery lubricated by palm oil employed them and produced the goods that made their economy 'the workshop of the world', while tins manufactured with palm oil canned their food, and palm kernels fed the cattle that produced the milk they drank with their tea.

In essence this process saw West African palm oil producers being integrated into the world market for oils and fats. The aim of this study has been to examine the precise impact of this world market on West Africa and how that impact varied over the century. Three issues have been thrown up by this. Firstly, it has raised the question of how far the development of the palm produce trade represented a break in West Africa's economic history. The argument has been that the development of this trade did accompany changes in trading and producing patterns in West Africa, but that it is difficult to see these as amounting to a systemic break or crisis in the region's social structure or economic life. What is more striking is the degree of continuity in the trading system and in West Africa's economic patterns that characterised the transition from slaving to palm oil. Indeed, it was precisely this continuity that enabled the new trade to develop as rapidly as it did. This can be seen clearly in the sphere of trading and, to a greater or lesser extent, in the organisation of production. Further work on the details of this transition remains to be done, especially on the impact of oil pro- duction on social structures and, above all, on gender, where only impres- sionistic conclusions have been offered here.

The second issue addressed by this study has been the difficulties that developed in the trade in the late nineteenth century. The argument has been that it was from the middle of the century that West Africa's trading relationships began to change significantly and the underlying theme here has been the impact of the steamship. It was the introduction of this new technology after 1852 that had the greatest impact on the palm oil trade, through opening the market to newcomers at a time of a changing pattern of world demand; this development led to overproduction and in turn contributed to the fall in prices of the later decades of the century. The problems of the ensuing depression were reinforced by the innovations in trading techniques and business organisation that were made necessary by the steamship. This crisis of restructuring – for crisis this clearly was – affected producer, broker, and trader alike, making this an immensely difficult period for all, and, not least, left producers vulnerable to the vagaries of the global market. More work is still needed on this depression and especially on the business and managerial changes that occurred during it. In particular more is needed on how individual British firms reacted to the pressures of restructuring and how they passed their costs on to their suppliers and customers. Important work has been done on the Krio and Gold Coast firms operating along the coast in the late nineteenth century, but of inestimable value would be similar analysis of how individ- ual broking businesses in, say, Old Calabar, Bonny, or Brass reacted to the pressures of these decades, not least their reaction to the competitive ten- sions within the broking market after the 1870s.

Finally, the crisis of restructuring threw up fundamental questions con- cerning the relationship between West African and European traders. It raised the central question of what was to be the place of West Africans in the trade. Were they to be brokers and producers, or simply producers? What were to be the powers of brokers in the trade? Until the arrival of the steamship this had been a commerce in which effective control of the mechanisms of trade had lain with African brokers. The struggle between European traders and African brokers over the utilisation of the technology of steam that developed after 1852 was to shift that balance firmly away from African traders, and in the long term, by pushing the trading frontier inland, reduced brokers to an essentially subsidiary role. Repeated efforts by brokers, not to mention by Krio traders, were made to exploit the advantages of steam for their own ends. These attempts, and their eventual failure, remain a critical turning-point in West Africa's economic history.

The restructuring of the market from the middle of the century also had an impact on the attitudes of British traders towards colonial conquest. Initially traders remained sceptical of talk of abandoning free trade and moving towards colonial rule. The fall in oil prices of the late 1880s, however, drove oil traders to look for economies and thus towards support for a policy that had hitherto been rejected, namely colonial expansion in West Africa. This is not to suggest that the origins of colonial conquest in West Africa lay in any simplistic sense in these problems in the palm oil trade. Complex factors developing beyond the region lay behind the move towards British imperial expansion in West Africa, but it is clear that, from the late 1880s, palm oil traders added their voices to those of others who urged colonial conquest as the solution to their problems on the African continent. From the point of view of the oil trade – the concern of this study – the significance of this was that, by demanding a move inland and a concomitant curtailing of African brokers' powers, British traders were urging an end to long-established structures and practices of palm oil trading. In doing this, traders were recognising the end of trading structures in both Britain and Africa that went back several centuries. In this sense the late nineteenth century truly marked the end of an era in West African trade.

Notes

INTRODUCTION

1. J. Barbot, 'A Description of the Coast of North and South Guinea and of Ethiopia Inferior, Vulgarly Angola', in A. Churchill and J. Churchill (eds.), *A Collection of Voyages and Travels*, 6 vols. (London, 1732), vol. V, 204.
2. C. W. S. Hartley, *The Oil Palm*, 3rd edn (London, 1988), 1; L. E. Andés, *Vegetable Fats and Oils* (London, 1897), 210. 'Pure fresh palm oil has an agreeable smell . . . resembling that of plum cake': 'The African Oil Palm', *Kew Bulletin of Miscellaneous Information* 55 (1891), 191.
3. Hartley, *Oil Palm*, 1–3; A. C. Zeven, 'The Origin of the Oil Palm', *Journal of the Nigerian Institute for Oil Palm Research* 4 (1965), 218–25; J. D. Clark, 'Prehistoric Populations and Pressures Favouring Plant Domestication', in J. R. Harlan, J. M. J. de Wet, and A. B. L. Stemler (eds.), *Origins of African Plant Domestication* (The Hague, 1976), 80; T. Shaw, 'Early Crops in Africa: A Review of the Evidence', *ibid.*, 113, 132; P. J. Munson, 'Archaeological Data on the Origins of Cultivation in the South-Western Sahara and Their Implications for West Africa', *ibid.*, 197.
4. Shaw, 'Early Crops in Africa', 138; D. Northrup, *Trade Without Rulers: Pre-Colonial Economic Development in South-Eastern Nigeria* (Oxford, 1978), 185. Northrup makes the point that the words for oil palms in the languages of the Niger Delta clearly developed in the very distant past. Equally, terms for the oil palm in Surinam, *obe* and *maba*, appear to be derived from the Yoruba *ope*, the Fanti–Twi *abe*, and the Kikongo *maba*: Zeven, 'Origin', 223.
5. G. R. Crone (ed.), *The Voyages of Cadamosto* (London, 1937), 42–4, 83; D. Pacheco Pereira, *Esmeraldo de Situ Orbis* (ed. by G. H. T. Kimble) (London, 1937), 126–8.
6. Hartley, *Oil Palm*, 5–8; G. G. Auchinleck, *The West African Oil Palm and Its Products* (Colombo, 1923), 9; J. W. Purseglove, 'The Origins and Migrations of Crops in Tropical Africa', in Harlan, de Wet, and Stemler, *African Plant Domestication*, 298. Northrup, *Trade Without Rulers*, 185, attributes this density in southeastern Nigeria to the 'semi-cultivation' practices that accompanied the penetration of cultivators into the primary rain forest of this region. See also A. C. Zeven, 'Oil Palm Groves in Southern Nigeria, Part I: Types of Groves in Existence', *Journal of the Nigerian Institute for Oil Palm Research* 4 (1965), 226–50, and 'Part II: Development, Deterioration, and Rehabilitation of Groves', 5 (1968), 21–39.
7. J. R. Harlan, J. M. J. de Wet, and A. B. L. Stemler, 'Plant Domestication and

191

Indigenous African Agriculture', in Harlan, de Wet, and Stemler, *African Plant Domestication*, 12–14.

8. Hartley, *Oil Palm*, 95–6; H. C. Billows and H. Beckwith, *Palm Oil and Kernels: The 'Consols of the West Coast'* (Liverpool, 1913), 13–14; 'Investigations in Connection with the African Palm Oil Industry', *Bulletin of the Imperial Institute* 7 (1909), 359–61.

9. J. H. J. Farquhar (ed. H. N. Thompson), *The Oil Palm and Its Varieties* (London, 1913), 17–20; G. C. Dudgeon, *The Agricultural and Forest Products of British West Africa* (London, 1911), 61; 'African Oil Palm'; J. M. Sarbah, 'The Oil Palm and Its Uses', *Journal of the African Society* 8 (1909), 236–7; P. Manning, 'The Economy of Early Colonial Dahomey, 1890–1914', in J. P. Smaldone (ed.), *Explorations in Quantitative African History* (Syracuse, 1977), 26.

10. B. W. Andah, 'Identifying Early Farming Traditions of West Africa', in T. Shaw, P. Sinclair, B. Andah, and A. Okpoko (eds.), *The Archaeology of Africa: Foods, Metals, and Towns* (London, 1993), 240–54; R. Oliver, *The African Experience* (London, 1991), 45; Clark, 'Prehistoric Populations and Pressures', 87. D. R. Harris, 'Traditional Systems of Plant Food Production and the Origins of Agriculture in West Africa', in Harlan, de Wet, and Stemler, *African Plant Domestication*, 338–9, stresses the ecological and dietary complementarity between the fat produced by the oil palm and the carbohydrates produced by yams: hence the spread of the two crops together in many parts of West Africa.

11. A. Falconbridge, *An Account of the Slave Trade on the Coast of Africa* (London, 1788), 16; E. J. Usoro, *The Nigerian Oil Palm Industry* (Ibadan, 1974), 1.

12. J. Corry, *Observations upon the Windward Coast of Africa* (London, 1807), 39.

13. E. D. Morel, *Affairs of West Africa* (London, 1902), 77.

14. Pacheco Pereira, *Esmeraldo*, 128.

15. N. H. Stilliard, 'The Rise and Development of Legitimate Trade in Palm Oil with West Africa', MA thesis, University of Birmingham (1938), 8–9.

16. M. Johnson, *Anglo-African Trade in the Eighteenth Century* (ed. J. T. Lindblad and R. Ross) (Leiden, 1990), 56.

17. *PP* 1845, XLVI (187), 481; 1854–5, LII (1987), 84.

18. *PP* 1899, XCV (9300), 32.

19. Annual Statement of the Trade and Navigation of the UK, *PP, passim*.

20. Billows and Beckwith, *Palm Oil and Kernels*, 3; 'Lagos Palm Oil', *Kew Bulletin of Miscellaneous Information* 69 (1892), 200–8; C. Wilson, *The History of Unilever*, 2 vols. (London, 1954), vol. I, 3–8; K. E. Hunt, 'Raw Materials', in J. H. van Stuyvenberg (ed.), *Margarine: An Economic, Social, and Scientific History, 1869–1969* (Liverpool, 1969), 44–5.

21. J. E. Flint and E. A. McDougall, 'Economic Change in West Africa in the Nineteenth Century', in J. F. A. Ajayi and M. Crowder (eds.), *History of West Africa*, 2 vols., 2nd edn (London, 1987), vol. II, 383.

22. A. G. Hopkins, 'The "New International Economic Order" in the Nineteenth Century: Britain's First Development Plan for Africa', in R. Law (ed.), *From Slave Trade to 'Legitimate' Commerce: The Commercial Transition in Nineteenth-Century West Africa* (Cambridge, 1995), 240–64.

23. A. McPhee, *The Economic Revolution in British West Africa* (London, 1926), esp. 30–6; Stilliard, 'Legitimate Trade'.
24. The historiography of the transition is laid out in R. Law, 'The Historiography of the Commercial Transition in Nineteenth-Century West Africa', in T. Falola (ed.), *African Historiography: Essays in Honour of Jacob Ade Ajayi* (Harlow, 1993), 91–115, and R. Law, 'Introduction', in Law, *From Slave Trade to 'Legitimate' Commerce*, 1–31.
25. K. O. Dike, *Trade and Politics in the Niger Delta, 1830–1885* (Oxford, 1956).
26. A. G. Hopkins, 'Economic Imperialism in West Africa: Lagos, 1880–1892', *Economic History Review* 21 (1968), 580–606. See also J. F. A. Ajayi and R. A. Austen, 'Hopkins on Economic Imperialism in West Africa', *Economic History Review* 25 (1972), 303–6, and the 'Rejoinder' by Hopkins in the same issue, 307–12.
27. A. G. Hopkins, *An Economic History of West Africa* (London, 1973), 124–66.
28. Ajayi and Austen, 'Hopkins on Economic Imperialism'; R. A. Austen, 'The Abolition of the Overseas Slave Trade: A Distorted Theme in West African History', *JHSN* 5 (1970), 257–74; J. F. Munro, *Africa and the International Economy, 1800–1960* (London, 1976), 46; P. Manning, 'Slaves, Palm Oil, and Political Power on the West African Coast', *African Historical Studies* 2 (1969), 279–88.
29. E. J. Alagoa, 'Nineteenth-Century Revolutions in the Eastern Delta States and Calabar', *JHSN* 5 (1971), 565–73; A. J. H. Latham, *Old Calabar, 1600–1891* (Oxford, 1973).
30. R. A. Austen, *African Economic History* (London, 1987), 100–2.
31. T. Zeleza, *A Modern Economic History of Africa*, vol. I, *The Nineteenth Century* (Dakar, 1993), 370–1.
32. C. Gertzel, 'John Holt: A British Merchant in West Africa in the Era of Imperialism', DPhil. thesis, University of Oxford (1959); C. J. Gertzel, 'Commercial Organisation on the Niger Coast, 1852–1891', *Proceedings of the Leverhulme Intercollegiate History Conference* (Salisbury, 1960), 1–16; P. N. Davies, *The Trade Makers: Elder Dempster in West Africa, 1852–1972* (London, 1973); Davies (ed.), *Trading in West Africa, 1840–1920* (London, 1976); Davies, *Henry Tyrer* (London, 1979).
33. P. Manning, 'Palm Oil and Kernel Exports from Nigeria, 1880–1905: A Study in Econometric History', MSc. thesis, University of Wisconsin (1966); Hopkins, *Economic History*, 133–64; Munro, *Africa and the International Economy*, 65–73; Austen, *Economic History*, 112–17; C. Newbury, 'On the Margins of Empire: The Trade of Western Africa, 1875–1890', in S. Förster, W. J. Mommsen, and R. Robinson (eds.), *Bismarck, Europe, and Africa: The Berlin Africa Conference, 1884–1885, and the Onset of Partition* (Oxford, 1988), 35–58.
34. S. M. Martin, *Palm Oil and Protest: An Economic History of the Ngwa Region of South-Eastern Nigeria, 1800–1980* (Cambridge, 1988); S. M. Martin, 'Slaves, Igbo Women, and Palm Oil in the Nineteenth Century', in Law, *From Slave Trade to 'Legitimate' Commerce*, 172–94; Law, '"Legitimate" Trade and Gender Relations in Yorubaland and Dahomey', *ibid.*, 195–214.
35. Northrup, *Trade Without Rulers*; J. N. Oriji, 'A Study of the Slave and Palm Produce Trade Among the Ngwa–Igbo of Southeastern Nigeria', *Cahiers d' études africaines* 23, 91 (1983), 311–28; A. Jones, *From Slaves to Palm Kernels:*

194   Notes to pages 7–15

A History of the Galinhas Country, 1730–1890 (Wiesbaden, 1983); G. I. Jones, *From Slaves to Palm Oil: Slave Trade and Palm Oil Trade in the Bight of Biafra* (Cambridge, 1989); L. E. Wilson, *The Krobo People of Ghana to 1892: A Political and Social History* (Athens, Ohio, 1992).

36. J. S. Hogendorn, 'The Vent-for-Surplus Model and African Cash Agriculture to 1914', *Savanna* 5 (1976), 15–28; W. M. Freund and R. W. Shenton, '"Vent-for-Surplus" Theory and the Economic History of West Africa', *Savanna* 6 (1977), 191–6.

1 THE WEST AFRICAN TRADE IN TRANSITION

1. P. D. Curtin, *The Atlantic Slave Trade: A Census* (Madison, 1969), 211.
2. J. D. Fage, *A History of West Africa* (Cambridge, 1969), 78–80.
3. M. McCarthy, *Social Change and the Growth of British Power in the Gold Coast: The Fante States, 1807–1874* (Lanham, MD, 1983), 82.
4. J. Sanders, 'Palm Oil Production on the Gold Coast in the Aftermath of the Slave Trade: A Case Study of the Fante', *IJAHS* 15 (1982), 49.
5. J. L. A. Webb, 'The Trade in Gum Arabic: Prelude to French Conquest in Senegal', *JAH* 26 (1985), 149–68.
6. Fage, *West Africa*, 120.
7. C. Fyfe, *A History of Sierra Leone* (London, 1962), 117, 125, 141–2; E. A. Ijagbemi, 'The Freetown Colony and the Development of "Legitimate" Commerce in the Adjoining Territories', *JHSN* 5 (1970), 243–56.
8. Curtin, *Slave Trade*, 221.
9. D. Eltis, 'Precolonial Western Africa and the Atlantic Economy', in B. L. Solow (ed.), *Slavery and the Rise of the Atlantic System* (Cambridge, 1991), 97–119, esp. 118.
10. D. Eltis and L. C. Jennings, 'Trade Between Western Africa and the Atlantic World in the Pre-Colonial Era', *American Historical Review* 93 (1988), 939–40.
11. Hopkins, *Economic History*, 125–35. Many of these commodities still await their historians.
12. S. Lambert (ed.), *House of Commons Sessional Papers of the Eighteenth Century* (Wilmington, 1975), vol. LXVII, 53–5; *PP* 1845, XLVI (187), 481.
13. Lambert, *Sessional Papers*, 65; Stilliard, 'Legitimate Trade', 9–10.
14. Johnson, *Anglo-African Trade*, 68–9.
15. CUST 5/153, PRO.
16. CUST 5/–, *passim*, PRO; *PP* 1890–1, LXXXIX (6457), 134–5.
17. CO 272/23, PRO.
18. Annual Statement of the Trade and Navigation of the UK, *PP*, *passim*. It should be noted that these are figures for 'nuts and kernels commonly used for expressing oil', rather than for palm kernels alone.
19. O. Philipps, 'Germany and the Palm Kernel Trade', *Journal of the African Society* 14 (1914–15), 193–8; A. H. Milbourne, 'Palm Kernels from West Africa', *Journal of the African Society* 15 (1915–16), 133–44; E. Hieke, *Zur Geschichte des deutschen Handels mit Ostafrika: das hamburgische Handelshaus Wm O'Swald & Co*, vol. I, *1831–1870* (Hamburg, 1939); E. Hieke, *G. L. Gaiser: Hamburg–Westafrika* (Hamburg, 1949).
20. L. Harding, 'Hamburg's West Africa Trade in the Nineteenth Century', in G.

Liesegang, H. Pasch, and A. Jones (eds.), *Figuring African Trade* (Berlin, 1986), 363–91.

21. N. R. Bennett and G. E. Brooks (eds.), *New England Merchants in Africa* (Boston, 1965), xxx; G. E. Brooks, 'American Trade as a Factor in West African History in the Early Nineteenth Century: Senegal and the Gambia, 1815–1835', in D. F. McCall, N. R. Bennett, and J. Butler (eds.), *Western African History* (New York, 1969), 133; G. E. Brooks, *Yankee Traders, Old Coasters, and African Middlemen* (Boston, 1970), 259, 281, 305–10.

22. B. Schnapper, *La Politique et le commerce français dans le Golfe de Guinée de 1838 à 1871* (Paris, 1961), 140.

23. CO 100/2–/6, PRO; Brooks, *Yankee Traders*, 307–10. Only nine casks, worth £150, were exported to the USA in 1831; this reached £2,156 and 27 per cent of Sierra Leone's total in 1839, but with this exception rarely did exports to the USA exceed 5 per cent of Sierra Leone's oil exports in the first half of the century.

24. One market for West African palm oil that does not receive attention is Brazil. Manning stresses that palm oil was reaching Brazil from the Slave Coast in this period but the total is unlikely to be large, not least given the availability of the native American oil palm: P. Manning, *Slavery, Colonialism, and Economic Growth in Dahomey, 1640–1960* (Cambridge, 1982), 51.

25. J. R. Hanson, *Trade in Transition: Exports from the Third World, 1840–1900* (New York, 1980), 13–15, 30; Eltis, 'Precolonial Western Africa', 104.

26. Eltis and Jennings, 'Trade Between Western Africa and the Atlantic World', 941, 946; C. W. Newbury, 'Prices and Profitability in Early Nineteenth-Century West African Trade', in C. Meillassoux (ed.), *The Development of Indigenous Trade and Markets in West Africa* (London, 1971), 92; J. E. Inikori, 'West Africa's Seaborne Trade, 1750–1850: Volume, Structure, and Implications', in Liesegang, Pasch, and Jones, *Figuring African Trade*, 60.

27. D. Eltis, *Economic Growth and the Ending of the Transatlantic Slave Trade* (Oxford, 1987), 170.

28. W. F. Hancock, *Survey of British Commonwealth Affairs*, 4 vols., vol. II, part 2, *Problems of Economic Policy* (London, 1942), 160.

29. *PP* 1831–2, XXXIV (514), 471; 1842, XXXIX (15), 53; 1854–5, LII (1987), 84; 1866, LXXIII (3675), 20–1.

30. For example, the market value of British imports of palm oil from West Africa in both 1819 and 1821 far exceeds the official value for all British imports from that region in *PP* 1824, XVII (269), 240.

31. Inikori, 'West Africa's Seaborne Trade'. Using official values, in 1828 palm oil made up 69 per cent of Britain's imports from West Africa and 70 per cent a year later. By 1831, still using official values, the proportion had reached 80 per cent: *PP* 1816, VII B (506), 12; 1830, X (661), 514–17; 1831–2, XXXIV (461), 201.

32. Inikori, 'West Africa's Seaborne Trade', 58. At a value of £400,000 palm oil represented less than 0.9 per cent of the official value of all British imports in 1833 and less than 0.7 per cent of the computed value: B. R. Mitchell, *Abstract of British Historical Statistics* (Cambridge, 1962), 282.

33. Eltis, *Economic Growth*, 228.

34. 'The Diary of Antera Duke', in D. Forde, *Efik Traders of Old Calabar*

(London, 1968), 42; J. Adams, *Remarks on the Country Extending from Cape Palmas to the River Congo* (London, 1823), 245; Latham, *Old Calabar*, 55.
35. Adams, *Remarks*, 247; Latham, *Old Calabar*, 65–6.
36. E. Aye, *Old Calabar Through the Centuries* (Calabar, 1967), 46; A. J. H. Latham, 'A Trading Alliance: Sir John Tobin and Duke Ephraim', *History Today* 24 (1974), 862–7.
37. Latham, *Old Calabar*, 66–7.
38. G. A. Robertson, *Notes on Africa* (London, 1819), 313–14, 363; Latham, *Old Calabar*, 66.
39. A. J. H. Latham, 'Price Fluctuations in the Early Palm Oil Trade', *JAH* 19 (1978), 213–18. Important in this process is the fact that oil palms, once planted, take several years before they bear fruit.
40. Robertson, *Notes on Africa*, 310, 363.
41. Stilliard, 'Legitimate Trade', 40–1; Latham, *Old Calabar*, 67.
42. Northrup, *Trade Without Rulers*, 183, 191–2. R. M. Jackson, *Journal of a Voyage to Bonny River* (London, 1934), 96–7, suggests that the growth in Bonny's exports was related to the 'opening' of the Bonny bar in 1826 which allowed larger oil ships to enter the Bonny River thereafter.
43. S. M. Hargreaves, 'The Political Economy of Nineteenth-Century Bonny: A Study of Power, Authority, Legitimacy, and Ideology in a Delta Trading Community, 1790–1914', Ph.D thesis, University of Birmingham (1987), 218–23.
44. *PP* 1842, XI (551), 244–5. Hutton was not a trader with Bonny, so his figures must be treated with caution.
45. T. J. Hutchinson, *Impressions of Western Africa* (London, 1858), 252; Dike, *Trade and Politics*, 50, 101.
46. E. J. Alagoa, *The Small Brave City-State: A History of Nembe–Brass in the Niger Delta* (Madison, 1964), 60.
47. This is confirmed by entries of palm oil from Brass in the Customs Bills of Entry at least as early as 1845: M. Lynn, 'Change and Continuity in the British Palm Oil Trade with West Africa, 1830–1855', *JAH* 22 (1981), 341.
48. W. E. Wariboko, 'New Calabar and the Forces of Change, c. 1850–1945', Ph.D thesis, University of Birmingham (1991), 68–72.
49. Lynn, 'Change and Continuity', 340–1; L. Z. Elango, 'Trade and Diplomacy on the Cameroon Coast in the Nineteenth Century, 1833–1879: The Case of Bimbia', in M. Njeuma (ed.), *Introduction to the History of Cameroon* (London, 1989), 32–62.
50. Adams, *Remarks*, 145; R. A. Austen, 'The Metamorphoses of Middlemen: The Duala, Europeans, and the Cameroon Hinterland, c. 1800–c. 1960', *IJAHS* 16 (1983), 1–24; M. Johnson, 'By Ship or by Camel: The Struggle for the Cameroons Ivory Trade in the Nineteenth Century', *JAH* 19 (1978), 539–49.
51. Robertson, *Notes on Africa*, 323; E. Bold, *The Merchants' and Mariners' Guide* (London, 1822), 83.
52. A. Wirz, 'La "Rivière du Cameroun": commerce pré-coloniale et contrôle du pouvoir en société lignagère', *Revue française d'histoire d'Outre-Mer* 60, 219 (1973), 172–95, esp. 182; Austen, 'Metamorphoses of Middlemen', 6–7.
53. W. F. W. Owen, *Narrative of Voyages to Explore the Shores of Africa...*, 2 vols. (London, 1833), vol. II, 357–9; Dike, *Trade and Politics*, 50; Eltis, *Economic Growth*, 170.

54. Log of the brig *Julian*, 22 March 1829 (in the possession of Prof. P. N. Davies; I am grateful to Prof. Davies for permission to consult this log); O. Ikime, *Merchant Prince of the Niger Delta* (Ibadan, 1968), 4–5.
55. J. Beecroft, 'On Benin and the Upper Course of the River Quorra or Niger', *JRGS* 11 (1841), 184–92.
56. Log of the brig *Julian*, 5 March 1829; R. S. Smith, *The Lagos Consulate, 1851–1861* (London, 1978), 12.
57. D. A. Ross, 'The Autonomous Kingdom of Dahomey, 1818–1894', Ph.D thesis, University of London (1967), 59–60; Manning, *Slavery, Colonialism, and Economic Growth*, 51. W. M. Hutton claimed his nephew opened the factory at Whydah in 1839–40, rather than 1838 (*PP* 1842, XI (551), 699; Hutton to Aberdeen, 20 December 1843, FO 84/501, PRO), though on another occasion he gave 1838 as the date, Hutton to Hawes, 6 July 1847, CALPROF 1/2/1, NNAE.
58. Hutton to Hawes, 25 March 1847, CO 96/12, PRO; C. W. Newbury, *The Western Slave Coast and Its Rulers* (Oxford, 1961), 37–43; C. Sorensen, 'Badagry, 1784–1863: The Political and Commercial History of a Pre-Colonial Lagoonside Community in South-West Nigeria', Ph.D thesis, University of Stirling (1995), 204–7.
59. Ross, 'Dahomey', 59–71; Manning, *Slavery, Colonialism, and Economic Growth*, 50–6; J. Reid, 'Warrior Aristocrats in Crisis: The Political Effects of the Transition from the Slave Trade to Palm Oil Commerce in the Nineteenth-Century Kingdom of Dahomey', Ph.D thesis, University of Stirling (1986), 178.
60. C. Coquery-Vidrovitch, 'De la traite des esclaves à l'exportation de l'huile de palme et des palmistes au Dahomey, XIXe siècle', in Meillassoux, *Development of Indigenous Trade*, 107–23.
61. D. A. Ross, 'The Career of Domingo Martinez in the Bight of Benin, 1833–1864', *JAH* 6 (1965), 79–90; Ross, 'The First Chacha of Whydah: Francisco Felix de Souza', *Odu* 2 (1969), 19–28; Manning, *Slavery, Colonialism, and Economic Growth*, 51.
62. B. Cruickshank, *Eighteen Years on the Gold Coast of Africa*, 2 vols. (London, 1853), vol. II, 41–2.
63. CUST 5/16, PRO; *PP* 1817, VI (431), 420; H. Meredith, *An Account of the Gold Coast of Africa* (London, 1812), 69, 73–5.
64. *PP* 1816, VII B (506), 15–17; 1817, VI (431), 420; Robertson's work, published in 1819, refers to oil exports from the Gold Coast, *Notes on Africa*, 362; Sanders, 'Palm Oil Production on the Gold Coast', 56.
65. Quoted in Sanders, 'Palm Oil Production on the Gold Coast', 56–7.
66. E. Reynolds, *Trade and Economic Change on the Gold Coast, 1807–1874* (Harlow, 1974), 69, 72–4; L. E. Wilson, *Krobo People*, 55–7.
67. CUST 5/16, CUST 5/19, CUST 5/29, PRO; Reynolds, *Trade and Economic Change*, 61, 134.
68. CUST 5/2, PRO; Corry, *Observations*, 39–40.
69. *PP* 1816, VII B (506), 53.
70. CO 272/1–/7, PRO.
71. CUST 5/24, CUST 5/29, PRO; Fyfe, *History*, 125; C. Fyfe, *A Short History of Sierra Leone* (London, 1979), 37–8, 57.
72. CO 272/7–/27, PRO.
73. CO 272/23, PRO.

74. CUST 5/1E; CO 90/4–/13: both PRO.
75. Bold, *Guide*, 49; Robertson, *Notes on Africa*, 43, 88, 92.
76. S. Daget, 'An Exceptional Document: Legitimate Trade of the Ship *Africain* on the West Coast of Africa in 1827', *Journal of African Studies* 2 (1975), 177–200; D. N. Syfert, 'The Liberian Coasting Trade, 1822–1900', *JAH* 18 (1977), 220–1.
77. CUST 5/20–/5, PRO.
78. CUST 5/16–/34, PRO.
79. T. E. Bowdich, *Mission from Cape Coast Castle to Ashantee* (London, 1819), 422–52; M. Lynn, 'British Business and the African Trade: Richard & William King Ltd of Bristol and West Africa, 1833–1918', *Business History* 34 (1992), 23–4.
80. Quantities of palm oil from Gabon were arriving in Britain by the 1850s: Lynn, 'Change and Continuity', 341.
81. R. T. Anstey, 'British Trade and Policy in West Central Africa Between 1816 and the Early 1880s', *THSG* 3 (1957), 50–1; R. T. Anstey, *Britain and the Congo in the Nineteenth Century* (Oxford, 1962), 10, 20–2; P. M. Martin, *The External Trade of the Loango Coast, 1576–1870* (Oxford, 1972), 136–57.
82. Lynn, 'Change and Continuity', 339–41.
83. These figures can be compared with D. Richardson, 'The Eighteenth-Century British Slave Trade: Estimates of Its Volume and Coastal Distribution in Africa', *Research in Economic History* 12 (1989), 151–95. The figures for Angola and for the Windward Coast in the later decades of the slave trade are slightly higher than the figures for the oil trade in the 1840s–1850s, but otherwise the totals are essentially comparable.
84. Liverpool's role in the slave trade is well set out in G. Williams, *History of the Liverpool Privateers and Letters of Marque* (London, 1897, reprint New York, 1966), and in *Liverpool and Slavery: An Historical Account of the Liverpool–African Slave Trade by a Genuine Dicky Sam* (Liverpool, 1884).
85. M. Lynn, 'Trade and Politics in Nineteenth-Century Liverpool: The Tobin and Horsfall Families and Liverpool's African Trade', *Transactions of the Historic Society of Lancashire and Cheshire* 142 (1993), 99–120.
86. B. K. Drake, 'Liverpool's African Commerce Before and After Abolition of the Slave Trade', MA thesis, University of Liverpool (1974), 106–7.
87. *PP* 1847–8, XXII (536), 474; Stilliard, 'Legitimate Trade', 14; Latham, *Old Calabar*, 56; Drake, 'Liverpool's African Commerce', 145.
88. H. Swanzy, 'A Trading Family in the Nineteenth-Century Gold Coast', *THSG* 2 (1956), 97; Drake, 'Liverpool's African Commerce', 159–60.
89. Stilliard, 'Legitimate Trade', 91; H. Swanzy, 'Trading Family'; F. J. Pedler, *The Lion and the Unicorn in Africa: The United Africa Company, 1787–1931* (London, 1974), 52–6.
90. Drake, 'Liverpool's African Commerce', 127–9.
91. M. Lynn, 'Bristol, West Africa, and the Nineteenth-Century Palm Oil Trade', *Historical Research* 64, 155 (1991), 359–74.
92. D. Richardson, *The Bristol Slave Traders: A Collective Portrait* (Bristol, 1985), 3.
93. Figures from *Annual Reports of the Bristol Chamber of Commerce* (Bristol, 1835–51), *passim*.
94. Though the evidence for the King family's involvement in the slave trade is ambiguous: Pedler, *Lion and Unicorn*, 13.

95. Lynn, 'British Business and the African Trade', 23–4.
96. B. Poole, *The Commerce of Liverpool* (London, 1854), 114–15; Lynn, 'Change and Continuity', 336–8. Figures for Liverpool's imports for the period 1842–8 are given in *PP* 1850, IX i (53), 225, from which it can be calculated that the port's share of total British imports fluctuated between 73 and 88 per cent.
97. Flint and McDougall, 'Economic Change in West Africa', 383.
98. 'The African Palm Oil Trade', *Friend of Africa* 25 (1842), 159.
99. G. F. Wilson, *On the Stearic Candle Manufacture* (London, 1852), 11–17; G. F. Wilson, *On the Manufactures of Price's Patent Candle Co.* (London, 1856), 19–21, 40.
100. W. L. Carpenter, *A Treatise on the Manufacture of Soap and Candles, Lubricants, and Glycerin* (London, 1885), 235–6, 128. E. Liveing (ed.), 'Living Bristol's Many Industries' (Bristol Central Library), 52; W. Ashworth, *An Economic History of England* (London, 1960), 78–9.
101. A. E. Musson, *Enterprise in Soap and Chemicals: Joseph Crosfield and Sons, Ltd, 1815–1965* (Manchester, 1965), 22, 27.
102. W. E. Minchinton, *The British Tinplate Industry* (Oxford, 1957), 28–9.
103. G. F. Wilson, *Manufactures of Price's Patent Candle Co.*, 46–7, 52.
104. A. J. H. Latham, 'Palm Produce from Calabar, 1812–1887, with a Note on the Formation of Palm Oil Prices to 1914', in Liesegang, Pasch, and Jones, *Figuring African Trade*, 280–1.
105. *PP* 1847–8, XXII (272), 181; Hancock, *Survey*, vol. II, pt 2, 159.
106. Musson, *Enterprise in Soap and Chemicals*, 91–2; Latham, 'Palm Produce from Calabar', 284–5.
107. Eltis and Jennings, 'Trade Between Western Africa and the Atlantic World', 942–4; H. A. Gemery, J. Hogendorn, and M. Johnson, 'Evidence on English/ African Terms of Trade in the Eighteenth Century', *Explorations in Economic History* 27 (1990), 157–77; D. Eltis, 'Trade Between Western Africa and the Atlantic World Before 1870: Estimates of Trends in Value, Composition, and Direction', *Research in Economic History* 12 (1989), 197–239.
108. Hopkins, *Economic History*, 132.
109. Eltis, *Economic Growth*, 183.
110. D. Northrup, 'The Compatibility of the Slave and Palm Oil Trades in the Bight of Biafra', *JAH* 17 (1976), 353–64.
111. M. Lynn, 'The West African Palm Oil Trade in the Nineteenth Century and "the Crisis of Adaptation"', in Law, *From Slave Trade to 'Legitimate' Commerce*, 57–77.

2 AFRICAN PRODUCERS AND PALM OIL PRODUCTION

1. Hopkins, *Economic History*, 128.
2. C. Punch, Report on the cultivation of the oil palm in Bonny District, 15 October 1908, CALPROF 14/3/801, NNAE.
3. Northrup, *Trade Without Rulers*, 185; Wariboko, 'New Calabar', 44. The fruit of oil palms in this area also had a higher oil content than most: D. S. Udom, 'Demand and Supply Analyses for Nigerian Oil-Palm Products with Policy Implications', Ph.D thesis, University of Reading (1980), 13.
4. W. B. Morgan, 'The Nigerian Oil Palm Industry', *Scottish Geographical*

Magazine 71 (1955), 174; E. Isichei, *A History of the Igbo People* (London, 1976), 94.

5. Latham, *Old Calabar*, 86–90; Northrup, *Trade Without Rulers*, 190–1.
6. A. Martin, *The Oil Palm Economy of the Ibibio Farmer* (Ibadan, 1956), 9; Northrup, *Trade Without Rulers*, 200.
7. Northrup, *Trade Without Rulers*, 200–2.
8. R. K. Oldfield, 'A Brief Account of an Ascent of the Old Calabar River in 1836', *JRGS* 7 (1837), 196–7.
9. J. B. Walker, 'Notes on the Old Calabar and Cross Rivers', *PRGS* 16 (1871–2), 135–7; J. B. Walker, 'Notes of a Visit, in May 1875, to the Old Calabar and Qua Rivers', *PRGS* 20 (1875–6), 224–30; Latham, *Old Calabar*, 86; Northrup, *Trade Without Rulers*, 200–2.
10. J. B. King, 'Details of Explorations of the Old Calabar River', *JRGS* 14 (1844), 260–83.
11. Northrup, *Trade Without Rulers*, 191–4; S. M. Hargreaves, 'Nineteenth-Century Bonny', 224–6.
12. H. Webber, Intelligence report on Bonny district (1931), CSO 26/3/27226, NNAI; Isichei, *Igbo People*, 95; S. M. Martin, *Palm Oil and Protest*, 28; Oriji, 'Study of the Slave and Palm Produce Trade', 316–17.
13. Northrup, *Trade Without Rulers*, 202–4.
14. *Ibid.*, 192; Wariboko, 'New Calabar', 44–72.
15. Alagoa, *Small Brave City-State*, 59–60.
16. G. I. Jones, *The Trading States of the Oil Rivers* (London, 1963), 146; Northrup, *Trade Without Rulers*, 205–7; F. K. Ekechi, 'Aspects of Palm Oil Trade at Oguta (Eastern Nigeria), 1900–1950', *AEH* 10 (1981), 35–65; G. I. Jones, *Slaves to Palm Oil*, 63.
17. Austen, 'Metamorphoses of Middlemen', 3.
18. V. G. Fanso, 'Trade and Supremacy on the Cameroon Coast, 1879–1887', in Njeuma, *Introduction to the History of Cameroon*, 63–87.
19. Latham, *Old Calabar*, 88.
20. Rowe to Kimberley, 24 January 1882, CO 96/137, PRO; H. J. Bevin, 'The Gold Coast Economy About 1880', *THSG* 2 (1956), 73–86; Sanders, 'Palm Oil Production on the Gold Coast', 61.
21. Fitzpatrick to Grey, 10 June 1849, CO 96/15, PRO.
22. J. A. Horton, *West African Countries and Peoples* (Edinburgh, 1969), 129.
23. L. E. Wilson, *Krobo People*, 72–99; L. E. Wilson, 'The "Bloodless Conquest" in Southeastern Ghana: The Huza and the Territorial Expansion of the Krobo in the Nineteenth Century', *IJAHS* 23 (1990), 269–97.
24. M. J. Field, 'The Agricultural System of the Manya–Krobo of the Gold Coast', *Africa* 14 (1943), 54–65; A. M. Kole, 'The Historical Background of Krobo Customs', *THSG* 1 (1955), 139.
25. Freeman to colonial secretary, 20 April 1859, SC 4/9, NAGA; M. Johnson, 'Migrants' Progress, Part I', *Bulletin of the Ghana Geographical Association* 9 (1964), 4–27; H. Huber, *The Krobo* (Bonn, 1963), 37–9.
26. L. E. Wilson, *Krobo People*, 72–7.
27. Quoted in L. E. Wilson, *Krobo People*, 78; Johnson, 'Migrants' Progress', 14; Huber, *Krobo*, 39, 59.
28. Merchants of Cape Coast to Freeling, 16 January 1878, in Freeling to

Carnarvon, 21 January 1878, CO 96/123, PRO; K. B. Dickson, 'The Development of Road Transport in Southern Ghana and Ashanti Since c. 1850', *THSG* 5 (1961), 33–42; in some parts of the Gold Coast the rolling of casks of oil to the coast became the method of transporting palm oil: Bevin, 'Gold Coast Economy', 75–6.

29. J. A. Croft, 'Exploration of the River Volta, West Africa', *PRGS* 18 (1873–4), 189; Huber, *Krobo*, 57–8; I. B. Sutton, 'The Volta River Salt Trade: The Survival of an Indigenous Industry', *JAH* 22 (1981), 43–61; L. E. Wilson, *Krobo People*, 87–91; D. E. K. Amenumey, 'Geraldo de Lima: A Reappraisal', *THSG* 9 (1968), 69.

30. F. Wolfson, 'A Price Agreement on the Gold Coast: The Krobo Oil Boycott, 1858–1866', *Economic History Review* 6 (1953), 68–77.

31. Johnson, 'Migrants' Progress', 21–2; L. E. Wilson, '"Bloodless Conquest"', 281.

32. Horton, *West African Countries*, 128; M. A. Kwamena-Poh, *Government and Politics in the Akuapem State, 1730–1850* (London, 1973), 3, 94; L. E. Wilson, '"Bloodless Conquest"', 281.

33. Freeman to colonial secretary, 20 April 1859, SC 4/9, NAGA; Johnson, 'Migrants' Progress', 17.

34. Quoted in Kwamena-Poh, *Government and Politics*, 95.

35. Johnson, 'Migrants' Progress', 21; P. Hill, *Migrant Cocoa-Farmers of Southern Ghana* (Cambridge, 1963), 163–4.

36. Ikime, *Prince*, 4–7; O. Ikime, *Niger Delta Rivalry* (London, 1969), 6, 59–68.

37. Dudgeon, *Agricultural and Forest Products*, 91.

38. S. O. Biobaku, *The Egba and Their Neighbours, 1842–1872* (Oxford, 1957), 17, 61; B. A. Agri, 'Aspects of Socio-Economic Changes Among the Awori Egba and Ijebu Remo Communities During the Nineteenth Century', *JHSN* 7 (1974), 472–3.

39. S. Johnson, *The History of the Yorubas* (Lagos, 1927), 227.

40. S. A. Akintoye, 'The Economic Background of the Ekitiparapo, 1878–1893', *Odu* 4 (1968), 44; B. Awe, 'Militarism and Economic Development in Nineteenth-Century Yoruba Country: The Ibadan Example', *JAH* 14 (1973), 69.

41. 'Lagos Palm Oil', 208.

42. Awe, 'Militarism and Economic Development', 69–72; Agri, 'Aspects of Socio-Economic Changes', 468–9.

43. Campbell to Clarendon, 30 August 1855, FO 84/975; Lodder to Malmesbury, 5 July 1859, FO 84/1088: both PRO; J. F. A. Ajayi, 'The Aftermath of the Fall of Old Oyo', in Ajayi and Crowder, *History of West Africa*, vol. II, 205–7.

44. R. S. Smith, *Lagos Consulate*, 51.

45. S. A. Akintoye, 'The North-Eastern Yoruba Districts and the Benin Kingdom', *JHSN* 4 (1969), 545; Akintoye, 'The Ondo Road Eastwards of Lagos, c. 1870–1895', *JAH* 10 (1969), 581–98.

46. Akintoye, 'Ekitiparapo', 44; Awe, 'Militarism and Economic Development', 66–8.

47. Ajayi, 'Fall of Old Oyo', 204; J. H. Kopytoff, *A Preface to Modern Nigeria: The 'Sierra Leonians' in Yoruba, 1830–1890* (London, 1965), 38–44, 86–110.

48. 'Investigations in Connection with the African Palm Oil Industry', 375; R.

Law, 'Royal Monopoly and Private Enterprise in the Atlantic Trade: The Case of Dahomey', *JAH* 18 (1977), 571; Manning, *Slavery, Colonialism, and Economic Growth*, 62; Reid, 'Warrior Aristocrats', 157–65.

49. E. A. Soumonni, 'Dahomean Economic Policy Under Ghezo, 1818–1858: A Reconsideration', *JHSN* 10 (1980), 6–8.
50. F. E. Forbes, *Dahomey and the Dahomans*, 2 vols. (London, 1851), vol. I, 54, 123.
51. Manning, *Slavery, Colonialism, and Economic Growth*, 54; Reid, 'Warrior Aristocrats', 199–200, 419–21.
52. Dudgeon, *Agricultural and Forest Products*, 22; M. T. Dawe and F. J. Martin, 'The Oil Palm Industry and Its Problems in Sierra Leone', *Proceedings of the First West African Agricultural Conference* (Lagos, 1927), 7–8.
53. Hanson to FO, 1 January 1855, FO 2/13; CO 272/–, *passim*: both PRO; Fyfe, *History*, 258.
54. Dudgeon, *Agricultural and Forest Products*, 19–20; J. I. Clarke (ed.), *Sierra Leone in Maps* (London, 1966), 79; J. Levi, *African Agriculture: Economic Action and Reaction in Sierra Leone* (Slough, 1976), 47, 50.
55. E. A. Ijagbemi, 'The Rokel River and the Development of Inland Trade in Sierra Leone', *Odu* 3 (1970), 45–70; A. M. Howard, 'The Relevance of Spatial Analysis for African Economic History: The Sierra Leone–Guinea System', *JAH* 17 (1976), 365–88; C. M. Fyle, *Commerce and Entrepreneurship: The Sierra Leone Hinterland in the Nineteenth Century*, Institute of African Studies, Fourah Bay College, Occasional Paper II (Freetown, 1977), 10.
56. C. Fyfe, 'European and Creole Influence in the Hinterland of Sierra Leone Before 1896', *Sierra Leone Studies* 6 (1956), 113–23; A. Howard, 'The Role of Freetown in the Commercial Life of Sierra Leone', in C. Fyfe and E. Jones (eds.), *Freetown: A Symposium* (Freetown, 1968), 40; A. Jones, *Slaves to Palm Kernels*.
57. Alldridge to colonial secretary, 7 January 1895, in Cardew to Ripon, 26 January 1895, CO 267/416, PRO; T. J. Alldridge, *The Sherbro and Its Hinterland* (London, 1901), 4; P. K. Mitchell, 'Trade Routes of the Early Sierra Leone Protectorate', *Sierra Leone Studies* 16 (1962), 204–17; M. E. Harvey, 'Bonthe: A Geographical Study of a Moribund Port and Its Environs', *Bulletin: The Journal of the Sierra Leone Geographical Association* 10 (1966), 60–75; G. Deveneaux, 'Trade Routes and Colonial Policy in Sierra Leone in the Nineteenth Century', *Journal of the Historical Society of Sierra Leone* 3 (1979), 71–95.
58. H. Myint, *The Economics of the Developing Countries* (London, 1964); Myint, 'The "Classical Theory" of International Trade and Underdeveloped Countries', *Economic Journal* 68 (1958), reprinted in I. Livingstone (ed.), *Economic Policy for Development* (Harmondsworth, 1971), 85–112.
59. Myint's view can be contrasted with interpretations that see force as 'the midwife of West African commodity production': K. Hart, *The Political Economy of West African Agriculture* (Cambridge, 1982), 112.
60. P. Wickins, *An Economic History of Africa from the Earliest Times to Partition* (Cape Town, 1981), 286.
61. Hopkins, *Economic History*, 231–6.
62. M. Johnson, 'Cotton Imperialism in West Africa', *African Affairs* 73, 291

(1974), 178–87; J. F. Munro, *Britain in Tropical Africa, 1880–1960* (London, 1984), 42–5.

63. Hogendorn, 'Vent-for-Surplus Model', 19–20; J. S. Hogendorn, 'Economic Initiative and African Cash Farming: Pre-Colonial Origins and Early Colonial Developments', in L. H. Gann and P. Duignan (eds.), *Colonialism in Africa, 1870–1960*, vol. IV, *The Economics of Colonialism* (Cambridge, 1975), 283–328; for a critical view, see Freund and Shenton, '"Vent-For-Surplus" Theory'.

64. A. F. B. Bridges, 'The Oil Palm Industry in Nigeria', *Farm and Forest* 7 (1946), 57.

65. 'African Oil Palm', 191; A. F. Mockler-Ferryman, *Up The Niger* (London, 1892), 16–17; Billows and Beckwith, *Palm Oil and Kernels*, 26–7; J. E. Gray, 'Native Methods of Preparing Palm Oil', in *First Annual Bulletin of the Agricultural Department, Nigeria* (Lagos, 1922), 30.

66. G. H. Hurst, *Soaps* (London, 1898), 125; A. F. Mockler-Ferryman, *British Nigeria* (London, 1902), 320; Billows and Beckwith, *Palm Oil and Kernels*, 24–6.

67. Oil from the Benin River differed according to its origin: oil from the right bank being soft, and from the left, hard: Minute by Governor Moloney on the eastern limit of the colony of Lagos, April 1888, FO 84/1882, PRO.

68. Mockler-Ferryman, *British Nigeria*, 320; A. C. Barnes, 'The Extraction of Oil Palm Products', in *Proceedings of the First West African Agricultural Conference, Ibadan, Nigeria, 1927* (Lagos, 1927), 38–51; 'Produce Goes to Market', *Statistical and Economic Review* 3 (1949), 5; P. Kilby, 'The Nigerian Palm Oil Industry', *Food Research Institute Studies* 7 (1967), 177–203.

69. O. T. Faulkner and C. J. Lewin, 'Native Methods of Preparing Palm Oil, II', in *Second Annual Bulletin of the Agricultural Department, Nigeria* (1923), 18. Other authorities give different figures for each category: Auchinleck, *West African Oil Palm*, 16; Bridges, 'Oil Palm Industry in Nigeria', 57.

70. 'Produce Goes to Market', 5.

71. For the differences between palm nuts, see Farquhar, *Oil Palm and Varieties*, 4–12; Billows and Beckwith, *Palm Oil and Kernels*, 14.

72. Kilby, 'Nigerian Palm Oil Industry', 182–91.

73. C. F. Coley, Assessment Report, Calabar Division, 1927, CSO 26/3/20689, NNAI; G. I. Jones, *Slaves to Palm Oil*, 49. Similar examples of the use of specialists to cut palm fruits could be found in the Gambia: 'Note on the Palm Kernel Industry in the Gambia', *Gambia Gazette* 62, 15 February 1945, CO 460/23, PRO.

74. Bold, *Guide*, 75; 'Lagos Palm Oil', 203; Sarbah, 'Oil Palm and Uses', 236; J. A. O. Oyewumi, 'The Development and Organisation of Palm Oil and Palm Kernel Production in Nigeria, 1807–1960', MSoc.Sc. thesis, University of Birmingham (1972), 30–1.

75. Corry, *Observations*, 39–40.

76. Sarbah, 'Oil Palm and Uses', 240–1.

77. Freeling to Carnarvon, 18 April 1877, ADM 1/2/21, NAGA; Sarbah, 'Oil Palm and Uses', 238; Johnson, 'Migrants' Progress', 21.

78. Palm oil production was more labour-intensive than cocoa farming: I. Sutton, 'Labour in Commercial Agriculture in Ghana in the Late Nineteenth and

Early Twentieth Centuries', *JAH* 24 (1983), 466–7; Barnes, 'Extraction of Oil Palm Products', 42; 'Produce Goes to Market', 5.

79. Gray, 'Native Methods of Preparing Palm Oil', 47–50; Usoro, *Nigerian Oil Palm Industry*, 142.

80. Methods of production in various parts of West Africa are detailed in Broadhurst to Kortright, 12 February 1877, in Kortright to Carnarvon, 15 February 1877, CO 267/331, PRO; Report on Oil Palms, Cultivation of (1908), CALPROF 14/3/801, NNAE; Farquhar to Thompson, 29 August 1918, CSE 5/13/17, NNAE; 'Report on the Oil Palm . . . ', 2 June 1910, CSO 14/2, A. 2061/1910, NNAI; H. N. Thompson, 'Notes on the Oil Palm (Elaeis Guineensis) of Southern Nigeria', *Southern Nigeria Government Gazette*, 5 February 1908, CO 591/5, PRO; Cruickshank, *Eighteen Years*, vol. II, 276; J. J. Monteiro, *Angola and the River Congo*, 2 vols. (London, 1875), vol. I, 96; 'African Oil Palm'; 'Lagos Palm Oil', 205; Gray, 'Native Methods of Preparing Palm Oil', 30–3; O. T. Faulkner and J. R. Mackie, *West African Agriculture* (Cambridge, 1933), 101–2; Kilby, 'Nigerian Palm Oil Industry', 182–3.

81. 'Lagos Palm Oil', 205; Sarbah, 'Oil Palm and Uses', 238–44; Alldridge, *Sherbro*, 66–7; Northrup, *Trade Without Rulers*, 186.

82. Meredith, *Account*, 75.

83. Sarbah, 'Oil Palm and Uses', 241–2.

84. Sarbah, *ibid.*, 240, notes that the Krobo used a wooden strainer to strain the oil from the fibre.

85. Farquhar, *Oil Palm and Varieties*, 24–5.

86. 'Oil Palm in Labuan: A Success and a Failure', *Kew Bulletin of Miscellaneous Information* 35 (1889), 262–4.

87. Hutchinson, *Impressions*, 194–5.

88. Manning, 'Palm Oil and Kernel Exports', 35–9; Sutton, 'Labour in Commercial Agriculture', 467.

89. Fraser to Rowan, 13 September 1826, CO 267/93, PRO; P. M. Martin, *Loango Coast*, 154.

90. *Missionary Record of the United Presbyterian Church* 82 (1 October 1872), 300; Hansen to Rowan, 17 September 1826, CO 267/93, PRO; Law, 'Introduction', 10.

91. H. N. Thompson, 'Notes on the Oil Palm', CO 591/5, PRO.

92. Kilby, 'Nigerian Palm Oil Industry', 177.

93. Auchinleck, *West African Oil Palm*, 6, 12.

94. Farquhar, *Oil Palm and Varieties*, 20–3; Kilby, 'Nigerian Palm Oil Industry', 186.

95. 'Lagos Palm Oil', 208; Farquhar, *Oil Palm and Varieties*, 21.

96. Kilby, 'Nigerian Palm Oil Industry', 186.

97. 'African Oil Palm', 190; Farquhar, *Oil Palm and Varieties*, 36–8.

98. S. M. Martin, *Palm Oil and Protest*, 51.

99. Manning, 'Palm Oil and Kernel Exports', 8–10; Manning, *Slavery, Colonialism, and Economic Growth*, 51. Manning stresses that, because the pericarp protects the kernel, oil output is more sensitive to rainfall than kernel output.

100. Hartley, *Oil Palm*, 96.

101. G. I. Jones, *Slaves to Palm Oil*, 48.

102. Faulkner and Lewin, 'Native Methods of Preparing Palm Oil, II', 22.
103. Farquhar, *Oil Palm and Varieties*, 30.
104. S. M. Martin, *Palm Oil and Protest*, 33–4, 101.
105. Sarbah, 'Oil Palm and Uses', 240–1.
106. S. M. Martin, *Palm Oil and Protest*, 33–4; G. I. Jones, *Slaves to Palm Oil*, 47–8.
107. J. Tosh, 'The Cash Crop Revolution in Tropical Africa: An Agricultural Reappraisal', *African Affairs* 79, 314 (1980), 79–94.
108. S. M. Martin, *Palm Oil and Protest*, 33–4.
109. Hopkins, *Economic History*, 232.
110. G. I. Jones, *Slaves to Palm Oil*, 49, 64–5; Wariboko, 'New Calabar', 46–7.
111. D. Northrup, 'Nineteenth-Century Patterns of Slavery and Economic Growth in Southeastern Nigeria', *IJAHS* 12 (1979), 9.
112. P. Lovejoy, *Transformations in Slavery* (Cambridge, 1983), 159–83.
113. As was recognised at the time: Dowell to Admiralty, 7 February 1869, FO 541/16, PRO.
114. Forbes, *Dahomey*, vol. I, 115; Lovejoy, *Transformations*, 171–3.
115. Lovejoy, *Transformations*, 162–3.
116. Agri, 'Aspects of Socio-Economic Changes', 468.
117. Northrup, 'Nineteenth-Century Patterns', 9–10; Lovejoy, *Transformations*, 173–7.
118. *PP* 1842, XI (551), 169, 171.
119. Reynolds, *Trade and Economic Change*, 82; Sutton, 'Labour in Commercial Agriculture', 467–8; G. M. McSheffrey, 'Slavery, Indentured Servitude, Legitimate Trade, and the Impact of Abolition in the Gold Coast, 1874–1901', *JAH* 24 (1983), 349–68.
120. Lovejoy, *Transformations*, 178; Northrup, 'Nineteenth-Century Patterns', 9–10. This is not to mention the increased use of slaves in trading for oil.
121. G. I. Jones, *Slaves to Palm Oil*, 64.
122. S. M. Martin, 'Slaves, Igbo Women', 180–1. Oriji, in contrast, suggests slave owning was extensive amongst the Ngwa: J. N. Oriji, 'A Re-Assessment of the Organisation and Benefits of the Slave and Palm Produce Trade Among the Ngwa–Igbo', *Canadian Journal of African Studies* 16 (1982), 536; Oriji, 'Study of the Slave and Palm Produce Trade', 317.
123. Sutton, 'Labour in Commercial Agriculture', 463, 466–8; L. E. Wilson, '"Bloodless Conquest"', 297. Sutton's views are supported by Griffith to Ripon, 12 June 1893, CO 96/234, PRO.
124. S. M. Martin, *Palm Oil and Protest*; S. M. Martin, 'Gender and Innovation: Farming, Cooking, and Palm Processing in the Ngwa Region, South-Eastern Nigeria, 1900–1930', *JAH* 25 (1984), 411–27; S. M. Martin, 'Slaves, Igbo Women'.
125. Section G, Johnson to Salisbury, 1 December 1888, FO 84/1882, PRO; Answers to questions on a report . . . (Obubra), by A. C. Douglas, 12 October 1908, CALPROF 14/3/801, NNAE; Report by the director of agriculture on palm oil and palm kernel production in the Gold Coast, 22 February 1940, CSO 216/34, NAGA.
126. *PP* 1850, IX i (53), 37; Hutchinson, *Impressions*, 194–5.
127. Alldridge, *Sherbro*, 66–7.
128. S. Johnson, *History of the Yorubas*, 124.

129. Quoted in Law, '"Legitimate" Trade and Gender Relations', 206.
130. Section G, Johnson to Salisbury, 1 December 1888, FO 84/1882, PRO.
131. Oyewumi, 'Palm Oil and Palm Kernel Production in Nigeria', 32–6; Wariboko, 'New Calabar', 45; Law, '"Legitimate" Trade and Gender Relations', 206.
132. S. M. Martin, *Palm Oil and Protest*, 32; E. M'Bokolo, 'From the Cameroon Grasslands to the Upper Nile', in *UNESCO General History of Africa*, vol. V, B. A. Ogot (ed.), *Africa from the Sixteenth to the Eighteenth Century* (Oxford, 1992), 541.
133. S. M. Martin, *Palm Oil and Protest*, 32; A. Martin, *Ibibio Farmer*, 10, stresses the injunctions that were designed to prevent women climbing palm trees.
134. *Missionary Record of the United Presbyterian Church* 43 (1 July 1869), 398; 62 (1 February 1871), 381.
135. Law, '"Legitimate" Trade and Gender Relations', 207–9.
136. S. M. Martin, *Palm Oil and Protest*, 47–8.
137. Report by the director of agriculture on palm oil and palm kernel production in the Gold Coast, 22 February 1940, CSO 216/34, NAGA; A. Martin, *Ibibio Farmer*, 16. For attempts by the Aro to prevent women cracking kernels on the grounds that it would make them barren, see Moor to secretary of state, 9 September 1899, CO 444/2, PRO.
138. L. E. Wilson, '"Bloodless Conquest"', 294.
139. Law, '"Legitimate" Trade and Gender Relations', 207–8; L. E. Wilson, *Krobo People*, 91–3.
140. S. M. Martin, 'Slaves, Igbo Women', 183.
141. L. E. Wilson, *Krobo People*, 91–3.
142. Oriji, 'Study of the Slave and Palm Produce Trade', 323.
143. G. B. A. Coker, *Family Property Among the Yorubas* (London, 1958), 27–8; L. T. Chubb, *Ibo Land Tenure* (Ibadan, 1961); T. O. Elias, *Ghana and Sierra Leone: The Development of Their Laws and Customs* (London, 1962), 152–9, 285–91; Levi, *African Agriculture*, 205–11; Hart, *West African Agriculture*, 91–2; T. Falola, *The Political Economy of a Pre-Colonial African State: Ibadan, 1830–1900* (Ife, 1984), 25–6.
144. S. M. Martin, *Palm Oil and Protest*, 27; Falola, *Ibadan, 1830–1900*, 49.
145. Material on ownership of palms in southern Nigeria can be found in Report on Oil Palms, Cultivation of (1908), CALPROF, 14/3/801, NNAE; A. Martin, *Ibibio Farmer*, 9.
146. Such as in the Degema area of Nigeria: Assessment report on Degema Division by Whitman, Brasher, and Stockley (1927), CSO 26/3, 20621, NNAI.
147. Report on Bende District by W. A. C. Cockburn, 8 October 1908, CALPROF 14/3/801, NNAE; Northrup, *Trade Without Rulers*, 187; Falola, *Ibadan, 1830–1900*, 49.
148. H. N. Thompson, 'Notes on the Oil Palm', CO 591/5, PRO; Zeven, 'Oil Palm Groves in Southern Nigeria, I, II'; Harlan, de Wet, and Stemler, 'Plant Domestication and Indigenous African Agriculture', 12–13; Harris, 'Traditional Systems of Food Production', 326; Oliver, *African Experience*, 45.
149. A. Martin, *Ibibio Farmer*, 9; Northrup, *Trade Without Rulers*, 185–6.
150. Northrup, *Trade Without Rulers*, 187; Oriji, 'Study of the Slave and Palm Produce Trade', 321–3; S. M. Martin, 'Slaves, Igbo Women', 186–7.
151. For the Gold Coast, see *PP* 1842, XI (551), 169.

152. Similarly, there are problems in using 'wild' to describe palms, since all palms are seen as belonging ultimately to someone, as is clear in Report on Oil Palms, Cultivation of (1908), CALPROF 14/3/801, NNAE.
153. Field, 'Agricultural System', 54–6.
154. Agri, 'Aspects of Socio-Economic Changes', 473; G. I. Jones, *Slaves to Palm Oil*, 47. For the Sierra Leone case, see Levi, *African Agriculture*, 220–2.
155. Northrup, *Trade Without Rulers*, 187.
156. Hopkins, *Economic History*, 125.
157. Northrup, *Trade Without Rulers*, 188; G. I. Jones, *Slaves to Palm Oil*, 56.
158. Hopkins, 'Economic Imperialism: Lagos', 588; though J. Clarke, 'Households and the Political Economy of Small-Scale Cash Crop Production in South-Western Nigeria', *Africa* 51 (1981), 807–23, takes a different view.
159. Manning, *Slavery, Colonialism, and Economic Growth*, 53–4; Reid, 'Warrior Aristocrats', 216–18; L. E. Wilson, '"Bloodless Conquest"', 292.
160. Hopkins, *Economic History*, 149–50; Reid, 'Warrior Aristocrats', 216–17; Law, '"Legitimate" Trade and Gender Relations', 199–200.
161. Quoted in R. Law, 'The "Crisis of Adaptation" Reconsidered: Dahomey and the Transition from the Slave Trade to "Legitimate" Commerce in the Nineteenth Century', unpublished seminar paper, School of Oriental and African Studies, London, 17 October 1990, 1.
162. Hopkins, *Economic History*, 126. In contrast, see Zeleza, *Modern Economic History of Africa*, vol. I, 370–1.
163. Sanders, 'Palm Oil Production on the Gold Coast', 60–3.
164. L. E. Wilson, '"Bloodless Conquest"', 297.
165. Reynolds, *Trade and Economic Change*, 174–81.
166. Hopkins, 'Economic Imperialism: Lagos', 587; Law, 'Historiography'.
167. Hopkins, 'Economic Imperialism: Lagos', 599–606.
168. Latham, 'Palm Produce from Calabar', 272–3.
169. Northrup, 'Compatibility', 355–8.
170. Hart, *West African Agriculture*, 111–12.
171. Law, 'Introduction', 10–11.
172. E. Isichei, *History of West Africa Since 1800* (London, 1977), 152; G. I. Jones, *Slaves to Palm Oil*, 65.
173. S. Berry, *Cocoa, Custom, and Socio-Economic Change in Rural Western Nigeria* (Oxford, 1975), 25–8; Law, 'Historiography', 107.
174. Northrup, *Trade Without Rulers*, 206–7.
175. *Ibid.*, 187–8; Oriji, 'Study of the Slave and Palm Produce Trade', 321–3; S. M. Martin, *Palm Oil and Protest*, 31.
176. Northrup, *Trade Without Rulers*, 187; S. M. Martin, 'Slaves, Igbo Women', 186.
177. Isichei, *Igbo People*, 95, 102.
178. Oriji, 'Study of the Slave and Palm Produce Trade', 323.

3 AFRICAN BROKERS AND THE GROWTH OF THE PALM OIL TRADE

1. G. I. Jones, *Trading States*, 82.
2. Northrup, 'Compatibility', 359.

3. Latham, 'Price Fluctuations', 216–17; Latham, 'Palm Produce from Calabar', 270–2. Northrup agrees that the organisation of the two trades coincided the nearer they got to the coast: *Trade Without Rulers*, 189.
4. C. W. Newbury, 'Trade and Authority in West Africa from 1850 to 1880', in Gann and Duignan, *Colonialism in Africa, 1870–1960*, vol. I, *The History and Politics of Colonialism, 1870–1914* (Cambridge, 1969), 91.
5. Latham, *Old Calabar*, 79–90.
6. Northrup, *Trade Without Rulers*, 191–202 (quote from 191).
7. Latham, *Old Calabar*, 113–23.
8. Latham, 'Trading Alliance', 863.
9. Latham, *Old Calabar*, 84. However, John Clarke identified some forty-two major Efik traders in 1845: Journal of John Clarke, Second Journey to Africa, II, 5 June 1845, Baptist Missionary Society Archives.
10. S. M. Hargreaves, 'Nineteenth-Century Bonny', 218–27.
11. Dike, *Trade and Politics*, 83–4.
12. G. I. Jones, *Trading States*, 51–62; S. M. Hargreaves, 'Nineteenth-Century Bonny', 77–120.
13. H. Crow, *Memoirs* (London, 1830), 238; S. M. Hargreaves, 'Nineteenth-Century Bonny', 218–20.
14. E. J. Alagoa and A. Fombo, *A Chronicle of Grand Bonny* (Ibadan, 1972), 17–21; M. Lynn, 'Factionalism, Imperialism, and the Making and Breaking of Bonny Kingship, c. 1830–1885', *Revue français d'histoire d'Outre-Mer* 82 (1995), 169–92.
15. Northrup, *Trade Without Rulers*, 114–45; G. I. Jones, *Slaves to Palm Oil*, 34–6.
16. Northrup, *Trade Without Rulers*, 206–8.
17. Ikime, *Rivalry*, 64, 71; O. Ikime, *The Isoko People: A Historical Survey* (Ibadan, 1972), xvii–xviii.
18. Wariboko, 'New Calabar', 49–65.
19. Austen, 'Metamorphoses of Middlemen', 1.
20. Wirz, 'La "Rivière du Cameroun"', 182–3, 190; D. Birmingham, *Central Africa to 1870* (Cambridge, 1981), 142–3. The other major broker of this area was King Bile of Bimbia: Elango, 'Trade and Diplomacy on the Cameroon Coast'.
21. Croft, 'Exploration of the River Volta'; Sutton, 'Volta River Salt Trade', 51–4; S. A. Greene, *Gender, Ethnicity, and Social Change on the Upper Slave Coast* (London, 1996), 102–3.
22. Fitzpatrick to Grey, 10 March 1850, CO 96/18, PRO.
23. S. B. Kaplow, 'The Mudfish and the Crocodile: Underdevelopment of a West African Bourgeoisie', *Science and Society* 41 (1977), 317–33; McCarthy, *Social Change*, 108.
24. Law, 'Royal Monopoly and Private Enterprise', 574; Soumonni, 'Dahomean Economic Policy', 6–7.
25. Reid, 'Warrior Aristocrats', 225–6, 241, 427.
26. Ross, 'First Chacha of Whydah'; Ross, 'Domingo Martinez'; Manning, *Slavery, Colonialism, and Economic Growth*, 46–7.
27. Newbury, *Western Slave Coast*, 36; Sorensen, 'Badagry', 175–7. This was also the case with Lagos after 1851: Campbell to Clarendon, 30 August 1855, FO 84/976, PRO.

28. P. M. Martin, *Loango Coast*, 154–6.
29. J. Vansina, *Paths in the Rainforests: Towards a History of Political Tradition in Equatorial Africa* (London, 1990), 207–11.
30. Anstey, *Britain and the Congo*, 19–21.
31. P. M. Martin, *Loango Coast*, 97–100, 144–6.
32. Howard, 'Role of Freetown', 44–6; Deveneaux, 'Trade Routes', 77–8.
33. Fyfe, 'European and Creole Influence', 119.
34. Ijagbemi, 'The Rokel River'; A. Jones, *Slaves to Palm Kernels*, 81–114.
35. M. Lynn, 'John Beecroft and West Africa, 1829–1854', Ph.D thesis, University of London (1979), 225.
36. *Missionary Record of the United Presbyterian Church* 82 (1 October 1872), 300.
37. Jackson, *Journal*, 95. A later attempt to penetrate the interior from Bonny was also firmly resisted: H. M. Waddell, 'Journal', VII, 5 February 1850, National Library of Scotland, Edinburgh.
38. G. I. Jones, *Slaves to Palm Oil*, 53.
39. Manning, 'Slaves, Palm Oil', 286.
40. Howard, 'Role of Freetown', 40–2.
41. R. Smith, 'The Canoe in West African History', *JAH* 11 (1970), 524.
42. Latham, 'Palm Produce from Calabar', 276.
43. C. N. de Cardi, 'A Short Description of the Natives of the Niger Coast . . . ', in M. Kingsley, *West African Studies* (London, 1899), 472; Manning, 'Palm Oil and Kernel Exports', 36–7.
44. Adams, *Remarks*, 130; G. O. Ogunremi, *Counting the Camels: The Economics of Transportation in Pre-Industrial Nigeria* (New York, 1982), 175–6; Law, 'Introduction', 10–11.
45. R. Smith, 'Canoe', 527; Northrup, *Trade Without Rulers*, 216.
46. Such as among the Agwa'aguna and the western Ijo: R. Smith, 'Canoe', 521; Latham, 'Palm Produce from Calabar', 275–6.
47. P. Manning, 'Merchants, Porters, and Canoemen in the Bight of Benin: Links in the West African Trade Network', in C. Coquery-Vidrovitch and P. E. Lovejoy (eds.), *The Workers of African Trade* (Beverley Hills, 1985), 51–74.
48. 'Report on Export Products of Calabar Province, 1915', CALPROF 5/4/472, NNAE; Reid, 'Warrior Aristocrats', 345–7.
49. H. Bindloss, *In the Niger Country* (Edinburgh, 1898), 68; Manning, 'Palm Oil and Kernel Exports', 36–7.
50. Northrup, *Trade Without Rulers*, 207.
51. Griffith to Ripon, 8 July 1893, CO 96/235, PRO; Bevin, 'Gold Coast Economy', 76; Manning, 'Merchants, Porters, and Canoemen', 65.
52. H. L. van der Laan, *The Lebanese Traders in Sierra Leone* (The Hague, 1975), 325, n 1; G. I. Jones, *Slaves to Palm Oil*, 53–4.
53. Reynolds, *Trade and Economic Change*, 86.
54. Howard, 'Role of Freetown', 42–3.
55. Huber, *Krobo*, 57–8.
56. Reynolds, *Trade and Economic Change*, 81–2; D. Northrup, 'Nineteenth-Century Patterns', 6–7; Sutton, 'Labour in Commercial Agriculture', 467.
57. Gabriel to Malmesbury, 15 April 1859, FO 541/2, PRO.
58. Bindloss, *Niger Country*, 176.
59. Wariboko, 'New Calabar', 50.

60. Ikime, *Rivalry*, 60, 74–5.
61. Latham, *Old Calabar*, 91–6; D. Northrup, 'Nineteenth-Century Patterns', 11–15; Austen, 'Metamorphoses of Middlemen', 7; Alagoa and Fombo, *Grand Bonny*, 69.
62. Latham, *Old Calabar*, 155; S. J. S. Cookey, *King Jaja of the Niger Delta: His Life and Times, 1821–1891* (New York, 1974); Wariboko, 'New Calabar', 163.
63. Newbury, 'Trade and Authority', 81–2; Newbury, 'Prices and Profitability', 97–8; C. W. Newbury, 'Credit in Early Nineteenth-Century West African Trade', *JAH* 13 (1972), 81–95; G. Austin, 'Indigenous Credit Institutions in West Africa, c. 1750–c. 1960', in G. Austin and K. Sugihara (eds.), *Local Suppliers of Credit in the Third World, 1750–1960* (London, 1993), 131.
64. M. Johnson, 'The Atlantic Slave Trade and the Economy of West Africa', in R. Anstey and P. E. H. Hair (eds.), *Liverpool, the African Slave Trade, and Abolition* (Widnes, 1976), 23.
65. Latham, *Old Calabar*, 27.
66. Bold, *Guide*, 79; Adams, *Remarks*, 245.
67. Lynslager to Clarendon, 3 March 1855, FO 2/13; Campbell to commercial agents, 18 October 1857, in Campbell to Clarendon, 3 November 1857, FO 84/1031; Day to Wise, 24 December 1857, in Admiralty to Foreign Office, 9 February 1858, FO 84/1068: all PRO; Cruickshank, *Eighteen Years*, vol. II, 35; Newbury, *Western Slave Coast*, 58; Ikime, *Rivalry*, 59–61.
68. Crow, *Memoirs*, 225; A. Swanzy, 'On Trade in Western Africa with and Without British Protection', *Journal of the Society of Arts* 22 (1874), 481.
69. Hutchinson to Clarendon, 21 February 1857, FO 84/1030, PRO; Newbury, 'Prices and Profitability', 98; Latham, *Old Calabar*, 80.
70. S. M. Hargreaves, 'Nineteenth-Century Bonny', 230–4.
71. Latham, *Old Calabar*, 115.
72. Bold, *Guide*, 60.
73. Quoted in M. Johnson, 'Cloth on the Banks of the Niger', *JHSN* 6 (1973), 354.
74. Northrup, *Trade Without Rulers*, 209–10.
75. Robertson, *Notes*, 314; Bold, *Guide*, 85; Adams, *Remarks*, 247; Crow, *Memoirs*, 191. Local salt was important in trade on the Volta: Sutton, 'Volta River Salt Trade'.
76. Latham, 'Palm Produce from Calabar', 268–70.
77. J. Harford, 'A Voyage to the African Oil Rivers Twenty-Five Years Ago', in Kingsley, *West African Studies*, 576; Northrup, *Trade Without Rulers*, 213.
78. Inikori, 'West Africa's Seaborne Trade', 64.
79. Robertson, *Notes*, 323; Bold, *Guide*, 58; Adams, *Remarks*, 244–9; G. I. Jones, *Slaves to Palm Oil*, 59–61.
80. Latham, *Old Calabar*, 74; Reynolds, *Trade and Economic Change*, 91–2; G. I. Jones, *Slaves to Palm Oil*, 60–1.
81. Robertson, *Notes*, 292; Brooks, *Yankee Traders*, 245, 257–8.
82. Inikori, 'West Africa's Seaborne Trade', 64–5.
83. W. I. Ofonagoro, *Trade and Imperialism in Southern Nigeria, 1881–1929* (New York, 1979), 80, 95; G. I. Jones, *Slaves to Palm Oil*, 58.
84. G. I. Jones, *Slaves to Palm Oil*, 61–3.
85. Adams, *Remarks*, 243; Crow, *Memoirs*, 191; C. Partridge, *Cross River Natives* (London, 1905), 253; E. K. Hawkins, 'The Growth of a Money Economy in Nigeria and Ghana', *Oxford Economic Papers* 10 (1958), 344.

86. Crow, *Memoirs*, 251; Hutchinson, *Impressions*, 255–6; G. I. Jones, 'Native and Trade Currencies in Southern Nigeria During the Eighteenth and Nineteenth Centuries', *Africa* 28 (1958), 45, 52; Newbury, 'Prices and Profitability', 102.

87. Jackson, *Journal*, 71; Hutchinson, *Impressions*, 255–6. There were twenty manillas to the bar in Bonny in the early nineteenth century, said Hutchinson, giving a value of 3d. It should be noted that there were several types of manilla in the Eastern Delta: W. Babington, 'Remarks on the General Description of the Trade on the West Coast of Africa', *Journal of the Society of Arts* 23 (1875), 248–9.

88. Adams, *Remarks*, 248; Partridge, *Cross River Natives*, 251; A. J. H. Latham, 'Currency, Credit, and Capitalism on the Cross River in the Pre-Colonial Era', *JAH* 12 (1971), 601; Northrup, *Trade Without Rulers*, 162.

89. A. H. M. Kirk-Greene, 'The Major Currencies in Nigerian History', *JHSN* 2 (1960), 132–50; A. Adomako, 'The History of Currency and Banking in Some West African Countries', *Economic Bulletin of Ghana* 7 (1963), 3–17.

90. Babington, 'Remarks', 250; Newbury, *Western Slave Coast*, 40–1.

91. J. Hogendorn and M. Johnson, *The Shell Money of the Slave Trade* (Cambridge, 1986), 65–7; M. Johnson, 'The Cowrie Currencies of West Africa, Parts I and II', *JAH* 11 (1970), 17–49, 331–53.

92. Cruickshank, *Eighteen Years*, vol. II, 43–4; C. W. Thomas, *Adventures and Observations on the West Coast of Africa* (London, 1864), 160.

93. Bold, *Guide*, 66; M. Laird and R. A. K. Oldfield, *Narrative of an Expedition into the Interior of Africa*, 2 vols. (London, 1837), vol. I, 166; G. I. Jones, 'Trade Currencies', 48; Hogendorn and Johnson, *Shell Money*, 106–7; Reid, 'Warrior Aristocrats', 216–17.

94. A. G. Hopkins, 'The Currency Revolution in South-West Nigeria in the Late Nineteenth Century', *JHSN* 3 (1966), 471–7; Hogendorn and Johnson, *Shell Money*, 69, 138; R. Law, 'Cowries, Gold, and Dollars: Exchange Rate Instability and Domestic Price Inflation in Dahomey in the Eighteenth and Nineteenth Centuries', in J. I. Guyer (ed.), *Money Matters* (London, 1995), 53–73.

95. Johnson, 'Cowrie Currencies', 340, 350; P. E. Lovejoy, 'Interregional Monetary Flows in the Precolonial Trade of Nigeria', *JAH* 15 (1974), 565, 575.

96. Walker, 'Notes on the Old Calabar and Cross Rivers'; Walker, 'Notes of a Visit'; Johnson, 'Cowrie Currencies', 24; Latham, *Old Calabar*, 85; P. M. Martin, 'Family Strategies in Nineteenth-Century Cabinda', *JAH* 28 (1987), 77; Wariboko, 'New Calabar', 50–1.

97. Crow, *Memoirs*, 238; Ikime, *Rivalry*, 61; E. J. Alagoa, *A History of the Niger Delta* (Ibadan, 1972), 156–7; Alagoa and Fombo, *Grand Bonny*, 75–6; Austen, 'Metamorphoses of Middlemen', 4–5.

98. Observations on Mr Holt's letter of 16 February 1884, FO 84/1660, PRO; Alagoa and Fombo, *Grand Bonny*, 74; Cookey, *Jaja*, 10, 19; Austen, 'Metamorphoses of Middlemen', 4.

99. Northrup, *Trade Without Rulers*, 97.

100. Alagoa and Fombo, *Grand Bonny*, 18.

101. Alagoa, *History of Niger Delta*, 157; Lynn, 'John Beecroft', 209–12, 225–9.

102. Northrup, *Trade Without Rulers*, 207.

103. Law, 'Introduction', 10–11.

104. Robertson, *Notes*, 305–13; Jackson, *Journal*, 74. The 'King Pepple' concerned would have been Opubo.

105. The temporary nature of such cask houses was seen in the Efik refusal to allow construction of an iron cask house even as late as 1862: supercargoes to Burton, 28 April 1862, in Burton to Russell, 22 May 1862, FO 84/1176, PRO.

106. *Ibid.*; Lynslager's Journal of a visit to the Cameroons, in Lynslager to Clarendon, 3 March 1855, FO 84/975, PRO; Bold, *Guide*, 78; Adams, *Remarks*, 247; Jackson, *Journal*, 67. The rent in the Cameroons was set at five crews per cask house in 1862: Byelaws for ... the River Cameroons, 19 May 1862, in Burton to Russell, 22 May 1862, FO 84/1176, PRO.

107. Adams, *Remarks*, 135; Jackson, *Journal*, 77.

108. Jackson, *Journal*, 73.

109. Hutchinson, *Impressions*, 257; Jackson, *Journal*, 64–5.

110. Byelaws for ... the River Cameroons, 19 May 1862, in Burton to Russell, 22 May 1862, FO 84/1176; Burton to Russell, 18 December 1862, FO 84/1176: both PRO; Hutchinson, *Impressions*, 257–8.

111. Average comey at Old Calabar was alternatively estimated at £200 per ship in Davies to Hutchinson, 13 October 1856, in Hutchinson to Clarendon, 1 November 1856, FO 84/1001, PRO; Adams, *Remarks*, 245, 248; de Cardi, 'Short Description', 443. S. M. Hargreaves, 'Nineteenth-Century Bonny', 203, notes that the cost of comey for European traders at Bonny declined in 1792–1840, due to the depreciation in the value of the bars it was paid in: P. Ehrensaft, 'The Political Economy of Informal Empire in Pre-Colonial Nigeria, 1807–1884', *Canadian Journal of African Studies* 6 (1972), 469.

112. De Cardi, 'Short Description', 446.

113. J. Smith, *Trade and Travels in the Gulph of Guinea* (London, 1851), 186; G. I. Jones, *Trading States*, 99.

114. De Cardi, 'Short Description', 523–5; A. A. Cowan, 'Early Trading Conditions in the Bight of Biafra, II', *Journal of the Royal African Society* 35 (1936), 54.

115. Hutchinson, *Impressions*, 258; G. I. Jones, *Trading States*, 100.

116. M. Johnson, 'The Ounce in Eighteenth Century West African Trade', *JAH* 7 (1966), 197–214; Newbury, *Western Slave Coast*, 59–60; Northrup, *Trade Without Rulers*, 162. A 'bar' was also used as a unit of account in the Sierra Leone area (Kennedy to Pakington, 21 December 1852, CO 267/229, PRO), while in the Cameroons the crew was used as a unit of account. Hutchinson, *Impressions*, 256, valued the crew at between 10s and £1.

117. Wariboko, 'New Calabar', 87.

118. Aye, *Old Calabar*, 46; Latham, 'Trading Alliance', 864.

119. Adams, *Remarks*, 144.

120. Dowell to Admiralty, 10 January 1869, FO 541/16, PRO; Austen, 'Metamorphoses of Middlemen', 7–8.

121. Waddell, 'Journal', IX, 14 July 1850; Austen, 'Metamorphoses of Middlemen', 4–5.

122. J. C. Langdon, 'Three Voyages to the West Coast of Africa, 1881–1884' (Bristol Central Library), 22; Latham, *Old Calabar*, 27; P. M. Martin, *Loango Coast*, 103.

123. 'A Pioneer of the West African Trade: A Brief Outline of Mr Harry Cotterell's Life', *Elder Dempster Magazine* 4, 13 (1925), 19; Latham, *Old Calabar*, 80–1.

124. Brooks, *Yankee Traders*, 281.
125. Bold, *Guide*, 41.
126. *Ibid.*, 46; Robertson, *Notes*, 35, 75.
127. Reynolds, *Trade and Economic Change*, 103–38; McCarthy, *Social Change*, 125–33.
128. Swanzy to Cardwell, 16 November 1864, CO 96/66; Bedingfield to Adams, 3 July 1854, in Admiralty to Wodehouse, 24 March 1855, FO 84/981; Campbell to Clarendon, 5 January 1857, FO 84/1031: all PRO; P. Leonard, *Records of a Voyage to the Western Coast of Africa* (Edinburgh, 1833), 23; P. Verger, *Bahia and the West Coast Trade, 1549–1851* (Ibadan, 1964); Manning, 'Merchants, Porters, and Canoemen', 66–7.
129. Fitzpatrick to Grey, 10 March 1850, CO 96/18, PRO; Cruickshank, *Eighteen Years*, vol. II, 35, 42; P. M. Martin, *Loango Coast*, 107–10.
130. McCoskry to Russell, 2 July 1861, FO 84/1141, PRO, covers charges at Porto Novo; A. Swanzy, 'On Trade in Western Africa', 481, paid £45 to the king of Dahomey for every ship; Reid, 'Warrior Aristocrats', 173–4; Vansina, *Paths in the Rainforests*, 205.
131. P. M. Martin, *Loango Coast*, 97–8, 114, 146.
132. Ofonagoro, *Trade and Imperialism*, 81.
133. Waddell, 'Journal', VII, 10 January 1850.
134. Hutchinson to Clarendon, 24 June 1856, FO 84/1001, PRO. King Eyo was said to owe £16,000–£18,000 in 1857: Hutchinson to Clarendon, 25 May 1857, FO 84/1030, PRO. 'Over entrusting' by traders was designed to create a monopoly position in a river: Hutchinson to Clarendon, 29 September 1856, FO 84/1001, PRO.
135. As faced Tyson & Richmond's ships in Old Calabar in 1859: Hearn to Hutchinson, 1 March 1859, in Hutchinson to Malmesbury, 21 March 1859, FO 84/1087, PRO.
136. Dike, *Trade and Politics*, 109–10. Chopping oil was also common along the Gold Coast: Conran to Cardwell, 10 March 1866, CO 96/70, PRO.
137. Price to Clarendon, 15 March 1847, FO 2/3, PRO.
138. M. Lynn, 'Law and Imperial Expansion: The Niger Delta Courts of Equity, c. 1850–1885', *Journal of Imperial and Commonwealth History* 23 (1995), 54–76.
139. Alagoa and Fombo, *Grand Bonny*, 74–6; G. I. Jones, *Trading States*, 115–16.
140. Ikime, *Prince*, 5–6; Alagoa, *Small Brave City-State*, 88–90.
141. Austen, 'Metamorphoses of Middlemen', 9.
142. Quoted in Law, 'Introduction', 12.
143. Dike, *Trade and Politics*, 153–65; J. B. Webster and A. A. Boahen, *The Revolutionary Years: West Africa Since 1800* (London, 1967), 193–210.
144. Alagoa, 'Nineteenth-Century Revolutions', 563–73; Latham, *Old Calabar*; Wariboko, 'New Calabar', esp. 110–11.
145. Latham, *Old Calabar*, 94, 118.
146. Austen, 'Metamorphoses of Middlemen', 9; Lynn, 'Factionalism, Imperialism', 172
147. Laird and Oldfield, *Narrative*, vol. I, 100; *Missionary Record of the United Presbyterian Church* 62 (1 February 1871), 381; Latham, 'Palm Produce from Calabar', 273–4.
148. G. I. Jones, *Slaves to Palm Oil*, 77.
149. S. M. Hargreaves, 'Nineteenth-Century Bonny', considers these issues in

chapter 2, 77–120; she notes that women were banned from travelling in the interior from Bonny until late in the century. Krio women from Sierra Leone do appear to have been very active in the oil trade, however: memo on a possible equalisation of tariffs by Governor Rowe, in Rowe to Hicks Beach, 13 October 1879, CO 879/17, PRO.

150. S. Biobaku, 'Madame Tinubu', in K. O. Dike (ed.), *Eminent Nigerians of the Nineteenth Century* (Cambridge, 1960), 33–41; K. Mann, 'Women, Landed Property, and the Accumulation of Wealth in Early Colonial Lagos', *Signs* 16 (1991), 682–706.

151. G. I. Jones, *Trading States*, 51–7; Northrup, *Trade Without Rulers*, 189–90.

152. Latham, *Old Calabar*, 115; Pepple to Beecroft, 17 January 1854, CALPROF 4/1, NNAI. Wariboko, 'New Calabar', 94, stresses that in Elem Kalabari all comey went to the *Amanyanabo*.

153. Latham, *Old Calabar*, 84.

154. Supercargoes to Burton, 28 April 1862, in Burton to FO, 22 May 1862, FO 84/1176; Livingstone to FO, 21 December 1867, FO 84/1277: both PRO; S. M. Hargreaves, 'Nineteenth-Century Bonny', 394–8.

155. Latham, 'Trading Alliance', 863.

156. Law, 'Historiography', 105–6.

4 BRITISH TRADERS, BRITISH PORTS, AND THE EXPANSION OF THE PALM OIL TRADE

1. Inikori, 'West Africa's Seaborne Trade', 69.

2. Quoted *ibid.*

3. G. Williams, *Liverpool Privateers*, 621.

4. Drake, 'Liverpool's African Commerce', 12–13; B. K. Drake, 'Continuity and Flexibility in Liverpool's Trade with Africa and the Caribbean', *Business History* 18 (1976), 85–97.

5. Drake, 'Liverpool's African Commerce', 91–121, 123.

6. *Ibid.*, 12, 61–2, 111, 195.

7. *Ibid.*, 106–7.

8. *PP* 1847–8, XXII (536), 471, 474; Stilliard, 'Legitimate Trade', 14, 24; R. T. Anstey, *The Atlantic Slave Trade and British Abolition, 1760–1810* (London, 1975), 291.

9. *Liverpool and Slavery*, 120–1; Dike, *Trade and Politics*, 49.

10. Drake, 'Liverpool's African Commerce', 251–2; see the burial inscription of Isaac Oldham Bold (1785–1853) in St James Cemetery, Liverpool: copy held in Liverpool Record Office.

11. *Liverpool and Slavery*, 119, 126–7; Dike, *Trade and Politics*, 108; Lynn, 'Trade and Politics', 103–4.

12. Lynn, 'Trade and Politics', 103–5; Lynn, 'Change and Continuity', 344–5.

13. *PP* 1847–8, XXII (536), 472–3; Lynn, 'Trade and Politics', 106–7.

14. Poole, *Commerce*, 115.

15. Lynn, 'Trade and Politics', 103–4, 107–8.

16. Poole, *Commerce*, 115.

17. Lynn, 'British Business and the African Trade', 21; 'Builders of the West African Trade: The King Family', *Elder Dempster Magazine* 6 (1927), 10–11.

18. Lynn, 'Change and Continuity', 337.

19. Though it must be noted that Bristol's slave trade had virtually disappeared by 1807: K. Morgan, *Bristol and the Atlantic Trade in the Eighteenth Century* (Cambridge, 1993), 133, 145.
20. Latham, 'Palm Produce from Calabar', 268–9. Latham stresses that salt did not play a major role in the slave trade at Old Calabar: *Old Calabar*, 24.
21. Lynn, 'Trade and Politics', 102. Important too were the major harbour and dock improvements on Merseyside in this period: S. Marriner, *The Economic and Social Development of Merseyside* (London, 1982), 30–2.
22. Lynn, 'Bristol, West Africa', 362; K. Morgan, *Bristol and the Atlantic*, 97.
23. *PP* 1837–8, XLV (223), 448–9.
24. T. Baines, *History of the Commerce and Town of Liverpool* (London, 1852), 768; C. Wilson, *Unilever*, vol. I, 15–18; G. F. Wilson, *On the Stearic Candle Manufacture*, 12–13; G. F. Wilson, *On the Manufactures of Price's Patent Candle Co.*, 11.
25. Musson, *Enterprise in Soap and Chemicals*, 11; Minchinton, *British Tinplate Industry*, 29.
26. Musson, *Enterprise in Soap and Chemicals*, 14.
27. Marriner, *Development of Merseyside*, 53–9; J. Langton, 'Liverpool and Its Hinterland in the Late Eighteenth Century', in B. L. Anderson and P. J. M. Stoney (eds.), *Commerce, Industry, and Transport: Studies in Economic Change on Merseyside* (Liverpool, 1983), 1–25.
28. *PP* 1837–8, XLV (223), 448–9.
29. Quoted in Musson, *Enterprise in Soap and Chemicals*, 14; F. E. Hyde, 'The Growth of Liverpool's Trade, 1700–1950', in W. Smith (ed.), *A Scientific Survey of Merseyside* (Liverpool, 1953), 157; F. E. Hyde, *Liverpool and the Mersey: An Economic History of a Port, 1700–1970* (Newton Abbot, 1971), 40.
30. C. Wilson, *Unilever*, vol. I, 11–13, 21; Musson, *Enterprise in Soap and Chemicals*, 13–14.
31. There were thirty-five soap manufacturers in the city in 1830: *Mathew's Bristol Directory, 1830* (Bristol, 1830); T. O'Brien, 'Christopher Thomas & Bros. Ltd', *Progress* (1949), 43–8; W. J. Corlett, *The Economic Development of Detergents* (London, 1958), 46; S. J. Diaper, 'Christopher Thomas & Brothers Ltd: The Last Bristol Soapmakers', *Transactions of the Bristol and Gloucestershire Archaeological Society* 105 (1987), 223–32.
32. Minchinton, *Tinplate Industry*, 25, 29; Lynn, 'Bristol, West Africa', 362.
33. Fyfe, *History*, 166.
34. Lynn, 'Change and Continuity', 343–6. Charles Sauerbray, a ship broker, noted that ships would call at Freetown to fill empty cargo space on their journey back to Britain: *PP* 1842, XI (551), 33, 205–9, 710.
35. Lynn, 'Change and Continuity', 337.
36. Forster to Bathurst, 19 January 1825, CO 267/69; Nicolls to Hay, 14 November 1830, CO 82/3; Blunt to Grey, 17 December 1838, CO 82/9: all PRO; Reynolds, *Trade and Economic Change*, 55.
37. *PP* 1842, XI (551), 205–6; R. B. Sheridan, 'The Commercial and Financial Organisation of the British Slave Trade, 1750–1807', *Economic History Review* 11 (1958), 249–63.
38. *PP* 1842, XI (551), 205; M. Stenton (ed.), *Who's Who of British Members of Parliament*, vol. I, *1832–1885* (Hassocks, 1976), 146. Forster, who sat in the

Whig interest, was unseated for bribery: R. Braithwaite, 'Matthew Forster of Bellsise', *Camden History Review* 19 (1995), 13–16. I am grateful to Christopher Fyfe for material on Forster & Smith.

39. P. D. Curtin, *Economic Change in Precolonial Africa: Senegambia in the Era of the Slave Trade*, 2 vols. (Madison, 1975), vol. I, 137.

40. Pedler, *Lion and Unicorn*, 52–5.

41. *PP* 1842, XI (551), 731; Reynolds, *Trade and Economic Change*, 122; Lynn, 'Change and Continuity', 345. According to F. Boyle, *Through Fanteeland to Coomassie* (London, 1874), 32, Forster & Smith had seventeen ships in their fleet at their peak.

42. *The Firm of Hutton* (n. d.), JHPL; obituary of J. F. Hutton, *Journal of Manchester Geographical Society* 7 (1891), 1–8; *Lancashire Men of the Period* (London, 1895), 67; W. B. Tracey and W. T. Pike, *Manchester and Salford at the Close of the Nineteenth Century* (Brighton, n. d.), 116.

43. A. Swanzy, 'On Trade in Western Africa', 479; Lynn, 'Change and Continuity', 344.

44. Hutton to Hawes, 6 July 1847, CALPROF 1/2/1, NNAE; *PP* 1842, XI (551), 243–4; Huttons were accused of facilitating slaving through selling goods to slavers on the coast; this can be seen in the amount of specie their ships would bring back from West Africa.

45. *Lancashire Men of the Period*, 67. The firm re-emerged in 1853 as a Manchester commission house, James F. Hutton & Co. See also James F. Hutton's entry in F. Boase, *Modern English Biography* (London, 1892).

46. Lynn, 'Change and Continuity', 337.

47. R. & W. King to Stanley, 7 June 1842, in Hope to Canning, 6 July 1842, FO 403/4; R. & W. King to Aberdeen, 3 March 1843, FO 403/4; Lucas, Gwyer, & Lucas to Stanley, 6 March 1843, CO 96/3; Campbell to Clarendon, 5 January 1857, FO 84/1031: all PRO; Kingsley, *West African Studies*, 70–4.

48. *PP* 1842, XI (551), 140–1.

49. It was still the pattern in 1881: Langdon, 'Three Voyages'.

50. Lynn, 'British Business and the African Trade', 23.

51. Drake, 'Liverpool's African Commerce', 128–9, 145–7.

52. M. Lynn, 'From Sail to Steam: The Impact of the Steamship Services on the British Palm Oil Trade with West Africa, 1850–1890', *JAH* 30 (1989), 238.

53. Lynn, 'Change and Continuity', 337.

54. Drake, 'Liverpool's African Commerce', 248–50; Horsfall & Co. were in partnership with Thomas Tobin for much of this period: Lynn, 'Change and Continuity', 344–5.

55. *PP* 1842, XI (551), 140, 206, 265.

56. *Ibid.*, 246.

57. McPhee, *Economic Revolution*, 70; Stilliard, 'Legitimate Trade', 89–90.

58. J. Whitford, *Trading Life in Western and Central Africa* (Liverpool, 1877), 288.

59. Nicolls to Hay, 3 July 1832, 30 August 1832, CO 8/5, PRO.

60. Hay to Stephen, 12 May 1834, CO 82/7; Burton to Russell, 15 April 1864, FO 2/45: both PRO; *PP* 1847–8, XXII (536), 485–94.

61. Affidavits by Capts. Gordon and Hemingway, 25 July 1830, CO 8/3, PRO; *PP* 1842, XI (551), 132, 265; 1850, IX i (53), 217–18.

62. *PP* 1842, XI (551), 140.

63. Masters were usually paid a fee, plus a percentage of the returns; in the slave trade era this stood at around 6 per cent: *PP* 1847–8, XXII (536), 473–4.
64. He imported, for example, eleven cargoes of oil, totalling 8,135 casks, on his own account in 1847: *Customs Bills of Entry*.
65. *PP* 1842, XI (551), 257, 499. It should be noted that the figures Hutton quotes in his examination differ from the figures given in the table he submitted to the committee.
66. Drake, 'Liverpool's African Commerce', 243–6.
67. Jackson, *Journal*, 80.
68. Stilliard, 'Legitimate Trade', 88.
69. *PP* 1850, IX i (53), 218; Jackson, *Journal*, 141. In contrast, later in the century Harford spoke of spending up to fifteen months in a Delta river waiting for oil: Harford, 'Voyage to the African Oil Rivers', 578.
70. R. G. Clough, *Oil Rivers Trader* (London, 1972), 39.
71. Babington, 'Remarks', 252; A. P. Crouch, *Glimpses of Feverland* (London, 1889), 45. Adams, *Remarks*, 248, stresses that mortality among European coopers was 'generally great, by reason of much of their duty being performed on shore'.
72. *PP* 1842, XI (551), 121, 269. Kru pay, in soap, alcohol, tobacco, and cloth, is outlined in 'The Voyages of the Schooner *Maria*', in *The Diary of John Holt*, ed. P. N. Davies (St John's, Newfoundland, 1993), 146–7. For material on Kru work in the oil trade, see G. E. Brooks, *The Kru Mariner in the Nineteenth Century* (Newark, 1972), 1–69; J. Martin, 'Krumen "Down the Coast": Liberian Migrants on the West African Coast in the Nineteenth and Early Twentieth Centuries', *IJAHS* 18 (1985), 401–23; E. Tonkin, 'Creating Kroomen: Ethnic Diversity, Economic Specialism, and Changing Demand', in J. C. Stone (ed.), *Africa and the Sea* (Aberdeen, 1985), 27–47.
73. Kru wages were between 5s and 14s plus provisions per month, in the middle of the century, compared to wages for British crew varying between £1 to £5: entry for William Harris, log of the *Belmont*, in the possession of Prof. P. N. Davies; Langdon, 'Three Voyages', First Voyage, 1; *PP* 1842, XI (551) 135; J. Smith, *Trade and Travels*, 103.
74. *PP* 1842, XI (551), 135, 143. Some Kru would remain in a Delta port over several years working for different ships: D. Frost, 'The Kru in Freetown and Liverpool: A Study of Maritime Work and Community During the Nineteenth and Twentieth Centuries', Ph.D thesis, University of Liverpool (1992).
75. *PP* 1842, XI (551), 42, 140.
76. Langdon, 'Three Voyages', First Voyage.
77. Pedler, *Lion and Unicorn*, 153.
78. J. Smith, *Trade and Travels*, 185; Harford, 'Voyage to the African Oil Rivers', 575–7; H. Cotterell, 'Reminiscences of One Connected with the West African Trade from 1863 to 1910', in Davies, *Trading in West Africa*, 24.
79. Adams, *Remarks*, 247; J. Smith, *Trade and Travels*, 185.
80. Langdon, 'Three Voyages', First Voyage, 8–12; J. Smith, *Trade and Travels*, 190; Babington, 'Remarks', 252. One of the major activities of the crew during this period was the boiling and 'trying' of palm oil for adulteration.
81. Babington, 'Remarks', 252–3.
82. Langdon, 'Three Voyages', First Voyage, 12.

83. Waddell, 'Journal', I, 11 April 1846. I am grateful to the World Mission and Unity Department of the Church of Scotland for permission to quote from Waddell's Journal.
84. Burton to Russell, 15 April 1864, FO 2/45, PRO.
85. Langdon, 'Three Voyages', Second Voyage, 28.
86. Quinine was already used on the coast to treat fever but it was not until 1854 that its value as a prophylactic was confirmed: W. B. Baikie, *Narrative of an Exploring Voyage* (London, 1856).
87. *PP* 1842, XI (551), 267, 379, 499; Jackson, *Journal*, 88–9, 142. Shipwrecks should not be ignored in this consideration of mortality: *PP* 1852, XLIX (284), 452–3, 460–1, observes that nine ships in the African trade were lost at sea in 1850 and five in 1851.
88. For contemporary medical practices, see H. Temperley, *White Dreams, Black Africa: The Antislavery Expedition to the River Niger, 1841–1842* (New Haven and London, 1991), 46–50, 114–16. For a ship's surgeon who appeared to be drunk for an entire voyage, see Langdon, 'Three Voyages', Second Voyage, 40.
89. J. Clarke, 'Journal', Second Journey, III, 19 August 1845, Baptist Missionary Society Archives; Hutchinson to Clarendon, 31 January 1856, FO 2/15 PRO; J. Smith, *Trade and Travels*, 202–3. For this reason it was usual for oil ships to load gunpowder at sea.
90. Beecroft to Hay, 26 July 1831, CO 82/4; Nicolls to Hay, 29 April 1831, CO 82/5: both PRO.
91. Langdon, 'Three Voyages', First Voyage, 20–2.
92. Waddell, 'Journal', I, 16 April 1846; VII, 21 January 50. The monotony of the trading life along the coast is underlined in J. F. N. Hewett, *European Settlements on the West Coast of Africa* (London, 1862), 83–6.
93. Burton to Russell, 15 April 1864, FO 2/45, PRO.
94. Langdon, 'Three Voyages', First Voyage, 16.
95. Waddell noted that Capt. Turner had a daughter of ten in Old Calabar whom he gave in marriage to King Eyo ('Journal', IX, 14 July 1851), while Clarke referred to a British trader in the Cameroons with eleven 'wives', and to the daughter of Captain Burnley and an Igbo woman living in Clarence ('Journal', First Journey, I, 3 February 1841; Second Journey, II, 18 March 1845). See Beecroft to Palmerston, 19 April 1851, FO 84/858, PRO, for an early reference to a wife from Britain living with her trader husband in a Delta river.
96. Waddell, 'Journal', I, 18 May 1846; IX, 28 August 1851; Clarke, 'Journal', Second Journey, I, 8 September 1844; *Diary of John Holt*, 98.
97. Crowther to Clegg, 3 January 1867, CA3/04/219; Annual Report on the Niger Mission, 1875, CA3/04/744: both CMSP; Waddell, 'Journal', IX, 14 July 1851.
98. Langdon's 'Three Voyages' is the only record available giving the view of an ordinary seaman and is characterised by a very limited understanding of the societies he visited.
99. J. B. Walker, 'Notes on the Politics, Religion, and Commerce of Old Calabar', *Journal of the Anthropological Institute of Britain and Ireland* 6 (1877), 119–24. Clarke makes several references to this practice and the privileges it ensured: 'Journal', First Journey, II, 7 February 1842; Second Journey, I, 29 March 1844; Second Journey, III, 3 August 1845. For an alleged equivalent practice in Bonny, see Annual Report on the Niger Mission, 1875, CA3/04/744, CMSP.

100. Jackson, *Journal*, 159.
101. J. Smith, *Trade and Travels*, 206–8.
102. Lynn, 'John Beecroft', 19–81.
103. This was particularly the case in the 1820s when the bar of the Bonny River made the port inaccessible to large ships: Owen to Croker, 13 October 1828, in Barrow to Hay, 3 February 1829, CO 82/2, PRO.
104. Lynn, 'John Beecroft', 82–123.
105. Roberts to African Company, 24 December 1780, T70/32, PRO; J. Holman, *Travels in Madeira, Sierra Leone*... (London, 1840), 242; Waddell, 'Journal', VII, 1 January 1850.
106. Lynn, 'John Beecroft', 108, 142–3.
107. G. Williams, *Liverpool Privateers*, 307–8.
108. W. E. Minchinton, 'The Voyage of the *Snow Africa*', *Mariners' Mirror* 37 (1951), 187–8; Drake, 'Liverpool's African Commerce', 142–4.
109. R. C. Reid, 'Annals of the Tobin Family of Liverpool and the Isle of Man', Liverpool City Library, 20–6; Pedler, *Lion and Unicorn*, 14–15.
110. Lynn, 'Change and Continuity', 342.
111. Lynn, 'Trade and Politics', 106.
112. Drake, 'Liverpool's African Commerce', 134–9.
113. R. H. Thornton, *British Shipping* (Cambridge, 1959), 40; F. Neal, 'Liverpool Shipping in the Early Nineteenth Century', in J. R. Harris (ed.), *Liverpool and Merseyside* (London, 1969), 162; Marriner, *Development of Merseyside*, 43.
114. *Customs Bills of Entry*, 16 September 1844, 2 January 1846.
115. Lynn, 'Change and Continuity', 337.
116. W. H. Fisher & Co. to Freeman, 22 November 1860, SC 4/172, NAGA; Freeman to Pine, 27 June 1857, CO 96/41, PRO.
117. Livingstone to Stanley, 1 October 1866, FO 2/47, PRO.
118. Drake, 'Liverpool's African Commerce', 142–4, 266–73; Latham, *Old Calabar*, 71–2; Newbury, 'Prices and Profitability', 100–4; E. Reynolds, 'Economic Imperialism: The Case of the Gold Coast', *Journal of Economic History* 35 (1975), 98.
119. *PP* 1847–8, XXII (366), 385–6; Clarke, 'Journal', 'First Journey', II, 22 February 1842.
120. 'Memoranda of the African trade ascribed to W. A. & G. Maxwell & Co., 1830–1840', Sydney Jones Library, University of Liverpool; M. Lynn, 'The Profitability of the Early Nineteenth-Century Palm Oil Trade', *AEH* 20 (1992), 77–97. These profitability figures are considerably higher than those suggested by some historians for the later years of the slave trade: Anstey, *Atlantic Slave Trade*, 46–7; S. Drescher, *Econocide: British Slavery in the Era of Abolition* (Pittsburgh, 1977), 30–2.
121. Latham, 'Price Fluctuations', 213–18.
122. Hancock, *Survey*, vol. II, part 2, 159.
123. Lynn, 'Change and Continuity', 342–7.
124. Isaac Bold, who inherited his firm from the slaving business of his father Jonas, was the largest importer of palm oil in Britain in 1840; he ceased trading in oil in 1847. Hamilton, Jackson, & Co. were the third largest oil importers in 1835 and fourth in 1840; their last importation of oil was in 1842: *Customs Bills of Entry*; Lynn, 'Change and Continuity', 344–5.

220 Notes to pages 97–105

125. *Liverpolitan* 4 (1935), 7; W. T. Pike, *Liverpool and Birkenhead in the Twentieth Century* (Brighton, 1911), 160; Drake, 'Liverpool's African Commerce', 248–50.
126. Lynn, 'Change and Continuity', 342–7.
127. *Liverpool Mercury*, 19 October 1832; Baines, *Town of Liverpool*, appendix, 11–12.
128. Lynn, 'Trade and Politics', 110–11.
129. Baines, *Town of Liverpool*, appendix, 11–12; obituary of James Aspinall Tobin, *Daily Post*, 17 April 1891; *Liverpool Poll Book, 1857*; *Liverpool Fifty Years Ago* (1878–9), 54–6.
130. *Bristol Times and Mirror*, 28 September 1874; A. B. Freeman, *Bristol Worthies* (Bristol, 1909), 48–9; 'Builders of the West African Trade: The King Family', 10–11; 'The Merchant Kings', *Bristol Evening Post*, 25 May 1945; W. G. Neale, *At the Port of Bristol*, 2 vols. (Bristol, 1968), vol. I, *Members and Problems*, 9, 11, 114–19; D. Large (ed.), *The Port of Bristol, 1848–1884* (Bristol, 1984), 1, 3, 38.
131. *Liverpool Review*, 23 October 1887, 7; *Clifton Chronicle*, 29 July 1863; *Western Daily Press*, 13 October 1893; Neale, *Port of Bristol*, vol. I, 127–8.
132. Hieke, *Zur Geschichte des deutschen Handles mit Ostafrika*; Schnapper, *La Politique et le commerce français*, 23, 144–8.
133. *Liverpool Citizen*, 26 September 1888, 3; L. Finigan, *The Life of Peter Stuart: The Ditton Doctor* (privately printed, 1920).
134. The firm was run from 1869 by the two sons of Thomas Worthington Cookson, Edward Hatton Cookson and Thomas Worthington Cookson, and became a limited liability company in 1901: *Liverpool Citizen*, 24 October 1888, 9; *Elder Dempster Magazine* 6 (1927), 133–4; E. A. Woods, 'Liverpool Fleet Lists', 159–65, MS, Liverpool Record Office; Lynn, 'Change and Continuity', 344–5.
135. *Clifton Chronicle*, 26 July 1863; *Western Daily Press*, 13 October 1893; G. E. Farr, *Records of Bristol Ships, 1800–1838* (Bristol, 1950), 212–13; Minchinton, 'The Snow *Africa*', 188–90; Neale, *Port of Bristol*, vol. I, 127–8.
136. *Sea Breezes* 23 (1939), 434; M. K. Stammers, *The Passage Makers* (Brighton, 1978), 120, 134–5; Lynn, 'Change and Continuity', 344–5.
137. Henry to Tudor, 1 March 1849, in Admiralty to FO, 26 May 1849, FO 2/3, PRO.
138. Neale, *Port of Bristol*, vol. I, 114–19; Lynn, 'Trade and Politics', 106–7.
139. Lynn, 'Change and Continuity', 346; based on a survey of every fifth year between 1830 and 1855.
140. Gertzel ('John Holt', 62) uses 'monopoly' to describe their control of the trade.
141. Newbury, 'On the Margins of Empire', 39.

5 TECHNOLOGICAL CHANGE, THE BRITISH MARKET, AND AFRICAN PRODUCERS

1. A. Sauerbeck, 'Prices of Commodities and the Precious Metals', *Journal of the Royal Statistical Society* 49 (1886), 641.
2. Heddle to Baikie, 8 May 1857, in Hill to Labouchere, 30 June 1857, CO 267/257, PRO.
3. W. H. Fischer & Co. to Freeman, 22 November 1860, SC 4/172, NAGA.

4. *Half-Yearly Report of the Bristol Chamber of Commerce, June 1853* (Bristol, 1853), 15–16.
5. Davies, *Trade Makers*, 41.
6. R. A. Austen and D. Headrick, 'The Role of Technology in the African Past', *African Studies Review* 26 (1983), 163–84; D. R. Headrick, *The Tools of Empire: Technology and European Imperialism in the Nineteenth Century* (Oxford, 1981); Headrick, *The Tentacles of Progress: Technology Transfer in the Age of Imperialism, 1850–1940* (Oxford, 1988); J. F. Munro, 'African Shipping: Reflections on the Maritime History of Africa South of the Sahara, 1800–1914', *International Journal of Maritime History* 2 (1990), 163–82.
7. G. S. Graham, 'The Ascendancy of the Sailing Ship, 1850–1885', *Economic History Review* 9 (1956), 74–88.
8. Thornton, *British Shipping*, 23; Headrick, *Tools of Empire*, 129–41; R. Hope, *A New History of British Shipping* (London, 1990), 296–7.
9. Headrick, *Tools of Empire*, 142–9, 170; Graham, 'Sailing Ship', 82–3, 87; Hope, *British Shipping*, 297, 300–1.
10. Governor of Sierra Leone to Grey, 29 January 1851: *PP* 1852, XLIX (284), 422.
11. 'Steam to Africa from England and the United States', *Colonial Magazine and East India Review* 19 (1850), 349–50.
12. Governor of Sierra Leone to Grey, 29 January 1851: *PP* 1852, XLIX (284), 422; Laird and Oldfield, *Narrative*, vol. II, 399.
13. *PP* 1852, XLIX (284); G. Chandler, *Liverpool Shipping: A Short History* (London, 1960), 165–84; P. N. Davies, 'The African Steam Ship Co. ', in Harris, *Liverpool and Merseyside*, 212–38.
14. Davies, *Trade Makers*, 35–51.
15. African Steam Ship Co., *Annual Report for 1853*, EDR. It should be noted that such steamers would have used sail for parts of their voyage: Davies, *Trade Makers*, 44.
16. African Steam Ship Co., *Annual Report for 1853*, EDR.
17. African Steam Ship Co., *Half Yearly Report, December 1858*, EDR; POST 29/133/PKT 1065R/1866.
18. Davies, *Trade Makers*, 56–69, 82–91; W. Thompson, 'Glasgow and Africa: Connexions and Attitudes, 1870–1900', Ph.D thesis, University of Strathclyde (1970), 128–34. In its early years the British & African was largely Scottish-owned.
19. Davies, *Trade Makers*, 95–107.
20. L. G. Fay, 'Ninety-Six Years in the West African Trade', *Sea Breezes* 6 (1948), 150–68; R. Fry, *Bankers in West Africa: The Story of the Bank of British West Africa Ltd* (London, 1976); P. N. Davies, *Sir Alfred Jones: Shipping Entrepreneur par excellence* (London, 1978), 47–61.
21. M. H. Kingsley, *Travels in West Africa* (London, 1897), 633; C. Leubuscher, *The West African Shipping Trade, 1909–1959* (Leiden, 1963), 14; Hopkins, *Economic History*, 149; Wickins, *Economic History of Africa*, 291–2. For material on Portuguese steam ship services, see Report by Consul Hopkins on the Trade . . . of Angola, *PP* 1875, LXXV (1132), 238; Cohen to Salisbury, 22 May 1880, FO 84/1566, PRO; W. G. Clarence-Smith, *Slaves, Peasants, and Capitalists in Southern Angola, 1840–1926* (Cambridge, 1979), 65, 95–6.
22. Leubuscher, *Shipping Trade*, 14–16; Davies, 'African Steam Ship Co.', 222–3. In effect this amounted to an interest-free loan by traders to the shipping firms.

23. Tramp steamers required a regular trade and good harbours to be successful (McPhee, *Economic Revolution*, 96), though they did try to enter the Delta trade at the turn of the century, A. C. Douglas, *Niger Memories by Nemo* (Exeter, 1927), 106.

24. *Customs Bills of Entry, passim*; POST 29/325/PKT 346H/1882.

25. African Steam Ship Co., *Annual Report for 1853*, EDR; the government contract in 1866 specified 1,228 hours for the voyage from Liverpool to Fernando Po and back: POST 29/133/PKT 1065R/1866; POST 29/325/PKT 346H/1882. POST 43/140 gives details of the lengths of voyages of all mail steamers, 1859–71.

26. African Steam Ship Co., *Annual Report for 1853*, EDR; Davies, *Trade Makers*, 40, 96–7.

27. J. A. O. Payne, *Lagos and West African Almanack for 1881* (London, 1880), 107–8.

28. P. N. Davies, 'The Impact of the Expatriate Shipping Lines on the Economic Development of British West Africa', *Business History* 19 (1977), 8–9; A. J. H. Latham, *The International Economy and the Undeveloped World* (London, 1978), 35.

29. Cotterell, 'Reminiscences', 38.

30. Lynn, 'From Sail to Steam', 233.

31. Leubuscher, *Shipping Trade*, 19–25; Davies, *Trade Makers*, 91.

32. Livingstone to Clarendon, 19 February 1870, FO 84/1326, PRO. Sailing ships continued to be used for cheaper, coarser cargoes: memo by Livingstone, 8 December 1871, FO 84/1343, PRO.

33. McPhee, *Economic Revolution*, 71; Lynn, 'From Sail to Steam', 234.

34. Sauerbeck, 'Prices of Commodities', 49 (1886), 641; 55 (1892), 119; 69 (1906), 225–6.

35. These figures are calculated from CUST 5/52–/162, PRO, using a strict definition of mainland West Africa. Islands like the Canaries and Madeira have been excluded – because of the possibility of these figures involving South American supplies – as have re-exports from Germany and the USA.

36. The figures are calculated from CUST 5/52–/162, covering West Africa only, and differ from the figures to be found in the *PP* which cover 'all parts'.

37. As early as 1872 observers were commenting on approaching difficulties for the palm oil trade: Livingstone to Granville, 9 July 1872, FO 84/1356, PRO.

38. Leubuscher, *Shipping Trade*, 14–16; Neal, 'Liverpool Shipping', 162; Marriner, *Development of Merseyside*, 43.

39. Hopkins, *Economic History*, 133, 151.

40. McPhee, *Economic Revolution*, 33–4.

41. Munro, *Africa and the International Economy*, 71–2.

42. 'Oil Palm in Labuan', 259–67.

43. Hartley, *Oil Palm*, 19–23.

44. The CUST 5/– figures record intermittent palm oil imports into Britain – albeit of limited quantity – from Borneo from 1873, Java from 1889, and Singapore from 1893. Also notable in the CUST 5/– figures are growing imports from Brazil after 1850; this oil was clearly from the South American oil palm.

45. Livingstone to Granville, 9 July 1872, FO 84/1356, PRO. By the 1920s these concerns had reached a considerable volume: Auchinleck, *West African Oil*

Palm, 1–2; *Palm Oil and Palm Kernels: Report of a Committee Appointed by the Secretary of State for the Colonies, September 1923* (London, 1925); Dawe and Martin, 'Oil Palm Industry', 5–29; F. M. Dyke, *Report on the Oil Palm Industry in British West Africa* (Lagos, 1927).

46. McPhee, *Economic Revolution*, 33; A. Nevins, *John D. Rockefeller: The Heroic Age of American Enterprise*, 2 vols. (New York, 1941), vol. I, 147.
47. Hancock, *Survey of Commonwealth Affairs*, vol. II, part 2, 159; E. C. Kirkland, *A History of American Economic Life*, 4th edn (New York, 1969), 295–6, 301; D. C. North, *Growth and Welfare in the American Past*, 2nd edn (Englewood Cliffs, NJ, 1974), 141–2.
48. H. U. Faulkner, *American Economic History*, 8th edn (New York, 1960), 331–2, 418–19.
49. Hopkins, *Economic History*, 133.
50. Carpenter, *Soap and Candles*, 32–6, 243; Hurst, *Soaps*, 123; Ashworth, *Economic History of England*, 78. Paraffin was first extracted in 1848.
51. Corlett, *Economic Development*, 65–7; R. Feron, 'Technology and Production', in van Stuyvenberg, *Margarine*, 83–121.
52. Minchinton, *Tinplate Industry*, 25, 58.
53. Milbourne, 'Palm Kernels', 134.
54. Campbell to Clarendon, 4 May 1856, FO 84/1002, PRO; Carpenter, *Soap and Candles*, 36–40. G. A. Moore had a kernel extracting machine in Brass from 1878 ('Lagos Palm Oil', 201), while de Cardi was operating one, also at Brass, by 1884, Craigie to Salmon, in Admiralty to FO, 9 September 1884, FO 84/1689, PRO.
55. Hurst, *Soaps*, 127–8; E. T. Webb, *Soap and Glycerine Manufacture* (London, 1927), 6–7; Corlett, *Economic Development*, 63.
56. C. Wilson, *Unilever*, vol. I, 21–44; I. C. Bradley, *Enlightened Entrepreneurs* (London, 1987), 174–201.
57. E. Williams, *Port Sunlight: The First Hundred Years, 1888–1988* (Kingston upon Thames, 1988).
58. Sunlight consisted of 42 per cent palm kernel oil; its formula is given in C. Wilson, *Unilever*, vol. I, 31.
59. Philipps, 'Germany and the Palm Kernel Trade'; Milbourne, 'Palm Kernels', 133–44.
60. C. Wilson, *Unilever*, vol. II, 24–7; van Stuyvenberg, *Margarine*.
61. W. Clayton, *Margarine* (London, 1920), 3–4; A. J. C. Andersen, *Margarine* (London, 1954), 1–5.
62. C. Wilson, *Unilever*, vol. II, 35–7; Feron, 'Technology and Production', 101.
63. C. Wilson, *Unilever*, vol. II, 26, 39–40; W. G. Hoffman, 'One Hundred Years of the Margarine Industry', in van Stuyvenberg, *Margarine*, 17.
64. CO 272/23, PRO; the figure behind the Sierra Leone kernels trade in this period was Charles Heddle: C. Fyfe, 'Charles Heddle: An African "Merchant Prince"', in *Laboratoire 'Connaissance du Tiers-Monde': Entreprises et entrepreneurs en Afrique, 19–20 siècles* (Paris, 1983), 235–47.
65. CO 272/–, *passim*, PRO; considerable quantities of kernels from the Sierra Leone area were exported to France in these years: Hanson to FO, 1 January 1855, FO 2/13, PRO.
66. CO 151/1; Campbell to Clarendon, 4 May 1856, FO 84/1002; CO 100/19: all PRO.

67. As Heddle claimed: Heddle to Baikie, 8 May 1857, in Hill to Labouchere, 30 June 1857, CO 267/257, PRO.
68. Manning, 'Palm Oil and Kernel Exports', 72, 76–8; Manning, 'Some Export Statistics for Nigeria, 1880–1905', *Nigerian Journal of Economic and Social Studies* 9 (1967), 229–34; the Delta was comparatively slow to start a kernel export trade, Livingstone to Clarendon, 24 November 1869, FO 84/1308; Hartley to Granville, 20 March 1874, FO 84/1401: both PRO.
69. Hanson to Russell, 17 January 1860, FO 2/33; Livingstone to Russell, 30 January 1865, FO 84/1249: both PRO; Brooks, *Yankee Traders*, 310.
70. Report of the Committee on Edible and Oil-Producing Nuts and Seeds: *PP* 1916, IV (8247), 27–9; McPhee, *Economic Revolution*, 33–4; C. Wilson, *Unilever*, vol. II, 102–4.
71. Philipps, 'Germany and the Palm Kernel Trade'; Harding, 'Hamburg's West Africa Trade', 378–80.
72. Combined palm oil and kernel imports into Hamburg fell from 10,931,990 marks in 1885 to 7,843,750 marks in 1886, before recovering to 11,796,040 marks by 1888: Harding, 'Hamburg's West Africa Trade', 380.
73. It must be noted that the British figures include nuts such as groundnuts.
74. Manning, 'Some Export Statistics', 231.
75. Newbury, 'On the Margins of Empire', 46.
76. *PP* 1861, LX (1), 83; 1890–1, LXXXIX (6457), 134–5; Manning, 'Palm Oil and Kernel Exports', 76; Hopkins, *Economic History*, 133.
77. Newbury, 'Margins of Empire', 46, 56.
78. Munro, *Africa and the International Economy*, 45–6, 72–3; Zeleza, *Modern Economic History of Africa*, vol. I, 379–82.
79. Hopkins, *Economic History*, 131–4; Eltis, 'Trade Between Western Africa and the Atlantic World Before 1870', 209–13; Eltis and Jennings, 'Trade Between Western Africa and the Atlantic World', 942–4.
80. P. Manning, 'Slave Trade, "Legitimate" Trade, and Imperialism Revisited: The Control of Wealth in the Bights of Benin and Biafra', in P. E. Lovejoy (ed.), *Africans in Bondage* (Madison, 1986), 211–12.
81. Hill, *Migrant Cocoa-Farmers*, 163–7; Manning, 'Palm Oil and Kernel Exports', 48; R. Dumett, 'The Rubber Trade of the Gold Coast and Asante in the Nineteenth Century', *JAH* 12 (1971), 79–101; R. Howard, *Colonialism and Underdevelopment in Ghana* (London, 1978), 70–1.
82. S. M. Martin, *Palm Oil and Protest*, 45–7.
83. Calculated from tables 5. 5 and 5. 7.
84. Hopkins, *Economic History*, 125.
85. Agri, 'Aspects of Socio-Economic Changes', 478.
86. S. M. Martin, 'Slaves, Igbo Women', 186.
87. Wariboko, 'New Calabar', 116.
88. 'Oil Palm in Labuan'; 'African Oil Palm'; Alldridge, *Sherbro*, 67; Dudgeon, *Agricultural and Forest Products*, 63, 92; E. Isichei, *The Ibo People and the Europeans* (London, 1973), 69. One of the earliest mentions of kernel oil production in the area of modern Nigeria is Campbell to Clarendon, 4 May 1856, FO 84/1002, PRO.
89. Memo on a possible equalisation of tariffs by Rowe, in Rowe to Hicks Beach, 13 October 1879, CO 879/17; Alldridge to Hay, 12 May 1890, in Hay to Knutsford, 6 June 1890, CO 267/383: both PRO.

90. Philipps, 'Germany and the Palm Kernel Trade'; Milbourne, 'Palm Kernels from West Africa'; Harding, 'Hamburg's West Africa Trade', 378–82.
91. CO 272/72, CO 100/45, PRO; Manning, 'Palm Oil and Kernel Exports', 73–9; Manning, *Slavery, Colonialism, and Economic Growth*, 352–4.
92. CO 272/38, PRO.
93. Broadhurst to Kortright, 12 February 1877, in Kortright to Carnarvon, 15 February 1877, CO 267/331, PRO; Dudgeon, *Agricultural and Forest Products*, 22–3; Dawe and Martin, 'Oil Palm Industry', 7; Mitchell, 'Trade Routes', 205.
94. Howard, *Colonialism and Underdevelopment*, 33, 69–79; Reynolds, *Trade and Economic Change*, 109, 135, 146; R. E. Dumett, 'African Merchants of the Gold Coast, 1860–1905: Dynamics of Indigenous Entrepreneurship', *Comparative Studies in Society and History* 25 (1983), 678; F. Agbodeka, *An Economic History of Ghana from the Earliest Times* (Accra, 1992), 40. Germany was the major destination of the Gold Coast's kernel exports: H. J. Bell, *The History, Trade, Resources, and Present Condition of the Gold Coast* (Liverpool, 1893), 30–2.
95. Manning, 'Economy of Early Colonial Dahomey'; Manning, *Slavery, Colonialism, and Economic Growth*, 14, 54, 69, 98–103, 332.
96. A. Macmillan (ed.), *The Red Book of West Africa* (London, 1920), 43.
97. CO 151/5, PRO.
98. S. A. Akintoye, *Revolution and Power Politics in Yorubaland, 1840–1893* (London, 1971), 149–50; Ofonagoro, *Trade and Imperialism*, 76.
99. Coomber to Venn, 2 May 1863, CA3/012/5, CMSP; Livingstone to Clarendon, 24 November 1869, FO 84/1308, PRO.
100. Latham, *Old Calabar*, 67; S. M. Martin, *Palm Oil and Protest*, 48; Manning, 'Slave Trade, "Legitimate" Trade, and Imperialism', 209–10.
101. Latham, *Old Calabar*, 67.
102. S. M. Martin, *Palm Oil and Protest*, 46–7, 51–4.
103. Calculated from tables 5. 7, 5. 9; CO 100/–, CO 151/–, CO 464/–, CO 272/–, PRO; Manning, *Slavery, Colonialism, and Economic Growth*, 332; Harding, 'Hamburg's West Africa Trade', 378–81.
104. Usoro, *Nigerian Oil Palm Industry*, 10; Manning, 'Slave Trade, "Legitimate" Trade, and Imperialism', 211; S. M. Martin, *Palm Oil and Protest*, 45–8; L. E. Wilson, *Krobo People*, 91–3; Law, '"Legitimate" Trade and Gender Relations', 204–7.

6 BRITISH TRADERS AND THE RESTRUCTURING OF THE PALM PRODUCTS TRADE

1. Zeleza, *Modern Economic History of Africa*, vol. I, 370–1.
2. See table 1.8.
3. Lynn, 'Bristol, West Africa', 361.
4. Lynn, 'British Business and the African Trade'; S. Chapman, *Merchant Enterprise in Britain* (Cambridge, 1992), 82, stresses the role of the African trade in Liverpool's mercantile challenge to London in the nineteenth century.
5. For one example, *PP* 1883, LXX (3637), 73.
6. Calculated from *Customs Bills of Entry*, 1880.
7. Chandler, *Liverpool Shipping*, 165–84.
8. Newbury, 'Prices and Profitability', 94. Little work has been done on such

frontiers but see H. L. van der Laan, 'Modern Inland Transport and the European Trading Firms in Colonial West Africa', *Cahiers d'études africaines* 21, 84 (1981), 547–75, and M. E. Noah, 'Inland Ports and European Trading Firms in South Eastern Nigeria', *African Affairs* 88, 350 (1989), 25–40.

9. A. G. Hopkins, 'An Economic History of Lagos, 1880–1914', Ph.D thesis, University of London (1964), 47.
10. Campbell to Clarendon, 5 January 1857, FO 84/1031, PRO; Lynn, 'Bristol, West Africa', 363–4.
11. Langdon, 'Three Voyages'.
12. Kingsley, *Travels in West Africa*, 632; Kingsley, *West African Studies*, 70–4.
13. According to Kingsley, Bristol traders were still coasting on the Ivory Coast in the 1890s but were loading their oil on to the steamship services for despatch to Liverpool: *West African Studies*, 70–4; Syfert, 'Liberian Coasting Trade'.
14. Livingstone's memo, 8 December 1871, FO 84/1343, PRO.
15. S. A. Crowther, Bonny mission, April 1865, CA3/O4/748, CMSP; 'The Trading Hulks', *Statistical and Economic Review* 1 (1948), 36–7.
16. Burton to Russell, 15 April 1864, FO 84/1221, PRO; Cotterell, 'Reminiscences', 26.
17. W. N. Thomas, 'On the Oil Rivers of West Africa', *PRGS* 17 (1873), 151.
18. Churchill to Hewett, 16 May 1876, in Admiralty to FO, 9 June 1876, FO 84/1464, PRO; R. Holt, 'Autobiography of Mr James Deemin', in Davies, *Trading in West Africa*, 100.
19. Whitford, *Trading Life*, 284–5.
20. Hartley to Derby, 24 November 1876, FO 84/1455; Johnston to Salisbury, 1 December 1888, 'Report on the . . . Oil Rivers', cap. G, FO 84/1882: both PRO.
21. Latham, *Old Calabar*, 72.
22. 'Pioneer of the West African Trade'; Cowan, 'Early Trading Conditions, I and II'; Laughland to Russell, 21 January 1861, FO 84/1147, PRO.
23. Cotterell was paid £300 p.a. as his basic salary in the early 1860s: Cotterell, 'Reminiscences', 34–5. Others continued to be paid a commission, as earlier in the century: one agent, C. J. S. Jackson, made £10,000 commission in eighteen months in the middle of the century, Davies, *Trading in West Africa*, 175.
24. Cowan, 'Early Trading Conditions, II', 61.
25. Journal for 16 October 1855, in Lynslager to Clarendon, 31 October 1855, FO 84/975, PRO.
26. Hewett, *European Settlements*, 83, makes this point for the Windward Coast.
27. These figures excluded the number of missionaries settled in the Delta: Burton to Russell, 15 April 1864, FO 2/45, PRO.
28. Disease was still a major problem for traders, as with the Yellow Fever epidemic of 1862–3 which killed 163 out of the 350 whites in Bonny and 175 out of the 278 in Elem Kalabari: Burton to Russell, 15 April 1864, FO 2/45, PRO.
29. *African Times*, 23 July 1868, 10–11; Journal of J. C. Taylor, 22 August 1861, CA3/O37/77, CMSP.
30. Johnston to Salisbury, 1 December 1888, 'Report on the . . . Oil Rivers', cap. G, FO 84/1882, PRO.
31. Livingstone to Granville, 16 February 1872, FO 84/1356, PRO.
32. Johnston to Salisbury, 1 December 1888, 'Report on the . . . Oil Rivers', cap. G, FO 84/1882; Burton to Russell, 15 April 1864, FO 2/45: both PRO; Cotterell, 'Reminiscences', 33.

33. D. C. Crowther's Report for 1879, CA 3/013/47, CMSP.
34. Factories had been longer established on the South Coast: Journal of Commander Need, in Admiralty to FO, 20 May 1856, FO 84/1009, PRO; K. D. Patterson, *The Northern Gabon Coast to 1875* (Oxford, 1975), 121–2.
35. Campbell to Clarendon, 24 March 1856, FO 84/1002, PRO.
36. Supercargoes to Burton, 28 April 1862, in Burton to Russell, 22 May 1862, FO 84/1176, PRO.
37. Latham, *Old Calabar*, 110–11.
38. Livingstone's memo, 8 December 1871, FO 84/1343, PRO. A higher estimate than Livingstone's is given in Frost, 'Kru in Freetown and Liverpool', 42. See also J. Martin, 'Krumen "Down the Coast"'.
39. Hutchinson to Clarendon, 24 January 1857, FO 2/19, PRO; Crouch, *Glimpses of Feverland*, 45; Cowan, 'Early Trading Conditions, II', 59–60; though white labour continued to be used in the rivers to at least the 1860s: Whitford, *Trading Life*, 285; Livingstone to Clarendon, 23 April 1866, FO 84/1265, PRO.
40. Johnston to Salisbury, 1 December 1888, 'Report on the . . . Oil Rivers', cap. G, FO 84/1882, PRO.
41. Brooks, *Kru Mariner*, 44–59. Kru were being transported direct to Fernando Po by John Holt in 1867: 'Report of Proceedings on Kru Coast on Board *Peep O'Day*', in Davies, *Diary of John Holt*, 192.
42. Harford, 'Voyage to the African Oil Rivers', 583.
43. D. C. Crowther, 'A Missionary Trip to Benin River', CA3/013/42, CMSP; W. N. M. Geary, *Nigeria Under British Rule* (London, 1927), 89. Cowan, 'Early Trading Conditions, I', 397, dates this move to the 1880s but there were already factories in Brass and Bonny before 1880, according to J. L. B. Wood, 'Report on a Visit to the Niger Mission', CA3/043/13, CMSP.
44. Whitford, *Trading Life*, 293; Latham, *Old Calabar*, 110–11.
45. African Association to Salisbury, 7 January 1890, FO 403/149, PRO; Cowan, 'Early Trading Conditions, I', 397.
46. Cowan, 'Early Trading Conditions, II', 53–4.
47. Hutchinson to Clarendon, 28 January 1858, FO 84/1061, PRO.
48. Memo on Egbo (Ekpe) by John Holt, n. d., 7/4, JHPO: 'at the present time Egbo is influencing greatly the trade of the river'.
49. Livingstone to Clarendon, 3 December 1869, FO 84/1308, PRO; 'Regulations with regard to the payment of comey in . . . Old Calabar, 29 October 1887', 9/1, JHPO.
50. Kingsley, *West African Studies*, 523–5.
51. Hopkins, *Economic History*, 149–51; Hogendorn and Johnson, *Shell Money*, 138–43.
52. Ussher to Hicks Beach, 3 May 1880, CO 879/18, PRO; memo to agents, 20 December 1889, 6/1, JHPO; Adomako, 'History of Currency and Banking', 6; Hopkins, 'Currency Revolution', 479.
53. Johnston to Salisbury, 1 December 1888, 'Report on the . . . Oil Rivers', cap. G, FO 84/1882, PRO.
54. Fry, *Bankers in West Africa*, 4–9.
55. Hopkins, *Economic History*, 150–1; Davies, 'Impact of the Expatriate Shipping Lines', 9.
56. For one example of such an arrangement, see agreement of Holt and Gibney, 4 January 1900, 1/1, JHPO.

57. Hopkins, 'Economic History of Lagos', 64–5.
58. Irvine & Woodward, 15/1, JHPO; Hopkins, 'Economic History of Lagos', 64–5.
59. BT 31/798/519C, PRO; *PP* 1865, V (412), 232–9; *African Times*, 23 July 1864, 17. Hatton & Cookson developed a commission house system on the South Coast: Hunt to Salisbury, 31 October 1878, FO 84/1505, PRO.
60. McPhee, *Economic Revolution*, 72–3.
61. The actual total in 1880 is likely to be higher since many traders' palm oil was labelled under 'sundry consignees'.
62. W. B. MacIver & Co. was founded in 1875 by two brothers from Dumfries and survived until going bankrupt in 1900: J. J. Rankin, *The History of the United Africa Co. Ltd to 1938* (privately printed, 1938), 56. For Brunnschweiller, see H. L. van der Laan, 'A Swiss Family Firm in West Africa: A. Brunnschweiller & Co. 1929–1959', *AEH* 12 (1983), 287–97; Zagury was bought out by the Congo & Central African Co. in 1882, Davies, *Henry Tyrer*, 30.
63. Rankin, *United Africa Co.*, 60–8; Thompson, 'Glasgow and Africa', 35–76; Pedler, *Lion and Unicorn*, 99–111; Gertzel, 'John Holt'.
64. Thompson, 'Glasgow and Africa', 76–97; 'G. B. Ollivant Ltd', *West African Review* 8, 120 (1937), 95–116; D. L. Johnson, 'A History of G. B. Ollivant' (typescript, 1976), UACP.
65. Swanzy Correspondence and Affidavits, 1845–54; Swanzy Correspondence, 1864–74; Swanzy Correspondence, 1866–71; Swanzy Correspondence, 1869–80: all UACP; A. Swanzy, 'On Trade in Western Africa'; J. D. Hay, *Ashanti and the Gold Coast and What We Know of It* (London, 1874), 8; H. Swanzy, 'Trading Family'.
66. *Journal of the Society of Arts* 22 (1874), 118.
67. A. Hamilton, 'On the Trade with the Coloured Races of Africa', *Journal of the Statistical Society of London* 31 (1868), 28.
68. Latham, *Old Calabar*, 106.
69. Burton to Russell, 15 April 1864, FO 2/45, PRO; Newbury, 'Credit', 90–1.
70. M. Lynn, 'Technology, Trade, and "a Race of Native Capitalists": The Krio Diaspora of West Africa and the Steamship, 1852–1895', *JAH* 33 (1992), 430.
71. Cash Book, 1875–86, G. B. Williams papers, SC 12/1, NAGA; Rhodes to Granville, 13 January 1883, FO 84/1654; Hay to Lees, 20 November 1878, in Herbert to Pauncefote, 25 June 1879, FO 403/12: both PRO.
72. Lynn, 'Technology, Trade', 430–1.
73. Prospectus, Niger Steam Ship Co. Ltd, n. d., f. 199, FO 84/1278, PRO; C. H. Fyfe, 'The Life and Times of John Ezzidio', *Sierra Leone Studies* 4 (1955), 213–23; Fyfe, *History*, 449; Gertzel, 'John Holt', 534.
74. Lynslager to Clarendon, 31 October 1855, FO 84/975; Hutchinson to Clarendon, 26 January 1857, FO 2/19; Hutchinson to Malmesbury, 25 May 1858, FO 84/1061: all PRO; C. Fyfe, 'Peter Nicholls: Old Calabar and Freetown', *JHSN* 2 (1960), 105–14.
75. Hutchinson to Clarendon, 29 September 1856, FO 84/1001, PRO.
76. *African Times*, 31 December 1874, 3.
77. I. K. Sundiatta, 'Creolization on Fernando Po: The Nature of Society', in M. L. Kilson and R. I. Rotberg (eds.), *The African Diaspora* (Cambridge, MA,

1976), 395; memorial of Scott, 27 June 1852, FO 2/7; Lynslager to Clarendon, 31 October 1855, FO 84/975: both PRO.

78. Hewett to Salisbury, 29 February 1888, FO 84/1881; 7 March 1889, FO 84/1941; Ledlum to Granville, 20 December 1883, FO 84/1655; Craigie to Salmon, 11 August 1884, in Admiralty to FO, 9 September 1884, FO 84/1689: all PRO.
79. Campbell to Clarendon, 30 August 1855, 2 October 1855, FO 84/976; 4 May 1856, FO 84/1002: all PRO.
80. *Lagos Times*, 9 August 1882; Gertzel, 'John Holt', 534; A. G. Hopkins, 'R. B. Blaize, 1845–1904: Merchant Prince of West Africa', *Tarikh* 1 (1966), 70–9.
81. Dumett, 'African Merchants', 672
82. Account Sales Book, 1880–9, Ocansey Papers, SC 8/2, NAGA; Dumett, 'African Merchants', 673–6; J. E. Ocansey (ed. K. Arhin), *An African Trading or the Trials of William Narh Ocansey of Addah, West Coast of Africa, River Volta* (Accra, 1989; originally published Liverpool, 1881).
83. Receipt of Ferguson, 8 May 1867, Ghartey Papers, SC7/15, NAGA; Dumett, 'African Merchants', 676–8.
84. Reynolds, *Trade and Economic Change*, 108–12.
85. Journal of J. M. Sarbah, 1869–76, SC 6/1, NAGA; R. E. Dumett, 'John Sarbah the Elder and African Mercantile Entrepreneurship in the Gold Coast in the Late Nineteenth Century', *JAH* 14 (1973), 653–79.
86. Burton to Russell, 15 April 1864, FO 2/45, PRO.
87. Régis had two launches at Whydah from 1859: Campbell to Malmesbury, 4 March 1859, FO 84/1088; Burton to Russell, 30 November 1863, FO 84/1203: both PRO; Hopkins, 'Economic History of Lagos', 72–3.
88. Schnapper, *La Politique et le commerce français*, 191–3.
89. Craigie to Salmon, 11 August 1884, in Admiralty to FO, 9 September 1884, FO 84/1689, PRO.
90. Wickins, *Economic History of Africa*, 292.
91. Memo respecting the trade etc. of the Cameroon River, 17 December 1883, FO 84/1681, PRO; Fanso, 'Trade and Supremacy on the Cameroon Coast', 64.
92. Hieke, *Zur Geschichte des deutschen Handels mit Ostafrika*; Hieke, *Gaiser*; Hopkins, 'Economic History of Lagos', 71–2.
93. Burton to Russell, 30 November 1863, FO 84/1203; Hopkins to FO, 28 April 1877, FO 84/1478: both PRO.
94. Boyle, *Fanteeland*, 34.
95. Livingstone to Stanley, 1 October 1866, FO 2/47; Livingstone to Granville, 9 July 1872, FO 84/1356: both PRO; *PP* 1873, LXV (828), 3–4.
96. Freeman to Pine, 27 June 1857, in Pine to Labouchere, 31 August 1857, CO 96/41; Burton to Russell, 15 April 1864, FO 2/45: both PRO.
97. *African Times*, 22 November 1862, 55.
98. Extract from Mr Edgar's letter, 5 May 1875, CA3/04/497A, CMSP.
99. Dike, *Trade and Politics*, 115; K. K. Nair, 'Trade in Southern Nigeria from 1860 to the 1870s: Expansion or Stagnation?', *JHSN* 6 (1973), 425–33.
100. Hutchinson to Clarendon, 29 September 1856, 24 September 1856, FO 84/1001, PRO.
101. Hedd and others to Hill, 25 September 1856, in Hill to Clarendon, 27 October 1856, FO 84/1003, PRO.

102. Crowther to Venn, 30 August 1862, CA3/04/115, CMSP.
103. *African Times*, 23 December 1871, 65; 30 September 1874, 29, 31–2.
104. Ledlum to Granville, 20 December 1883, FO 84/1655; Rhodes to Salisbury, 21 March 1888, FO 84/1917: both PRO.
105. Macdonald to FO, 26 March 1895, FO 2/83, PRO.
106. McPhee, *Economic Revolution*, 95–6.
107. Fry, *Bankers in West Africa*, 4–5.
108. Reynolds, 'Economic Imperialism', 115.
109. E. Reynolds, 'The Rise and Fall of an African Merchant Class on the Gold Coast, 1830–1874', *Cahiers d'études africaines* 14, 54 (1974), 253–64; Kaplow, 'Mudfish and Crocodile', 329.
110. Lynn, 'Change and Continuity', 344–5.
111. Newbury, 'Trade and Authority', 84.
112. Gertzel, 'John Holt', 497.
113. Moloney to Knutsford, 27 February 1889, CO 147/69, PRO.
114. Holt's circular of 19 January 1888, 5/3, JHPO.
115. Livingstone's memo of 8 December 1871, FO 84/1343; minute by Governor Moloney on the eastern limit of . . . Lagos, April 1888, FO 84/1882: both PRO; Langdon, 'Three Voyages'.
116. E. A. Cookson's Notes on Hatton & Cookson, 7 May 1936, UACP.
117. Minute by Governor Moloney on the eastern limit of . . . Lagos, April 1888, FO 84/1882, PRO.
118. Livingstone to Clarendon, 31 March 1870, FO 84/1326, PRO; Whitford, *Trading Life*, 316; tramp steamers were rare in the West African trade because of the lack of natural harbours, but were not unknown: Douglas, *Niger Memories*, 106.
119. Holt to Miller, 18 January 1895, 4/5, JHPL.
120. E. A. Cookson's Notes on Hatton & Cookson, 7 May 1936, UACP; *Sea Breezes* 23 (February 1939), 434.
121. This process was encouraged by the deferred rebate system introduced by the shipping ring in 1895: Leubuscher, *Shipping Trade*, 14.
122. E. A. Cookson's Notes on Hatton & Cookson, 7 May 1936, UACP.
123. Croft, 'Exploration of the River Volta', 183.
124. Burton to Russell, 15 April 1864, FO 2/45, PRO; Anstey, *Britain and the Congo*.
125. Monteiro, *Angola and the River Congo*, vol. I, 81–6, 100.
126. Campbell to Clarendon, 8 February 1856, FO 2/17, PRO.
127. J. Pinnock, *Benin: The Surrounding Country, Inhabitants, Customs, and Trade* (Liverpool, 1897), 30.
128. Livingstone to Clarendon, 31 March 1870, FO 84/1326, PRO.
129. Hartley to Derby, 27 March 1875, FO 84/1418, PRO.
130. S. A. Crowther, 'Steamers on the Niger', CA3/014/4B, CMSP; agreement between J. Holt, J. C. Holt, and G. Watts, 22 October 1885, 1/1, JHPO.
131. E. A. Cookson's Notes on Hatton & Cookson, 7 May 1936; Cleaver to Swanzy, 18 September 1871, Swanzy Correspondence, 1864–74: both UACP.
132. *Lagos Times*, 21 January 1881; Holt's circular, 19 January 1888, 5/3, JHPO; Newbury, 'On the Margins of Empire', 42.
133. Billows and Beckwith, *Palm Oil and Kernels*, 71. However, S. R. Pearson, 'The

Economic Imperialism of the Royal Niger Co.', *Food Research Institute Studies* 10 (1971), 69–88, shows that large profits could still be achieved in these years.

134. P. Lemberg, 'The Commerce of Sierra Leone', in Rowe to CO, 24 June 1885, CO 267/358, PRO.
135. Holt to Miller, 29 March 1886, 4/5, JHPL.
136. Minute Book of Hatton & Cookson, Ltd, 1901–22, UACP; 'Builders of the African Trade: Edward Hatton and Thomas W. Cookson', *Elder Dempster Magazine* 6 (1927), 133–4.
137. They were the second largest firm in the oil rivers by 1889: 'Statistics and Calculations prior to the formation of the African Association Ltd', 6/1, JHPO; the founders of the firm, Peter Douglas and Peter Stuart, died in 1883 and 1888 respectively, Finigan, *Peter Stuart*.
138. The other problem for Horsfalls was the lack of younger family members available to take over the firm by the 1870s: Lynn, 'Trade and Politics', 113.
139. Boyle, *Fanteeland*, 33–4.
140. British & Continental African Co. Ltd, BT 31/1860/7323, PRO.
141. Capper to Holt, 1 August 1878, 15/1, JHPO; Cotterell, 'Reminiscences', 39–40; Davies, *Henry Tyrer*, 30; H. Swanzy, 'Trading Family', 116; Pedler, *Lion and Unicorn*, 99–111.
142. 'Memo regarding the suspension of Taylor, Laughland, April 1896', 5/4, JHPO; 'W. B. MacIver & Co. ', 8/8, JHPO; *African Times*, 1 June 1886, 82; 2 January 1888, 4.
143. Co. of African Merchants Ltd, BT 31/798/519C, PRO.
144. D. Chinery, *West African Slavery* (London, 1864), 18.
145. Thompson, 'Glasgow and Africa', 93.
146. *African Times*, 2 January 1888, 4; E. A. Cookson's Notes on Hatton & Cookson, 7 May 1936, UACP.
147. Newbury, 'Margins of Empire', 57.
148. Latham, *Old Calabar*, 64.
149. Deposition of agents in Opobo, n. d., CALPROF 5/8/6, NNAE.
150. Holt to Watts, 9 January 1885, 4/5; Holt to Williams, 18 November 1887, 4/5, both JHPL; 'Old Calabar Agreement', c. 1885, 3/11, JHPO.
151. Miller to Holt, 17 October 1895, 4/1, JHPO; agreement between African Association and the Niger Co., 1 May 1900, UACP.
152. Couper to Holt, 6 June 1884, 5/3; Miller to Holt, 11 August 1887, 4/1: both JHPO. This period has been termed 'the era of the Great Amalgamations in the West African trade': 'Merchandise Trading in British West Africa', *Statistical and Economic Review* 5 (1950), 5.
153. Davies, *Trade Makers*, 97–101.
154. Companies House, London, 29140; the negotiations to form the African Association can be followed in 5/3, 5/5, JHPO, and Pedler, *Lion and Unicorn*, 139, while the agreements between the various firms can be seen in UAB/2/8–16, UACP.
155. 'Statistics and Calculations prior to the formation of the African Association Ltd', 6/1, JHPO; *Sea Breezes* 23 (February 1939), 434.
156. The reason for Millers' refusal to join, after George Miller had been an earlier

advocate, lies in the legacy of the disputes between British traders over Opobo in the mid-1880s: Pedler, *Lion and Unicorn*, 142–4.
157. Gertzel, 'John Holt', 211; Pedler, *Lion and Unicorn*, 148, 225–39.

7 AFRICAN BROKERS AND THE STRUGGLE FOR THE PALM PRODUCTS TRADE

1. Eltis and Jennings, 'Trade Between Western Africa and the Atlantic World', 940.
2. CO 151/1, CO 151/28, PRO.
3. Eltis and Jennings, 'Trade Between Western Africa and the Atlantic World', 955–6.
4. Lynn, 'From Sail to Steam', 240; it must be noted that the 1850 figure may be an underestimate due to the practice of ships in entering 'Africa' as their origin before the 1860s.
5. See chapter 1, pp. 17–26.
6. S. M. Hargreaves, 'Nineteenth-Century Bonny', 307–9. In 1878, Hopkins described Bonny as 'a ruined and impoverished town': Hopkins to FO, 23 November 1878, FO 84/1508, PRO.
7. Akassa developed as a major oil port during the 1870s because of its access to the Niger trade: Johnson to Hutchinson, 14 December 1877, CA3/023/1, CMSP.
8. A. Jones, *Slaves to Palm Kernels*, 104–7; though it should be noted that output from most of Sierra Leone increased in these years.
9. Reid, 'Warrior Aristocrats', 470–6; Manning, *Slavery, Colonialism, and Economic Growth*, 50–6.
10. P. M. Martin, *Loango Coast*, 147–54; Vansina, *Paths in the Rainforests*, 210–13.
11. Eltis and Jennings, 'Trade Between Western Africa and the Atlantic World', 946.
12. Macmillan, *Red Book*, 43–7; CO 272/77, CO 100/50, PRO; Agbodeka, *Economic History*, 40, gives much higher figures for the Gold Coast.
13. This issue is discussed in C. Chamberlin, 'Bulk Exports, Trade Tiers, Regulation, and Development: An Economic Approach to the Study of West Africa's "Legitimate Trade"', *Journal of Economic History* 39 (1979), 419–38.
14. Hopkins, 'Economic History of Lagos', 20–97; Hopkins, 'R. B. Blaize'; R. S. Smith, *Lagos Consulate*, 38–40.
15. Campbell to Clarendon, 4 May 1856, FO 84/1002; Campbell to Malmesbury, 28 January 1859, FO 84/1088: both PRO.
16. Gertzel, 'John Holt', 534.
17. *Ibid.*, 69.
18. Cited in Kopytoff, *Preface to Modern Nigeria*, 170.
19. Hopkins, 'Economic History of Lagos', 59–64.
20. K. Mann, 'The Rise of Taiwo Olowo: Law, Accumulation, and Mobility in Early Colonial Lagos', in K. Mann and R. Roberts (eds.), *Law in Colonial Africa* (London, 1991), 85–107.
21. Account Sales Book, 1880–9, SC 8/2, Ocansey Papers, NAGA.
22. Mills to Sarbah, 27 February 1877, Letter Book, 1874–89, SC 6/4, Sarbah Papers, NAGA.

23. Letter Book, incoming, 1887–8, SC 8/64, Ocansey Papers, NAGA.
24. Dumett, 'African Merchants', 691.
25. S. B. Kaplow, 'African Merchants of the Nineteenth-Century Gold Coast', Ph.D thesis, Columbia University (1971), 122–3; Kaplow, 'Mudfish and Crocodile', 329; Dumett, 'Rubber Trade', 82.
26. Thompson, 'Glasgow and Africa', 65.
27. Caesar to Horsfield, Berry, & Co., 21 March 1899, Duplicate Letter Book, 1888–99, SC 13/17, J. H. Caesar's Trading Papers, NAGA.
28. Journal (ledger), 1886–94, SC 13/1, Caesar Trading Papers, NAGA.
29. Visit to the Kittam by Edwards, September 1878, in Meade to Pauncefote, 30 December 1878, FO 403/11; memo on a possible tariff equalisation by Rowe, in Rowe to Hicks Beach, 13 October 1879, CO 879/17: both PRO.
30. A. Jones, *Slaves to Palm Kernels*, 104.
31. Cohen to Granville, 3 January 1883, FO 403/14, PRO.
32. Lynslager to Clarendon, 31 October 1855, FO 84/975; Hutchinson to Clarendon, 2 January 1857, FO 84/1030: both PRO.
33. Lynslager to Clarendon, 31 October 1855, FO 84/975; Hutchinson to Clarendon, 12 March 1856, FO 84/1001: both PRO.
34. Hutchinson to Clarendon, 29 April 1857; Hutchinson to Clarendon, 20 August 1857, FO 84/1030: both PRO.
35. Hutchinson to Clarendon, 2 January 1857; Cuthbertson and others to Hutchinson, 19 April 1857, in Hutchinson to Clarendon, 29 April 1857; super-cargoes to Hutchinson, 25 July 1857, in Hutchinson to Clarendon, 31 August 1857, FO 84/1030: all PRO.
36. S. M. Hargreaves, 'Nineteenth-Century Bonny', 282.
37. Hopkins to FO, 23 November 1878, FO 84/1508, PRO; Mockler-Ferryman, *Up the Niger*, 3.
38. J. D. Hargreaves, 'The Atlantic Ocean in West African History', in Stone, *Africa and the Sea*, 5–13; the issue of trading frontiers is well laid out in Chamberlin, 'Bulk Export, Trade Tiers'.
39. Latham, *Old Calabar*, 105–8. Jaja's similar moves to control the actions of Krio in Opobo is outlined in *African Times*, 2 December 1878, 145–6.
40. Palmerston to Beecroft, 30 June 1849, FO 84/775, PRO.
41. Dike, *Trade and Politics*, 88–91.
42. Lynn, 'Law and Imperial Expansion', 59
43. Wilmot to Admiralty, 25 December 1864, FO 541/9, PRO.
44. Livingstone to Clarendon, 3 December 1869, FO 84/1308, PRO; Ehrensaft, 'Informal Empire', 469.
45. Dike, *Trade and Politics*, 118–19.
46. Livingstone to Granville, 30 August 1870, FO 84/1326, PRO.
47. Livingstone to Stanley, 23 December 1867, FO 84/1277; Livingstone to Clarendon, 22 November 1869, FO 84/1308: both PRO.
48. Livingstone to Stanley, 25 February 1868, FO 84/1290, PRO.
49. Walker to chairman of the Court of Equity, 23 July 1874, CALPROF 3/2, NNAI; *PP* 1873, LXV (828), 4.
50. Freeman to Russell, 10 April 1863, FO 84/1201, PRO.
51. Hutchinson to Clarendon, 12 March 1856, FO 84/1001; Burton to FO, 22 May 1862, FO 84/1176: both PRO.

52. Burton to FO, 14 January 1862, FO 84/1176, PRO.
53. Livingstone to Stanley, 21 December 1867, FO 84/1277, PRO.
54. *PP* 1873, LXV (828), 4; minute by Wylde on Livingstone to Stanley, 25 February 1868, FO 84/1290, PRO.
55. Hutchinson to Clarendon, 31 January 1856, FO 84/1001, PRO.
56. Supercargoes to Hutchinson, 30 June 1856, in Hutchinson to Clarendon, 28 July 1856, FO 84/1001, PRO.
57. Campbell to Clarendon, 3 November 1857, FO 84/1031; Livingstone to Clarendon, 2 January 1866, FO 84/1265: both PRO.
58. Livingstone to Stanley, 22 April 1867, FO 84/1277; Livingstone to Stanley, 25 February 1868, FO 84/1290: both PRO.
59. Treaty with Elem Kalabari, 2 October 1850, and treaty with Bonny, 3 October 1850, in Beecroft to Palmerston, 15 October 1850, FO 84/816; agreement with Old Calabar, 5 May 1862, and Bye-laws for the River Cameroons, 19 May 1862, in Burton to FO, 22 May 1862, FO 84/1176: all PRO. These were not the first commercial treaties with Delta states, but they were the first to regularise the trade on a Delta-wide basis.
60. Lynn, 'Law and Imperial Expansion', 61.
61. Code of Bye-laws for Old Calabar, in Hutchinson to Clarendon, 24 September 1856, FO 84/1001, PRO.
62. List of vessels laying in the River Old Calabar, in Lynslager to Clarendon, 31 October 1855, FO 84/975, PRO. These figures include journey times.
63. Livingstone to Russell, 3 June 1865, FO 84/1249; Livingstone to Stanley, 21 December 1867, FO 84/1277: both PRO.
64. In a reversal of the picture usually painted, clashes within the British trader community could also cause African brokers to stop trade until such disputes were settled: Livingstone to Clarendon, 23 April 1866, FO 84/1265, PRO.
65. Burton to Russell, 22 May 1862, FO 84/1176; Livingstone to Stanley, 21 December 1867, FO 84/1277; Livingstone to Clarendon, 22 November 1869, FO 84/1308; Livingstone to Granville, 30 August 1870, FO 84/1326: all PRO.
66. Livingstone to Granville, 30 August 1870, FO 84/1326, PRO.
67. Hutchinson to Clarendon, 20 February 1857, FO 84/1030; Livingstone to Granville, 24 August 1870, FO 84/1326, both PRO.
68. Nair, 'Trade in Southern Nigeria', 427
69. Ofonagoro, *Trade and Imperialism*, 78–81, 114–20.
70. A marked increase in adulterated produce was noted from the early 1880s: Fynn to Owen, 1 February 1883, CALPROF 3/2, NNAI; Farquhar, *Oil Palm and Varieties*, 32–3; Billows and Beckwith, *Palm Oil and Kernels*, 20–1, 43.
71. Burton to Russell, 26 August 1862, FO 84/1176; Livingstone to Clarendon, 23 November 1869, FO 84/1308: both PRO.
72. Baikie to Russell, 29 February 1860, FO 2/34; memo by Wylde, 8 January 1862, FO 97/434: both PRO.
73. Livingstone to Granville, 14 January 1873, FO 84/1377; Hopkins to FO, 4 December 1878, FO 84/1508; Tait to Derby, 27 August 1877, FO 84/1487: all PRO; Johnson to Hutchinson, 14 December 1877, CA3/023/1, CMSP.
74. Latham, *Old Calabar*, 81.
75. *Missionary Record of the United Presbyterian Church* 82 (1 October 1872), 300.
76. Burton to Russell, 22 May 1862, FO 84/1176, PRO.
77. Livingstone to Russell, 3 June 1865, FO 84/1249, PRO.

78. Livingstone to Clarendon, 16 March 1870, FO 84/1326, PRO.
79. Wariboko, 'New Calabar', 118–20.
80. Supercargoes to Burton, 28 April 1862, in Burton to Russell, 22 May 1862, FO 84/1176; Livingstone to FO, 21 December 1867, FO 84/1277; Hart to Granville, 20 March 1874, FO 84/1401: all PRO.
81. Latham, *Old Calabar*, 84.
82. Wariboko, 'New Calabar', 53–4.
83. Hewett to Rosebery, 12 July 1886, FO 84/1749, PRO. S. M. Hargreaves, 'Nineteenth-Century Bonny', 392, argues that individual traders could increasingly challenge house heads in these years in a process that led to the breakdown of house authority, but adds that this was not generated primarily by the transition to the oil trade.
84. Ikime, *Prince*, 10–11.
85. Austen, 'Metamorphoses of Middlemen', 8–9, though Wirz, 'La "Rivière du Cameroun"', 172–95, takes a contrary view; see also Gertzel, 'John Holt', 500.
86. Austen, 'Metamorphoses of Middlemen', 10.
87. Hewett to Granville, 5 February 1883, 11 June 1883, FO 84/1634, PRO.
88. Livingstone to Russell, 3 June 1865, FO 84/1249, PRO; Walker, 'Notes of a Visit'; G. I. Jones, *Slaves to Palm Oil*, 68.
89. Law, 'Introduction', 10–11.
90. Hopkins to FO, 23 November 1878, FO 84/1508, PRO; Mockler-Ferryman, *Up the Niger*, 3; Minute Book of the African Association Ltd, vol. II, 28 September 1894, UAA/1/21, UACP; Ocansey, *An African Trading*.
91. G. I. Jones, *Trading States*, 145–50.
92. Livingstone to Stanley, 25 April 1867, and Livingstone to Stanley, 23 December 1867, FO 84/1277; Hopkins to Granville, 27 October 1871, FO 84/1343; Livingstone to Granville, 16 December 1873, FO 84/1377: all PRO.
93. Wariboko, 'New Calabar', 110–80.
94. Cookey, *Jaja*, 59–77.
95. There is little information on profit margins for brokers, though in 1927 a figure of 8–10 per cent was calculated for oil 'middlemen' in Warri Division: W. E. Hunt, Assessment Report, Warri Division, 1927, CSO 26/3/20653, NNAI.

8 THE COMING OF COLONIAL RULE AND THE ENDING OF LEGITIMATE TRADE

1. Gertzel, 'John Holt', 240–2.
2. Lynn, 'Technology, Trade', 434.
3. A. Swanzy, 'On Trade in Western Africa', 480.
4. Gertzel, 'John Holt', 235–40.
5. J. D. Hargreaves, *Prelude to the Partition of West Africa* (London, 1963), 284–8, 294–301.
6. Fanso, 'Trade and Supremacy on the Cameroon Coast', 74–84.
7. Edward Cookson, John Holt, and A. L. Jones were among the British traders who visited Berlin during the conference.
8. Newbury, 'Trade and Authority', 93–4.
9. *Annual Report of the Board of Directors of Manchester Chamber of Commerce* 1881, 15–16; 1882, 9–10; 1883, 11–13; *Annual Report of the Bristol Chamber*

of Commerce 1885, 103; *Report of the Council of Birmingham Chamber of Commerce* 1885, 13–16; *Chamber of Commerce Journal*, 5 November 1884, 320; A. Redford, *Manchester Merchants and Foreign Trade*, vol. II, *1850–1939* (Manchester, 1956), 59–78.

10. Minutes of the West African Section of the London Chamber of Commerce, vol. I, 27 October 1884, Guildhall Library, London.

11. Manchester Chamber of Commerce to Granville, 13 November 1882, FO 84/1631; Hutton to Granville, 20 March 1883, FO 403/15A; Stuart & Douglas to Granville, 16 November 1883, FO 403/36; Stuart to Granville, 1 December 1882, in Whitby to Granville, 2 December 1882, FO 403/14: all PRO.

12. W. G. Hynes, *The Economics of Empire* (London, 1979), 66–7.

13. African Trade Section of Liverpool Chamber of Commerce to Granville, 8 October 1884, FO 84/1690, PRO; Minutes of the West African Section of the London Chamber of Commerce, vol. I, 7 October 1884, Guildhall Library, London.

14. R. & W. King to Granville, 23 December 1884, FO 403/48, PRO; *Annual Report of the Bristol Chamber of Commerce* 1885, 9–10, 102.

15. Stuart to Granville, 1 October 1884, 10/7, JHPO.

16. J. C. Anene, *Southern Nigeria in Transition, 1885–1906* (Cambridge, 1966), 67–8.

17. Manchester Chamber of Commerce to Granville, 4 April 1884, FO 84/1684; London Chamber of Commerce to Granville, 21 January 1885, FO 84/1732; Liverpool Chamber of Commerce to FO, 5 February 1885, FO 84/1781: all PRO; Minutes of West African Section, London Chamber of Commerce, vol. I, 21 April 1886, Guildhall Library, London; *Annual Report of the Council of Liverpool Chamber of Commerce* 1888, 71–3.

18. Minutes of West African Section, London Chamber of Commerce, vol. I, 12 January 1887.

19. *Annual Report of the Council of Liverpool Chamber of Commerce* 1889, 80–7; Minutes of the Bristol Chamber of Commerce, vol. VIII, 27 November 1889, *Annual Report of the Bristol Chamber of Commerce* 1890, 14, 90–2.

20. *African Times*, 1 February 1882, 19; 1 April 1882, 43; 1 October 1883, 114; 1 September 1885, 131; *West African Reporter*, 9 August 1884.

21. *Lagos Times*, 27 April 1882; 26 April 1882; *Lagos Observer*, 4 May 1882.

22. *African Times*, 1 September 1888, 137–8.

23. Lagos Chamber of Commerce to colonial secretary, 15 September 1888, in Moloney to Knutsford, 27 February 1889, CO 147/69, PRO.

24. Fynn to Owen, 1 February 1883, CALPROF 3/2, NNAI; MacDonald to FO, 26 November 1894, FO 2/64, PRO.

25. Hopkins, 'Economic History of Lagos', 98–167; Hopkins, 'Economic Imperialism: Lagos', 597–602.

26. Fyfe, *Short History*, 92.

27. Harris to Rowe, 5 November 1880, in Rowe to CO, 10 November 1880; Rowe to CO, 21 October 1880, CO 879/18: both PRO.

28. Moseley to colonial secretary, 15 March 1888, in Rowe to Knutsford, 27 July 1888, CO 879/27, PRO.

29. C. Gertzel, 'Relations Between African and European Traders in the Niger Delta, 1880–1896', *JAH* 3 (1962), 361–6.

30. Hewett to Salisbury, 10 November 1888, FO 84/1881, PRO.
31. Newbury, 'On the Margins of Empire', 44.
32. Miller to Holt, 11 August 1887, 4/1, JHPO; P. Lemberg, 'The Commerce of Sierra Leone', in Rowe to CO, 24 June 1885, CO 267/358, PRO.
33. *Lagos Times*, 21 January 1881; Holt to Miller, 29 March 1886, 4/5, JHPL; Holt's circular, 19 January 1888, 5/3, JHPO.
34. Pearson, 'Economic Imperialism', 84.
35. J. E. Flint, *Sir George Goldie and the Making of Nigeria* (London, 1960), 96.
36. Regulation 9 of the National African Company, 30 July 1886; G. Goldie, 'Concise History of the Royal Niger Company, 20 May 1887', UACP. Goldie to Agents, 23 March 1887, UACP, outlines Goldie's determination to drive produce prices down; see also Gertzel, 'John Holt', 337–8; Pedler, *Lion and Unicorn*, 128–9.
37. Moloney to Knutsford, 7 June 1888, CO 147/64; Merchants . . . of Lagos to Moloney, 12 March 1889, in MacDonald Report, chap. 8, 9 January 1890, FO 84/2109: both in PRO.
38. Hewett's remarks on a letter of the Liverpool African Association of 27 March 1884, FO 84/1660; African Association to Salisbury, 3 October 1891, in Whitley to Salisbury, 8 October 1891, FO 403/171: both PRO; Gertzel, 'John Holt', 329.
39. Hewett to Salisbury, 10 November 1888, FO 84/1881, PRO.
40. Hewett to Salisbury, 26 December 1888, FO 84/1881, PRO; Wariboko, 'New Calabar', 210–27; Ekechi, 'Aspects of Palm Oil Trade', 37.
41. Gertzel, 'John Holt', 340–1, 481; Alagoa, *Small Brave City-State*, 91–2.
42. Hewett to Salisbury, 10 November 1888, FO 84/1881, PRO.
43. Statement of Grievances . . . by A. A. Whitehouse, in MacDonald Report, chap. 6, 9 January 1890, FO 84/2109, PRO.
44. Johnston to Salisbury, 11 September 1888, FO 84/1882, PRO.
45. Thompson, 'Glasgow and Africa', 35–76.
46. Holt to Theorin, 31 July 1888, 4/5, JHPL; Holt to Knutsford, 28 April 1892, 9/1, JHPO; Holt to Granville, 28 October 1881, 7/1, JHPO; Gertzel, 'John Holt', 218–20, 270.
47. Holt to Granville, 16 February 1882, FO 403/18, PRO.
48. Holt to Miller, 29 March 1886, 4/5, JHPL; Miller to Holt, 9 December 1887, 4/1, JHPO.
49. Latham, *Old Calabar*, 82–3.
50. Austen, 'Metamorphoses of Middlemen', 11.
51. S. M. Hargreaves, 'Nineteenth-Century Bonny', 363–7.
52. Memo on the Spiff case, Brass River, 15 August 1887, FO 84/1867, PRO.
53. S. M. Hargreaves, 'Nineteenth-Century Bonny', 375–6.
54. Hewett to Granville, 5 February 1883, FO 84/1634, PRO; Gertzel, 'John Holt', 268–70; Cookey, *Jaja*, 103–32.
55. Johnston to Salisbury, 15 January 1886, FO 84/1750; agents in Opobo, n. d., in Admiralty to FO, 27 January 1886, FO 84/1780; Hewett to Salisbury, 29 February 1888, FO 84/1881: all PRO; H. H. Johnston, *The Story of My Life* (London, 1923), 190–4.
56. De Cardi, 'Short Description', 540–6; Cookey, *Jaja*, 125.
57. Hewett to Rosebery, 19 April 1886, FO 84/1749, PRO.

58. Couper to Salisbury, 23 June 1887, FO 403/73; Couper, Johnstone, & Co. to Salisbury, 13 September 1887, FO 403/73: both PRO.
59. Johnston to Salisbury, 1 August 1887, 12 August 1887, 20 August 1887, FO 84/1828, PRO.
60. African Association to Salisbury, 10 August 1887, 23 August 1887, FO 403/73; Millers to Salisbury, 27 August 1887, FO 403/73: both PRO.
61. Johnston to Salisbury, 24 September 1887, FO 84/1828, PRO; R. Oliver, *Sir Harry Johnston and the Scramble for Africa* (London, 1957), 107–23.
62. Anene, *Southern Nigeria*, 115–21.
63. Holt to Miller, 6 February 1888, 4/5, JHPL.
64. Miller to Holt, 12 March 1884, 4/1, JHPO; Holt to Miller, 20 December 1884, 15 January 1885, 4/5, JHPL.
65. Moore to Derby, 19 January 1885, in Herbert to Lister, 28 January 1885, FO 403/49, PRO.
66. Gertzel, 'John Holt', 321–44.
67. Goldie to Miller, 13 November 1887, 3/7, JHPO; Holt to Goldie, 13 January 1888, 4/5, JHPL.
68. Miller to Holt, 11 August 1887, 4/1; Holt to Goldie, 26 November 1887, 3/6: both JHPO; African Association to Salisbury, 6 November 1888, FO 403/76, PRO.
69. Holt to Goldie, 7 January 1888, 3/6, JHPO.
70. Shipping cos. to FO, 27 February 1888, FO 403/74; Graves to Salisbury, 9 April 1888, FO 403/76; CO to FO, 14 November 1888, FO 403/76: all PRO.
71. Holt to Goldie, 23 April 1888, 3/6, JHPO; Holt to Goldie, 6 April 1888, 4/5, JHPL; Davies, *Trade Makers*, 92–101.
72. African Association to Salisbury, 7 January 1890, FO 403/149, PRO.
73. 'Preliminary Statement: Oil Rivers Charter', n. d., 5/6, JHPO.
74. African Association to Salisbury, 7 January 1890, FO 403/149, PRO.
75. MacDonald to Salisbury, 12 June 1889, FO 84/1940; MacDonald Report on the Administration of the Royal Niger Co. territories, 9 January 1890, FO 84/2109: both PRO.
76. Miller Bros. to Rogerson, 11 February 1890, UACP.
77. *Lagos Observer*, 12 May 1888; Liverpool Chamber of Commerce to Salisbury, 8 March 1890, FO 403/149; Pickering & Berthoud to Salisbury, 27 March 1890, FO 403/149: both PRO.
78. Gertzel, 'John Holt', 415–16.
79. Anene, *Southern Nigeria*, 131–77.
80. MacDonald to FO, 4 May 1891, FO 84/2111; Proclamation imposing Customs Duties, 10 August 1891, FO 84/2111: both PRO.
81. Minutes of the African Association Ltd, vol. II, 20 November 1896, UAA/1/21, UACP.
82. Gertzel, 'John Holt', 491–500.
83. Pedler, *Lion and Unicorn*, 144–7.
84. Johnston to Salisbury, 26 September 1888, FO 84/1882; MacDonald to Salisbury, 17 October 1891, FO 84/2111: both PRO.
85. *African Times*, 1 November 1888, 167.
86. Gertzel, 'John Holt', 287–98.
87. MacDonald to Salisbury, 17 October 1891, FO 84/2111, PRO.

88. Minutes of the African Association Ltd, vol. I, 23 December 1892, UAA/1/20, UACP.
89. MacDonald to FO, 8 February 1893, FO 2/51, PRO.
90. Royal Niger Co. to FO, 19 June 1891, FO 403/171; MacDonald to FO, 18 March 1892, FO 84/2194: both PRO.
91. Gertzel, 'John Holt', 480–91.
92. FO to Liverpool Chamber of Commerce, 2 February 1892, FO 84/2241, PRO.
93. Harford, 'Voyage to the African Oil Rivers', 594–611.
94. Minutes of the African Association Ltd, vol. II, 30 January 1895, UAA/1/21, UACP.
95. Minutes of the African Association Ltd, vol. I, 10 January 1893, 7 November 1893, UAA/1/20, UACP.
96. Minutes of the African Association Ltd, vol. I, 15 December 1893, *ibid.*
97. Minutes of the African Association Ltd, vol. I, 24 October 1893, *ibid.*
98. Dickson, 'Development of Road Transport', 36; A. M. Hay, 'The Development of Road Transport in Nigeria, 1900–1940', *Journal of Transport History* 1 (1971), 95–107; van der Laan, 'Modern Inland Transport'; Noah, 'Inland Ports and European Trading Firms', 30.
99. Minutes of the West African Section of the London Chamber of Commerce, 24 February 1892, Guildhall Library, London; Alldridge to Hay, 12 May 1890, in Hay to Knutsford, 6 June 1890, CO 267/383, PRO.
100. *African Times*, 2 February 1880, 18; 2 March 1880, 30.
101. *Manchester Guardian*, 18 March 1892, 3/1, JHPL.
102. Holt to MacDonald, 1 August 1893, 4/5, JHPL.
103. Holt to Moor, 1 May 1896, 4/5, JHPL.
104. Anene, *Southern Nigeria*, 182.
105. Gallwey's Report, in MacDonald to Salisbury, 11 December 1891, FO 84/2111, PRO; Ikime, *Prince*.
106. Coxon to Pinnock, 1 July 1894, FO 2/63, PRO.
107. Moor to FO, 6 August 1894, FO 2/63, PRO; Ikime, *Prince*, 97–164.
108. MacDonald to FO, 4 February 1896, FO 2/83; correspondence respecting the grievances of Brass chiefs, FO 2/100: both PRO.
109. Anene, *Southern Nigeria*, 165–73; Alagoa, *Small Brave City-State*, 91–116.
110. A. I. Nwabughuogu, 'From Wealthy Entrepreneurs to Petty Traders: The Decline of African Middlemen in Eastern Nigeria, 1900–1950', *JAH* 23 (1982), 365–79.
111. Ofonagoro, *Trade and Imperialism*, 196–201; G. I. Jones, *Slaves to Palm Oil*, 76–8, 90–3.
112. Nwabughuogu, 'Wealthy Entrepreneurs to Petty Traders', 365–70.

Select bibliography

I UNPUBLISHED SOURCES

I OFFICIAL RECORDS

National Archives of Ghana, Accra
ADM 1/2, 1/10, 6/1, 11/1
CSO Colonial Secretary's Office, Accra
SCT 5/4 Judicial Assessors Court, Cape Coast
Special collections:
  Blankson Papers, Bannerman Papers, Rev. T. B. Freeman Papers, Sarbah Papers,
    Ghartey Papers, Ocansey Papers, G. B. Williams Papers, J. H. Caesar Papers

National Archives of Nigeria, Enugu
Records of the Chief Secretary's Office, Enugu
  CSE 1, 2, 3, 4, 5, 35
Rivers Province Papers
  RIVPROF 3, 8, 14
Calabar Province Papers
  CALPROF 1, 5, 8, 9, 13, 14, 53

National Archives of Nigeria, Ibadan
Records of the Chief Secretary's Office, Lagos
  CSO 8, 14, 15, 16, 17
Calabar Province Papers
  CALPROF 2, 3, 4, 6
Intelligence reports (CSO 26)
  Bonny District, Okrika Clan, Jekri sub-tribe
Assessment reports (CSO 26)
  Calabar Division, Opobo Division, Warri Division, Degema Division, Bende
    Division, Ikot Ekpene District

Public Record Office, Kew
Colonial Office records
  CO 82, CO 87, CO 90, CO 96, CO 100, CO 147, CO 151, CO 272, CO 267, CO
    271, CO 442, CO 444, CO 460, CO 464, CO 591, CO 879
Foreign Office records
  FO 2, FO 47, FO 84, FO 403, FO 541

240

HM Customs & Excise records
CUST 5
Board of Trade records
BT 31 Dissolved Companies: Swanzy Estates & Gold Mining Co. Ltd, F. & A.
Swanzy Ltd, Rio Bento Kernel Co. Ltd, Co. of African Merchants Ltd,
Sulymah Trading Co. Ltd, Sulymah & Sherbro Trading Co. Ltd

Companies House, London
Registrar of Companies' files
African Association Ltd, Co. of African Merchants Ltd, Richard & William
King Ltd

Principal Registry, Families Division, The High Court ('Somerset House')
Wills of Thomas Horsfall, Robert Jamieson, Mervyn King, Richard King,
William King, Thomas Tobin

Post Office Archives, London
POST 29/133/PKT 1065R/1866 Contract with the African Steamship Co. 1866
29/325/PKT 346H/1882 Timetables of Sailings to West Africa, 1883 43/140
West African Mail Packets Outward & Homeward, 1859–71

II CHAMBER OF COMMERCE RECORDS

a Minutes
Minutes of the Council of Birmingham Chamber of Commerce 1876–1900
(Birmingham Chamber of Industry and Commerce)
Minutes of the Bristol Chamber of Commerce 1826–1901 (Bristol Record Office)
Minutes of the Council of London Chamber of Commerce 1888–95 (Guildhall
Library)
Minutes of the West African Section of London Chamber of Commerce 1884–1903
(Guildhall Library)
Minutes of the Council of Liverpool Chamber of Commerce 1860–95 (Liverpool
Record Office)
Minutes of the African Trade Section, Liverpool Chamber of Commerce 1902–3
(Liverpool Record Office)
Minutes of the Board of Directors of Manchester Chamber of Commerce
1858–1901 (Manchester Central Library, Archives Dept)
Minutes of the African Sectional Committee of Manchester Chamber of
Commerce 1892–9 (Manchester Central Library, Archives Dept)

b Annual reports
Reports of the Council of Birmingham Chamber of Commerce 1865–1901
(Birmingham Public Library)
Annual Reports of the Bristol Chamber of Commerce 1825–1901 (Bristol Library
and Bristol Record Office)
Annual Reports of the Council of Liverpool Chamber of Commerce 1851–99
(Merseyside Chamber of Commerce)
Annual Reports of the London Chamber of Commerce 1882–95 (British Library)

Annual Reports of the Board of Directors of Manchester Chamber of Commerce
1869–89 (Manchester Central Library)

III BUSINESS RECORDS

United Africa Co. Papers, Unilever Archives, Port Sunlight
  UAA/1/20, 21, 22, Committee Minute Books of the African Association Ltd,
    1891–1903
  UAB/2/8, 9, 10, 11, 12, 13, 14, 16, Agreements between the African Association
    and founding firms, 1890
  Regulations of the Royal Niger Co., 1887–1900; Minute Book of Hatton &
    Cookson Ltd, 1901–22; The West African Trade by Lord Leverhulme; Papers
    of the National African Co., 1886; Concise History of the Royal Niger Co. by
    George Goldie; Misc. agreements between the Royal Niger Co. and other
    trading firms, 1899–1900; Niger Navigation Regulations, 1894; F. & A. Swanzy
    papers, 1845–74; Trade Book, Senegal/Gambia, 1826–7
Royal Niger Co. papers (Scarbrough papers), Rhodes House, Oxford
  vols. 1, 4, 10 and 18
John Holt Papers, Rhodes House, Oxford
  Boxes 1–24 Correspondence & Pamphlets, 1863–1923
John Holt Papers, Liverpool Record Office
  1/– Letters, 1861–1915; 3/– Newscuttings, 1876–1933; 4/– Letter books,
    1867–1914; 6/– Trade diaries, 1875–1905; 7/– Notes on the Niger, 1900–3; 11/–
    Photographs
Lintott, Spink, & Co. papers, 1857–1907, Guildhall Library, London
  MSS 10624, 10625, 10626, 10626A, 12054
Elder Dempster Records, Merseyside Maritime Museum, Maritime Records
    Centre, Liverpool
  2C 2336 African Steam Ship Co. *Annual Reports* 1853–99
Memoranda of the African Trade ascribed to W. A. & G. Maxwell, 1830–1940,
    Sydney Jones Library, University of Liverpool

IV MISSIONARY RECORDS

Church Missionary Society Records, University of Birmingham Library
  CA3 Niger Mission, 1857–80
  G3 A3 Niger Mission, 1880–1934
Baptist Missionary Society Archives
  Journal of J. Clarke, 1840–6
National Library of Scotland, Edinburgh
  Journal of W. Anderson, 1851–2
  Journal of H. M. Waddell, 1846–55

V SHIPS LOGS

National Maritime Museum, Greenwich
  Journal of the merchant ship *Magistrate* to Calabar, 1840–1
  Voyage of the *Celma* to Calabar, 1847

In the possession of Prof. P. N. Davies
Log of the *Belmont*, 1810–25
Log of the brig *Julian*, 1828–30

VI PERSONAL PAPERS

Thomas Fowell Buxton papers, Rhodes House, Oxford
vols. 17, 19, 20, 27, 29, 30, 31, 32, 33, 34
Medlycott Papers, Somerset Record Office, Taunton
Journal of Mervyn B. Medlycott, 1852–75
'Annals of the Tobin family of Liverpool and the Isle of Man', by R. C. Reid (1940),
MS Liverpool Record Office
Extracts from the Diary kept on the Voyage from Liverpool to Lagos by Edmund
Rushton, 1863, Liverpool Record Office
T. H. Bickerton Papers, vol. A, Liverpool Record Office
Papers of J. C. Langdon ('Jerry'), Bristol Central Library
'Three Voyages to the West Coast of Africa, 1881–1884'; 'Our Bust Up with the
Nigger of Sassandrew River, West Coast of Africa, 1883–1884'; 'Tales of the
Deep from an Old Salt's Log'; 'Barter Trade from Bristol Ships, West Coast of
Africa, 50 Years Ago'; Diary and Notebook, 1883–4

VII MISCELLANEOUS RECORDS

'Vessels sailed from Liverpool to West Africa, 1842–1846' (in the possession of Prof.
P. N. Davies)
Peet Papers, Sydney Jones Library, University of Liverpool
XIV African Trade Papers, 1799–1804
Liverpool obituary notices, Liverpool Record Office
'Liverpool Fleet Lists', by E. A. Woods (typescript), Liverpool Record Office
British Library Additional MSS
38416 Liverpool papers relating to the slave trade, 1787–1823
1162A, 1162B Egerton Collection
Rhodes House Oxford, MSS Afr s
1491 'History of the Nigeria Marine' by F. W. Skutil (1953)
697 'Report on Oil Palm Survey, Ibo, Ibibio, & Cross River Areas' by A. F. B.
Bridges (1938)

II PUBLISHED SOURCES

I OFFICIAL

Parliamentary Papers
1816, VII B (506); 1817, VI (431); 1824, XVII (269); 1826–7, VII (312, 552); 1830,
X (661); 1830–1, X (344); 1831–2, XXXIV (461, 514, 551); 1835, XXVI (116);
1837–8, XLV (223); 1842, XI (551); 1842, XII (551); 1842, XXXIX (15); 1845,
XLVI (187); 1845, L (634); 1847–8, XXII (272, 366, 536, 623); 1849, XIX (308);
1850, IX i (53); 1852, XXXI (46); 1852, XLIX (284); 1852–3, LXII (1693);
1854, LXV (296); 1854–5, LII (1987); 1854–5, LVI (406); 1856, XLII (433);
1856, LXII (01); 1856, LXII (02); 1857, XVI (2201); 1857, XLIV (2281); 1857,

XLIV (2282); 1857–8, LXI (2443); 1861, LX (1); 1862, LVIII (3054); 1862, LXI
(2958); 1864, XLI (424); 1864, LXVI (3339); 1865, V (412); 1865, XXXVII
(3523); 1865, LVI (3503); 1866, LXXIII (3675); 1873, LXV (828); 1874, XLVI
(1113); 1875, LII (1343); 1875, LXXV (1132); 1876, LXXVII (1573); 1880,
LXVII (2484); 1881, XCIV (2936); 1883, LXX (3637); 1884–5, LXXXIII
(4225); 1888, LXXIV (5365); 1890–1, LXXXIX (6457); 1895, CIV (7875);
1898, C (8992); 1899, LXIII (9223); 1899, XCV (9300); 1909, XLVII (4670);
1909, XLVIII (4685); 1916, IV (8247)

II PRIMARY

Adams, J. *Remarks on the Country Extending from Cape Palmas to the River Congo*
(London, 1823)
'The African Palm Oil Trade', *Friend of Africa* 25 (1842), 159
Alexander, J. E. *Narrative of a Voyage of Observation*, 2 vols. (London, 1837)
Alldridge, T. J. *The Sherbro and Its Hinterland* (London, 1901)
Allen, W., and Thompson, T. R. H. *Narrative of the Expedition... to the River Niger
in 1841* (London, 1848)
'Autobiography of Mr James Deemin', in Davies, *Trading in West Africa*, 97–136
Babington, W. 'Remarks on the General Description of the Trade on the West Coast
of Africa', *Journal of the Society of Arts* 23 (1875), 245–57
Baines, T. *History of the Commerce and Town of Liverpool* (London, 1852)
Bell, H. J. *The History, Trade, Resources, and Present Condition of the Gold Coast*
(Liverpool, 1893)
Bindloss, H. *In the Niger Country* (Edinburgh, 1898)
Bold, E. *The Merchants' and Mariners' Guide* (London, 1822)
Bowdich, T. E. *Mission from Cape Coast Castle to Ashantee* (London, 1819)
Boyle, F. *Through Fanteeland to Coomassie* (London, 1874)
Carnes, J. A. *Journal of a Voyage from Boston to the West Coast of Africa* (Boston,
1852)
Clarke, J. 'On the Mouths of the River Jamoor', *JRGS* 16 (1847), 255–8
Cole, W. *Life in the Niger or the Journal of an African Trader* (London, 1862)
Corry, J. *Observations upon the Windward Coast of Africa* (London, 1807)
Cotterell, H. 'Reminiscences of One Connected with the West African Trade from
1863 to 1910', in Davies, *Trading in West Africa*, 13–92
Croft, J. A. 'Exploration of the River Volta, West Africa', *PRGS* 18 (1873–4),
183–94
Crouch, A. P. *Glimpses of Feverland* (London, 1889)
Crow, H. *Memoirs* (London, 1830)
Cruickshank, B. *Eighteen Years on the Gold Coast of Africa*, 2 vols. (London, 1853)
Daniell, W. F. 'On the Natives of Old Callebar', *Journal of the Ethnological Society*
1 (1848), 210–27
'The Diary of Antera Duke', in D. Forde, *Efik Traders of Old Calabar* (London,
1968), 27–65
The Diary of John Holt, ed. Davies, P. N. (St John's, Newfoundland, 1993)
Douglas, A. C. *Niger Memories by Nemo* (Exeter, 1927)
Dupuis, J. *Journal of a Residence in Ashantee* (London, 1824)
Falconbridge, A. *An Account of the Slave Trade on the Coast of Africa* (London,
1788)

Fawckner, J. *Narrative of Capt. James Fawckner's Travels on the Coast of Benin* (London, 1837)
Forbes, F. E. *Dahomey and the Dahomans*, 2 vols. (London, 1851)
Gordon, C. A. *Life on the Gold Coast* (London, 1874)
Gore's Liverpool Directory (Liverpool, 1810–1900)
Hamilton, A. 'On Trade with the Coloured Races of Africa', *Journal of the Statistical Society of London* 31 (1868), 25–48
Hay, J. D. *Ashanti and the Gold Coast and What We Know of It* (London, 1874)
Hewett, J. F. N. *European Settlements on the West Coast of Africa* (London, 1862)
Holman, J. *Travels in Madeira, Sierra Leone . . .* (London, 1840)
Huntley, H. V. *Seven Years' Service on the Slave Coast of Western Africa*, 2 vols. (London, 1860)
Hutchinson, T. J. *Impressions of Western Africa* (London, 1858)
Ten Years' Wanderings Among the Ethiopians (London, 1861)
'On the General Features of West African Trade from Senegal to St Paul de Loanda', *Journal of the Society of Arts* 22 (1874), 314–23
Hutton, W. *A Voyage to Africa* (London, 1821)
Jackson, R. M. *Journal of a Voyage to Bonny River* (London, 1934)
Kingsley, M. H. *Travels in West Africa* (London, 1897)
West African Studies (London, 1899)
Laird, M., and Oldfield, R. A. K. *Narrative of an Expedition into the Interior of Africa*, 2 vols. (London, 1837)
Latimer, J. *Annals of Bristol in the Nineteenth Century* (Bristol, 1887)
Leonard, P. *Records of a Voyage to the Western Coast of Africa* (Edinburgh, 1833)
Liverpool and Slavery: An Historical Account of the Liverpool–African Slave Trade by a Genuine Dicky Sam (Liverpool, 1884)
McCulloch, J. R. *Dictionary of Commerce* (London, 1859)
Macdonald, G. *The Gold Coast: Past and Present* (London, 1898)
Mann, G., and Wendland, H. 'On the Palms of Western Tropical Africa', *Transactions of the Linnean Society* 24 (1864), 421–39
Mathew's Bristol Directory (Bristol, 1830–95)
Meredith, H. *An Account of the Gold Coast of Africa* (London, 1812)
Mockler-Ferryman, A. F. *Up the Niger* (London, 1892)
British Nigeria (London, 1902)
Monteiro, J. J. *Angola and the River Congo*, 2 vols. (London, 1875)
Ocansey, J. E. *An African Trading or the Trials of William Narh Ocansey of Addah, West Coast of Africa, River Volta* (Liverpool, 1881; ed. K. Arhin, Accra, 1989)
Owen, W. F. W. *Narrative of Voyages to Explore the Shores of Africa . . .*, 2 vols. (London, 1833)
Payne, J. A. O. *Lagos and West African Almanack for 1881* (London, 1880)
Pinnock, J. *Benin: The Surrounding Country, Inhabitants, Customs, and Trade* (Liverpool, 1897)
Poole, B. *The Commerce of Liverpool* (London, 1854)
Robertson, G. A. *Notes on Africa* (London, 1819)
Sampson, M. J. *Gold Coast Men of Affairs* (London, 1937)
Sarbah, J. M. 'The Oil Palm and Its Uses', *Journal of the African Society* 8 (1909), 232–50
Sauerbeck, A. 'Prices of Commodities and the Precious Metals', *Journal of the

Royal Statistical Society 49 (1886), 581–648; 55 (1892), 110–20; 69 (1906), 211–26

Smith, J. *Trade and Travels in the Gulph of Guinea* (London, 1851)

'Steam to Africa from England and the United States', *Colonial Magazine and East India Review* 19 (1850), 349–62

Swanzy, A. 'On Trade in Western Africa with and Without British Protection', *Journal of the Society of Arts* 22 (1874), 478–87

Thomas, C. W. *Adventures and Observations on the West Coast of Africa* (London, 1864)

Thomas, W. N. 'On the Oil Rivers of West Africa', *PRGS* 17 (1873), 148–55

Waddell, H. M. *Twenty-Nine Years in the West Indies and Central Africa* (London, 1863)

Walker, J. B. 'Notes on the Old Calabar and Cross Rivers', *PRGS* 16 (1871–2), 135–7

'Notes of a Visit, in May 1875, to the Old Calabar and Qua Rivers', *PRGS* 20 (1875–6), 224–30

'Notes on the Politics, Religion, and Commerce of Old Calabar', *Journal of the Anthropological Institute of Britain and Ireland* 6 (1877), 119–24

Whitford, J. *Trading Life in Western and Central Africa* (London, 1877)

Williams, G. *History of the Liverpool Privateers and Letters of Marque* (London, 1897; reprint, New York, 1966)

Wilson, G. F. *On the Stearic Candle Manufacture* (London, 1852)

On the Manufactures of Price's Patent Candle Co. (London, 1856)

III SECONDARY

Adomako, A. 'The History of Currency and Banking in Some West African Countries', *Economic Bulletin of Ghana* 7 (1963), 3–17

'The African Oil Palm', *Kew Bulletin of Miscellaneous Information* 55 (1891), 190–2

Agbodeka, F. *African Politics and British Policy in the Gold Coast, 1868–1900* (London, 1971)

An Economic History of Ghana from the Earliest Times (Accra, 1992)

Agboola, S. A. 'Agricultural Changes in Western Nigeria, 1850–1910', in Akinjogbin, I. A., and Osoba, S. O. (eds.), *Topics on Nigerian Economic and Social History* (Ife, 1980), 128–45

Agri, B. A. 'Aspects of Socio-Economic Changes Among the Awori Egba and Ijebu Remo Communities During the Nineteenth Century', *JHSN* 7 (1974), 465–83

Ajayi, J. F. A. 'The Aftermath of the Fall of Old Oyo', in Ajayi and Crowder, *History of West Africa*, vol. II, 174–214

Ajayi, J. F. A., and Austen, R. A. 'Hopkins on Economic Imperialism in West Africa', *Economic History Review* 25 (1972), 303–6

Ajayi, J. F. A., and Crowder, M. (eds.). *History of West Africa*, 2nd edn, 2 vols. (London, 1987)

Akintoye, S. A. 'The Economic Background of the Ekitiparapo, 1878–1893', *Odu* 4 (1968), 30–52

'The Ondo Road Eastwards of Lagos, c. 1870–1895', *JAH* 10 (1969), 581–98

Alagoa, E. J. *The Small Brave City-State: A History of Nembe–Brass in the Niger Delta* (Madison, 1964)

'Long-Distance Trade and States in the Niger Delta', *JAH* 11 (1970), 319–29

'Nineteenth-Century Revolutions in the Eastern Delta States and Calabar', *JHSN* 5 (1971), 565–73

A History of the Niger Delta (Ibadan, 1972)

Alagoa, E. J., and Fombo, A. *A Chronicle of Grand Bonny* (Ibadan, 1972)

Amenumey, D. E. K. 'Geraldo de Lima: A Reappraisal', *THSG* 9 (1968), 65–78

Andah, B. W. 'Identifying Early Farming Traditions of West Africa', in Shaw, T., Sinclair, P., Andah, B., and Okpoko, A. (eds.), *The Archaeology of Africa: Foods, Metals, and Towns* (London, 1993), 240–54

Andersen, A. J. C. *Margarine* (London, 1954)

Andés, L. E. *Vegetable Fats and Oils* (London, 1897)

Anene, J. C. *Southern Nigeria in Transition, 1885–1906* (Cambridge, 1966)

Anstey, R. T. 'British Trade and Policy in West Central Africa Between 1816 and the Early 1880s', *THSG* 3 (1957), 47–71

Britain and the Congo in the Nineteenth Century (Oxford, 1962)

Auchinleck, G. G. *West African Oil Palm and Its Products* (Colombo, 1923)

Austen, R. A. 'The Abolition of the Overseas Slave Trade: A Distorted Theme in West African History', *JHSN* 5 (1970), 257–74

'The Metamorphoses of Middlemen: The Duala, Europeans, and the Cameroon Hinterland, c. 1800–c. 1960', *IJAHS* 16 (1983), 1–24

African Economic History (London, 1987)

'Tradition, Invention, and History: The Case of the Ngondo', *Cahiers d'études africaines* 32, 126 (1992), 285–309

Austen, R. A., and Headrick, D. 'The Role of Technology in the African Past', *African Studies Review* 26 (1983), 163–84

Austin, G. A. 'Indigenous Credit Institutions in West Africa, c. 1750–c. 1960', in Austin, G. A., and Sugihara, K. (eds.), *Local Suppliers of Credit in the Third World, 1750–1960* (London, 1993), 93–159

Avezathe, G. H. 'Calabar and the Cross River Trade', *Sea* 1 (1954), 1–3

Awe, B. 'Militarism and Economic Development in Nineteenth-Century Yoruba Country: The Ibadan Example', *JAH* 14 (1973), 65–77

Aye, E. *Old Calabar Through the Centuries* (Calabar, 1967)

Barnes, A. C. 'The Extraction of Oil Palm Products', in *Proceedings of the First West African Agricultural Conference, Ibadan, Nigeria, 1927* (Lagos, 1927), 38–51

Bevin, H. J. 'The Gold Coast Economy About 1880', *THSG* 2 (1956), 73–86

'Some Notes on Gold Coast Exports, 1886–1913', *Economic Bulletin of Ghana* 4 (1960), 13–20

Billows, H. C., and Beckwith, H. *Palm Oil and Kernels: The 'Consols of the West Coast'* (Liverpool, 1913)

Braithwaite, R. 'Matthew Forster of Bellsise', *Camden History Review* 19 (1995), 13–16

Bridges, A. F. B. 'The Oil Palm Industry in Nigeria', *Farm and Forest* 7 (1946), 54–8

Brooks, G. E. 'American Trade as a Factor in West African History in the Early Nineteenth Century: Senegal and the Gambia, 1815–1835', in McCall, D. F., Bennett, N. R., and Butler, J. (eds.), *Western African History* (New York, 1969), 132–52

Yankee Traders, Old Coasters, and African Middlemen (Boston, 1970)

The Kru Mariner in the Nineteenth Century (Newark, 1972)

'Builders of the African Trade: Edward Hatton and Thomas W. Cookson', *Elder Dempster Magazine* 6 (1927), 133–4

'Builders of the West African Trade: The King Family', *Elder Dempster Magazine* 6 (1927), 10–11

Cameron, J. *Soaps and Candles* (London, 1888)

Carpenter, W. L. *A Treatise on the Manufacture of Soap and Candles, Lubricants, and Glycerin* (London, 1885)

Chamberlin, C. 'Bulk Exports, Trade Tiers, Regulation, and Development: An Economic Approach to the Study of West Africa's "Legitimate Trade"', *Journal of Economic History* 39 (1979), 419–38

Chandler, G. *Liverpool Shipping: A Short History* (London, 1960)

Chauveau, J.-P. 'Une histoire maritime africaine est-elle possible?', *Cahiers d'études africaines* 26, 101 (1986), 173–235

Clarke, J. 'Households and the Political Economy of Small-Scale Cash Crop Production in South-Western Nigeria', *Africa* 51 (1981), 807–23

Clayton, W. *Margarine* (London, 1920)

Clough, R. G. *Oil Rivers Trader* (London, 1972)

'The Company's River Fleet and Port, Nigeria', *Statistical and Economic Review* 2 (1948), 33–48

Cookey, S. J. S. *King Jaja of the Niger Delta: His Life and Times, 1821–1891* (New York, 1974)

Coquery-Vidrovitch, C. 'De la traite des esclaves à l'exportation de l'huile de palme et des palmistes au Dahomey, XIXe siècle', in Meillassoux, *Development of Indigenous Trade*, 107–23

Les Africaines: histoire des femmes d'Afrique Noire du XIXe au XXe siècle (Paris, 1994)

Corlett, W. J. *The Economic Development of Detergents* (London, 1958)

Cowan, A. A. 'Early Trading Conditions in the Bight of Biafra, Part I', *Journal of the Royal African Society* 34 (1935), 391–402; 'Part II', 35 (1936), 53–64

Curtin, P. D. *The Atlantic Slave Trade: A Census* (Madison, 1969)

Economic Change in Precolonial Africa: Senegambia in the Era of the Slave Trade (Madison, 1975)

Daget, S. 'An Exceptional Document: Legitimate Trade of the Ship *Africain* on the West Coast of Africa in 1827', *Journal of African Studies* 2 (1975), 177–200

Davies, P. N. 'The African Steam Ship Co.', in Harris, *Liverpool and Merseyside*, 212–38

The Trade Makers: Elder Dempster in West Africa, 1852–1972 (London, 1973)

'The Impact of the Expatriate Shipping Lines on the Economic Development of British West Africa', *Business History* 19 (1977), 3–17

Sir Alfred Jones: Shipping Entrepreneur par excellence (London, 1978)

Henry Tyrer (London, 1979)

Davies, P. N. (ed.). *Trading in West Africa, 1840–1920* (London, 1976)

Dawe, M. T., and Martin, F. J. 'The Oil Palm Industry and Its Problems in Sierra Leone', in *Proceedings of the First West African Agricultural Conference* (Lagos, 1927), 5–29

Deveneaux, G. 'Trade Routes and Colonial Policy in Sierra Leone in the Nineteenth Century', *Journal of the Historical Society of Sierra Leone* 3 (1979), 71–95

Dickson, K. B. 'The Development of Road Transport in Southern Ghana and Ashanti Since c. 1850', *THSG* 5 (1961), 33–42

Dike, K. O. *Trade and Politics in the Niger Delta, 1830–1885* (Oxford, 1956)

Drake, B. K. 'Continuity and Flexibility in Liverpool's Trade with Africa and the Caribbean', *Business History* 18 (1976), 85–97

'The Liverpool–African Voyage c. 1790–1807: Commercial Problems', in Anstey, R., and Hair, P. E. H. (eds.), *Liverpool, the African Slave Trade, and Abolition* (Widnes, 1976), 126–56

Dudgeon, G. C. *The Agricultural and Forest Products of British West Africa* (London, 1911)

Dumett, R. E. 'African Merchants and Trader's Agents of the Major Towns of Ghana During the Late Nineteenth Century', *THSG* 8 (1972), 261–4

'John Sarbah the Elder and African Mercantile Entrepreneurship in the Gold Coast in the Late Nineteenth Century', *JAH* 14 (1973), 653–79

'African Merchants of the Gold Coast, 1860–1905: Dynamics of Indigenous Entrepreneurship', *Comparative Studies in Society and History* 25 (1983), 661–93

Dyke, F. M. *Report on the Oil Palm Industry in British West Africa* (Lagos, 1927)

Ehrensaft, P. 'The Political Economy of Informal Empire in Pre-Colonial Nigeria, 1807–1884', *Canadian Journal of African Studies* 6 (1972), 451–90

Ekechi, F. K. 'Aspects of Palm Oil Trade at Oguta (Eastern Nigeria), 1900–1950', *AEH* 10 (1981), 35–65

Elango, L. Z. 'Trade and Diplomacy on the Cameroon Coast in the Nineteenth Century, 1833–1879: The Case of Bimbia', in Njeuma, *Introduction to the History of Cameroon*, 32–62

Eltis, D. *Economic Growth and the Ending of the Transatlantic Slave Trade* (Oxford, 1987)

'Trade Between Western Africa and the Atlantic World Before 1870: Estimates of Trends in Value, Composition, and Direction', *Research in Economic History* 12 (1989), 197–239

'Precolonial Western Africa and the Atlantic Economy', in Solow, B. L. (ed.), *Slavery and the Rise of the Atlantic System* (Cambridge, 1991), 97–119

Eltis, D., and Jennings, L. C. 'Trade Between Western Africa and the Atlantic World in the Pre-Colonial Era', *American Historical Review* 93 (1988), 936–59

Falola, T. *The Political Economy of a Pre-Colonial African State: Ibadan, 1830–1900* (Ife, 1984)

Fanso, V. G. 'Trade and Supremacy on the Cameroon Coast, 1879–1887', in Njeuma, *Introduction to the History of Cameroon*, 63–87

Farquhar, J. H. J. (ed. H. N. Thompson). *The Oil Palm and Its Varieties* (London, 1913)

Faulkner, O. T., and Lewin, C. J. 'Native Methods of Preparing Palm Oil, II', in *Second Annual Bulletin of the Agricultural Department, Nigeria* (1923), 3–22

Faulkner, O. T., and Mackie, J. R. *West African Agriculture* (Cambridge, 1933)

Fay, L. G. 'Ninety-Six Years in the West African Trade', *Sea Breezes* 6 (1948), 150–68

Feron, R. 'Technology and Production', in van Stuyvenburg, *Margarine*, 83–121

Field, M. J. 'The Agricultural System of the Manya–Krobo of the Gold Coast', *Africa* 14 (1943), 54–65

Finigan, L. *The Life of Peter Stuart: The Ditton Doctor* (privately printed, 1920)

Flint, J. E., and McDougall, E. A. 'Economic Change in West Africa in the

Nineteenth Century', in Ajayi and Crowder, *History of West Africa*, vol. II, 379–402

Freund, W. M., and Shenton, R. W. '"Vent-for-Surplus" Theory and the Economic History of West Africa', *Savanna* 6 (1977), 191–6

Fry, R. *Bankers in West Africa: The Story of the Bank of British West Africa Ltd* (London, 1976)

Fyfe, C. 'European and Creole Influence in the Hinterland of Sierra Leone Before 1896', *Sierra Leone Studies* 6 (1956), 113–23

   A History of Sierra Leone (London, 1962)

   'Charles Heddle: An African "Merchant Prince"', in *Laboratoire 'Connaissance du Tiers-Monde': Entreprises et entrepreneurs en Afrique, 19–20 siècles* (Paris, 1983), 235–47

Fyle, C. M. *Commerce and Entrepreneurship: The Sierra Leone Hinterland in the Nineteenth Century*, Institute of African Studies, Fourah Bay College, Occasional Paper II (Freetown, 1977)

   History and Socio-Economic Development in Sierra Leone (Freetown, 1988)

   'G. B. Ollivant & Co.', *West African Review* 8, 120 (1937), 95–116

Gann, L. H., and Duignan, P. (eds.). *Colonialism in Africa, 1870–1960*, vol. I, *The History and the Politics of Colonialism, 1870–1914* (Cambridge, 1969); vol. IV, *The Economics of Colonialism* (Cambridge, 1975)

Geary, W. M. N. 'Jaja, an African Merchant Prince', *West Africa* (14 January 1922), 1709–13

Gemery, H. A., Hogendorn, J., and Johnson, M. 'Evidence on English/African Terms of Trade in the Eighteenth Century', *Explorations in Economic History* 27 (1990), 157–77

Gertzel, C. J. 'Commercial Organisation on the Niger Coast, 1852–1891', in *Proceedings of the Leverhulme Intercollegiate History Conference* (Salisbury, 1960), 1–16

   'Relations Between African and European Traders in the Niger Delta, 1880–1896', *JAH* 3 (1962), 361–6

Goerg, O. *Commerce et colonisation en Guinée, 1850–1913* (Paris, 1986)

   'Deux modalités d'adaptation à l'abolition de la traite atlantique: le Rio Nunez et le Rio Pongo', in Daget, S. (ed.), *De la traite à l'esclavage*, 2 vols. (Paris, 1988), vol. II, 557–73

Graham, G. S. 'The Ascendancy of the Sailing Ship, 1850–1885', *Economic History Review* 9 (1956), 74–88

Gray, J. E. 'Native Methods of Preparing Palm Oil', in *First Annual Bulletin of the Agricultural Department, Nigeria* (Lagos, 1922), 29–50

Hancock, W. F. *Survey of British Commonwealth Affairs*, 4 vols., vol. II, part 2, *Problems of Economic Policy* (London, 1942)

Hanson, J. R. *Trade in Transition: Exports from the Third World, 1840–1900* (New York, 1980)

Harding, L. 'Hamburg's West Africa Trade in the Nineteenth Century', in Liesegang, Pasch, and Jones, *Figuring African Trade*, 363–91

Hargreaves, J. D. 'The Atlantic Ocean in West African History', in Stone, *Africa and the Sea*, 5–13

Hargreaves, R. A. 'A Short History of Bonny', *Nigerian Field* 40 (1975), 40–6

Harris, J. R. (ed.). *Liverpool and Merseyside* (London, 1969)

Hart, K. *The Political Economy of West African Agriculture* (Cambridge, 1982)
Hartley, C. W. S. *The Oil Palm*, 3rd edn (London, 1988)
Hawkins, E. K. 'The Growth of a Money Economy in Nigeria and Ghana', *Oxford Economic Papers* 10 (1958), 339–54
Hay, A. M. 'The Development of Road Transport in Nigeria, 1900–1940', *Journal of Transport History* 1 (1971), 95–107
Hieke, E. *Zur Geschichte des deutschen Handels mit Ostafrika: das hamburgische Handelshaus Wm O'Swald & Co.*, vol. I, *1831–1870* (Hamburg, 1939)
  G. L. Gaiser: Hamburg–Westafrika (Hamburg, 1949)
Hill, P. *Migrant Cocoa-Farmers of Southern Ghana* (Cambridge, 1963)
Hilling, D. 'The Evolution of the Major Ports of West Africa', *Geographical Journal* 135 (1969), 365–78
Hoffman, W. G. 'One Hundred Years of the Margarine Industry', in van Stuyvenberg, *Margarine*, 9–36
Hogendorn, J. S. 'Economic Initiative and African Cash Farming: Pre-Colonial Origins and Early Colonial Developments', in Gann and Duignan, *Colonialism in Africa*, vol. IV, 283–328
  'The Vent-for-Surplus Model and African Cash Agriculture to 1914', *Savanna* 5 (1976), 15–28
  'Vent-for-Surplus Theory: A Reply', *Savanna* 6 (1977), 196–9
Hope, R. *A New History of British Shipping* (London, 1990)
Hopkins, A. G. 'The Currency Revolution in South-West Nigeria in the Late Nineteenth Century', *JHSN* 3 (1966), 471–83
  'R. B. Blaize, 1845–1904: Merchant Prince of West Africa', *Tarikh* 1 (1966), 70–9
  'Economic Imperialism in West Africa: Lagos, 1880–1892', *Economic History Review* 21 (1968), 580–606
  'Economic Imperialism in West Africa: A Rejoinder', *Economic History Review* 25 (1972), 307–12
  An Economic History of West Africa (London, 1973)
  'The "New International Economic Order" in the Nineteenth Century: Britain's First Development Plan for Africa', in Law, *From Slave Trade to 'Legitimate' Commerce*, 240–64
Howard, A. 'The Role of Freetown in the Commercial Life of Sierra Leone', in Fyfe, C., and Jones, E. (eds.), *Freetown: A Symposium* (Freetown, 1968), 38–64
Huber, H. *The Krobo* (Bonn, 1963)
Hunt, K. E. 'Raw Materials', in van Stuyvenberg, *Margarine*, 37–82
Hurst, G. H. *Soaps* (London, 1898)
Hyde, F. E. *Liverpool and the Mersey: An Economic History of a Port, 1700–1970* (Newton Abbot, 1971)
Hynes, W. G. *The Economics of Empire* (London, 1979)
Ijagbemi, E. A. 'The Freetown Colony and the Development of "Legitimate" Commerce in the Adjoining Territories', *JHSN* 5 (1970), 243–56
  'The Rokel River and the Development of Inland Trade in Sierra Leone', *Odu* 3 (1970), 45–70
Ikime, O. *Merchant Prince of the Niger Delta* (Ibadan, 1968)
  Niger Delta Rivalry (London, 1969)
Inikori, J. E. 'Market Structure and the Profits of the British African Trade in the Late Eighteenth Century', *Journal of Economic History* 41 (1981), 745–76

'West Africa's Seaborne Trade, 1750–1850: Volume, Structure, and Implications',
in Liesegang, Pasch, and Jones, *Figuring African Trade*, 49–88

'The Credit Needs of the African Trade and the Development of the Credit
Economy in England', *Explorations in Economic History* 27 (1990), 197–231

'Investigations in Connection with the African Palm Oil Industry', *Bulletin of the
Imperial Institute* 7 (1909), 357–94

Isichei, E. *The Ibo People and the Europeans* (London, 1973)

A History of the Igbo People (London, 1976)

Johnson, M. 'Migrants' Progress, Part I', *Bulletin of the Ghana Geographical
Association* 9 (1964), 4–27

'The Ounce in Eighteenth-Century West African Trade', *JAH* 7 (1966), 197–214

'The Cowrie Currencies of West Africa, Part I', *JAH* 11 (1970), 17–49; 'Part II',
331–53

'Cotton Imperialism in West Africa', *African Affairs* 73, 291 (1974), 178–87

Anglo-African Trade in the Eighteenth Century (ed. J. T. Lindblad and R. Ross)
(Leiden, 1990)

Jones, A. *From Slaves to Palm Kernels: A History of the Galinhas Country,
1730–1890* (Wiesbaden, 1983)

Jones, G. I. 'Native and Trade Currencies in Southern Nigeria During the
Eighteenth and Nineteenth Centuries', *Africa* 28 (1958), 43–54

The Trading States of the Oil Rivers (London, 1963)

From Slaves to Palm Oil: Slave Trade and Palm Oil Trade in the Bight of Biafra
(Cambridge, 1989)

Kaplow, S. B. 'The Mudfish and the Crocodile: Underdevelopment of a West
African Bourgeoisie', *Science and Society* 41 (1977), 317–33

'Primitive Accumulation and Traditional Social Relations on the Nineteenth-
Century Gold Coast', *Canadian Journal of African Studies* 12 (1978), 19–36

Kilby, P. 'The Nigerian Palm Oil Industry', *Food Research Institute Studies* 7 (1967),
177–203

Kirk-Greene, A. H. M. 'The Major Currencies in Nigerian History', *JHSN* 2
(1960), 132–50

Klein, M. A. 'Slavery, the Slave Trade, and Legitimate Commerce in Late
Nineteenth-Century Africa', *Etudes d'histoire africaine* 2 (1971), 5–28

Laan, H. L. van der. *European Commercial Enterprise in Colonial Sierra Leone,
1896–1961: A Preliminary Survey* (Leiden, 1978)

'Modern Inland Transport and the European Trading Firms in Colonial West
Africa', *Cahiers d'études africaines* 21, 84 (1981), 547–75

'A Swiss Family Firm in West Africa: A. Brunnschweiller & Co., 1929–1959',
AEH 12 (1983), 287–97

'Lagos Palm Oil', *Kew Bulletin of Miscellaneous Information* 69 (1892), 200–8

Latham, A. J. H. 'Currency, Credit, and Capitalism on the Cross River in the Pre-
Colonial Era', *JAH* 12 (1971), 599–605

Old Calabar, 1600–1891 (Oxford, 1973)

'A Trading Alliance: Sir John Tobin and Duke Ephraim', *History Today* 24
(1974), 862–7

'Price Fluctuations in the Early Palm Oil Trade', *JAH* 19 (1978), 213–18

'Palm Produce from Calabar, 1812–1887, with a Note on the Formation of Palm

Oil Prices to 1914', in Liesegang, Pasch, and Jones, *Figuring African Trade*, 265–96

Law, R. 'Royal Monopoly and Private Enterprise in the Atlantic Trade: The Case of Dahomey', *JAH* 18 (1977), 555–77

'The "Crisis of Adaptation" Reconsidered: Dahomey and the Transition from the Slave Trade to "Legitimate" Commerce in the Nineteenth Century', unpublished seminar paper, School of Oriental and African Studies, London, 17 October 1990

'The Historiography of the Commercial Transition in Nineteenth-Century West Africa', in Falola, T. (ed.), *African Historiography: Essays in Honour of Jacob Ade Ajayi* (Harlow, 1993), 91–115

'Cowries, Gold, and Dollars: Exchange Rate Instability and Domestic Price Inflation in Dahomey in the Eighteenth and Nineteenth Centuries', in Guyer, J. I. (ed.), *Money Matters* (London, 1995), 53–73

'Introduction', in Law, *From Slave Trade to 'Legitimate' Commerce*, 1–31

'"Legitimate" Trade and Gender Relations in Yorubaland and Dahomey', in Law, *From Slave Trade to 'Legitimate' Commerce*, 195–214

Law, R. (ed.). *From Slave Trade to 'Legitimate' Commerce: The Commercial Transition in Nineteenth-Century West Africa* (Cambridge, 1995)

Leubuscher, C. *The West African Shipping Trade, 1909–1959* (Leiden, 1963)

Levi, J. *African Agriculture: Economic Action and Reaction in Sierra Leone* (Slough, 1976)

Liesegang, G. 'Introduction', in Liesegang, Pasch, and Jones, *Figuring African Trade*, 1–24

Liesegang, G., Pasch, H., and Jones, A. (eds.). *Figuring African Trade* (Berlin, 1986)

Liveing, E. (ed.). 'Living Bristol's Many Industries' (Bristol Central Library)

Lovejoy, P. E. 'Interregional Monetary Flows in the Precolonial Trade of Nigeria', *JAH* 15 (1974), 563–85

Transformations in Slavery (Cambridge, 1983)

Lynn, M. 'Change and Continuity in the British Palm Oil Trade with West Africa, 1830–1855', *JAH* 22 (1981), 331–48

'From Sail to Steam: The Impact of the Steamship Services on the British Palm Oil Trade with West Africa, 1850–1890', *JAH* 30 (1989), 227–45

'Bristol, West Africa, and the Nineteenth-Century Palm Oil Trade', *Historical Research* 64, 155 (1991), 359–74

'British Business and the African Trade: Richard & William King Ltd of Bristol and West Africa, 1833–1918', *Business History* 34 (1992), 20–37

'British Business Archives and the History of Business in Nineteenth-Century West Africa', *Business Archives* 7, 62 (1991), 28–39

'The Profitability of the Early Nineteenth-Century Palm Oil Trade', *AEH* 20 (1992), 77–97

'Technology, Trade, and "a Race of Native Capitalists": The Krio Diaspora of West Africa and the Steamship, 1852–1895', *JAH* 33 (1992), 421–40

'Trade and Politics in Nineteenth-Century Liverpool: The Tobin and Horsfall Families and Liverpool's African Trade', *Transactions of the Historic Society of Lancashire and Cheshire* 142 (1993), 99–120

'Factionalism, Imperialism, and the Making and Breaking of Bonny Kingship c. 1830–1885', *Revue française d'histoire d'Outre-Mer* 82 (1995), 169–92

'Law and Imperial Expansion: The Niger Delta Courts of Equity, c. 1850–1885', *Journal of Imperial and Commonwealth History* 23 (1995), 54–76

'The West African Palm Oil Trade in the Nineteenth Century and "the Crisis of Adaptation"', in Law, *From Slave Trade to 'Legitimate' Commerce*, 57–77

McCarthy, M. *Social Change and the Growth of British Power in the Gold Coast: The Fante States, 1807–1874* (Lanham, MD, 1983)

MacInnes, C. M. *A Gateway of Empire* (Bristol, 1939)

Macmillan, A. *The Red Book of West Africa* (London, 1920)

McPhee, A. *The Economic Revolution in British West Africa* (London, 1926)

McSheffrey, G. M. 'Slavery, Indentured Servitude, Legitimate Trade, and the Impact of Abolition in the Gold Coast, 1874–1901', *JAH* 24 (1983), 349–68

'The Manilla Problem', *Statistical and Economic Review* 3 (1949), 44–56

Mann, K. 'The Rise of Taiwo Olowo: Law, Accumulation, and Mobility in Early Colonial Lagos', in Mann, K., and Roberts R. (ed.), *Law in Colonial Africa* (London, 1991), 85–107

'Women, Landed Property, and the Accumulation of Wealth in Early Colonial Lagos', *Signs* 16 (1991), 682–706

Manning, P. 'Some Export Statistics for Nigeria, 1880–1905', *Nigerian Journal of Economic and Social Studies* 9 (1967), 229–34

'Slaves, Palm Oil, and Political Power on the West African Coast', *African Historical Studies* 2 (1969), 279–88

'The Economy of Early Colonial Dahomey, 1890–1914', in Smaldone, J. P. (ed.), *Explorations in Quantitative African History* (Syracuse, 1977), 25–52

Slavery, Colonialism, and Economic Growth in Dahomey, 1640–1960 (Cambridge, 1982)

'Merchants, Porters, and Canoemen in the Bight of Benin: Links in the West African Trade Network', in Coquery-Vidrovitch, C., and Lovejoy, P. E. (eds.), *The Workers of African Trade* (Beverley Hills, 1985), 51–74

'Slave Trade, "Legitimate" Trade, and Imperialism Revisited: The Control of Wealth in the Bights of Benin and Biafra', in Lovejoy, P. E. (ed.), *Africans in Bondage* (Madison, 1986), 203–33

Marfaing, L. *L'évolution du commerce au Sénégal, 1820–1930* (Paris, 1991)

Marriner, S. *The Economic and Social Development of Merseyside* (London, 1982)

Martin, A. *The Oil Palm Economy of the Ibibio Farmer* (Ibadan, 1956)

Martin, J. 'Krumen "Down the Coast": Liberian Migrants on the West African Coast in the Nineteenth and Early Twentieth Centuries', *IJAHS* 18 (1985), 401–23

Martin, P. M. *The External Trade of the Loango Coast, 1576–1870* (Oxford, 1972)

Martin, S. M. 'Gender and Innovation: Farming, Cooking, and Palm Processing in the Ngwa Region, South-Eastern Nigeria, 1900–1930', *JAH* 25 (1984), 411–27

Palm Oil and Protest: An Economic History of the Ngwa Region of South-Eastern Nigeria, 1800–1980 (Cambridge, 1988)

'Slaves, Igbo Women, and Palm Oil in the Nineteenth Century', in Law, *From Slave Trade to 'Legitimate' Commerce*, 172–94

Martin, W. A. G. *A Century of Liverpool's Commerce* (Liverpool, 1950)

M'Bokolo, E. *Noirs et Blancs en Afrique équatoriale: les sociétés côtières et la péné-tration française, vers 1820–1874* (Paris, 1981)
Meillassoux, C. (ed.). *The Development of Indigenous Trade and Markets in West Africa* (London, 1971)
'Merchandise Trading in British West Africa', *Statistical and Economic Review* 5 (1950), 1–36
Meredith, D. 'Government and the Decline of the Nigeria Oil-Palm Export Industry, 1919–1939', *JAH* 25 (1984), 311–29
Milbourne, A. H. 'Palm Kernels from West Africa', *Journal of the African Society* 15 (1915–16), 133–44
Minchinton, W. E. *The British Tinplate Industry* (Oxford, 1957)
Mitchell, P. K. 'Trade Routes of the Early Sierra Leone Protectorate', *Sierra Leone Studies* 16 (1962), 204–17
Morel, E. D. *Affairs of West Africa* (London, 1902)
Morgan, K. *Bristol and the Atlantic Trade in the Eighteenth Century* (Cambridge, 1993)
Morgan, W. B. 'The Nigerian Oil Palm Industry', *Scottish Geographical Magazine* 71 (1955), 174–7
Mouser, B. L. 'Trade, Coasters, and Conflict in the Rio Pongo from 1790 to 1808', *JAH* 14 (1973), 45–64
Munro, J. F. *Africa and the International Economy, 1800–1960* (London, 1976)
Britain in Tropical Africa, 1880–1960 (London, 1984)
'African Shipping: Reflections on the Maritime History of Africa South of the Sahara, 1800–1914', *International Journal of Maritime History* 2 (1990), 163–82
Musson, A. E. *Enterprise in Soap and Chemicals: Joseph Crosfields and Sons, Ltd, 1815–1965* (Manchester, 1965)
Myint, H. 'The "Classical Theory" of International Trade and Underdeveloped Countries', in Livingstone, I. (ed.), *Economic Policy for Development* (Harmondsworth, 1971), 85–112
The Economics of the Developing Countries (London, 1964)
Nair, K. K. 'Trade in Southern Nigeria from 1860 to the 1870s: Expansion or Stagnation?', *JHSN* 6 (1973), 425–33
Neal, F. 'Liverpool Shipping in the Early Nineteenth Century', in Harris, *Liverpool and Merseyside*, 147–81
Neale, W. G. *At the Port of Bristol*, vol. I, *Members and Problems* (Bristol, 1968)
Newbury, C. W. *The Western Slave Coast and Its Rulers* (Oxford, 1961)
'Credit in Early Nineteenth-Century West African Trade', *JAH* 13 (1972), 81–95
'Trade and Authority in West Africa from 1850 to 1880', in Gann and Duignan, *Colonialism in Africa*, vol. I, 66–99
'Prices and Profitability in Early Nineteenth-Century West African Trade', in Meillassoux, *Development of Indigenous Trade*, 91–106
'On the Margins of Empire: The Trade of Western Africa, 1875–1890', in Förster, S., Mommsen W. J., and Robinson R. (eds.), *Bismarck, Europe, and Africa: The Berlin Africa Conference, 1884–1885, and the Onset of Partition* (Oxford, 1988), 35–58
Njeuma, M. (ed.). *Introduction to the History of Cameroon* (London, 1989)

Njoku, O. N. 'Oil Palm Syndrome in Nigeria: Government Policy and Indigenous Response, 1918–1939', *Calabar Historical Journal* 2 (1978), 78–97

Noah, M. E. 'Inland Ports and European Trading Firms in South Eastern Nigeria', *African Affairs* 88, 350 (1989), 25–40

Northrup, D. 'The Growth of Trade Among the Igbo Before 1800', *JAH* 13 (1972), 217–36

'The Compatibility of the Slave and Palm Oil Trades in the Bight of Biafra', *JAH* 17 (1976), 353–64

Trade Without Rulers: Pre-Colonial Economic Development in South-Eastern Nigeria (Oxford, 1978)

'Nineteenth-Century Patterns of Slavery and Economic Growth in Southeastern Nigeria', *IJAHS* 12 (1979), 1–16

Nwabughuogu, A. I. 'From Wealthy Entrepreneurs to Petty Traders: The Decline of African Middlemen in Eastern Nigeria, 1900–1950', *JAH* 23 (1982), 365–79

Ofonagoro, W. I. *Trade and Imperialism in Southern Nigeria, 1881–1929* (New York, 1979)

Ogundana, B. 'The Fluctuating Significance of Nigerian Seaports Before 1914', *Odu* 3 (1967), 44–71

Ogunremi, G. O. *Counting the Camels: The Economics of Transportation in Pre-Industrial Nigeria* (New York, 1982)

'Oil Palm in Labuan: A Success and a Failure', *Kew Bulletin of Miscellaneous Information* 35 (1889), 259–67

Oliver, R. *Sir Harry Johnston and the Scramble for Africa* (London, 1957)

Oriji, J. N. 'A Re-Assessment of the Organisation and Benefits of the Slave and Palm Produce Trade Among the Ngwa–Igbo', *Canadian Journal of African Studies* 16 (1982), 523–48

'A Study of the Slave and Palm Produce Trade Among the Ngwa–Igbo of Southeastern Nigeria', *Cahiers d'études africaines* 23, 91 (1983), 311–28

Palm Oil and Palm Kernels: Report of a Committee Appointed by the Secretary of State for the Colonies, September 1923 (London, 1925)

Partridge, C. *Cross River Natives* (London, 1905)

Patterson, K. D. *The Northern Gabon Coast to 1875* (Oxford, 1975)

Pearson, S. R. 'The Economic Imperialism of the Royal Niger Co.', *Food Research Institute Studies* 10 (1971), 69–88

Pedler, F. J. *The Lion and the Unicorn in Africa: The United Africa Company, 1787–1931* (London, 1974)

Philipps, O. 'Germany and the Palm Kernel Trade', *Journal of the African Society* 14 (1914–15), 193–8

'A Pioneer of the West African Trade: A Brief Outline of Mr Harry Cotterell's Life', *Elder Dempster Magazine* 4, 13 (1925), 15–23

'Produce Goes to Market', *Statistical and Economic Review* 3 (1949), 1–37

'The Production of Palm Oil and Kernels in Nigeria', *Statistical and Economic Review* 1 (1948), 15–31

Rankin, J. J. *History of the United Africa Co. Ltd to 1938* (privately printed, 1938)

Redford, A. *Manchester Merchants and Foreign Trade*, vol. II, *1850–1939* (Manchester, 1956)

Reynolds, E. 'The Rise and Fall of an African Merchant Class on the Gold Coast, 1830–1874', *Cahiers d'études africaines* 14, 54 (1974), 253–64

Trade and Economic Change on the Gold Coast, 1807–1874 (Harlow, 1974)

'Economic Imperialism: The Case of the Gold Coast', *Journal of Economic History* 35 (1975), 94–116

'Abolition and Economic Change on the Gold Coast', in Eltis, D., and Walvin, J. (eds.), *The Abolition of the Atlantic Slave Trade: Origins and Effects in Europe, Africa, and the Americas* (Madison, 1981), 141–51

Richardson, D. 'The Eighteenth-Century British Slave Trade: Estimates of Its Volume and Coastal Distribution in Africa', *Research in Economic History* 12 (1989), 151–95

Root, J. W. 'British Trade with West Africa', *Journal of the African Society* 1 (1901), 40–63

Ross, D. A. 'The Career of Domingo Martinez in the Bight of Benin, 1833–1864', *JAH* 6 (1965), 79–90

'The First Chacha of Whydah: Francisco Felix de Souza', *Odu* 2 (1969), 19–28

Ryder, A. F. C. *Benin and the Europeans, 1485–1897* (London, 1969)

Sanders, J. 'Palm Oil Production on the Gold Coast in the Aftermath of the Slave Trade: A Case Study of the Fante', *IJAHS* 15 (1982), 49–63

Sayers, E. F. 'French and English Trade Rivalry on the West Coast in 1824', *Sierra Leone Studies* 21 (1939), 110–18

Schnapper, B. *La Politique et le commerce français dans le Golfe de Guinée de 1838 à 1871* (Paris, 1961)

Sheridan, R. B. 'The Commercial and Financial Organisation of the British Slave Trade, 1750–1807', *Economic History Review* 11 (1958), 249–63

Smith, E. H. G. 'The Oil Palm (Elaeis Guineensis) at Calabar', in *Eighth Annual Bulletin of the Agricultural Dept* (Lagos, 1929), 5–42

Smith, R. 'The Canoe in West African History', *JAH* 11 (1970), 515–33

Soumonni, E. A. 'Dahomean Economic Policy Under Ghezo 1818–1858: A Reconsideration', *JHSN* 10 (1980), 1–11

'The Compatibility of the Slave and Palm Oil Trades in Dahomey, 1818–1858', in Law, *From Slave Trade to 'Legitimate' Commerce*, 78–92

Stone, J. C. (ed.). *Africa and the Sea* (Aberdeen, 1985)

Stuyvenberg, J. H. van (ed.). *Margarine: An Economic, Social, and Scientific History* (Liverpool, 1969)

Sutton, I. 'Labour in Commercial Agriculture in Ghana in the Late Nineteenth and Early Twentieth Centuries', *JAH* 24 (1983), 461–83

Swanzy, H. 'A Trading Family in the Nineteenth-Century Gold Coast', *THSG* 2 (1956), 87–120

Syfert, D. N. 'The Liberian Coasting Trade, 1822–1900', *JAH* 18 (1977), 217–35

Szereszewski, R. *Structural Changes in the Economy of Ghana, 1891–1911* (London, 1965)

Thornton, R. H. *British Shipping* (Cambridge, 1959)

Tonkin, E. 'Creating Kroomen: Ethnic Diversity, Economic Specialism, and Changing Demand', in Stone, *Africa and the Sea*, 27–47

Tosh, J. 'The Cash Crop Revolution in Tropical Africa: An Agricultural Reappraisal', *African Affairs* 79, 314 (1980), 79–94

'The Trading Hulks', *Statistical and Economic Review* 1 (1948), 36–7

Udo, R. K., and Ogundana, B. 'Factors Influencing the Fortunes of Ports in the Niger Delta', *Scottish Geographical Magazine* 82 (1966), 169–83

Usoro, E. J. *The Nigerian Oil Palm Industry* (Ibadan, 1974)
Vansina, J. 'Long-Distance Trade-Routes in Central Africa', *JAH* 3 (1962), 375–90
    *Paths in the Rainforests: Towards a History of Political Tradition in Equatorial
    Africa* (London, 1990)
Verger, P. *Bahia and the West Coast Trade, 1549–1851* (Ibadan, 1964)
Webb, E. T. *Soap and Glycerine Manufacture* (London, 1927)
Wickins, P. *An Economic History of Africa from the Earliest Times to Partition*
    (Cape Town, 1981)
Wilson, C. *The History of Unilever*, 2 vols. (London, 1954)
Wilson, L. E. 'The "Bloodless Conquest" in Southeastern Ghana: The Huza and
    the Territorial Expansion of the Krobo in the Nineteenth Century', *IJAHS* 23
    (1990), 269–97
    The Krobo People of Ghana to 1892: A Political and Social History (Athens, Ohio,
    1992)
Wirz, A. 'La "Rivière du Cameroun": commerce pré-coloniale et contrôle du
    pouvoir en société lignagère', *Revue française d'histoire d'Outre-Mer* 60, 219
    (1973), 172–95
Wolfson, F. 'A Price Agreement on the Gold Coast: The Krobo Oil Boycott,
    1858–1866', *Economic History Review* 6 (1953), 68–77
Young, J. M. S. *The Coaster at Home* (London, 1916)
    The Iniquitous Coaster (London, 1917)
Zeleza, P. T. *A Modern Economic History of Africa*, vol. I, *The Nineteenth Century*
    (Dakar, 1993)
Zeven, A. C. 'Oil Palm Groves in Southern Nigeria, Part I: Types of Groves in
    Existence', *Journal of the Nigerian Institute for Oil Palm Research* 4 (1965),
    226–50; 'Part II: Development, Deterioration, and Rehabilitation of Groves',
    5 (1968), 21–39
    'The Origin of the Oil Palm', *Journal of the Nigerian Institute for Oil Palm
    Research* 4 (1965), 218–25

III NEWSPAPERS

African Times
Bristol Presentments or Bill of Entry
Clyde Bill of Entry
Customs Bills of Entry, series A
Gold Coast Leader
Lagos Observer
Lagos Times and Gold Coast Colony Advertiser
Liverpool Courier
Liverpool Journal of Commerce
Liverpool Mercury
The Times
Trader
West Africa
West African Herald
West African Reporter

IV UNPUBLISHED THESES

Drake, B. K. 'Liverpool's African Commerce Before and After Abolition of the Slave Trade', MA thesis, University of Liverpool, 1974

Frost, D. 'The Kru in Freetown and Liverpool: A Study of Maritime Work and Community During the Nineteenth and Twentieth Centuries', Ph.D thesis, University of Liverpool, 1992

Gertzel, C. 'John Holt: A British Merchant in West Africa in the Era of Imperialism', DPhil. thesis, University of Oxford, 1959

Hargreaves, S. M. 'The Political Economy of Nineteenth-Century Bonny: A Study of Power, Authority, Legitimacy, and Ideology in a Delta Trading Community, 1790–1914', Ph.D thesis, University of Birmingham, 1987

Hopkins, A. G. 'An Economic History of Lagos, 1880–1914', Ph.D thesis, University of London, 1964

Howard, A. M. 'Big Men, Traders, and Chiefs: Power, Commerce, and Spatial Change in the Sierra Leone–Guinea Plain, 1865–1895', Ph.D thesis, University of Wisconsin, 1972

Inikori, J. E. 'English Trade to Guinea: A Study in the Impact of Foreign Trade on the English Economy, 1750–1807', Ph.D thesis, University of Ibadan, 1973

Kaplow, S. B. 'African Merchants of the Nineteenth-Century Gold Coast', Ph.D thesis, Columbia University, 1971

Lynn, M. 'John Beecroft and West Africa, 1829–1854', Ph.D thesis, University of London, 1979

Manning, P. 'Palm Oil and Kernel Exports from Nigeria, 1880–1905: A Study in Econometric History', MSc. thesis, University of Wisconsin, 1966

Oyewumi, J. A. O. 'The Development and Organisation of Palm Oil and Palm Kernel Production in Nigeria, 1807–1960', MSoc.Sc. thesis, University of Birmingham, 1972

Reid, J. 'Warrior Aristocrats in Crisis: The Political Effects of the Transition from the Slave Trade to Palm Oil Commerce in the Nineteenth-Century Kingdom of Dahomey', Ph.D thesis, University of Stirling, 1986

Ross, D. A. 'The Autonomous Kingdom of Dahomey, 1818–1894', Ph.D thesis, University of London, 1967

Sorensen, C. A. 'Badagry, 1784–1863: The Political and Commercial History of a Pre-Colonial Lagoonside Community in South West Nigeria', Ph.D thesis, University of Stirling, 1995

Stilliard, N. H. 'The Rise and Development of Legitimate Trade in Palm Oil with West Africa', MA thesis, University of Birmingham, 1938

Thompson, W. 'Glasgow and Africa: Connexions and Attitudes, 1870–1900', Ph.D thesis, University of Strathclyde, 1970

Tigwell, R. E. 'James Deemin and the Organisation of West African Trade, 1880 to 1915', MPhil. thesis, University of Liverpool, 1978

Udom, D. S. 'Demand and Supply Analyses for Nigerian Oil-Palm Products with Policy Implications', Ph.D thesis, University of Reading, 1980

Wariboko, W. E. 'New Calabar and the Forces of Change, c. 1850–1945', Ph.D thesis, University of Birmingham, 1991

Index

Other books in the series

Printed in the United States
By Bookmasters